The

Book

The Bible? That's the book indeed,
The Book of Books
On which who looks,
As he should do, aright, shall never need
Wish for a better light
To guide him in the night

George Herbert

The Book of Books

AND

AN INTRODUCTION TO A SELECTION OF THE CHRISTIAN CLASSICS

by

Roland Burrows

ISBN 978-1-913133-19-1

The Book of Books

Published by the Wakeman Trust

Distributed by Roland Burrows,
27, Beauty Bank, Cradley Heath B64 7HZ

* * *

* * *

* * *

Typeset using Minion Pro 11/12

Contents

Foreword

The following is a selection of forty-five, some longer, some shorter reflections on the themes and messages of renowned Christian writings.

Beginning with an introduction to the Book of Books, the Word of God, the Holy Spirit inspired Scriptures, the source and motivation of all the works cited and introduced in this collection.

Many will have already read the writings included; others will have heard of them but perhaps have never had time to read them. I have no claim to be a literary scholar, but my intention is to give a sample, or a taste of some of these great classics and hopefully open a door of understanding into their message and worth.

My further purpose is directed toward the young and others who may not yet have realised and appreciated what a rich, profitable and wide ranging legacy of Christian literature exists and is now so widely and easily accessible to us.

The following exhortations are from past worthies to stretch ourselves in the area of reading. We are not to spend all our time in reading, we have much to do for the extension of the Kingdom of God. However, reading is an important means to equip and make ourselves better soldiers and servants of our Saviour and King.

The Apostle Paul in prison writes to Timothy, "When thou comest, bring with thee the books, but especially the parchments" (2 Timothy 4:13). Beside the Hebrew Scriptures Paul was a great reader of books, of various sorts both Jewish and Gentile, as we can see from his quotations from heathen poets and the Jewish records. (Acts 17:28, 1 Corinthians 15:33, 2 Timothy 3:8, Titus 1:12) He is at this point old and in prison, but he is still concerned about his books, and desires to read them and have them read, also to set an example to Timothy and others to do the same. When he refers to the *parchments* here, he means the Scriptures.

Richard Baxter said: "Books are if well-chosen domestic, present, constant, judicious, pertinent, yea, powerful sermons; and are always a very great use to your salvation; but especially when the vocal preaching faileth, and preachers are ignorant, ungodly, or dull, or when they are persecuted, and forbidden to preach ...You have need of a judicious teacher at hand, to direct you what books to use or to refuse."

John Wesley said: "that one could never be a deep preacher without extensive reading, any more than a thorough Christian."

To read Spurgeon's *Commenting and Commentaries*, and his book reviews in the *Sword and Trowel* is ample evidence of the depth and breadth of his own personal reading.

My aim in producing this book, is to seek to open a door to the vast and varied library of Christian literature available to us, and to show something of its great significance and value.

Roland Burrows

1. The Bible, the Book of Books

Holy Bible, Book divine, precious treasure, thou art mine. For well over a thousand years this nation has been privileged to possess this treasure and to have access to an ever increasing part of it in its own tongue and language. It was the possession of those half-forgotten saints of the first millennium who treasured it and knew it and lived it, preached it and planted it deep in the national psyche.

Time fails to tell all we could say of its first translators such as Caedman, the cowherd poet, King Alfred the Great our Christian King, who believed that Christianity alone can rightly make and preserve a nation. There was Bede, the scholar monk of Jarrow, Father of English history, Bible translator and expositor. Also Aelfric the Abbot of Eynsham near Oxford, who was referred to at the time of the Reformation to prove that the early English Church did not hold to the doctrine of transubstantiation, and King Athelstan, of whom William Tyndale recollected in 1528: "Except my memory fails me and that I have forgotten what I read when I was a child thou shalt find in the English Chronicle how that King Athelstan (924–939) caused the Holy Scripture to be translated into the tongue that then was in England and how the prelates exhorted him thereto." We can add to this list Guthlac who translated the Psalms in the 7th century, and also Eadfrith and the *Lindisfarne Gospels* of AD 680. Not forgetting in Ireland, the *Book of Kells* and the *Book of Durrow*. The Scriptures we cannot fail to see have since those early centuries inspired our song, our literature, our laws, our fighting spirit (it was said a part of the reason why Aelfric translated the historical books of Joshua and Judges was in order to inspire Englishman of the need to defend their realm).

As early as 1175 Robert Grosseteste, Bishop of Lincoln, insisted on the authority of Scripture over the authority of the Pope. He, a convinced Augustinian, believed in salvation by grace alone and laid a strong emphasis on preaching, saying a priest's chief task is not to perform the mass but to preach the Word of God. Wycliffe is said to have been encouraged by reading the writings of Grosseteste. We may also remember the influence of Richard Fitzralph, Archbishop of Armagh, Chancellor of Oxford University. Fitzralph was the first to speak of the doctrine of dominion or lordship, arguing that God was the only ultimate source of authority, and the rulers in Church and State can only legitimately exercise dominion if they themselves are living a life of faithful service to God. This concept was later taken up and expanded upon by John Wycliffe.

At this time also we may remember the influence of Thomas Bradwardine, chaplain to Edward III of England who was regarded in his day as the greatest English theologian of all time. He accompanied Edward III and his expeditionary force to France, and preached to the gathered troops numbering thousands, salvation through grace alone.

The Bible influenced men of literature such as William Langland, author of *Piers Ploughman* which in turn it is said influenced John Bunyan in his writing of *The Pilgrim's Progress*. The ethic of *Piers Ploughman*, with its emphasis on godliness and honest toil, lives on in the Nonconformist conscience. Of the massive influence of John Wycliffe and William Tyndale and others we will speak later, but here we must at least mention Cranmer, Ridley and Latimer great figures of the English Reformation and the founders of our National Church of England, and of John Knox and his role in establishing the Church of Scotland. Sufficient to say that the Bible has influenced our nation for good since the early centuries. Our history stands as evidence of the fact that whenever the Bible is read, revered, studied, believed and acted upon it has produced extraordinary good by which our nation has been mightily enriched and blessed.

Of the tremendous potency and power of this book which we call the Bible we can be in no doubt. Alongside its measureless and wide ranging influence for good in the realm of mankind's spiritual and moral well-being, we may trace its influence in the area of legal and political thought and organisation, in its influence on linguistics and the development of language, of its influence on science and of course it's widespread influence on literature, art and music, all of which it is impossible to calculate or overstate.

The English classical scholar Benjamin Jowett did not exaggerate when he stated that:"The moral feelings of men have been deepened and strengthened, and also softened, and almost created by the Jewish prophets" (*The Bible and Civilisation*, 1973, p.3).

To record the impact of the Bible on the culture of the world would occupy the study of a lifetime. Focusing only on its impact on Western civilisation we can observe that for 2000 years the Old and New Testaments of Scripture have influenced all levels of Western Society. They have formed the bedrock of Western civilisation and exerted an influence far greater in extent than even the valuable inheritance of ancient Greece and Rome.

T.S. Eliot in his *Notes Toward the Definition of Culture* first published in 1948 states: "The dominant force in creating a common culture between peoples each of which has its distinct culture, is religion". Speaking in regard to European culture he makes no hesitation in saying:

> "It is Christianity which has made Europe what it is. It is in Christianity that our arts have developed; it is in Christianity that the laws of Europe have—until recently—been rooted. It is against a background of Christianity that all our thought has significance. An individual European may not believe that the Christian Faith is true, and yet what he says, and makes, and does, will all spring out of his heritage of Christian culture and depend upon that culture for its meaning. I do not believe that the culture of Europe could survive the complete disappearance of the Christian Faith. And I am convinced of that fact, not merely because I am a Christian myself, but as a student of social biology. If Christianity goes, the whole of our culture goes. Then you must start painfully again, and you cannot put on a new culture ready-made. You must wait for the grass to grow to feed the sheep to give the wool out of which your new coat will be made. You must pass through many centuries of barbarism. We should not live to see the new culture, nor would our great, great grandchildren: and if we did, not one of us would be happy in it.
>
> To our Christian heritage we owe many things besides religious faith. Through it we trace the evolution of our arts, through it we have our conception of Roman law which has done so much to shape the Western World, through it we have our conceptions of private and public morality. And through it we have our common standards of literature, in the literatures of Greece and Rome. The Western world has its unity in this heritage, in Christianity and in the ancient civilisations of Greece, Rome and Israel, from which, owing to 2000 years of Christianity, we trace our descent."
>
> Ibid pp. 122–123

There is an old story, involving a man who dreamt or we might say experienced a nightmare in which he turned to read his Bible but found only blank pages. Alarmed and dismayed he turned to his neighbours to find a Bible with the script still intact. To his utter despair and alarm, he found all their copies were the same.

There is so much that we take for granted in everyday life that we would not possess if our Bibles were nothing but blank pages.

As one has said: "If by some hideous accident at the divine computer keyboard, the 'delete' key were pressed for the Bible, much of the content of Western culture would disappear and it would shrivel like a deflated balloon."

Certainly we might say that the growth of our British character, the growth of our constitution and national identity have grown up alongside and been profoundly influenced by and intertwined with the translation of the English Bible. The Bible has clearly been the greatest and most formative influence on the development of our nation.

THE INFLUENCE OF THE BIBLE ON OUR UNDERSTANDING OF HISTORY

Turning to the opening pages of the Book of Genesis we see this very clearly. For example, the opening chapter of the Bible gives us a unique concept of history. The Bibles first words are: *In the beginning God...* They remind us that to attain any true understanding of life and its meaning and purpose we must begin with God.

John Calvin in his famous *Institutes* said: "nearly all the wisdom we possess, that is to say, true and sound wisdom, consists of two parts: the knowledge of God and the knowledge of ourselves."

It was also Dr Martyn Lloyd-Jones who reminded us that the Bible always starts with God; he reminded us of the great opening statement of Scripture "in the beginning God." He went on to say that we will not make any sense or find any meaning or purpose anywhere unless we begin with God. When we begin with God we begin with a right concept of history itself.

The Christian view of history is that time has a beginning and an end. The Bible takes us from Genesis to Revelation, and through its pages we see time has a beginning and time has an end, a climax and a purpose.

History is linear—it is not cyclic as many in the ancient pagan world believed it to be. History has a purpose, a goal, a direction, a significance. God is sovereign over it, as the hymn writer points out: *God is working his purpose out, as year succeeds to year.* Christ is the great theme of history, the Alpha and the Omega, the beginning and the end of it.

The futility of the cyclic view of history as referred to in Ecclesiastes chapter 1 verses 1 to 11 is portrayed as something profoundly depressing.

> Vanity of vanities, saith the Preacher, Vanity of vanities; all is vanity.
>
> What profit hath a man of all his labour which he taketh under the sun?
>
> One generation passeth away, and another generation cometh: but the earth abideth forever.
>
> The sun also ariseth, and the sun goeth down, and hasteth to his place where he arose.
>
> The wind goeth toward the south, and turneth about unto the north; it whirleth about continually, and the wind returneth again according to his circuits ...
>
> Is there anything whereof it may be said, See, this is new? It hath been already of old time, which was before us."
>
> Ecclesiastes 1:2–6 also v. 10.

Modern secular theories of history are equally depressing. Take for example the view of history advocated in the 20th century by H.A.L. Fisher who said, that there is no purpose whatsoever in history.

These non-biblical views and others like them are inevitably depressing and seem to be saying, life is futile. Whatever man achieves he ultimately loses and ultimately the whole exercise of living is pointless. These views are demoralising and destroy all incentive, leading us inevitably to the conclusion "eat, drink and be merry for tomorrow we die,"

The Christian view of history, as our Lord reminds us tells us that our strivings and efforts are not in vain, and the Gospels reminds us that, "even a cup of cold water given in my name shall not lose its reward." The Biblical view reminds us that at last we shall stand before the judgement seat of God and give account. Moreover, we are made in the image and likeness of God, we are responsible beings, we have an immortal soul, God's providence governs history, there is purpose and meaning in all that we do.

The Bible teaches us that it is God who is good and has created all things

This inspires us to create and to use the resources and skills God has given to us. It reminds us again that we are not engaged in vain, hopeless and futile endeavour. There is also the truth contained in this that brings us comfort and encouragement. God is the Creator of the heavens and the earth, therefore there is hope and help. This same God has given his only begotten Son to die to redeem us from our sin and condemnation This hymn, though written for little children is profound.

> God who made the earth,
> The air, the sky, the sea,
> Who gave the light its birth,
> Careth for me.
>
> God who sent his Son
> To die on Calvary,
> He, if I lean on him,
> Will care for me.

The Opening Chapters of the Bible give the Lie to Materialism

The materialist holds that the only thing that exists is matter.

The German materialist Feuerbach said:

> No hand holds the earth in its course; no prayer can arrest the sun or lull the fury of the storm; no voice can raise the dead from their eternal sleep; no angel can deliver the captive: no hand stretched forth from the clouds can feed the hungry; no sign from heaven can tell us that we know anything beyond nature. Beyond there is nothing; and nature [cries Feuerbachwith all the ferocious exultation of despair] Nature has no answer she can make to the griefs or the prayers of man; she drives him back inexorably upon himself.
>
> H.P. Liddon, *Sermons on Old Testament Subjects*, p.5.

The Bible gives the Lie to Pantheism. (*i.e. that everything is God*)

While the atheist insists that there is no God, the pantheist answers “Everything is God.” The pantheist believes the universe is not made by God, it is God.

For the pantheist there is no personal God.

For the pantheist the universe is its own judge, therefore there is in pantheism no clear standard of right and wrong. For the pantheist might, becomes right. For the pantheist there can be no personal life beyond this one.

There can be no prayer.

Sin does not exist.

THE BIBLE GIVES US THE RIGHT VIEW OF THE NATURE OF MANKIND

Mankind is made in the image and likeness of God.

We are capable of knowing God.

We are fallen creatures.

Yet we are capable of redemption.

God so loved the world, that he gave his only begotten Son, that whosoever believeth in him should not perish, but have everlasting life.

To sum up, the secular worldview says:

God probably does not exist.

The universe is a product of chance.

Man is not significant ultimately.

There is no plan, only chaos and chance.

There is no such thing as absolute truth.

There is no way of escape.

The Bible teaches us i.e. the Christian worldview says:

God exists.

The universe is created and ordered.

Mankind is significant.

God has a plan for the universe.

There is such a thing as absolute truth.

There is a way of escape, there is hope, there is salvation through Jesus Christ alone.

THE BIBLE'S INFLUENCE ON BRITISH LAW

When Christianity appeared and began to be established in Europe the Greco/Roman worldview was, philosophically, in a state of collapse. Society was desperately in need of a new foundation for social order. As a result, Christian philosophers such as Justin Martyr (c.100-c.165) and Tatian (c.160) turned to Christianity to resolve the crisis of meaning and order.

Other Christian apologists such as Tertullian who was a lawyer by profession, saw that the very foundations of Roman law were in imminent danger of collapse. Roman law was a man-made product. It was ostensibly based on Roman religion, but that in turn was also man-made. The Roman state effectively made the Roman gods. Tertullian pointed this out. He said:

> To say a word about the origin of the laws of the kind to which we now refer, there was an old decree that no god should be consecrated by the Emperor till first approved by the Senate.
>
> R.J. Rushdoony, quoted in Edward J. Murphy *In Your Justice*, p.ii

The implication was that the laws were based on Roman religion but as the state made the gods, the real god was the state.

Thus, as Rushdoony comments: "Rome's humanistic laws had become an expression, not of justice, but of popular (and changing) mores." (Ibid).

In many cases the law was but an expression of a corrupt and corrupting society. Edward J. Murphy comments:

> Tertullian and other Christian lawyers attacked the "pagan, state invented, religious" foundations of Roman law. The issue was *lordship*, or to use the more modern term *sovereignty*: Who is the Lord, Christ or Caesar, God or the state."
>
> Law-making is an attribute of sovereignty. Hence, the hostility of the modern state to Biblical law, and to Christ's Church."
>
> Ibid.

What Tertullian and others achieved when Christianity became the state religion of the Roman Empire was to make Christian principle the basis of Roman law. It was these very principles which were later to be absorbed into the legal codes of Western Europe.

In his book, *Under God and Under the Law*, Richard O'Sullivan, KC, points out:

> That there were three great systems of law which have moulded Western civilization as a whole: Roman Canon Law, Roman Civil Law and English Common Law. He is speaking as a lawyer, and not as a theologian, when he says: "like the three languages of Latin,

> Greek and Hebrew which Pilate used in the words of the inscription placed over the head of the Lord Jesus on the cross, all three of these systems of law, in turn, paid homage to the Lord Jesus Christ."
>
> Common Law is that which has grown up through common usage and experience over hundreds of years. It is that which has grown through long tradition and has not been imposed by Kings or governments. It is one of the great antidotes to tyranny and centralization. In England it early imbibed the spirit of Christianity and liberty. It meant that though the wind and rain might enter a man's house the King could not without the owner's permission. (Every man's house is his castle). It meant as one put it, "that no man could be persecuted for conscience sake, so that there should be an end of human sacrifice for mere faith or opinion".

The influence of Christianity on law led in due course to the abolition of the heathen laws of barbarian people and to the remodelling of their savage customs on more humane lines.

This Christianizing of Roman law reached its highest peak during the time of the Emperor Justinian (AD 527–565) when he drew up the great body of civil law called the *Corpus juris civilis.* Almost everything in the body of civil law which was new was the consequence of Christian moral principles.

It was these elements of Common Law combined with widely accepted elements of Roman law that King Alfred the Great brought together in his famous book of Domes or Laws.

The profound Biblical spirit which governed King Alfred and his times appears from the fact that's his Book of Laws, *Liber Judicialis* began with the Ten Commandments, and was followed by many of the Mosaic precepts, added to which were the sayings of our Lord Jesus Christ such as: "do not think that I am come to destroy the law, or the prophets; I am not come to destroy but to fulfil."

After this Alfred speaks of the divine commandment:

> "As ye would that men should do unto you do ye also unto them" and then declares "from this one doom, a man may remember that to judge everyone righteously, he need heed no other dome-book."

In 1066 William the Conqueror brought with him into England jurists and clerics thoroughly imbued with the spirit of the civil law and distinctly averse to English Common Law. However, the ancient laws and customs of England rooted in Christian truth and precept prevailed and withstood the shock and stress of opposition and remained very largely in place.

It was these ancient Christian laws that became further established and enshrined in the Magna Carta of 1215.

> Throughout the creative centuries of the common law, the orientation of the mind and life of England was towards God.
>
> Richard O Sullivan KC, *Christian Philosophy in the Common Law.*

> The practice whereby a witness takes the oath on the Bible indicates the Bible's penetration into the legal procedure, as well as concepts of law.
>
> Gabriel Sivan, *The Bible and Civilization* (1973) p.139.

The King is under the Law

One particular aspect of English law needs to be emphasized and pointed out. In the course of their history, the English accepted monarchs of French, Scottish, Welsh, Dutch and German origin and even monarchs like George I who spoke no English. They accepted them largely because they viewed their monarchs as creatures, and not creators, of the law. Each sovereign represented himself as entitled by law to his dominion, and more importantly, as subject to the law and bound to uphold it.

Henry de Bracton

The point was made by the 13th century judge Henry de Bracton, in his *De Legibus et Consuetudinibus Angliae* (Of the Laws and Customs of England c. 1220, revised c. 1250). The king, Bracton argued, lies under the law, since it is the law that appoints him. Directly and without philosophizing he was transcribing the route to English understanding of law, as something objective and that became part of the character of English law, something not to be invented and imposed but discovered and obeyed.

In Bracton's work the emphasis was not upon the power of the crown, but on the crowns responsibility. The monarch was the subject of God, to the law of the land and to his feudal court. In Bracton, the King owed some responsibility to listen to his lords. Bracton's writings later became a *de facto* antidote to the absolutism of the Tudors and Stuarts.

That the king is subservient to the law is discovered in the Holy Scriptures, not so much discovered as revealed. Braxton said:

> And that he (the King) ought to be under the law appears clearly in the analogy of Jesus Christ, whose vice regent on earth he is, for though many ways were open to him for his ineffable redemption of the human race, the true mercy of God chose this most powerful way to destroy the devils work, he would not use the power of force but the reason of justice.

In other words, comments Francis Schaeffer

> God in his sheer power could have crushed Satan in his revolt by the use of that sufficient power. But because of God's character, justice came before the use of power alone. Therefore, Christ died that justice, rooted in what God is, would be the solution. Bracton codified this as follows: Christ's example, because of who he is, is our standard, our rule, our measure. *Therefore, power is not first, but justice is first in society and law.* The Prince may have the power to control and to rule, but he does not have the right to do so without justice. This was the basis of English Common Law. The Magna Carta (1215) was written within 35 years (or less) after Bractons' De Legibus and in the midst of the same universal thinking in England at that time."
>
> Francis Schaeffer, *A Christian Manifesto*, 1981 p.28

The Reformation (300 years after Bracton) refined and clarified this further. It got rid of the encrustations that had been added to the Judeo-Christian world-view and clarified the point of authority with authority resting in Scripture rather than church and Scripture. This not only had meaning in regard to doctrine but clarified the base for law.

That base was God's written Law, and the content and authority of that written Law is rooted back to him who is the final reality. Thus, neither church nor state were equal to, let alone, above, that Law. The bases for law is not divided, and no one has the right to place anything, including king, state or church, above the content of God's Law.

Schaeffer further observes:

> The humanists push for "freedom", but having no Christian

> consensus to contain it, that "freedom" leads to chaos or to slavery under the state (or under an elite). Humanism, with its lack of any final base for values or law, always leads to chaos. It then naturally leads to some form of authoritarianism to control the chaos. Having produced the sickness, humanism gives more of the same kind of medicine for a cure. With its mistaken concept of final reality, it has no intrinsic reason to be interested in the individual, the human being. Its natural interest is the two collectives: the state and society.
>
> Ibid, p.30–29

The founding Fathers of the United States understood well the relationship between one's world-view and government. John Witherspoon (1723–1794) the only pastor to sign the Declaration of Independence saw that the linkage of Christian thinking and the concept of government were not incidental but fundamental. John Witherspoon a Presbyterian knew and stood consciously in the stream of Samuel Rutherford (1600–1661), who wrote *Lex Rex* in 1644. Lex Rex means law is king. The Stuart monarchs were firm believers in Rex Lex; that is the king is law. In the Declaration of Independence, we see Bracton's and Rutherford's Biblical view entering American law.

Another great influence in the founding of American democracy was William Penn (1644–1716) the Quaker founder of Pennsylvania, who wrote, "If we are not governed by God then we will be governed by tyrants." Ibid p.33–34

In the fullness of time these great principles became identified with and preserved by the authority of the Authorised Bible. The high regard in which it was held, its universally accepted authority and precepts made it the bastion of righteous law and true liberty. The Authorised Version came to be regarded as the safeguard of our liberties and our defence against tyranny.

British character was profoundly influenced by this concept of Common Law. For the British people the law was an objective reality: it did not (as we have seen) depend on the will of sovereigns or parliaments, but on the authority of God's Word stood and applied to the king and his subjects alike and equally.

> "It was to be likened to the Holy Spirit—always present, always vigilant, always personal, always benign. As the late Master of the Rolls Lord Denning expressed it, justice is above all merely human law. The policemen on his beat was its real embodiment,

> kindly, impartial and the guardian of the community. When a felon transgressed it was not the state but the Law which pursued him, and the essential goodness of the Law was symbolized by the fact that the policemen carried no arms. The American sociologist Geoffrey Gorer, exploring English character in 1955, found universal enthusiasm for the English police as role models, distinguished by their fairness, gentleness, decency and devotion to duty."
>
> Roger Scruton, *England an Elegy* (2006), p.57

These are concepts of priceless worth and we owe their existence to the influence of this book of the Holy Scriptures.

THE INFLUENCE OF THE BIBLE ON ENGLISH CHARACTER

A Sense of Duty

Stanley Baldwin (1867–1947), three times Conservative Prime Minister between the two World Wars writing in *British Life and Thought* (1941), comments on the fact that leaving aside the many defects in our national character there is one notable and persistent and worthy characteristic i.e. the instinct of the English mind to find out what is unjust among us and undo it, to know what is our duty and to do it, as God's bidding. He traces some of its origins in Caedmon, "For us it is very right that we praise with our words, love in our minds the Keeper of the Heavens, Glory King of Hosts". It was the same spirit that worked in Chaucer's time that worked in the Vision of Pier's Plowman and spoke through the voice of Gower the poet, a contemporary of Chaucer who called him Gower the Moral, as one crying in the wilderness, "Prepare ye the way of the Lord." It needed not in those days that a man should be a Wyclifite to see the griefs of the Church and people, and to trace them in their root to duties unperformed. (*British Life and Thought*, p. 442–3)

This sense of duty manifested itself in many ways down the years through literature and prose e.g. in Nelson's famous words at Trafalgar, "England expects that every man will do his duty." We have it in Wordsworth's, Ode to Duty, "Not, once nor twice in our rough Island's story the path of duty has been the road to glory". In Mrs Heman's famous *Casabianca*, "The flames rolled on, he would not go without his father's word." It was Baldwin's affirmation that "where an Englishman sees his duty, he will follow to the gates of hell."

Political Liberty and Justice

The Bible certainly played a profoundly important part in securing the political liberty which has characterized these islands over the years. As men, women and children read the great themes of Scripture, Justice (Abraham at Sodom and Gomorrah), liberty, (the Exodus), righteousness (the Ten Commandments) mercy, forgiveness, self-sacrifice, service, loyalty and many other great precepts were fixed in the hearts and consciences of the population.

Humility and Dependence on God

> But what was the effect of the Bible on the character of the Englishman? I should describe the effect on the common Englishman, as generation after generation that amazing truth of the Bible fell on his ears, Sunday after Sunday, was something like this. He became soaked unconsciously in the Hebrew tradition which in some strange way accorded to his native temper and disposition.
>
> The Hebrew spirit was always conscious of the mystery of life, and of human weakness. From that consciousness necessarily arose the sense of dependence on a higher power, God, whose ways were past finding out. Given that attitude to a Creator, unless a man is completely indifferent, he seeks to reconcile his conduct to what he believes is the will of God; that is to reckon his conduct by a standard of right and wrong ... the generations which received this impress have long been dust, but consciously or unconsciously we of today are still their children and their heirs.
>
> Stanley Baldwin, *British Life and Thought*, p.443

Responsibility

Built into this Biblical outlook on life was also the firm belief that individuals must take responsibility for their own lives and suffer the consequences of their actions. Staying on the right side of the Law was therefore not merely a duty it was also a liberation, for it guaranteed that you were safe, that no busybody could give you orders or force you to comply with a routine that you had not chosen. The Law was not to coerce you or to shape you into regiments obedient to the state. It was there to free you from the state and its officials, and to allow you to "get on with your own life" in private. Those who minded their own business and attended to their duties were rewarded with inalienable rights. The most important of these was the right to do what you ought.

Freedom and Independence of Spirit

The extraordinary result of this was that, while the English believed in law and authority, they despised officialdom and distrusted the state. English society was the creation of amateur initiatives; its most valuable institutions were the result either of private patronage or people making common cause in clubbing together. Such networks of self-help are natural, and are the fruit of the Christian conscience, they exist wherever the state does not extinguish them—as it extinguished them in Revolutionary France and later in Nazi Germany and Communist Russia. In England, however, private foundations, amateur circles, clubs and friendly societies sprang up not merely from the normal superfluity of social energy, but in response to social problems, calling upon the resources and consciences of Christian men and women to resolve them. It was not the state but friendly societies and building societies which provided industrial workers with housing. It was not the state but People's Dispensaries and volunteer hospitals which first brought the benefits of modern medicine to the poor. Schools, universities and colleges began as private foundations and, when it came to leisure, every village was a centre of spontaneous institution building, but it's football club and cricket club, its Boy Scouts and Girl Guides, its Women's Institutes and its circles of amateurs devoted to needlework, music, photography, theatricals, brass bands, jam making etc. almost always centred on the village church. (Based on Scruton, *England an Elegy*, p. 58).

A number of tributes to the influence of the Authorized Bible on British social life

The first from a surprising source, Thomas Huxley, the biologist and Darwinian evolutionist. Writing in his *Educational Essays* (1874) he draws attention to

> the great historical fact that for three centuries this book has been

> woven into the life of all that is best and noblest in English history; that it has become a national epic of Britain, and is familiar to noble and simple, from John O'Groats to Land's End; that it is written in the noblest and purest English, and abounds in exquisite beauties... By the study of what other book could children be so much humanized, and made to feel that each figure in that vast historical process fills, like themselves, but a momentary space in the interval between the Eternities; and earns the blessings or curses of all time according to its effort to do good and hate evil?
>
> The Bible has been the Magna Carta of the poor and of the oppressed; down to modern times no state has had a constitution in which the interests of the people are so largely taken into account, in which the duties so much more than the privileges of the rulers are insisted upon, as that drawn up for Israel in Deuteronomy and Leviticus; nowhere is the fundamental truth that the welfare of the state, in the long run, depends on the uprightness of the citizen so strongly laid down.
>
> Quoted by Gabriel Sivan, *The Bible and Civilization*, p.77

John Milton said:

> There are no songs compatible to the songs of Zion; no orations equal to those of the prophets; and no politics like those which the Scriptures teach.

Looking further afield we might notice that it was pre-eminently the use of the English Bible by the first Puritan Colonists that enforced the primacy of English as the language of the new continent nation which was to become the United States of America. It was in a spiritual sense the prime factor which gave its citizens a deep loyalty to the Christian faith and their consequent love of liberty and justice. The influence of the Holy Scriptures remains in "the land of the free" right up to the present day. The President in the White House still begins each day with prayer and the reading of Holy Scripture.

> The grip Protestantism has on the United States is strong and fundamentally influential in its political practices. The majesty of the language so transparently established in America's great public spoken moments, such as Lincoln's Gettysburg address, informs and is embraced by the leading democratic nation on the planet. Through this Bible the Protestant voice in English became the ruling

> tongue of two successive world empires. It also said to the world that Christianity was the leading faith, the Christian God, the one true God and Christ the true and only Redeemer. This Bible has had more impact on the ideology of the last four centuries than any other creed, manifesto or dogma.
>
> Ibid p.282

Later through the influence of the 18th Century Revival and the founding of the *British and Foreign Bible Society* the influence of the Authorized Version was carried to the four corners of the globe. It is perfectly legitimate to speak of the Authorized Version as the Book that changed the world.

It was in Protestant England that democratic theory was first put to the test and in time the results of that experiment rippled out to the margins of the globe.

Daniel Webster once remarked:

> that the tavern was the headquarters of the American Revolution—meaning, in part, that ideas of self-determination could only emerge in a setting where free discussion naturally took place. That discussion was free because the English Reformation had established the right to it, by virtue of the place the English Bible had in people's lives.
>
> Before the advent of the vernacular Bible, which was made available to the general public by printing, most people did not know what the Bible said. Thereafter, they could read it for themselves and decide for themselves what it meant. Their free discussions about the authority of the church and state-fostered concepts of constitutional government in England, which in turn were the indispensable prerequisites for the American colonial revolt. Without the vernacular Bible—and the English Bible in particular, through its impact on the reformation of English politics—there could not have been democracy as we know it, or even what we call today the "Free World."
>
> Benson Bobrick, *The Making of the English Bible*, p. 277

The Bible and the Birth of the Popular Press

Popular Bible reading marked the origin of a culture belonging to the man in the street which increasingly reached towards popular and democratic institutions. This awakened the minds of ordinary people and brought about in turn the birth of the popular press. The popular press first began to develop in London in September 1513. Between 1590 and 1610 at least 450 English news-books, as they were first called, appeared.

THE INFLUENCE OF THE AUTHORISED VERSION ON THE MORAL ETHOS OF BRITISH SOCIETY

Grotius, the Dutch theologian, after returning home from a visit to England in 1613 wrote: *theology rules there.* Casaubon made a similar report after his visit to the court of James I. This was a period when the nation was saturated with biblical truth.

This was to have an extraordinary moral affect. It certainly manifested itself in the literature of Jeremy Taylor, George Herbert, Milton and Bunyan. It certainly lay behind the high moral tone of Cromwell and his parliament and the ministers of the English and Scottish Puritans. At that time, it was said that ordinary men took their Bibles with them to the marketplace and to the work-shop; they bought and sold with its words on their lips and in their hearts. It was their guide in every part of their life; and when duty called them to take up arms they charged the enemy with the sword of the Lord and of Gideon in their hands, and David's psalms on their lips. It made men like Faithful and Greatheart and Gaius, and women like Mercy and Christiana in Bunyan's *Pilgrim's Progress.*

> "From the very first the spread of the Authorized Version made for progress and freedom. It was the study of the English Bible which in a single generation raised so many in the 17th century from the puerilities, superstitions, and prejudices of the Middle Ages, and made them strong, far-seeing men; and tender heroic women. It raised the nation at one bound to the foremost place among the nations of Europe, and more than all else kept it there. It taught us that the only enduring national prosperity is that which is based on loyalty and obedience to the word of God. Piety which is nourished on manuals of devotion and the lives of the saints is of the hot house order. It is those alone who are nourished on the Bible who can stand the storm and flourish in the open-air. It is they who become explorers and reformers, colonists and pioneers of . . . truth."
>
> William Muir, *Our Grand Old Bible*, p. 178

It reappeared at the time of the 18th century revival as it did again in the philanthropic and social reforms of the 19th century.

Even in the late 19th century the Roman Catholic writer F.W. Faber penned this unexpected compliment to the influence of Authorized Version on the character and morals of the nation.

> It lives on the ear like in music that can never be forgotten, like the sound of church bells which the convert scarcely knows how he can forgo. Its felicities often seem to be things rather than words. It is part of the national mind, and the anchor of the national seriousness. Nay, it is worshiped with a positive idolatry, in extenuation of whose fanaticism its intrinsic beauty pleads availingly with the scholar. The memory of the dead passes into it. The potent traditions of childhood are stereotyped in its verses. It is the representative of a man's best moments; all that there has been about him of soft and gentle and pure and penitent and good, speaks to him for ever out of his English Bible. It is his sacred thing which doubt never dimmed and controversy never soiled; and in the length and breadth of the land there is not one Protestant with one spark of religiousness about him whose spiritual biography is not in his Saxon Bible.
>
> Quoted by F.W. Farrar, *The Bible its Meaning and Supremacy*, p.251

It is well known that the Evangelical Revival of the Eighteenth Century brought about a moral transformation of Britain and we forget many other countries. Canon Overton wrote of its effect as follows:

> Of the faith which enabled a man to abandon the cherished habits of a lifetime and to go forth ready to spend and be spent in his Master's service; which nerved him to overcome the natural fear of death, and, indeed, to welcome the last enemy as his best friend who would introduce him to the better land he had long been living for; which made the selfish man self-denying, the discontented happy, the worldling spiritually minded, the drunkard sober, the sensual chaste, the liar truthful, the thief honest, the proud humble, the thriftless thrifty and the godless godly.
>
> *The Evangelical Revival of the Eighteenth Century*, p.131

In 1787 George III issued a proclamation for the "Encouragement of Piety and Virtue, and for the Preventing and Punishing of Vice, Profaneness, and Immorality". Others followed, the Society for the Preservation of Public Morals, Society for the Suppression of Public

Lewdness, The Society for the External Observance of the Lord's Day. The British and Foreign Bible Society was formed at this time in 1807, the forerunner of the Trinitarian Bible Society in 1832.

In the early and mid-Victorian era, the Bible held massive sway in our nation. On the Sunday of the 1851 census records showed half of the population were in church. On the same day over two million of the nation's children were in Sunday School and the figure continued to rise through the century. The crime rate was falling every year in spite of the increase in population. Serious crime fell by 60% between 1850 and 1890. In 1888 three out of every four children attended Sunday School. Illegitimacy fell by the end of the 19th century to 4%, divorce was almost unknown, and single parent families in the modern sense virtually unheard of. Drunkenness was a decreasing problem.

The virtues of self-control, self-help, self-discipline, hard work, independence, thrift, propriety, cleanliness is next to Godliness, temperance, honesty, promptness, regularity etc. were held in the highest regard.

It was said of the England of that time that it was a domestic country. Here the home is revered and the hearth is sacred.

> We have come to regard the Crown as the head of morality. The virtues of Queen Victoria or the virtues of George III have sunk deep into the popular understanding of monarchy. We have come to believe that it is natural to have a virtuous prince, and that the domestic virtues are as likely to be found on thrones as they are eminent else where.
>
> Gertrude Himmelfarb, *The De-Moralization of Society*, p.55, quoting from Karl Beckson, *London in the 1890s.*

It was to the eternal truths of God's Word and the unchanging law of righteousness that Arthur Mee turned the thoughts of his readers in the dark days of 1940. He wrote:

> If for one day the common people of these islands lose their faith in God the cause of freedom must perish.
>
> *Our Finest Hour*, 1940, p.27

THE BIBLE AND SPIRITUAL REVIVAL

Latourette, the renowned church historian reminds us that for some time prior to the 16th century Christianity had appeared to be on the wane. He writes:

> At the beginning of the 1500s the outlook for Christianity appeared unpromising. In many respects what remained of Christianity, seemed a diminishing force. Was Western Europe shedding its Christianity? Christianity, although driven out of much of the Mediterranean world by Islam, had been a tutor to bring civilization to the barbarian peoples of Northern Europe. Were these peoples outgrowing their teacher? Now that they were coming to manhood's estate were these rude folk whom the Church had taught the rudiments of culture to regard Christianity as something outworn, as swaddling clothes which should now be cast aside? Were a thousand years of certainty to be followed by centuries of decisive and final decay. As the world had witnessed the decline and fall of the Roman Empire, was it now to see the decline and disappearance of the faith with which the Roman Empire in its latter years had been so closely identified. The facts prove to be quite the opposite to the gloomy prognosis. Never had the influence of Christianity been so pronounced and widespread as it was after AD 1500.
>
> K.S. Latourette's *History of the Expansion of Christianity 1500–1800*. Introduction

Clearly it was the translation of Scripture into the common tongue of the European people's that brought about the extensive revival and expansion of the Church in that period. We see here that the translation of the Authorized Version was one of the ripe fruits of that period of spiritual awakening. The widespread reading and the periods of the widespread preaching of the Authorized Version in the 17th, 18th and 19th centuries again brought extensive revival of the church.

It is often remarked that this great era of Bible translation and the spiritual revival it produced also unlocked and stimulated all that was best and most noble in the human spirit. It was a revival of literature, science, of discovery and art and music etc. to a most remarkable degree.

In regard to the Authorized Version and revival we remember the accounts of George Whitefield on his knees, hour after hour, day after day in that early period of his Christian life, drinking in the Authorized text with Matthew Henry's comments. Those truths he was soon to preach over the length and breadth of Britain and in the American colonies as well.

THE BIBLE AND SOCIAL REFORM

It is not infrequently that we hear the charge levelled against Evangelicalism that it has no social concern and that its pursuit of the salvation of souls excludes any interest in the everyday problems of society. Those who level such a charge only reveal their ignorance of history. It has been said that social reform in our own and other countries owes more to Biblical Christianity than to any other influence. Kathleen Heasman in her study *Evangelicals in Action, an Appraisal of their Social Work* states, that in the 19th century a good three quarters of the charitable and voluntary societies which were set up were evangelical in character. Many of the functions of the Welfare State were recognized and met, not by social economists and Socialists, but by practical and practicing Christians, whose action was characterized by an intensely personal concern for the individual and his family, for prostitutes, cripples, drunkards, and even navvies and cabmen.

It was John Wesley, William Wilberforce, Thomas Clarkson, Granville Sharp, Thomas Fowler Buxton, and William Knibb, who fought the slave traffic, and they were all evangelicals.

It was John Howard and Elizabeth Fry, both evangelicals, who championed the cause of prison reform.

To the memory of the great reformer, Lord Shaftesbury, a pioneer emancipator of industrial England, and also an evangelical, stands the Eros monument in Piccadilly Circus, purchased with the pennies of the grateful poor.

It was John B. Gough, Frances Willard, and Sir Wilfrid Lawson—all evangelicals—who attacked the entrenched interests of the drink traffic, and whose labours resulted in many Temperance Societies for both old and young.

It was Robert Raikes, an evangelical, who inaugurated Sunday Schools in this country, which, says J.R. Green the historian, "were the beginnings of popular education".

It was Benjamin Waugh, George Muller, William Quarrier, C. H. Spurgeon, J.W.C. Fegan, and T.J. Barnado, all pronounced evangelicals, who espoused the cause of the children, and established orphanages in England and Scotland, some of which continue to the present day.

It was William and Catherine Booth who brought into being the vast and worldwide organization of the Salvation Army; Sir George Williams who originated the Young Men's Christian Association; Arthur Broome who founded the Royal Society for the Prevention of Cruelty to Animals (R.S.P.C.A.); and Florence Nightingale who was the great reformer of hospital nursing. All of these were deeply rooted and grounded in the Word God.

> What is not so often remembered is that, particularly towards the end of the 19th century, individual churches and chapels engaged in a tremendous amount of social work in their immediate vicinities. A pamphlet published in 1883 by the Rev. W. C. Preston, a Congregational minister entitled *The Bitter Cry of the Outcast Poor*, did a great deal to stimulate this work.
>
> The publication of *The Bitter Cry* would probably have caused less concern had it not appeared at the time when the unemployment and under-employed of the 1870s was beginning to gain the attention of the public. Widespread discussion of social conditions was taking place both among the workers and the intellectuals, and socialist ideas were being revived. *The Bitter Cry* was the response of those evangelicals who appreciated the situation and who wished to apply similar remedies with an evangelical emphasis. This method of approach was quickly seized upon. Williams Stead made it the basis of an article in the *Pall Mall Gazette*, and it inspired the *Liverpool Daily Press* to publish some vivid accounts of "squalid Liverpool". It also suggested the lines which were followed in 1890 by William Booth', *In Darkest England and The Way Out*—a book which was widely read in the last decade of the century and roused not only the Salvation Army, but other groups of evangelicals to recognise their social duties."
>
> Kathleen Heasman, *Evangelicals in Action*, p.49

Notable amongst churches to take up this kind of direct social action was the Metropolitan Tabernacle, London.

Some of this work was very innovative. For example, the societies set up to rescue women from prostitution established by men such as the Rev. Baptist Noel and Theophilus Smith. The London Female Mission with a home in White Lion Square, London held periodic midnight mission meetings to which hundreds of prostitutes attended to hear the message of the Gospel and receive practical help.

If there had been no Word of God little of this work would have ever started. Britain would have remained in the condition it was in the early part of the 18th Century as described in great detail in Dr Bready's famous book, *England Before and After Wesley.*

As Stanley Baldwin summarises:

> It's was just about 200 years ago that one of the great spiritual revivals of Christian history broke over England. Two men, Whitefield and Wesley, devoted themselves to the evangelistic work. From early morning to late at night, in fields and byways, amongst crowds of miners, in the roughest quarters of our towns they preached and taught and organized. Their preaching changed for the better countless lives, lives were liberated and there was a stirring of the dry bones far beyond the bounds of the Societies which they founded. Their work incalculable in its results.
>
> When Wesley created the organisation which was to bind his followers together, he came to rely more and more on lay helpers for the day to day administration of that great body. The results of this was throughout the whole country there were found earnest and sincere men, many of them of the working classes, who were giving all their spare time, and some, all of their time to definitely Christian work among their fellows, I used the word "incalculable" of the results of this movement: incalculable indeed was the result of the example of such men in that rough industrial world that was so swiftly growing up.
>
> In point of time I should perhaps have spoken of the religious revival of the 18th century before I sketched for you to the development of co-operation in the industrial age, but I put it last so as to try to impress it on your mind, and will make clear what I meant by insisting on the use of the word "incalculable" with reference to that Revival. No one, a hundred and fifty years ago, could have foreseen the rapid development of democracy, the shifting, as it were, of the political sense of gravity, in democratic States: far less could anyone have foretold the political developments within the different countries during the last quarter of a century. But in all these movements that have grown up among the working classes you will find their foundations are laid on a Christian basis. Amongst these the Friendly and Co-operative Societies and the Trade Union Movement are the most conspicuous and successful examples of self-

help and self-government among the working classes. They embody and are naturally determined by the Christian social philosophy which prevailed throughout the greater part of the 19th century.

You will find amongst the creators of these organisations and amongst the workers in them, generation after generation, men who are themselves workers in the various Christian denominations to which they belong, men of markedly Christian lives, and their general aim, consciously or unconsciously, is to make life itself more worth living for themselves and for their fellows to build up rather than to pull down. It has been a revolutionary spirit more in the religious than in the political sense. Here in my view lies the profound difference between our outlook and that which governs some of the current movements on the Continent, and so long as that outlook, temper, tradition, or whatever you like to call it, remains in England, so long will the Englishman fight to the end any attempt to subject them to a way of life which to him is death."

"British Life and Thought", Article by Stanley Baldwin. (Written 1940) pp 454–5

THE BIBLE AND SCIENCE

Undoubtedly Biblical Christianity is the mother of modern science because it insists that the God who created the universe has revealed himself in the Bible to be the kind of God he is. Consequently, there is a sufficient basis for science to study the universe.

This must be emphasized as much current popular opinion would hold that science grew thanks to the Classical and in spite of the Biblical tradition. Much is made of the retarding influence of the medieval church on the development of science. The role played by medieval Biblical exegesis in offering resistance to new scientific spirit on the movements of the earth and the planets has been emphasized again and again. In the first place, we might say, just as it would be wrong to blame Aristotle for all the prejudiced, dogmatic and even silly interpretations of his philosophy put forward by his medieval scholastic followers, so it would be wrong to lay to the account of the Biblical authors the short sighted interpretations of those who used the Scriptures to oppose legitimate scientific opinions and discoveries.

It is of the utmost significance and note that the era of modern science coincided with the period of new translation of Scripture from the original tongues. That period of the widespread reading and discussion of Scripture that culminated in the translation of the Authorized Version.

As R. Hooykaas observes:

> "In the epoch when modern science arose, religion was one of the most powerful factors in cultural life. What people thought about God influenced their conception of nature, and this in turn influenced their method of investigating nature, that is their science."
>
> *Religion and the Rise of Modern Science*, 1973, p. xiii

Herbert Butterfield, Regis Professor of history at Cambridge, wrote in his *The Origins of Modern Science*, that

> modern scientific investigation is firmly rooted in the Reformation. Scientific thinkers amongst the French Huguenots, the Dutch and English Protestants and the later Puritans believed that they should come to the book of God's works with the same reverence as they came to the book of God's words.
>
> They believed that as God had made all things in order, so the natural laws of creation are orderly and therefore the subject of scientific investigation.
>
> Just as God at the beginning of the Bible caused Adam to name the animals and creatures, so all living things could be classified and studied in an orderly fashion.
>
> As in the Bible God displays moral cause and effect, so the natural laws of creation can be studied as to their cause and effect.
>
> As God has promised the stability of natural laws in his Word; therefore, the natural laws are stable and can be the subjects of rational study.
>
> Finally, God the Creator is good, so the creation is for the benefit of mankind and we should therefore learn all that we can about the laws of nature and use this knowledge for the good of man's estate.

The essential difference between the ancient Greek concepts of science which dominated in the world up until the time of the Reformation was largely that scientific thinking was bound up within the confines of human reason. Whilst human reason plays an important part in scientific investigation, the process of bringing all observations to the bar of human reason tended to put a straitjacket of traditional thinking and circularity on all scientific investigation.

Francis Bacon (1561–1626) who is often called the *Father of Modern Science* expressed this difficulty along these lines.

In Bacon's opinion the root of all evil in science is the violation of the truth of nature by rationalistic prejudice.

> We copy the sin of our first parents ... they wished to be like God, but their posterity wished to be even greater. For we create worlds, we direct and domineer over nature, we will have it that all things are as in our folly we think they should be, not as it seems fittest to the divine wisdom, or as they are found to be in fact ... we clearly impressed the stamp of our own image on the creatures and the works of God, instead of carefully examining and recognizing in them the stamp of the Creator Himself. Thus we lost our dominion over nature, "because we decided to be like God and to follow the dictates of our own reason".

And then Bacon implores his readers to

> discount these preposterous philosophies which have led millions captive and triumphed over the works of God, and to approach with humility and adoration the works of God, to reverently un-role the volume of creation and read what it says.

Bacon criticized the inadequate intellectual reasoning of the Greeks, their neglect of experiments and their premature construction of theories, as spinning out of laborious webs of learning upon a too narrow basis of facts.

Sir Francis Bacon was one of the most influential of the founders of modern science, which was squarely based on Christian thought. He rightly advocated experiments to find out how the world worked, and was opposed to dependency on leading philosophers such as Aristotle (384–322 BC). But Bacon's writings contain many puzzling inconsistencies. Like many early modern scientists, such as Kepler (1571–1630) and Newton (1642–1727), he wrote explicitly of his belief in the literal six-day creation.

However, Bacon made a tragic error that had baneful consequences. Not only did he oppose building science on Greek philosophers, but he also rejected the Bible itself as a basis of scientific knowledge. He stated,

> yet some of the moderns have indulged this folly with such

> consummate inconsiderateness, that they have endeavoured to build a system of natural philosophy on the first chapter of Genesis, the Book of Job, and other parts of Scripture; seeking thus the dead among the living. And this folly is the more to be prevented and restrained, because not only fantastical philosophy, but theoretical religion spring from the absurd mixture of matters divine and human.

The Bible and the English Physicist Robert Boyle

> Boyle considered science to be an excellent school for religion. He pointed out that both science and religion are based on fundamentals that are incomprehensible, and that both are founded on facts "historical" rather than rationally cogent. The scientist finds much in nature that he does not thoroughly understand and he has therefore a special aptitude for accepting things that seem to be beyond belief to the "vulgar philosopher"—the man who thinks that he understands all things and that nothing which does not conform to his philosophy could be true. The scientist is prepared to learn even from unlearned people; just as it would be possible to learn more about the natural history of America from a companion of Columbus than from a hundred Schoolmen, so too one could learn more about God from those unlearned men, the Apostles, who were in close contact with "Him who was at the heart of the Father", than from any philosopher.
>
> R. Hooykaas, *Religion and the Rise of Modern Science* (1973), p.48

The fact that a Christian understanding of the world has made true scientific advance possible is well summed up as follows:

> Our Modern understanding of the structure of the physical world originates in the scientific revolution of the 17th century. It has been argued persuasively by Michael Foster and others that it was the Christian doctrine of creation which enabled this step to be taken in Western Europe, a step which had not proved possible in the equally technically advanced setting of, say, Chinese culture.
>
> To the Christian, God is reasonable and so the works of the Creator are intelligible and open to rational inspection. Yet, because God is free, there is a contingency in creation which means that its order cannot be determined by *a priori* thought (in this case simple going over what has been thought up to this time by others i.e. simply

> relying on man-made philosophies, as did the ancient Greeks, but must be discerned through experimental observation. Torrance puts this very well when he says: "The intelligibility of the universe provides science with its confidence, but the contingency of the universe provides science with its challenge."
>
> The separation which Christian theology maintains between Creator and creation de-sacralises the world and so makes its contingency open to empirical inquiry, free from the danger of impiety.
>
> Because the universe is God's creation, it is a fit subject for study. Thus it was that in the 17th century Christian theology provided the ideological setting in which science could embark on its task of investigating the pattern and structure of the physical world.
>
> "Creation and the Structure of the Physical World" in *Readings in Modern Theology*, Ed. Robin Gill, John Polkinghorn, 1995, p.25

As thinkers such as Herbert Butterfield and A. N. Whitehead have shown convincingly, science grew up within a Christian tradition: and for many years it was in no sense distinct or separate. The founder of science in Oxford, in the early 13th century, was Robert Grosseteste, author of *A Compendium Scientiarum* and later Bishop of Lincoln. He had no hesitation in saying that it was "impossible to understand Nature without experiment or described her without geometry." By this he clearly implies the unity of science and faith, just as much as his distinguished pupil, the Somerset friar Roger Bacon who in his *Opus Maius,* sought to show that the new knowledge, so far from being an enemy of Christian faith, was actually an aid, even in the business of evangelising mankind.

This same wholeness of outlook lasted well into the beginning of modern science. Our Royal Society was founded in 1645, and to its growth in importance much of the dissemination of knowledge, without which science cannot live, is due. Among its members were John Wilkins and Seth Ward, both bishops; John Wallace, Doctor of Divinity and mathematician; Robert Boyle the chemist bequeathed the sum of £50 a year to found a lectureship for "proving the Christian religion against notorious infidels," and "chiefly recommending to his sister" (his executor), the leaving of the greatest part of his estate for, "the advance or propagation of the Christian religion among infidels"; John Rae, the founder of systematic botany and zoology, whose great book *The Wisdom of God Manifested in the Works of Creation* exercised a profound influence among thinking people and was even used in a shortened form by John Wesley in training his travelling preachers; Christopher Wren, astronomer and architect of St Paul's Cathedral; as well as the greatest figure of them all, Isaac Newton, who claimed that his theological studies were at least as important as his strictly scientific ones. It may be true that religious discussions as such were not permitted at meetings of the Society, but this was balanced in their second Charter, where the Fellows were commanded to direct their studies "to the glory of God our Creator, and the advantage of the human race. "Any doubts regarding the relation between the Society and the Church was dispelled by its first historian, Sprat, who wrote:

> I do here in the beginning most sincerely declare that if this design of (a Royal Society) should in the least diminish the reverence that is due to the doctrine of Jesus Christ, it was so far from deserving protection that it ought to be abhorred by all the polite and prudent, as well as by the devout, part of Christendom."
>
> C.A. Coulson, *Science and Christian Belief* (1958), p.23

> Adam was thought to have possessed a perfect knowledge of all sciences, a knowledge lost to posterity when he fell from grace and was expelled from the Garden of Eden. The goal of 17th century scientists such as Francis Bacon and his successors in the Royal Society of London was to regain the scientific knowledge of the first man. Indeed, for these individuals, the whole scientific enterprise was an integral part of the redemptive enterprise that, along with the Christian religion, was to help restore the original race to its original perfection. The biblical account of the creation thus provided these scientists with an important source of motivation, and in an age still thoroughly committed to traditional Christianity, the new science was to gain social legitimacy on accounts of these religious associations.
>
> Internet article, "The Biblical Roots of Modern Science"

THE BIBLE AND ENGLISH LITERATURE

It is not an exaggeration to state that but for the Bible the English language and English literature as they are today would never have been. The language of the Authorized Version has been recently described as: *that incomparable masterpiece which has defeated all attempts at vulgar modernization. Besides the AV the language of modern versions read like the language of a plumber's manual.* (Simon Sharma BBC 4 lecture on the Authorized Version January 9th 2011.) It came about at a time of great literary excellence. 1611 was the year of Shakespeare swansong, *The Tempest.* It was also the year in which John Donne the preacher poet first began to rise to prominence. The language of the Authorized Version has also been described as sacred truth clothed in flesh and blood, its language has been described as powerful, muscular and sinewy. Its very language brings us a consciousness of the God who is awesome but never remote, always present. Another has described its language as that which lodges in the mind and disturbs the temporal with the haunting sound of the eternal.

Peter Hitchens has given us the following examples of the grandeur of its English commenting; "that other versions in comparison are as flat as Kansas and as dreary as the plains of Karagander."

"And the king was much moved, and went up to the chamber over the gate, and wept: and as he went, thus he said, O my son Absalom, my son, my son Absalom! Would God I had died for thee, O Absalom my son, my son!" This doesn't seem to me to be in any way hard for a 21st-century person to understand. Indeed, you can hear and feel the woe and regret in it across the centuries, an old man weeping and alone. Whereas take a few modern versions:"the king was deeply moved and went up to the chamber over the gates and wept. And thus he said as he walked, 'O my son Absalom, my son, my son Absalom! Would I had died instead of you, O Absalom, my son, my son!'" (New American Standard Version). Or "the king was shaken. He went up to the room over the gateway and wept. As he went, he said: 'O my son Absalom! My son, my son Absalom! If only I had died instead of you—oh Absalom, my son, my son!'" (New International Version).

Also, where the Authorized Version has: "And a man shall be as an hiding place from the wind, and a covet from the tempest; as rivers of water in a dry place, as the shadow of a great rock in a weary land," The *New International Reader's Version* becomes: "A king will come who will do what is right. His officials will govern fairly. Each man will be like a place to get out of the wind, he will be like a place to hide from storms. He'll be like streams of water flowing in the desert. He'll be like the shadow of a huge rock in a dry and thirsty land."

No contest, really, is there? The new versions tend only to be tolerable at all when they stick closely to the Authorized Version's poetic text.

As for *thee* and *thou* and *ye,* these remind the reader or listener that they are in a poetic and eternal context, not reading Harry Potter or listening to the radio news. And, as it happens, almost every other major language has retained these important distinctions. And isn't "would God I had died for thee" immediately more poignant than "would God I had died for you?" "Thee" (as any Yorkshireman knows) can refer only to one person. "You" can refer to a whole room full of people.

Sir Arthur Quiller-Couch referring to the Authorized Version of the Bible comments:

> The Scriptures in our Authorized Version are part and parcel of English.
>
> The Authorized Version has set a seal on our natural style, thinking, and speaking; it is in everything we see, hear, and feel, because it is in us, in our blood.

Speaking of the Authorized Versions effect upon English Literature he describes it as:

> "The most majestic thing in our literature, a well of English undefiled."
>
> *Cambridge Lectures on the English Language,* J.M. Dent, 1943

In his *History of the English People,* J. R. Green comments:

> As a mere literary monument, the English Version of the Bible remains the noblest example of the English tongue, while its perpetual use made it, from the instant of its appearance, the standard of our language.

Macaulay said of the English Bible:

> If everything else in our language should perish, it would alone suffice to show the whole extent of its beauty and power.

It is difficult to think of literate people who have not been influenced by the Authorised Version. We may think of the influence of the Authorized Version on writers such as John Bunyan. Edmund Goss said of his writings:

> It is the matchless and inimitable crystallization into imaginative art the whole system of Puritan Protestantism.

All of which we may note based on the Bible.

We may add the names of Crashaw, Quarles, Jeremy Taylor, Milton, Andrew Marvell, Addison, Defoe, Dean Swift, Samuel Johnson, William Cowper among the 17th and 18th century men of literature, profoundly influenced by the Authorized Version.

In the 19th century we may include the names of Wordsworth, Tennyson, Browning, Carlyle, Ruskin, Coleridge, Scott, Thackeray, Charles Reade, the Bronte's, Hawthorne, Longfellow and Southey, Christina Rossetti, Harriet Beecher Stow and many more.

In the 20th century we find its influence in Kipling, Auden, McLeish, T.S. Eliot, G. K. Chesterton, John Betjemen, Alistair Cooke, C. S. Lewis

An index of Bible references in the writings of Ruskin makes a volume of over three-hundred pages and in Van Dyke's book on Tennyson there is a list of the poet's biblical quotations and allusions which covers twenty-four pages.

David Lyle Jeffrey published a massive work in 1992 which was sixteen years in the making, comprising of a *Dictionary of Biblical Tradition in English Literature* covering 960 pages. In his introduction he states:

> The Bible is foundational for Western literature. To understand something of the Bible, and of its transmission in and through English literature is to reckon sympathetically with the development of English cultural consciousness in its richest and most coherent levels of expression.
>
> p. xi, xiii

The influence of the Authorised Version on everyday speech

The influence of the Authorised Version on everyday speech can be illustrated by such expressions as: highways and byways; lick the dust: a broken reed; the root of all evil; weighed and found wanting; the sweat of his brow; a word in season; heap coals of fire; a pearl of great price; the burden and heat of the day; wars and rumours of wars; an eye for an eye and a tooth for a tooth; casting one's pearls before swine; and hundreds more.

Whenever we sing, The National Anthem, *God save the King/Queen* we are using biblical language. (1 Samuel 10:24). The inscription over the portico of the Royal Exchange is from Psalm 24, *The earth is the*

Lord's and the fullness thereof. The motto of the University of Oxford is *Dominus illuminatio mea,* "The Lord is my light", Psalm 27.

To return to Sir Arthur Quiller Couch's Cambridge lecture on reading the Bible. On one occasion he read to his students the following sentences from Scripture.

> "Thine eyes shall see the king in his beauty: they shall behold the land that is very far off.
>
> And a man shall be as a hiding place from the wind, and a covert from the tempest; as rivers of water in a dry place and as the shadow of a great rock a weary land.
>
> So when this corruptible shall have put on incorruption, and this mortal shall put on immortality …
>
> Then observed that: when a nation has achieved this manner of diction these rhythms for its dearest beliefs, its literature is surely established … the Authorized Version set a seal on our national style … It has cadences homely and sublime, yet so harmonizes them that the voice is always one. The language of the Bible has shaped the speech of England.
>
> *The Outline of Literature*, ed. John Drinkwater p. 78

THE INFLUENCE OF THE AUTHORIZED VERSION ON MUSIC AND ART

If there had been no Bible there would be no Psalms and who can tell the influence that the 150 Psalms have had on countless lives, and through their inspirational strength and impact, at times, turned the whole course of history; (study for example the influence of Psalm 46 on European history). What a loss never to be able to sing: *Ye gates lift up your heads on high, I will lift up mine eyes unto the hill; O send thy light forth and thy truth; All people that on earth do dwell; O God our help in ages past; Let us with a gladsome mind; The Lord's my shepherd I'll not want.*

We might think of the great hymns of the New Testament, *The Magnificat*, the *Benedictus*, the *Gloria in Excelsis*, and the *Nunc Dimittis.*

The Church of Christ has always sung. The song began in the Upper Room at the institution of the Lord's Supper when our Lord and his Disciples sang part of Psalms 113–118. Paul teaches us that the early

Christians sang not only with their spirit but with their understanding. Also that they joined together in the singing of Psalms and hymns and spiritual songs.

Time and space permits only a reference to the vast treasures of Scripturally inspired hymnody. Watts and Wesley alone have enriched the songs of the Christian world beyond measure.

Amongst the British composers of sacred cantatas and oratorios we might mention Purcell's *Jubilate,* Sullivan's *The Light of the World,* Stainer's *Crucifixion* and Maunder's *Olivet to Calvary.* The libretto of Handel's famous *Messiah* is almost entirely taken from the Authorized Version. It is a fact that Jennings the compiler of the libretto of the great oratorio, by demonstrating that the coming of Christ the Messiah was long prophesied in the Old Testament, and the fact that God is sovereign over all the events of history, was directly refuting the teaching of the Deists. These were fundamentally ahistorical, claiming that "natural religion" has nothing to do with divinely revealed biblical history.

> "It has been said that no area of high culture was more profoundly influenced by the Reformation than music. Luther himself was a gifted musician, and he strove to compose singable hymns with a strongly Biblical content. He did a stanza by stanza recital of the Ten Commandments as a hymn, and his best known hymn "A mighty fortress is our God", was incorporated into the fourth movement of Felix Mendelssohn's Fifth Symphony and is a free rendering of the Psalm 46, "God is our refuge and strength."
>
> Jaroslav Pelican (2005), 177

This great tradition was clearly carried on in our own country through the influence of the Authorised Version.

As far as the Authorized Version has influenced Art we might just list some of the notable British artists and the paintings that have been influenced by the Scripture narrative.

Sir John Everett Millais 1829–1896, "Jephthah"

Lord Leighton 1830–1896, "Elijah in the Wilderness"

Sir Joshua Reynolds 1723–1792, "The Infant Samuel Kneeling at Prayer"

Ford Madox Brown 1821–1893, "Elijah Restoring the Widows Son"

Sir Edward Burne Jones 1833–1898, "David giving directions to Solomon for the Building of the Temple"

Gabrielle Dante Rossetti 1828–1882, "David as King"
G. F. Watts 1817–1904 "Samson"
Holman Hunt, "The Light of the World"
Joshua to Job the Art and Life Library, W. Shaw Sparrow

THE BIBLE AND THE INDIVIDUAL

Profound and far reaching as the influence of the Bible has been on public life, incalculable has been its influence on the private and devotional life of countless individuals. Wesley wrote:

> When quiet in my house I sit,
> Thy book be my companion still
> My joy thy sayings to repeat
> Talk o'er the record of thy will
> And search the oracles divine,
> Till every heartfelt word be mine.

Innumerable are the testimonies to the saving, strengthening, consoling, purifying power of the Scriptures in the lives of the saints through the centuries.

From the very beginning we read of how Timothy was early taught the Scriptures at home by his mother and grandmother.

Tertullian tells us that reading the Bible aloud in the home was one of the common practices of the early Christian families.

When Oliver Cromwell was dying he asked for Philippians 4:11–13 to be read to him.

He repeated the words of the text:

> Not that I speak in respect of want: for I have learned, in whatsoever state I am therewith to be content.
>
> I know both how to be abased and how to abound: everywhere and in all things I am instructed both to be full and to be hungry, both to abound and to suffer need.
>
> I can do all things through Christ which strengtheneth me.

Then he said:

> It is true, Paul, you have learned this, and attained to this measure of grace, but what shall I do? Ah, poor creature, it is a hard lesson for me to take out! I find it so.

But when he came to the words which followed, faith began to work, and his heart found comfort and support, and he said, "He that was Paul's Christ is my Christ too."

The story of Sir Walter Scott when dying is also well known.

He said to his son-in-law, Lockart, "Bring me the Book." "What book?" replied Lockhart? "The Book," said Sir Walter: "The Bible, there is but one Book."

Katharine Chorley, reminiscing on her Manchester upbringing in the early years of the 20th century, speaks of her parent's beliefs as follows:

> As I look back on Sunday at Ferns I see very clearly that I must distinguish between a materialist philosophy of life and a belief in the economics of capitalism as a basis for one's activities in the world. Father and mother believed, as I have said in the capitalist system, and the outer setting of their lives was framed on its harsh and impersonal economic assumptions, but they and most of their friends were not materialists. For them the inward personal life of a human being was directed to values sanctioned by some authority even more august and compelling than the inexorable law of the market. Although she might never talk about it, mother I know lived with a sense of a last reckoning, the final judgment, in the course of which men's motives and actions would be assessed and explained on a standard of absolute and unshakable values and by an Authority whose verdict admitted of no appeal. In short, most of them believed in absolute and objective values and were immune from the rotting miasma of subjectivism which has soaked into the vision of their successors. We their successors, have been pleased to regard absolute values as out of date because we have cheapened and made superficial the speculations of thinkers, whose researches we have only half understood, and half understanding have erected into the laws of life. And so, encouraged by the determinists that we really could not help ourselves since circumstances and environment and heredity shaped our characters and controlled our actions numbers of which were reflex anyway, and by the psycho-analysts who told us that what we are derives from recondite happenings of our remote childhood, we have substituted a sentimental subjectivism for the virile and uncompromising conviction of personal responsibility to which our parents subscribed. And further enlightened by the creative evolutionists who explained to us that conscience and ethics are simply varying products of the experience of countless

> generations of human beings striving to bond themselves into societies in order to live, we have obliterated the distinction between social morality and personal sin. My generation makes mistakes and does not commit sin. Their generation may have broken and stunted men's bodies in the interests of economic success, but we have extinguished men's souls, and that for no real purpose or goal whatsoever.
>
> Katharine Chorley, *Manchester Made Them*, p. 180–81

We may conclude by saying of Holy Scripture, that it never leaves a man where it finds him, because it bestows privilege, opens up opportunities, and creates responsibilities every time we consult its pages.

Being of Divine origin, it speaks with sovereign authority, and each of us turns aside from it at the cost of our present and eternal ruin.

Let us take this precious Word to our hearts and to our family life, our business life, our church life, our national life, indeed, to every aspect of our lives; let it in all things lead us to Christ the only Saviour and it will prove itself indeed to be the very Word of the living God, the fount of all life and blessedness.

> "Holy Bible book divine precious treasure thou art mine."
>
> Tolle Lege, Tolle Lege— Take and read, take and read

Bibliography

Gabriel Sivan, *The Bible and Civilisation* (Quadrangle, 1973)
Katherine Chorley, *Manchester Made Them* (n.d.).
Jeroslav Pelikan, *Whose Bible Is It?* (Penguin Books, 2005)
T. S. Eliot, *Notes towards the Definition of Culture* (Faber and Faber, 1948)
H.P. Liddon, *Sermons on Old Testament Subjects* (London: Longmans and Green, 1904)
Edward J. Murphy, *In Your Justice* (Ross House Books, 1982)
Francis Schaeffer, *A Christian Manifesto* (Wheaton, IL: Crossway Books, 1981)
Stanley Baldwin, *British Life and Thought* (Hodder and Stoughton, 1928)
Roger Scruton, *England, An Elegy* (Bloomsbury, 2006)
Benson Bobrick, *The Making of the English Bible* (Phoenix, 2003)

William Muir, *Our Grand Old Bible* (Morgan, and Scott, 1911)
F. W. Farrar, *The Bible its Meaning and Supremacy* (Longmans, Green, and Co. 1901)
J.H. Overton, *The Evangelical Revival of the 18th Century* (Longmans, Green and Co. 1900)
Karl Beckinson, *London in the 1890s* (W.W. Norton and Co., 2011)
Arthur Mee, *Our Finest Hour, 1940* (Hodder and Stoughton, 1941)
K.S. Latourette, *The Expansion of Christianity 1500 to 1800*
Kathleen Heaseman, *Evangelicals in Action* (Geoffrey Bles, 1962)
R.Hookaas, *Religion and the Rise of Modern Science* (Vancouver: Regent College Publishing, 2008)
Readings in Modern Theology, Ed. Robin Gill (SPCK, 1995)
C.A. Coulson, *Science and Christian Belief* (Fontana Books, 1958)
J.R. Green, *History of the English Speaking People* (Macmillan and Co., 1920)
David Lyle Jeffrey, *Dictionary of Biblical Tradition in English Literature* (Eerdmans, 1992)
John Drinkwater, *The Outline of Literature* (London: George Newness, n.d.)

2. The Apostolic Fathers and The Early Church Fathers

THE TITLE CHURCH FATHERS IS A GENERAL TERM APPLIED TO THE great figures of the church during the first 5 centuries AD.

> The Apostolic Fathers is the title given since the later 17th century to those Fathers of the age immediately succeeding the New Testament period, whose works in whole or in part, have survived. They are, Clement of Rome, AD 1–96, Ignatius of Antioch, AD 35–110, Hermas, AD c.150, Polycarp of Smyrna, AD 69–155, and Papius, AD c. 150 and in addition the authors of the Epistle of Barnabas, of the Epistle of Diogetus, of the 2nd Epistle of Clement, and The Didache. Sometimes Justin Martyr, AD 103–165 and Irenaeus, AD 100–200 are included in this group
>
> *The Oxford Dictionary of the Christian Church*, p. 76

The Apostolic Fathers are the first generation of Early Church Fathers, and they are those individuals who led the church from about the year AD 95 to AD 140.

When we come to the second century the age of the Early Church Fathers is sometimes called the Early Catholic Fathers, The Patristic Fathers or the Age of the Apologists. Many historians see this period as commencing with Justin Martyr and Irenaeus, and ending with Gregory the Great c. 540–604. Others as we have seen above list Justin Martyr with the Apostolic Fathers

The Early Church Fathers are often listed under the headings of the Greek Fathers and the Latin Fathers, the chief of these are as follows:

The Greek Fathers		*The Latin Fathers*	
Irenaeus	AD 100–200	Tertullian	AD 160–225
Clement of Alexandria	AD 150–216	Hippolytus of Rome	AD 170–235
Origen of Alexandria	AD 185–254	Cyprian of Carthage	AD 200–258
Eusebius of Caesarea	AD 263–339	Ambrose of Milan	AD 338–397
Athanasius of Alexandria	AD 293–373	Jerome	AD 347–420

Cyril of Jerusalem	AD 313–386	Augustine of Hippo	AD 354–430
John Chrysostom	AD 347–407	Leo the Great	AD 391–461
Cyril of Alexandria	AD 378–444	Gregory the Great	AD 540–604
John of Damascus	AD 676–749		

The writings of these individuals vary from the sublime and the excellent to qualities far below that standard. Their writings, even at their very best, fall far below that of the Inspired writers of the New Testament. As James Buchanan puts it, "there is a wide difference between the Historical Theology of Scripture, and the writings of the Fathers. These writings, whether of ancient or more modern date, posses, no divine authority in matters of faith and their teaching on these subjects has no claim on our belief, except insofar as it can be proved to be in conformity with the unerring standard of God's Word". My chief purpose in referring to these writings is that they in spite of their imperfections, sometimes confused, sometimes contradictory, nevertheless, they bear witness to the fact that the great doctrines of the faith were cherished and taught amongst them, i.e. the nature of the Trinity, the creation of the world, the fall of mankind, the grace of God, the divinity and manhood of Jesus Christ the Son of God, the need of salvation, and the doctrine of justification by faith alone etc.

To this end, I have included a series of quotations from this period bearing testimony to the fact that these great doctrines were known and taught.

Alongside this, I have included part of a discourse of Tertullian's on the subject of *The Beauty of Patience*, based on James 1:4. This extract illustrates something of the high standard of Christian living characteristic of the believers of that time.

The following examples are given also with the view of countering the argument of T.F. Torrance's influential book, *The Doctrine of Grace in the Apostolic Fathers*, first published in 1948. Torrance argued that in this period the Apostolic Fathers abandoned Paul's teaching on justification by faith and instead advocated various forms of "works righteousness." A very useful book by Brian J. Arnold published in 2018, examines the writings of Clement of Rome, Ignatius of Antioch, Justin Martyr as well as the Epistle to Diogetus and the Odes of Solomon, in order to refute the arguments of Torrance. Sadly, today there are those who, being misinformed have in the back of their minds the notion that the early Church Fathers either misunderstood or were not interested in the doctrine of grace. It needs to be made known that Christianity in its earliest post apostolic ages held to the essence of Pauline soteriology and that faith alone in the atoning death of Christ is the only prerequisite for justification. The following are sample of the teachings of the Fathers.

The Attributes of God

> Nothing is impossible with God, except to lie… All things are open before Him. Nothing can be hidden from His counsel.
>
> Clement of Rome, c. AD 96

> According to strict truth, God is incomprehensible, and incapable of being measured. For whatever the knowledge is that we are able to obtain about God—either by perception or by reflection—we must of necessity, believe that he is far better by many degrees than what we perceive him to be.
>
> Origen, c. AD 225

> Is anyone greater than God, or more merciful than God's goodness?
>
> Cyprian, c. AD 250

> We will not serve God as though he stood in need of our service, or as though he would be made unhappy if we ceased to serve him. Rather, we do it because we ourselves are benefited by the service of God. And we do it because we are freed from griefs and troubles by serving the Most-High God through his Only Begotten, the Word and Wisdom.
>
> Origen, c. AD 248

> God knows all things. He not only knows those things that presently exist, but also those things that will exist. He knows how each thing will be.
>
> Clement of Alexandria, AD c. 195

The Trinity

He commands them to baptise into the Father, the Son, and the Holy Spirit—not into an unpersonal God.

Tertullian, c. AD 213

It is protected by the power of God the Father, and the blood of God the Son, and the dew of the Holy Spirit.

Clement of Alexandria, c. AD 195

It is after the image and likeness of the uncreated God: The Father planning everything well and giving his commands, the Son carrying these into execution and performing the work of creating, and the Spirit nourishing and increasing.

Irenaeus, c. AD 180

If, then, the Word was with God, and was also God, what follows? Would one say that I speak of two Gods? I will not indeed speak of two Gods, but of one. I speak of two Persons, however, and of a third Economy—the grace of the Holy Spirit. For the Father, indeed, is one but there are two Persons, because there is also the Son. And then there is the third, the Holy Spirit. The Father decrees, the Word executes, and the Son is manifested, through whom the Father is believed on. The Economy of harmony is led back to one God. For God is one. It is the Father who commands, and the Son who obeys, and the Holy Spirit who gives understanding. The Father is above all, the Son is through all, and the Holy Spirit is in all.

Hippolytus, c. AD 205

Creation

God completed all his works in a specified order. At first, he laid them out in their uniform elements, so to speak. Then he arranged them in their finished beauty. For he did not inundate the light all at once with the splendour of the sun, nor did he immediately temper darkness with the moon's soothing beam. He did not adorn the heaven, all at once with constellations and stars. Nor did he at once fill the seas with all their teeming monsters. He did not endow the earth all at once with its various kinds of vegetation. Rather, he first gave it existence; then he filled it.

Tertullian, AD C. 200

The other works of creation he made by the word of command alone. But man, he framed by himself, by his own hand.

Clement of Alexandria, c. AD 195

God formed Adam, not as if he stood in need of man, but so that he might have (someone) upon whom to confirm his benefits.

Irenaeus, c. AD 180

Providence

Those who do not admit that the world was made by divine providence, either say that it is composed of atoms coming together randomly, or that it suddenly came into existence naturally.

Lactantius, c. AD 314

Who can bear to hear it said that this mighty habitation, which is composed of heaven and earth, and is called the "Cosmos," ...was established in all its order and beauty by those atoms that hold their course—devoid of order and beauty? Or, that this same state of disorder has grown into this true cosmos of order?

Dionysius of Alexandria, c. AD 262

When a house or city is built, it does not take on its stones, as though some of them placed themselves spontaneously upon the foundations, and other stones lifted themselves up to the various stories. Rather, the builder carefully places the skilfully prepared stones in their proper positions. In contrast, if the structure happens to give way, the stones are separated, cast down, and scattered about.

Dionysius of Alexandria, c. AD 262

Let Celsus (a pagan critic) then say distinctly that the great diversity among the products of the earth is not the work of providence, but that a certain fortuitous concurrence of atoms gave birth to qualities that are so diverse. Let him say that it was due to chance, that so many kinds of plants, trees, and herbs resemble one another. Let him say that no governing Reason gave existence to them and that they do not derive their origin from an understanding that is beyond all admiration. In contrast, we Christians feel grateful for these things, but we are devoted to the worship of the only God, who created them.

Origen, c. AD 248

Incarnation

The loving Lord became man for us.

Clement of Alexandria, c. AD 195

God suffers himself to be conceived in the mother's womb, and awaits the time of birth. And, when born, he bears the delay of growing up… Furthermore, he is baptised by His own servant.

Tertullian, c. AD 197

He took up man unto himself. Thereby, the invisible became visible; the incomprehensible was made comprehensible; the impassable became capable of suffering. So the Word was made man, and thereby summed up all things in himself.

Irenaeus, p. AD 180

He received testimony from everyone that he was very man and that he was very God.

Irenaeus, c. AD 180

The First Begotten of all creation would become incarnate by the virgin's womb, and be a child.

Justin Martyr, c. AD 160

The holy, pre-existent spirit Person who created every creature, God made to dwell in flesh, which he chose.

Hermas, c. AD 150

He is both the Son of man and the Son of God.

Ignatius, c. AD 105

The Divinity of Christ

He is Lord of all the world, to whom God said at the foundation of the world: "let us make man after our image, and after our likeness."

Barnabas. c. AD 70

God himself was manifested in human form for the renewal of eternal life.

Ignatius. c. AD 105

Continue in intimate union with Jesus Christ our God.

Ignatius. c. AD 105

Truly God himself, who is Almighty, the Creator of all things, and invisible, has sent from heaven, and placed among men, the One who is the truth, and the holy and incomprehensible Word… God did not, as one might imagine, send to men any servant, angel, or ruler… Rather, he sent the very Creator and Fashioner of all things—by whom He made the heavens… As a king sends his son, who is also a king, so God sent him. He sent him as God.

Letter to Diogenetus, AD c. 125–200

The Son ministered to the will of the Father. Yet, nevertheless, He is God, in that He is the First Begotten of all creatures.

Justin Martyr, c. AD 160

Salvation

A man cannot otherwise enter into the kingdom of God, than by the name of his beloved Son.

Hermas, c. AD 150

Open your heart to the Lord, believing that you can be saved by no other name than by his great and glorious name.

Hermas, c. AD 150

But there is no other way than this: to become acquainted with this

Christ, to be washed in the Fountain, spoken of by Isaiah for the remission of sins, and for the rest, to live sinless lives.

Justin Martyr, c. AD 160

No man can know God without both the goodwill of the Father and the agency of the Son.

Irenaeus, c. AD 180

All of these persons, therefore, were highly honoured, and were made great. This was not for their own sake or for their own works, or for the righteousness which they wrought, but through the operation of his will. And we, too, being called by his will in Christ Jesus, are not justified by ourselves. Nor are we justified by our own wisdom, understanding, godliness, or works that we have done in holiness of heart. Rather, we are justified by that faith through which, from the beginning, Almighty God has justified all men.

Clement of Rome, c. AD 96

Into this joy, many persons' desire to enter. They know that "by grace ye are saved, not of works," (Eph. 2:8–9) but by the will of God through Jesus Christ… But he who raised him from the dead will raise up us also—if we do his will, and walk in his commandments, and love what he loved, keeping ourselves from all unrighteousness.

Polycarp, c. AD 135

Atonement

In this manner, the Lord has redeemed us through his own blood, giving his soul for our souls, and his flesh for our flesh. He has also poured out the Spirit of the Father for the union and communion of God and man, actually imparting God to men by means of the Spirit. On the other hand, he has joined man to God by his own incarnation. And he will truly and lastingly bestow immortality upon us at his coming—through communion with God.

Irenaeus, c. AD 180

By his own passion, he rescued us from offences and sins.

Clement of Alexandria, c. AD 180

You have already been ransomed by Christ—and that at a great price!
Tertullian, c. AD 211

When our Lord was suffering upon the Cross, the tombs were burst open, exposing Hades. The souls leaped forth, the dead return to life, and many of them were seen in Jerusalem… Therefore, how great the effect of Christ's death was. For no creature endured his demise with equal mind, nor did the elements of his Passion. Furthermore, the earth did not retain his body, nor Hades his Spirit.
Clement of Alexandria, c. AD 324

The Son was willing to be sent and to become the Son of man, so that he could make us sons of God… He underwent death so that he could present immortality to mortals… At his coming, the Lord cured those wounds that Adam had borne. He healed the old poisons of the serpent. Thereafter, he gave a law to the sound man and bade him to sin no more, lest a worse thing should befall the sinner… Those sins that had been previously committed and purged by the blood and sanctification of Christ.
Cyprian, c. AD 250

Scripture

We have learned the plan of our salvation from no-one else other than from those through whom the Gospel has come down to us. For they did at one time proclaim the Gospel in public. And, at a later period, by the will of God, they handed the Gospel down to us in the Scriptures—to be "the ground and pillar of our faith."
Irenaeus, c. AD 180

I have demonstrated that the Scriptures which we believe are valid from their omnipotent authority.
Clement of Alexandria, c. AD 195

The heretics go the length of impiety by disbelieving the Scriptures!
Clement of Alexandria, c. AD 195

In order that we might acquire an ampler and more authoritative knowledge of himself, his counsels, and his will, God has added a

> written revelation. For the benefit of everyone whose heart is set on seeking him.
>
> Tertullian, c. AD 197

> The heretics have boldly falsified the sacred Scriptures, rejecting the canons of the ancient faith, and ignored Christ.
>
> Eusebius, c. AD 215

> We … believe that it is possible in no other way to explain and bring within the reach of human knowledge this higher and diviner Logos as the Son of God, than by means of those Scriptures, which alone were inspired by the Holy Spirit: the Gospels and Epistles, and the Law and the Prophets, according to the declaration of Christ himself.
>
> Origen, c. AD 225

The following is an extract from the writings of Tertullian who is often ranked next to Augustine, among the orators and theologians of the early Christian church. He was a man of extensive learning, educated in the Greek and Latin classics as well as in all the literature of the church existent at that time. He was born in Carthage, in Africa, about AD 150, some claim educated in the law. His family were pagans, and it was only after he had grown to mature manhood that he became a Christian. Much of his life was passed in Rome. Among his many works on Christianity is his celebrated *Apology* which he wrote in defence of Christianity during the persecution under the Emperor Severus.

The title of this sermon extract is *The Beauty of Patience* based on the text James 1:4.

> In this world we carry about us our very souls and bodies exposed to injury from all men, and under this injury we submit to be patient. Shall we be grieved by taking thought of the things of lesser moment?
>
> Away with such defilement from the servant of Christ, that his patience, made ready for greater temptations, should fall away in trifling ones. If any shall try to provoke thee by open violence, the admonition of the Lord is at hand: "To him that smiteth thee on the face, saith he, turn the other cheek also." Let his wickedness be wearied out by thy patience. Be the blow what it may, bound up with pain and insult, he will suffer a heavier one from the Lord. Thou beatest that wicked man the more by bearing with him, for

he shall be beaten by Him for whose sake thou barest with him. If the bitterness of the tongue should break out in cursing or railing, reflect on that which hath been said: "Rejoice when men shall curse you." The Lord himself was cursed under the law, and yet is the only Blessed. Wherefore let us his servants follow our Lord, and let us take cursing patiently, that we may be able to be blessed. If I hear, not with unruffled mind any wanton or naughty words spoken against me, must I needs myself also render bitter speech in my turn, or shall I be tortured by silent impatience. When, therefore, I have smitten another with evil speaking, how shall I be found to have followed the teaching of the Lord, wherein it is delivered unto us that a man is defiled not by the pollution of vessels, but of those things which proceed out of the mouth. And, again, that there remaineth an account to be given by us for every vain and idle word. It followeth, therefore, that what God forbideth us to do, he also admonisheth us to bear patiently from another.

Here would I now say a word of the pleasure of patience. For every wrong, whether inflicted by the tongue or the hand, when it hath encountered patience, will be finally disposed of in the same manner as any weapon launched and blunted against a rock of most enduring hardness. For it will fall upon the spot, its labour rendered vain and unprofitable and sometimes recoiling back, will wreak its fury by a violent reaction upon him who sent it forth. For a man injureth thee on purpose that thou mayest be pained; for the gain of the injuries lieth in the pain of the injured. When, therefore, thou hast overthrown his gain by being pained, he must himself needs be pained in missing his gain; and then wilt thou come off not only unhurt, which even itself is sufficient for thee, but besides this, both pleased by the disappointment of thine adversary, and avenged by his pain. Such is the profit and the pleasure of patience …

As respecteth the rule of that peace, which is so pleasing unto God, who is there at all, that is of his own nature impatient, who will forgive his brother even once, not to say seven times, and still less seventy time seven? Who while he is in the way with his adversary to the judge will end the matter by agreeing with him, except he first sever from himself that vexation, that harshness, that the bitterness, which are in fact the venom of impatience? How wilt thou forgive and it shall be forgiven thee, if for lack of patience thou be retentive of an injury? No man divided in spirit against his brother will offer his gift upon the altar, except first by being reconciled with his brother, he return to patience. If the sun goes down upon our wrath, we are in danger. We may not continue even for one day without patience. And since it directeth every kind of wholesome discipline, what wonder if it administers also repentance, which is wont to come to the succour of the fallen!

When, in a separation between man and wife (for some cause, that is, for which it is lawful either for a man or a woman to persevere in continuing in a state of widowhood) this patience waiteth for, desireth, urgeth, their salvation, as for those who will one day begin to repent. How much good doth it confere on both? The one it hindereth from adultery, the other it amendeth. In the same manner it is present also in those holy examples of patience in the Lord's parables. It is the patience of the shepherd, which seeketh and findeth the sheep which was gone astray; for impatience might easily despise that one sheep. But through patience he undertaketh the labour of the search, yea, and moreover carrieth on his shoulders the deserted offender, a patient bearer of his burden. Again, it is the patience of the father which both receiveth and clotheth and feedeth the Prodigal Son, and excuseth him to the impatience of his angry brother. He, therefore, which has been lost is saved, because he began to repent. His repentance is not lost, because it meeteth with pleasure. For by whose rules save those of patience is charity instructed; that chief mystery of the faith, that treasure of the Christian name, which the Apostle commendeth with all the power of the Holy Spirit. Charity, saith he, suffereth long; therefore, she useth patience. She is kind. Patience doth no unkindness. She envieth not; this indeed, properly belongs to patience. She savoureth not of wantonness: she hath derived her modesty from patience. She is not puffed up, doth not insult, for this belongeth not to patience. And she seeketh not her own, she beareneth with her own, so she may profit another. Nor is she easily provoked; for otherwise what would she have left for impatience to do? Wherefore, saith, he, charity beareth all things, endureth all things: that is, because she is patient. With good cause, therefore, she shall never fail: for all other things shall be cleared away, brought to a close. Tongues, knowledge, prophecies are exhausted. Faith, hope, charity abide. Faith, which the patience of Christ has produced: hope, which the patience of man waiteth for; charity, which patience acompanieth, God being its master …

In this strength of patience, Isaiah is sawn asunder, and ceaseth not to speak concerning the Lord: Stephen is stoned, and asketh forgiveness for his enemies. Oh, how exceedingly blessed is he also, who against the whole power of the devil worked out in full every sort of patience! Whom neither the driving away of his herds, nor all that abundance of cattle, nor his sons taken away by a single blow of ruin, nor, finally, the torment of his body in its wounded state, deprived of his patience, the integrity which he devoted to the Lord: whom the devil smote with all his might, in vain? For he was not moved away by so many afflictions from his reverence of God, but he was set as an example for us, and the testimony of the working out of patience, both in the spirit and in the flesh, both in the mind, and in the body; so that we may neither sink under the damage of our worldly goods, nor the loss of those most-dear to us, nor even the afflictions of our own bodies. How did God in this man build up a trophy over the devil! How did he set up his banner over the adversary of his glory! When this man, in reply to all the mass of tidings brought to him, uttered nothing from his mouth save thanks to God! When he denounced his wife, already wearied out with afflictions, and advising a wicked remedy! Well! God was rejoiced. Well! the evil one was cut asunder, while Job was wiping away, with great patience, the filthy discharged from his boils, which he was bringing back, in mockery the worms broke out from them into the same holes and pastures of his perforated flesh. Wherefore this labourer for the victory of God, having beaten back all the darts of his temptations by the coat of mail and shield of patience, presently both recovered from God the soundness of his body, and had in possession twice as much as he had lost; nay, if he had wished that his sons should be restored he would have been again called their father. But he had rather that they should not be given back to him at that day. Having full confidence in the Lord, he deferred a joy so great to another season. He endured this voluntary bereavement that he might not live without some kind of patience.

Thus is God an abundantly sufficient depository of patience. If thou placest a wrong in his hands, he is an avenger; if a loss, he is a restorer; if pain, he is a physician: if death, he is the resurrection.

What a licence, hath patience, in having God for her debtor! And not without cause; for she observeth all his pleasure, she interposeth her aid in all his commands. She fortifieth faith, guideth peace, assisteth charity, instructeth humility, waiteth for patience, setteth her mark upon confession, ruleth the flesh, preserveth the spirit, bridleth the tongue, restraineth the hand, treadeth temptations underfoot, driveth away offences, perfecteth martyrdom, consoleth the poor, ordereth the rich, straineth not the weak, wasteth not the strong, delighteth the believer, inviteth the heathen, commendeth the servant to his master, his master to God: adorneth the woman, approveth the man; is loved in the boy; praised in the young man; respected in the old; is beautiful in every sex, in every age. Come, now, let us describe her form and her demeanour. She hath a countenance serene and placid, a forehead smooth, contracted with no wrinkle of grief and anger, her brows evenly and smoothly relaxed, her eyes cast down in humility, not in melancholy. Her mouth beareth the seal of honourable silence. Her colour is such as those have who are free from care and crime. Her head is often shaken at the devil, with a smile of defiance. For the rest, her clothing about her bosom is white and closely fitted to the body, as being neither puffed out nor ruffled. For she sitteth on the throne of that most kind and gentle Spirit who is not in the gathering of the whirlwind, nor in the whole blackness of the cloud, but belongeth to the soft, calm, and simple Voice, such as Elias knew at the third time. For where God is, there is also his foster child, to wit, Patience. When, therefore, the Spirit of God, descendeth, patience never divideth from him, acompanieth him. If we receive her not together with the Spirit, will he abide with us always? Nay, I know not whether he would continue any longer. Without his companion and handmaid, he must needs be grieved at every place and time. Whatever his enemy inflicted he cannot endure alone, lacking the instrument of endurance. This is the way, this the rule, these the words of the heavenly and true, that is, a Christian patience.

International University Course, editor Ernest Barker, p. 402–406

Bibliography

The Oxford Dictionary of the Christian Church, F. L. Cross and EA Livingston, eds. (Oxford University Press, London, 1974)

A Dictionary of Early Christian Beliefs, David W. Bercot, ed. (Hendrickson publishers, 1998)
N.R. Needham, *2000 years of Christ's Power* (Grace Publications, 1998)

3. The Apostles Creed

THE QUESTION IS SOMETIMES ASKED WHAT RIGHT THIS CREED HAS TO be called the Apostles Creed? Does it have any direct connection with the original Apostles? Can we accept the opinion of Rufinus of Aquileia who writing in the year AD 400, gives the following explanation of how the creed came to be composed?

> After our Lord's Ascension (so runs the tradition of our forefathers) with the coming of the Holy Spirit tongues of fire settled on the Apostles, individually. They were thus enabled to speak a variety of different languages, with the result that they found no nation strange to them, and no foreign speech beyond their powers of comprehension. The Lord then commanded them to journey separately to different countries, to preach the Word of God. When they were on the point of taking leave of each other, they first settled on a common form for their future preaching, so that they might not find themselves, widely dispersed as they would be, delivering diverging messages to the people they were persuading to believe in Christ. So they all assembled in one spot and, filled with the Holy Spirit, drafted this short summary, as I have explained, of their future preaching, each contributing the clause he judged fitting: and they decreed that it should be handed out as standard teaching to converts.

This account of its origins was certainly prevalent in the Middle Ages. See page 109 of this work, John Wycliffe's *Exposition of the Apostles Creed.*

Many would argue that the Apostles Creed is an expansion of Matthew 28:19: "Go ye therefore, and teach all nations, baptizing them in the name of the Father, and of the Son, and of the Holy Ghost:"

It is precisely the Church's belief about the Father, the Son and the Holy Spirit that is expressed in this ancient creed. It is a concise expression, summing up the great basic foundations of the faith, which were to perform the basis of all apostolic, missionary preaching.

Long before Rufinus it is evident that the faith of the Apostles Creed was the faith of the Church. Tertullian, writing in the first quarter of the Third Century, (*De Virg.* Vol. 1) affirms that the basic faith of the church was "believing in one God, Almighty, maker of the world, and in his Son Jesus Christ, born of Mary the virgin, crucified under Pontius Pilate; the 3rd day raised from the dead, received in the heavens, sitting now at the right hand of the Father, about to come to judge quick and dead, through the resurrection also of the flesh."

This affirmation dates back to around the year AD 230 but it is possible to trace the origins of this creed to at least the year AD 100.

The baptismal confession of the church in Rome at this time is extremely similar to what we now know as the Apostles Creed. It runs:

> I believe in God the Father Almighty:
> And in Christ Jesus, his only Son our Lord,
> Who was born of the Holy Ghost, and the Virgin Mary,
> Crucified under Pontius Pilate and buried,
> The third day he rose from the dead,
> He ascended into heaven,
> Sitteth at the right hand of the Father,
> Thence he shall come to judge living and dead.
> And in the Holy Ghost,
> The holy Church,
> The remission of sins,
> The resurrection of the flesh.

We see therefore, that these words, from the very first generation after the close of the New Testament were the basic statement of the church's faith. That they summarised the teaching given to new converts, and the affirmation that they were required to make before they were admitted to baptism and the partaking of the Lord's Supper.

It is unlikely that it was written down, and probably slightly varied in its wording from congregation to congregation. No, one reading it however, could doubt its obvious connection with what we now know as the Apostles Creed.

While we cannot with any degree of certainty affirm Ruffinus' account of its first composition, we can trace it back to a very early date. When we read it or repeat the Apostles Creed we can know that we are using a form of words and summary of belief that for more than nineteen centuries has been held by the people of God.

The following notes on the Apostles Creed are taken from Charles Wheatley's work on the *Book of Common Prayer*:

> Though the Scriptures be a perfect revelation of all divine truths necessary to salvation; yet the fundamental articles of our faith are

so dispersed there, that it was thought necessary to collect out of those sacred writings one plain and short summary of fundamental doctrines, which might easily be understood and remembered by all Christians.

This summary, from the first word in Latin, Credo, is commonly called the Creed; though in Latin it is called Symbolum, for which several reasons are given: as, first, that it is an allusion to the custom of several persons meeting together to eat one common supper, wither every one brings something for his share to make up that common meal, which from hence was called Symbolum, which comes from the Greek, which signifies to throw or cast together: even so, say some, the Apostles met together, and each one put in or threw in his article to compose this symbol.

Another signification of the word is fetched from military affairs, where it is used to denote those marks, signs, or watchwords, etc., whereby the soldiers of an army distinguished and knew each other: in like manner, as some think, by this Creed the true soldiers of Jesus Christ were distinguished from all others, and discerned from those who were only false and hypocritical pretenders.

But the most natural signification of the word seems to be derived from the pagan symbols, which were secret marks, words, or tokens communicated at the time of initiation, or a little before, unto those who were consecrated or entered into their reserved or hidden rites, and to none else; by the declaration, manifestation, or pronunciation whereof, those more devout idolaters knew each other, and were with all freedom and liberty of access admitted to the more intimate mysteries, i.e. to the secret worship and rights of that god, whose symbols they had received: from whence the multitude in general were kept out and excluded: which said symbols, those who had received them were obliged carefully to conceal, and not, on any account whatsoever, to divulge or reveal. And for the same reasons, the Apostles Creed is thought by some to have been termed a symbol, because it was studiously concealed from the pagan world, and not revealed to the catechumens themselves, till just before their baptism or initiation in the Christian mysteries; when it was delivered to them as that secret note, mark, or token, by which the faithful in all parts of the world might, without any danger, make themselves known to one another.

That the whole Creed, as we now use it was drawn up by the Apostles themselves, can hardly be proved: but that the greatest part of it was derived from the very days of the Apostles, is evident from the testimonies of the most ancient writers; particularly of St Ignatius, in whose epistles, most of its articlcs arc to bc found: though there are some reasons to believe, that some few of them, vis. that of the descent into hell, the communion of saints, and the life everlasting, were not added till some time after, in opposition to some gross errors and heresies that sprang up in the Church. But the whole form, as it now stands in our Liturgy, is to be found in the works of St Ambrose and Ruffinas.

It is true indeed that primitive Christians, by reason, always concealed this and their other mysteries, nor did their assemblies publicly recite the Creed, except at the times of baptism; which unless in cases of necessity, were only at Easter and Whitsuntide. From whence it came to pass, that the constant repeating of the Creed in the church was not introduced till five hundred years after Christ: about which time Petrus Gnapheus, Bishop of Antioch, prescribed the constant recital of the Creed at the public administration of divine service.

The place of it in our Liturgy may be considered with respect both to what goes before, and what comes after it. That which goes before it are the Lessons taken out of the Word of God: for faith cometh by hearing; and therefore, when we have heard God's Word, it is fit that we should profess our belief in it, there setting our seals as it were, to the truth of God, … What follows the Creed are the prayers which are grounded upon it: for we cannot call on him in whom we have not believed. And therefore, since we are to pray to God the Father, in the name of the Son, by the assistance of the Holy Ghost, for remission of sins, and a joyful resurrection; we must first declare that we believe in God the Father, Son, and Holy Ghost, and that there is remission here, and the resurrection to life hereafter, for all true members of the Catholic Church; and then we may be said to pray in faith.

Both minister and people are appointed to repeat this Creed: because it is the profession of every person present, and ought for that reason to be made by everyone in his own person; the more expressly to declare their belief of it to each other, and consequently to the whole Christian world, with whom they maintain communion.

It is to be repeated standing, to signify our resolution to stand up stoutly in the defence of it. And in Poland and Lithuania the nobles used formally to draw their swords, in token that, if need were, they would defend and seal the truth of it with their blood."

Charles Wheatly, *A Rational Illustration of the Book of Common Prayer* (London: Henry G. Bohn, 1862), p.147.

Bibliography

Charles Wheatly, *A Rational Illustration of the Book of Common Prayer* (London: Henry G, Bohn, 1862)

William Barclay, *The Plain Man looks at the Apostles' Creed* (London: Fontana Books, 1967)

4. Augustine—*The City of God*

It has been said "that if any work deserves the title of a classic of Christian literature, it is most certainly Saint Augustine's *City of God*." (*Masterpieces of Christian Literature*, p141).

It is the first major philosophy of history, and its influence spills over into literature, philosophy, and theology. In its size and scope, it can only be described as monumental, entering into and engaging with every aspect of Christian doctrine. Augustine's purpose is nothing less than to define God, man, and the world. To accomplish this goal, he chooses the metaphorical image of the city, because the city was in his day the centre and model of cultural and political life.

Augustine seems to have been daunted by the thought of what was required of him as he sets out to complete this monumental

work. (He began when he was fifty-nine and completed it when he was seventy-two.) Here he is undertaking to expound the Christian faith, and to justify to enlightened and educated men its superiority to all those forms of belief, philosophical or popular, which were then striving for the mastery, or at least for standing-room in the world of that day. He is attempting to set before the world a vision of glory that might win the regard even of men who were dazzled by the fascinating splendour of a world-wide Empire. He recognised that a task was laid before him to which even his own extensive powers might prove unequal, a task certainly which would afford ample scope for his learning, dialectic, philosophical grasp, acumen, eloquence, and faculty of exposition. He fully acknowledged that without the help of God he could do nothing. He later wrote: "With the help of the Lord, I seem to have paid off my debt, in this, a giant of a book."

Peter Brown in his biographical work, *Augustine of Hippo* recognises that Augustine's immediate concern, as he puts it, was to reach the educated pagans, "through their libraries" (p. 305). He realised that many of the pagans of his day were "fanatical antiquarians."

> They preferred every form of religion and philosophy that could boast an immemorial origin preserved for them in literary classics. It is just this body of literature which Augustine dissects. He intercepts the pagans in their last retreat to the past; he will expose the tainted origins of the cults that were most ancient, and that figured most in the classics; he will play upon the inconsistencies, and hint at the secret incredulity of the writers who preserve this past, their poet, Virgil, their antiquarian, Varro. His discussion of Roman history, also, gravitates around the origins of Rome. These early days had particularly interested the learned pagans of the previous century; and Augustine followed their taste closely.

Augustine himself was thoroughly and deeply acquainted with the pagan ideas, histories, and philosophies he was arguing against. This must have not only impressed his critical readers, but presented them with a challenge, by way of an intellectual *tour de force*. What Augustine was doing was giving Christian answers to pagan questions or as we may put it, countering pagan answers, with superior Christian answers.

Some have also seen the work as revealing an inner dialogue within the mind of Augustine himself, as he wrestles with the pagan ideas he himself in earlier life once embraced. Why was it, for instance, that some of the more noble pagans of Greek and Roman history not only advocated and in some cases exemplified virtues such as frugality, self-denial, chastity, sobriety, courage in the face of death, keeping their sworn word to their fellow-citizens, and even to their enemies.

> By allowing himself to be challenged by these exempla, Augustine transforms the Roman view of their own past. He goes behind the appearance of the conduct of these noble ancestors, to find out why they actually behaved as they did. He answers with a single all-embracing explanation: The Romans had been moved to an outstanding show of virtue by one force alone, by an overweening

> love of praise: they wanted to hoard glory. This is what they loved so whole-heartedly; for this they lived, for this they did not hesitate to die: all other lusts, they battered down with his overwhelming desire.
>
> Peter Brown, *Augustine of Hippo*, p. 310.

It is at this point we need to remember that an important factor in Augustine's producing this great work, at least in part, was to refute the claim of the pagans that the sack of Rome by Alaric and his Visigoths was the result of the abandoning of the Roman gods and the embracing of Christianity.

Here we can appropriately quote Augustine's own preface to the work where he summarises his reasons for writing as follows:

> Rome having been stormed and sacked by the Goths under Alaric, their king (AD 410), the worshippers of false gods, or pagans, as we commonly call them, made an attempt to attribute this calamity to the Christian religion, and began to blaspheme the true God with even more than their wonted bitterness and acerbity. It was this which kindled my zeal for the house of God, and promoted me to undertake the defence of the City of God against the charges and misrepresentations of its assailants. This work was in my hands for several years, owing to the interruptions occasioned by many other affairs which had a prior claim on my attention, and which I could not defer. However, this great undertaking was at last completed in twenty-two books. Of these, the first five refute those who fancy that the polytheistic worship is necessary in order to secure worldly prosperity, and that all these overwhelming calamities have befallen us, in consequence of its prohibition. In the following five books I address myself to those who admit such calamities have at all times attended, and will at all times attend, the human race, and that they constantly recur in forms, more or less disastrous, varying only in the scenes, occasions, and persons on whom they light, but, while admitting this, maintain that the worship of the gods is advantageous for the life to come. In these ten books, then, I refute these two opinions, which are as groundless as they are antagonistic to the Christian religion.
>
> But that no one might have occasion to say, that though I had refuted the tenets of other men, I had omitted to establish my own, I devote to this object the second part of this work, which comprises twelve books, although I have not scrupled, as occasion offered, either to

> advance my own opinions in the first ten books, or to demolish the arguments of my opponents in the last twelve. Of these twelve books, the first four contain an account of the origin of these two cities—the city of God, and the city of the world. The second four treat of their history or progress; the third and the last four, of their deserved destinies. And so, though all these twenty-two books refer to both cities, yet I have named them after the better city, and call them: The City of God.

Such is the account given by Augustine himself, on the occasion and plan of this his greatest work.

In relation to its title, *The City of God* (taken from the Psalms), he explains that this city has a temporal stage here below (where it's citizens are journeying as pilgrims among sinners) and an eternal stage (that is, the heavenly home of perfect peace). In contrast, the earthly city is dominated by a passion for dominion, and from this city, the enemies of the City of God launch their attacks.

The inhabitants of the earthly city, however successful here, will not participate in the joys of the world to come, prepared by Divine Providence.

Moreover, the good and evil things of this life are divided aright between the just and the unjust. Yet the good and bad who suffer are different, even though they suffer the same trials. Though what they endure is the same, their virtues and vices are different. The tide of troubles tests, purifies, and improves the good, whereas it beats down, crushes, and sweeps away the wicked.

At the same time, he notes that every man deserves some temporal affliction, no matter how good he has been, although the good will escape eternal punishment. The fact that the good often fail to speak out against evil, for fear of the loss of some temporal advantage, indicates that the good, as well as the bad, love and are attached to an earthly life. As God tested Job before, so the good must now stand adversity as a test of their mettle and of their love of God. Whatever good men lose in this life, it is always possible for such men to preserve their faith, their piety, and the treasures of the inner life. In the midst of adversity, the good still have more than those who are evil.

Both good and bad men must sooner or later die. Neither has any basic advantage here. Death preceded by a good life, however, is never evil; nothing makes death evil except what is to follow it. This earthly life is a school in which the servant of God is training for life eternal.

Refusing to be enslaved by temporal goods, he uses them as a pilgrim would. Yet, as long as it is here, the City of God cannot be sure who belongs to it. Some who appear to be its members here will not be associated in the eternal felicity of the saints. Among even its notorious adversaries here on earth are men destined to be its friends, however little they know of it now. On earth, the earthly and the heavenly cities are linked and fused together, to be separated at the Last Judgement.

As we have seen above, the first five books major on showing that the sack of Rome was due to internal reasons, corruptions which justly brought about this result.

We may summarise them as follows:

The First Part, Books I–V

A critique of pagan religion

Book I: A criticism of the pagans, who attributed the sack of Rome to Christianity, despite being saved by taking refuge in Christian churches. The book also explains good and bad things happen to righteous and wicked people alike, and consoles the women violated in the recent calamity.

Book II: A proof that because of the worship of the pagan gods, Rome suffered the greatest calamity of all, that is, moral corruption.

Book III: A proof that the pagan gods failed to save Rome numerous times in the past from worldly disasters, long before the sack of Rome by the Visigoths.

Book IV: A proof that the power and long duration of the Roman Empire was due not to the pagan gods but to the providential purposes of the one true God.

Book V: A refutation of the doctrine of Fate and an explanation of the doctrine of Providence, together with an affirmation of God's sovereignty and man's responsibility.

The Second Part, Books VI–X.

A criticism of pagan philosophy

Book VI: A refutation of the assertion that the pagan gods are to be worshipped for eternal life (rather than for temporal benefits). Augustine claimed that even the esteemed pagan theologian Varro held the gods in contempt.

Book VII: A demonstration that eternal life is not granted by Janus, Jupiter, Saturn, and other select gods.

Book VIII: An argument against the Platonists and their natural theology, which Augustine views as the closest approximation of Christian truth, and a refutation of Apulieus' insistence of the worship of Demons as mediators between God and man.

Book IX: A proof that all demons are evil and that only Christ can provide man with eternal happiness.

Book X: A teaching that the good angels desire that God alone is worshipped and a proof that no sacrifice can lead to purification except through the blood of Christ.

The Third Part, Books XI–XIV

The origins of the two cities

Book XI: The origins of the two cities from the separation of the good and bad angels, and a detailed analysis of Genesis 1.

Book XII: Answers to why some angels are good and others bad, and a close examination of the creation of man.

Book XIII: Teaching that death originated as a penalty for Adam's sin.

Book XIV: Teachings on the original sin as the cause for future lust and shame as a just punishment for lust.

The Fourth Part, Books XV–XVIII

The history or progress of the two cities, including the foundational theological principles regarding the part played by Jews

Book XV: An analysis of the events in Genesis between the time of Cain and Abel to the time of the Flood.

Book XVI: The progress of the two cities from Noah to Abraham, and the progress of the heavenly city from Abraham to the kings of Israel.

Book XVII: The history of the City of God from Samuel to David and to Christ, and Christological interpretations of the prophecies in Kings and Psalms.

Book XVIII: The parallel history of the earthly and heavenly cities from Abraham to the end of time. Doctrine of witnesses, that Jews received prophecy predicting Christ, and that the Jews are dispersed among the nations to provide independent testimony of the Hebrew Scriptures.

The Fifth Part: Books XIX–XXII

The final destinies of the two cities

Book XIX: The end of the two cities, and the final glory of the people of Christ.

Book XX: The prophecies of the Last Judgement in the Old and New Testaments.

Book XXI: The eternal punishment of the worldly city.

Book XXII: The eternal happiness and felicity of the saints and explanations of the resurrection of the body.

https:\\en. wikipedia. org/wiki/The City of God

In summing up, we may say that Augustine views history as the sphere of interaction between two cities or societies, an Earthly and a Heavenly, which though contrasting sharply in character run their course concurrently and inseparably. God, the Transcendent, has made all things good. Especially he has made man good and endowed him with every gift that should have ensured virtue and happiness, peace and justice, and eternal blessedness in fellowship with God. Not by nature but by free choice did man fall into his present state of sin and misery, from which redemption comes only by the grace of God. Hence, for while history continues there are two strands in it—the complex strand made up of the multifarious activities of sinful man under the influence of Love of Self; and the simple strand of the work of Grace, whereby "the Love of God is shed abroad in our hearts through the Holy Ghost, who is given to us." Of these the latter, though hidden from most men, is the golden thread running through history, giving it coherence, meaning and a final goal. The Society of mortals dispersed throughout the world is bound together by common descent and by sharing a common nature, and would have remained one and at peace had it pursued its chief good. It divided against itself, because each one follows his own utilities and lusts. But there are not sufficient worldly goods to satisfy all demands, hence the history of sinful man has been a tale of war and strife, conquest and subjection, dominance and slavery, wealth and poverty. Such are politics and economics under the reign of Love of Self. Nay, even the development of the arts and civilisation, intellectual and moral culture, while it is a token of the goodness of man's nature as created, it has been blighted by being subordinated to false ends. All this tends to nought, and would be brought to nought were it not for God's purpose of grace, his

Revelation and Redemption. Another more hopeful story runs side-by-side with that which historians tell, the story of the Promise of God fulfilled in Christ Jesus to his Church.

It is also interesting to note Augustine's hope for the future. Unlike modern secular writers he doesn't greet the future as bright with new inventions, gadgets and amenities. The wonderful achievements of man are not made the basis of a hope of still greater achievements to come. Rather, they are offered as proofs of the goodness of God who bestows these gifts on a condemned race, and his power to bestow even greater gifts on his redeemed in a life wholly spiritual.

History as such, has an end rather than goal. It is a process rather than a progress. Its purely human structures rise and pass away, the earthly city will cease to be a city, and the goods it sought and of which it was inordinately proud fall into corruption and decay. Yet history is not a vain whirl. In it there is accomplished something that will never be destroyed. Throughout its duration there runs the line of Prophets and Apostles, Saints and Martyrs, predestined citizens of the Eternal City, predestined to pass this way to their appointed end. The modern conception of progress as the increasing attainment of security and pleasure is at most the secularised version of the City of God, looked for not in the future life, but now, not in heaven, but here. It is "false eternal" which, when its falsity becomes apparent, leads to bitterness and despair. By Christian faith alone is the relation of the temporal to the eternal rightly understood, so that the temporal receives the respect that it is due, but no more, and its vicissitudes neither exalt nor dismay beyond measure.

Moreover, we may note that Augustine completely refutes the ancient theory of cyclic history. The Stoics believed that the empty aeons of time past and future were filled with endless cycles. Whatever happens, has already happened innumerable times before and will happen innumerable times again. Augustine reasons against this, citing the central affirmation of the Christian faith that Christ died, "Once for all, for our sins."

Again we may note Augustine's emphasis upon the importance of the individual. It has been noted that Augustine would have agreed with Thomas Carlyle's assertion that "*history is the essence of innumerable biographies.*" Christianity, pre-eminently insists upon the worth of the individual. Augustine never loses sight of the individual. Again and again he describes the world of history as a place where the dying give place to those who have been born, which aptly describes the pathos of human life from the personal and individual point of view. He feels passionately that it would be the final intolerable misery to have to believe that there was no possible escape from historical experience, or rather no salvation for the individual. And if the doctrine of the Fall and Original Sin seem to rob the individual of responsibility and freedom, and to this extent merges him in the generality of mankind, the doctrine of predestination assured the believer of God's interest in him from all eternity, and of God's continual care over him until his destiny is fulfilled.

Finally, the life of the saints is a social life, not one of absorption into the One, whether it be the Mystical One without the multiplicity of distinction, or a collectivist One which suppresses diversity. It is the life of redeemed and perfected persons, join together by sharing a common love of God, their Highest Good, and a mutual love one for the other in God.

History is meaningful because by its disciplines God has fitted his people in all generations for fellowship and citizenship in His Eternal City. Individuality and Society are accorded their rightful place. Society is a partnership of persons, and persons reach their true goal in union and reconciliation with God.

History comes to an end when God's purpose of grace has been fulfilled. The end must be the fulfilment and not the destruction of whatever of good has been attained throughout its course. Faith, hope and charity, humility and self-abnegation, strength and patience acquired through suffering, are all taken up and glorified in the Eternal City of God. Here they are lifted free and brought to their goal, that is, happiness in the knowledge and love of God their Creator and Redeemer.

Evil cannot frustrate God's design, for it is met and outmatched by his redemptive power. History is real and earnest at every point, because God originated it and overrules it so that it fulfils his redeeming purpose.

This final summary is based on the concluding chapter of John H.S. Burleigh's work, *The City of God*:

> Unless love for God has priority in our lives the realities we seek—wealth, power, honour, pleasure—become idols. As false gods, they cannot give peace to persons who are "made toward" God. All people seek happiness, and complete happiness is to be found only in the

> supreme good, which is eternal life. "Where God shall be all in all, where eternity shall be firm, and peace most perfect and absolute."
>
> This happiness is visible only to the eyes of faith and is to be received from God for the asking.

Book XIX.20

Bibliography

Frank N. Magill, *Masterpieces of Christian Literature* (Harper and Row, n.d.)

Peter Brown, *Augustine of Hippo, A Biography* (Faber and Faber, 1985)

Augustine of Hippo selected Writings, ed. Mary T. Clark (London: SPCK, 1984)

The City of God, translated by Marcus Dods (Edinburgh: T & T Clark, 1949)

John H. S. Burleigh, *The City of God* (Nisbet and Co. Ltd, Croall Lectures, 1944, this edition, 1949)

5. Boethius—*The Consolations of Philosophy*

Anicus Manlius Torquatus Severinus Boethius, or simply Boethius for short, was the son of an old senatorial family, born most likely in Rome about AD 480 and died in AD 525 or 526. Some have described him as a tragic figure, who at an early age lost his father and was taken into guardianship of another immensely powerful family, that of Quintus Aurelius Memmius Symmachus. In spite of his difficult start by AD 510 he achieved the office of consul, and by AD 522 his two sons were also made consuls. In the same year he became Master of the Offices at the Ostrogothic court in Ravenna under King Theodoric. It was while he was serving in this capacity that Boethius was accused of treason, imprisoned, tried and later executed. It remains very unclear to this day whether he was actually guilty of treason, or as seems much more likely, was simply the victim of the instability of imperial politics at that time.

Boethius' contributions to Western civilisation in general and to theology in particular, in spite of his short life, are wide ranging and most significant. He was highly educated, able to read Greek, and may have studied in Athens. His talents were prodigious, stretching to mathematics and musical theory, logic, theology and philosophy. Whilst imprisoned he wrote, over a period of months, his famous work, *The Consolations of Philosophy*, in which he argued the complete injustice of his fate. It is often remarked that there are no overt references to the Christian faith in this work, and since Boethius was facing almost certain death some have questioned his allegiance to it. It seems clear, however, that he opposed corruption in the state at every level, thereby making himself enemies—when he defended

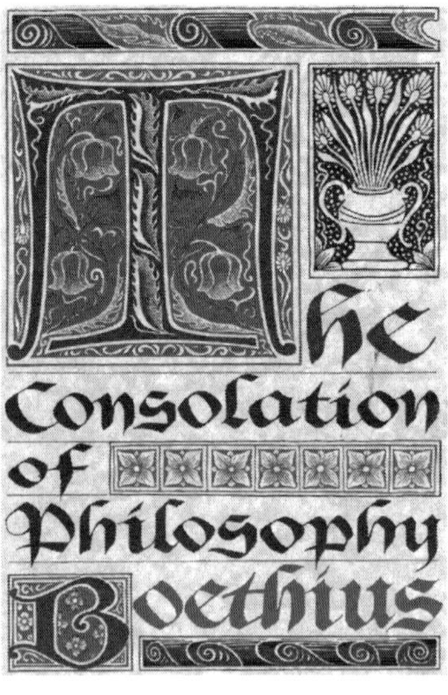

the Senator, Albinus, who was accused of treason on behalf of the Eastern Emperor Justin, Boethius was implicated in the scandal and condemned, unheard, with Albinus. It is also said that he was tortured before execution.

Boethius' theological works give the lie to the suggestion that he was not a true Christian. The first of these was the *Opuscular Sacra,* which covers issues relating to the doctrines of the Trinity, the nature of the Catholic Faith, and the Incarnation. Boethius' work on the Trinity was to be a standard textbook in the Middle Ages, and that writing a commentary upon it was to be a basic part of theological education, the importance of his work in this area cannot be overestimated.

Peter McEnhill summarises Boethius' theological works as follows:

Boethius' work on Christian doctrine deals with the unity of the *Trinity* (conceived in broadly Augustinian terms), the consubstantiality of Father, Son, and Holy Spirit, the importance of Substance, and the Catholic Faith, and includes a work against Eutyches and Nestorius. In this work, Boethius, defends the "Chalcedonian, two natures in one person." account of Christ. His work *On Catholic Faith* gives a short and precise account of Augustine's doctrine of redemption, stressing the uniqueness of the Christian Gospel as a challenge to the philosopher. He is perhaps most known for its famous definition of a person—"a person is the individual substance of a rational nature".

In his *Consolation* Boethius developed a somewhat austere understanding of God as the ultimate unknown mystery, drawing heavily on Aristotle. This inheritance enabled him to make an influential contribution to the thought about God's nature in action—notably in the issues of free will and *universals.* God foresees the free acts of the free will, but this does not destroy their freedom and contingency, for foreknowledge of the act does not imply the necessitation of an act. God sees all things concurrently and eternally, even though they take place through the succession of time in the created world. Boethius draws too on Augustine and Plato in developing an argument for the existence of God as the supreme good, beyond the varying degrees of goodness in human nature. This concept of God, than whom nothing better can be conceived, was to be taken up by Anselm in his famous ontological argument.

The argument of the Consolations of Boethius can be summarised as follows:

1. In Book One of the *Consolations* Boethius is composing mournful verse when a vision of the lady Philosophy appears, to guide him in his hour of need. "Then was the dark night dispelled, the shadows fell away, and my eyes received returning power as before … He who has calmly reconciled his life to fate, and set proud death beneath his feet can look fortune in the face, unbending to good and bad."

2. Book Two brings on Rhetoric, to persuade him not to let his happiness depend on anything that Fortune can give or take away. "Nothing is to be sought in her, and it is plain she has no innate good for she is not always joined with good men, nor does she make good those with whom she is joined."

3. Book Three then raises the issue of the nature of the Supreme Good. God is the supreme good. "Have we not shown that complete satisfaction exists in true happiness, and we have agreed that God is happiness itself, have we not?"

4. Why, then, asks Book Four, do the wicked flourish—Job's question? Good and bad deeds will produce their own eternal rewards. "A man who lacks good cannot justly be described as a good man; therefore, we may say that good habits never miss their rewards. As honest itself is the reward of the honest, so wickedness is itself the punishment of the wicked."

5. Book Five asks whether, then, there is such a thing as Chance. All is under the providence of God, and man must live remembering that he is always in the presence of God. "Hopes are not put vainly in God, nor prayers in vain offered: if these are right, they cannot but be answered."

Throughout the work there is stress on the unreality of earthly greatness, and the superiority of things of the mind. There is no overt reference to Christianity—perhaps at this point, Boethius wishes to distract himself with pure philosophy; we simply do not know.

Boethius's *Consolation* was one of the most influential books of the Middle Ages. It was translated into Old German and Anglo-Saxon, and influenced a range of writers from Alfred the Great, to Chaucer to Dante. His specifically Christian writings and themes were to be much discussed and commented upon by Aquinas and others during the later Middle Ages. Boethius was executed by an Arian King, and this has resulted in his veneration as a martyr saint of the Catholic Church—St Severinus.

(Partly adapted from Peter McEnhill and George Newlands, *Fifty Key Christian Thinkers*, 2004)

Bibliography

Peter McEnhill and George Newlands, *Fifty Key Christian Thinkers* (Routledge, 2004)

Vishal Mangalwadi, *The Book that Made Your World* (Nashville: Thomas Nelson, 2011)

6. Gregory the Great—*Regular Pastoralis*

Gregory the Great (540–604) ruled as Pope AD 590—March 604. He lived at a period of great political turbulence; there was no Emperor in Rome at the time, the Lombards were on the attack, laying waste vast areas of the country, famine, sickness and distress filled the land.

Gregory's labours were immense. He brought about many useful reforms in the Church, checking heresy, and preventing a schism in Constantinople. He brought Spain back from Arianism, and was responsible for sending Augustine to England.

His writings were numerous and important, including his Exposition of Job, Twenty Homilies on the Prophet Ezekiel, a Life of St Benedict, a collection of pastoral letters numbering in the region of eight or nine-hundred. A number of liturgical works and the *Regular Pastoralis*, the subject of this chapter.

The nature and intent of this great work was to teach and instruct bishops, whom he saw as pre-eminent pastors of the flock of Christ, that which was required of them in their high calling. From the outset its value in this respect was seen. The Emperor Charlemagne used it widely in his Church reforms. Hincmar, Archbishop of Reims records that when a bishop was consecrated he was required to kneel before the altar, taking in his hand. *The Regular Pastoralis* and swearing that "he would so live, so teach, and so judge as was therein prescribed and set forth."

The Regular Pastoralis/Pastor Pastoralis was translated into English in the ninth century—so, it is said, by no less a person than King Alfred the Great. The manuscript of this translation copied under the eye of Alfred himself still exists in the Bodleian Library, Oxford. In Alfred's preface, he writes:

> That it had very often come into his mind that there were formally throughout England, wise men, both of the sacred and secular order; and what happy times there were then throughout the country; and how the Kings in those days obeyed God and His ministers; how they preserved peace and morality and order at home, and at the same time enlarged their territory abroad; how they prospered, both with war and wisdom; and also, the sacred orders, how zealous they were both in teaching and in learning and in the service of

> God; how foreigners came to this land in search of wisdom and instruction—and "that we now should have to go abroad for them!" So general, he says, was this decay that there were very few on this side of the Humber who could understand their rituals in English, or translate a letter from Latin into English; and he believed that there were not many beyond the Humber; "so few there were," he continues. "That I do not remember any south of the Thames when I began to reign. It is God Almighty's grace that we have any teachers among us now." "I remember," he goes on, "how I saw, before it had all been ravaged and burnt, how the churches throughout the whole of England stood filled with treasures and books, and there was also a great multitude of God servants; but they had very little knowledge of the books, because they were not written in their own language… And I wondered extremely that the good and wise men who were formally all over England, and had perfectly learned all the books, did not wish to translate them into their own language." Thus he was induced, as he continues to explain, to conclude that it would be a good thing if certain books which were needed for all men to know were to be translated into English, and that all the English youth—if, he significantly adds, we have "stillness" (peace) enough—that all the free English youths that are rich enough, to be set to learn until they are well able to read English writing; let those afterwards go on to Latin, who are to continue learning, and to be promoted to higher places. "So I began," he pursues, "among other various and manifold troubles of this kingdom to translate into English the book that is called "Pastoralis" in Latin, and "Herd-Book" (or Shepherd's Book) in English, sometimes word by word, and sometimes according to the sense, as I have learned it from Pregmund my Archbishop and Asser my Bishop and Grimbold my Mass-priest. And I will send a copy to every bishopric in my kingdom. And on each there is a clasp worth fifty man-cuses. And I command in God's name, that no man take the clasp from the book, nor the book from the minister.
>
> John Cuthbert Headley, *Lex Levitarum* (Westminster Art and Book Co. Ltd. 1906), p.xix–xx

The Plan and Content of Regular Pastoralis

In the first book is considered what kind of men should aspire to the pastoral office; in the second, how the pastor should live and behave;

in the third, how he should teach and direct souls, and in the fourth, which is extremely short, how the pastor, who lives as he should do and teaches wisely and well, should consistently, "return upon himself," (examine himself) by humility, lest his very virtues prove his ruin.

The First Book

This section opens with Gregory's oft repeated remark, "The cure of souls is the noblest of arts or professions." No-one would seek to undertake an ordinary secular profession or vocation without having first studied it and looked into it. No man should aspire to the pastoral office who has not examined whether or not he is truly called by God and considered whether his motives must be pure and his learning sufficient for the task. He must at the same time be someone who has made progress in Christian things and has reached a state of maturity and stability of character. "No one," says Gregory, "does more harm in the Church, then a man who, in name and by his order is holy, and yet leads a bad life." Gregory goes on to speak in serious tones of the weight of pastoral responsibility and the absolute necessity for a pastor to keep a careful watch upon his own soul. He warns those who seek the office simply to gratify themselves or to gain some advantage for themselves that they are committing a grave fault and must fail in the work of God.

The Second Book speaks to those who are already in the pastoral office

First, such an individual must be "pure in thought," (by which he means single-minded), or free from the three chief defiling stains, impurity, vanity and avarice. Next, he must be careful to show a good example to his people; he must preach, by action, as much as by his words. Thirdly, he must know when to speak and when to keep silence. Fourthly, he must unite active sympathy with private meditation and reflection. Fifthly, he must know how to be kind to the good and firm with those who require rebuke. Sixthly, busyness and activity must not diminish his private times of spiritual devotion; he must learn to leave the care of the temporal in the hands of those who are not priests. The seventh point refers to the duty of making oneself liked by the flock—not for self-gratification but for the good of the flock itself. In the eighth place there is a long chapter on the method of correcting or passing over, the faults of others. The ninth and last chapter is on the theme of admonition and is concerned with the pastor's obligation to keep up continually his reading and study of Scripture and other spiritually helpful books.

In the Third Book, he gives instructions on how the pastor is to teach

This section consists of forty chapters. In in a sense, this is a book in itself and takes up more than half of the whole treatise. It is made up of a series of admonitions whose purpose it is to help the pastor to suit his teaching to the kind of people with whom he has to deal. He first summarises his points as follows: "Men are to be admonished differently from women; the young from the old; the poor from the rich; the servant from the master; the prelate from the subject; the bold from the timid; the innocent from the corrupt"—and so on through some thirty-six pairs of antitheses, each of which has a chapter to itself. This book became the principal pastoral manual of the Middle Ages.

> It's wise and pregnant philosophy, its beautiful zeal for souls, its wealth of Scriptural illustration and its finished literary form have justly made it one of the classics of patristic tradition.
>
> John Cuthbert Headley, p. xxiv

The Fourth Book is entitled: How the preacher, all things being duly and well done, is to examine himself, lest either his own virtuous life or his practice may lift him up to pride.

This is a singular chapter, its main emphasis being that a pastor must continuously watch his soul, fight temptation, know his own weakness and be aware of his own faults.

It has been said of *Pastor Pastoralis* that every book on pastoral practice and responsibility that has ever been produced since its production has been indebted in some way to this great book.

Philip Schaff comments:

> The work is well worthy of its old repute, being the best of its kind, and profitable for all ages.
>
> Gregory had not studied in vain the Pastoral Epistles of St Paul. Remarkable indeed is his own discriminating insight, displayed

throughout, into human characters and motives and his perception of the temptations to which circumstances or temperament render various people—pastors as well as members of their flocks—peculiarly liable. No less striking, in this as in other works of his, is his intimate acquaintance with the whole of Holy Scripture. He knew it indeed, through the Latin version only; his critical knowledge is frequently at fault; and his far-fetched mystical interpretations, such as he delighted in, abound. But as a true expounder of its general moral and religious teaching he well deserves his name as one of the great Doctors of the Church. And, further, notwithstanding all his reverence for Councils and Fathers, as paramount authorities in matters of faith, it is to Scripture that he ever appeals as the final authority for conduct and belief."

Philip Schaff, www. ccel.org NPNF-212

Bibliography

John Cuthbert Hedley, *Lex Levitarum* Westminster Art and Book Company Limited, 1906

Philip Schaff, www.ccel.org NPNI-212

7. Bede—*The Ecclesiastical History of the English Nation*

THE VENERABLE BEDE OFTEN CALLED "THE FATHER OF ENGLISH history", was a priest and monk at the Benedictine monastery at Jarrow, Northumberland. It seems likely that he came from a noble and fairly well-to-do family. At the age of seven he was sent to the monastery for his education, which at the time did not necessarily herald the life of a solitary priesthood; but this indeed was the life which he would eventually take up, spending most of his years within the monastery walls and working tirelessly as a scholar.

Jarrow was a new monastery founded by Benedict Biscop (c. 485–c. 580) who had brought back from Rome a good library and a chanter. Bede says, "I wholly applied myself to the study of Scripture, and amid the observance of monastic discipline, and the daily care of singing in the church, I always took delight in learning, teaching, and writing."

A list of his writings includes, besides *The Ecclesiastical History*, numerous biblical commentaries, lives of saints and churchmen, and treatises on the arts and sciences. The latter, in particular were widely influential, not merely in England but also in France, prompting Continental scholars, such as Professor Etienne Gilson, to place Bede alongside Cassiodorus (c.485–c. 580) as an important source of Mediaeval learning.

In regard to his *Ecclesiastical History of the English Nation* it is said that he wrote with "conscientious regard for the truth." For information concerning the centuries prior to the coming of Augustine of Canterbury, he depended upon books written by others; for the critical years during which Augustine and his successors were evangelising the nation, he drew upon documents—such as the correspondence between Gregory I and Augustine—obtained for him from Canterbury and from Rome; for more recent developments he made a point of consulting "Men of good credit" from different

provinces. "I humbly beseech the reader," he says, "that if he shall find anything set down other than truth in this that I have written, he will not impute it unto us, as the which I have endeavoured with all sincerity to put in writing to the instruction of our after comers such things as we have gathered by common report, which is the true law of history."

Much has been written about where Bede's sympathies lay in his account and interpretation of the events he records. One might say, he wrote from the perspective of a supporter of the status quo of his day, but as we shall note further on, he includes some discreetly worded criticisms. He certainly recognised that there was a Church in Britain before the arrival of Augustine. He writes with appreciation the story of its famous martyr St Alban, who was beheaded during the Diocletian persecution. In regard to the indigenous Britons however he draws on Gilda's interpretation, that because of their sinful apostasy God judged them by sending the Saxon invasion. Bede criticises the ancient British Church for its non-evangelisation of the Anglo-Saxons, but this must be balanced as modern historians point out, reminding us that the Saxon invasion was one of great savagery in its first beginning. Having made his criticism of the former British Church, Bede does acknowledge that the Saxons were evangelised by the Irish missionaries who had journeyed from Columba's settlement on the Island of Iona, on the west coast of Scotland, and that they had succeeded in bringing large portions of the northern part of Britain to the faith of the Gospel.

Bede's history was translated from its Latin original into Saxon English by Alfred the Great, assisted by the most able and respected scholars of his day, which of course added to the power and prestige of the translation. The project was a key part of Alfred's translation and educational program undertaken towards the end of the ninth century with the aim of rebuilding the spiritual and moral foundations of his kingdom. Many regard Alfred's translation of *The Ecclesiastical History* as having also the underlying purpose of uniting the peoples of Britain, ancient Britons and Angles-Saxons-Jutes together under a common English Christian identity. A further important aspect of the translation was to encourage his people not to lose faith in the face of the Scandinavian invasions.

Among the many accounts in these writings that have become commonplace in the history of Christianity in these islands we may note his account of the coming of Augustine of Canterbury to Kent in

AD 596 and his reception by Ethelbert, King of Kent, who had married the Christian Princess Bertha, daughter of Charibert, King of the Franks, and who had built for her St Martin's Church in Canterbury.

Bede also recounts the meeting of Augustine with the leaders of the ancient British Church at Aust (Austercliffe) on the banks of the River Severn in Gloucestershire.

Bede records that Augustine warned the ancient British Church leaders that if they did not join with him, "that if they would not have peace with brethren, they should have war with their enemies." This, Bede said, was fulfilled when many of the ancient British monks and priests were slaughtered by the pagan King Ethelfrith at Bangor on Dee, near Chester.

He also records the account of the marriage of Edwin, King of Northumbria, to the daughter of the now Christian King Ethelbert of Kent and the subsequent ministry of Paulinus and King Edwin's subsequent conversion. The sermon was preached in the great hall where the preacher referred to the sparrow flying through the window on a cold winter's night, out of the dark into the light of the hall, and then out again into the darkness as being illustrative of man's ignorance of his origins, destiny and darkness without Christ, not knowing whence he came, or whither he was going and without the knowledge of salvation. He then records the response of the pagan priest Coifi, who, after the sermon encouraged all present to believe what had been spoken, and his subsequent going out and destroying the pagan sanctuary, an account that has been forever impressed upon the English memory.

Likewise, Bede records the events of the Synod of Whitby, and the subsequent part union of the ancient British Church with that emanating from the mission of Augustine.

Foxe in his famous *Book of Martyrs* speaks highly of Bede and his work. There was great interest at the time of the Reformation in the work of the Ancient British and Saxon Churches, as the Reformers sought to illustrate by these histories that the Reformation was simply a restoring of what had been the faith of England in former years.

At the same time, in 1565, the Roman Catholic Thomas Stapleton brought out a new translation of Bede's *History* with the aim of seeking to prove that the Reformers were moving from what he described as "the pattern of that sound and Catholic Faith planted first among Englishmen by holy St Augustine, our apostle, and his virtuous company, described truly and sincerely by the Venerable Bede, so-called in all Christendom for his surpassing virtues and rare learning.".

While it is true that Bede had a high regard for Augustine of Canterbury, and was faithful to the Roman Church of his day, he does at the same time very discreetly reveal the corruptions that were creeping in even at that time. This reveals itself in the way that Bede records the ministry of such a figure as Wilfred. It is nearly certain that Bede had access to Eddius' *Life of Wilfred*. Eddius relates many miracles, said to have been performed by Wilfred, and also describes how he believed God fought on Wilfred's side in his struggle for Episcopal power. At the same time Eddius records that Wilfred was rich and determined to preserve his riches, and his style of life seems to have been much like that of the great secular lords of his day.

In contrast, Bede shows great reserve in his description of Wilfred, he says nothing of Wilfred's wealthy lifestyle, his quarrels, his time of imprisonment, and his many conflicts with other bishops. He does record Wilfred's part in the conversion of Sussex, but nevertheless we find a marked reserve in Bede's account.

The same can be said of his treatment of Theodore of Tarsus, the then Archbishop of Canterbury. Although he refers to Theodore as "of blessed memory," he says nothing by way of a description of his personal holiness or way of life, neither does he attribute to him any miracles. It is surprising that Bede should have so little to say about such an important figure as Theodore was at that time.

When we read Bede's account of some of the former saints of the English Church such as Aidan, Chad and Cuthbert, his reserve in regard to Wilfred and Theodore becomes all the more evident.

In Bede's *Letter to Egbert,* Aidan's way of life was, he says, very different from the idleness of our days. In describing Cuthbert's reception when he went about preaching, he says that in those days' people flocked to the preacher. The implication being that in his day they did not.

> "The Ecclesiastical History has many lessons for the laity; it has more for the clergy. One of its principal functions is to set them good examples. Bede's account of what the Church of England had been in the past is affected by his judgement of what it was and what it ought to have been in his own day. In The Ecclesiastical History, Bede has very little to say about events in England after 690 and he does not

make his views on the contemporary Church explicit. But, thanks to the preservation of his "Letter to Egbert" we know that some of the laity left much to be desired. Avarice, neglect, and ignorance were all too prevalent. His biblical commentaries shed further light on his attitude. They showed him to have held strict views on the proper conduct of the clergy, and in particular on clerical poverty. How rich the clergy may properly be was, and remains, a subject for argument. Bede was adamant that they ought to be poor. Granted Bede's preference for praising the good rather than denouncing the bad, and his belief is made quite clear in his commentaries, that it is wrong publicly to denounce the clergy, be they never so wicked, it seems that his reticence in his history on the recent past of his Church is largely to be explained by his disapproval of some of its members and their acts.".

Bede, *The Ecclesiastical History of the English People*, Ed. H. Trevor Roper pp. xx–xxi

Note on Bede's emphasis on the importance of the date of Easter

Bede has a long account of the Easter controversy in each of the first four books of his history. It is at first sight not easy to understand why he should have given so much attention to what appears to us to be a mere technical issue; for the practice of the Celts seems to have been simply that which had been used elsewhere in the past, but which had become superseded.

But Bede makes it very clear that the calculation of the date of Easter was not merely a technical or isolated issue. However, for Bede and the Church of his day the matter was loaded with significance.

Easter had to be just at the Equinox, for the lengthening of days represented Christ's triumph over the powers of darkness.

It had to be in the first month of the lunar year, for this was the month in which the world had been created and in which it ought to be newly created.

It had to be as the moon was about to wane, for the moon turns from the earth toward the sun as it wanes, just as we should turn from earthly to heavenly things.

It was appropriate that Easter should always fall within the space of seven days, for seven was a number of divine significance.

Considered from another point of view, Easter was to be calculated in such a way as to fulfil both the Old Law of the Jews and the New Law of Christ. If it was celebrated at exactly the right time, then all was in harmony.

Nothing can illustrate the gulf between Bede's thought world and ours more vividly than his views on Easter. Such views were not simple popular piety. They formed part of an elaborate and not unsophisticated system of thought, which brought all knowledge into unity and to Divine ends, and whose power depended on the capacity to see an allegory as a mysterious truth, rather than as an illustration, or a coincidence. Divergences between churches on such a matter as Easter was not a trivial matter. It was a rent in the seamless garment, and it is not surprising that Bede, who was by far the most learned man of his day in regard to computation, should have devoted much of his history to this issue.

Based on: Bede, *The Ecclesiastical History of the English People*, edited by H. R. Trevor Roper, p.xvii–xviii

Bibliography

Bede, *The Ecclesiastical History of the English People*, edited by H. R. Trevor Roper (New York: Washington Square Press, n.d)

8. Anselm—*Cur Deus Homo?* *Why Did God Become Man?*

Anselm, Archbishop of Canterbury from 1093–1109, is known for his works, *Monologian* and *Prosologian,* being demonstrations by rational proofs for the existence of God. *Prosologian* contains Anselm's famous ontological argument for the existence of God, arguing not only that God exists but also that he is a being of which non-greater can be thought.

> Everyone must grant that God is to be understood as a being than whom non greater can be conceived.
>
> A being than whom no greater can be conceived must be conceived of as existing in reality and not merely in thought, for that which is conceived of as having real existence is greater than that which is thought of as only a concept.
>
> Because God cannot be thought not to be, He necessarily exists.
>
> God is at one and the same time compassionate and passionless, just and merciful, sensible and incorporeal, omnipotent and unable to do wrong, unified in being and existing as the Trinity of Father, Son, and Holy Spirit.
>
> Magill, *Masterpieces of Christian Literature,* p. 198

Anselm lived at a time when a need was felt to systematise and demonstrate the inherent rationality of Christian theology. Anselm gave expression to this need in two phrases, i.e. "*faith seeking understanding.*" And "*I believe in order to understand.*" This basic belief was that while faith came before understanding, the content of the faith was rational. These formulae demonstrated the priority of faith over reason, just as they at the same time asserted that faith is not unreasonable. Anselm however was no rationalist, for he believed that reason has its limits. He taught that a demonstration of the reasonableness of faith would be a powerful apologetic tool for convincing nonbelievers at that time, particularly Moslems, of the truth of Christianity.

Turning to what is usually regarded as Anselm's greatest work, *Cur Deus Homo? Why did God become Man?* with our introductory remarks in mind; we are able to understand why there are so few Scriptural quotations included in the setting out of his argument.

> In it, he set out to "prove" the rational necessity of Christ's incarnation and death, but although he thought the sheer reasonableness of his argument should be compelling for unbelievers, he insisted that the proof was not meant to establish faith, but was rather to serve as an example of "faith seeking understanding."
>
> *Masterpieces of Christian Literature*, p. 202

However, in regard to the significance of this work we can heartily agree with Philip Schaff when he tells us with the writing of *Cur Deus Homo?;*

> A new chapter opens in the development of the doctrine of the Atonement.
>
> Philip Schaff, *History of the Christian Church*, Vol. 5, Hendrickson reprinted 1996 p.604

Through the dialogue of Anselm and Boso his pupil, it has pleased the Holy Spirit to lead the Church more fully into an understanding of this great doctrine.

Certainly we can agree with J.K. Mosley's comment that;

> If any one Christian work outside the Canon of the New Testament may be described as "epoc–making", it is the *Cur Deus Homo?* of Anselm.
>
> Quoted by Arthur Pollard in "Anselm's Doctrine of the Atonement", *The Churchmen*, Internet.

Looking at the Main outline of the Book

The main premises of the work can be identified under the following headings:

1. That mankind though made perfect without sin and able not to sin is now fallen and lost and the only way to save him is by the Incarnation and the Atonement.

Anselm's understanding of mankind is thoroughly biblical and orthodox. Through the fall of Adam man is now wholly ruined and given over to the power of the devil, his sin brings with it death. Man is now under the just judgement of God; he has not, in himself, power to avoid sin or its punishment. All men are conquered by sin and unable to save themselves.

Man is now both helpless and hopeless, he has sinned against God, robbed God of his honour and grievously offended against the supreme justice and holiness of God. (book 1:9; Book 2: 2).

2.God has willed to save lost mankind Book II:1

Anselm states that it is clear that God wills to save mankind.

Anselm argues that God is good, so man, his creature, must choose good and hate evil. Since it is inconsistent with the wisdom of God that he should have made man rational and moral but not enabled him to fulfil the end of his creation, (i.e. the enjoyment of God), and inconsistent with the power of God that he should so wish but not effect it, it is clear that God will enable man to be happy in enjoying him.

> *Anselm.* Hence it is easy to perceive, that either God will affect in human nature, that which he began, or he made so exalted a nature for so great good, in vain. But if it be acknowledged that God has made nothing more precious than a rational nature formed to rejoice in him, it is very unlike him to suffer that nature to perish utterly.
>
> *Boso.* No heart informed by reason could think otherwise.
>
> *Anselm.* Thus it is needful that he should complete what he designed in human nature; but, as we said before, he cannot do this, except through an entire satisfaction for sin, which no sinner can make.
>
> *Boso.* I understand it to be certainly necessary for God to carry out what he designed, lest he should appear to give up his intention in a manner inconsistent with himself.

A further motive of course is mentioned by Anselm, and that is God's love. Clearly the love of God is active in providing man's salvation.

3. Anselm's third assertion is that all other ways of salvation are impossible

Mankind cannot be saved without satisfaction for sin.

This part of the argument may be summarised as:

Man cannot save himself.

Neither can angelic beings save him.

Neither can God's compassion save him without justice being satisfied.

> *Boso*. If this deliverance were said to be affected by anyone else, rather than by God himself (whether by angel or by man), in what way matters not, the human intellect would accept the fact much more readily. For God might have made some one-man without sin, not of the sinful mass of humanity, nor from any one man, but as he made Adam: by such a one it would appear that this same work might have been accomplished.
>
> *Anselm*. Don't you understand that whatever other person should save man from eternal death, to him would man rightly belong? If that was so, he could in no wise be restored to that place of dignity, which he would have filled had he not sinned; since he was to have been the servant of God only, and equal in all things to the good angels, he would be the slave of one who was not God and to whom the angels owned no service.
>
> Book 1:5

> For God to put away sin by compassion alone, without any payment of the honour taken from him, he variously describes as "not right," "not fitting," "not proper," "unbecoming," "incongruous" and "inconsistent".
>
> Book 1:12

Only one who is both God and man can save. Herein is the necessity for God to take flesh and dwell amongst us in the Person of Jesus Christ, the God–Man. Anselm's Christ is the authentic biblical, Chalcedonian Christ,

> Very God and very man, one person in two natures, and two natures in one person, and that Person is the eternal Son of God.

Anselm goes on to answer three questions:

1. Why was Christ formed of a woman? Book 2:8

Answer: it serves as a comfort to women, whom I despair of salvation, since the Fall was occasioned by a woman.

2. Why must it be that the Son was sent? Book 2:9

Answer: It must be the Son, and not the Father who comes, because the Son, who is the image of the Father, is the one who restores that image ruined by the Fall.

3. Can God experience suffering? Book 1:8, 2:12, Book 2:18

Answer: Since God is "beyond doubt impassable," Christ had to be man in order to endure suffering.

Anselm also considers the question of the number of the elect

In regard to the number of the elect, Anselm maintains that the number would be equivalent to the number of the angels that did not fall. Book 1:16–18

This we may say is speculation and not accepted by all.

In summing up the points raised by Anselm so far, it is very clear that he teaches that God's redeeming mercies are unmerited and made ours through grace alone.

> "And when we say that God doth anything as by a necessity of avoiding inconsistency; since he feareth it not, this is rather to be understood as that he does it by the necessity of preserving integrity; which necessity is nothing else than his own immutable integrity, which he hath from himself, and not from another; and therefore it is but improperly called necessity. Let us say, then, that it is necessary that the goodness of God, on account of his own unchangeableness, should be perfect in man, what he began, although all the benefits he bestows are of free grace."
>
> 2:5

Anselm's work is most significant in that he emphasises the "satisfaction" element in our Lord's atoning sacrifice.

He moved the Church away from the inadequate concept that had arisen of seeing Christ's atonement as being the price that God the Father paid in order to ransom the lost from the devil.

Anselm brings the Church back to an understanding based on the scriptural truth of satisfaction.

Book 1:19

> That mankind cannot be saved without satisfaction for sin.

Book 1:20

> That the satisfaction should be proportionate to the transgression, nor can man make it for himself.

What however may be seen as the flaw in Anselm's understanding is that he understood the atonement in terms of it being a satisfaction of God's slighted honour.

The Reformers clearly built on Anselm's reaffirmation of the element of satisfaction in their understanding of this great central doctrine of the atonement. They however again got closer to the biblical teaching in showing that it was a satisfaction not to God's slighted honour, but to God's broken law.

In Conclusion

There is a most helpful article posted on the Internet, outlining the content and importance of Anselm's great work. The article is posted by Rev. Angus Stewart and this present summary has drawn heavily on his work in this article. I quote his conclusion in full:

> "Anselm's *Cur Deus Homo?*, is an epoch-making book, a masterpiece of theological learning," declares Louis Berkof, combining "metaphysical depth with clearness of presentation." In many ways it is a model of doctrinal development. Anselm builds his doctrine of the atonement on the previous work of the Church: her formulations of the doctrine of the Trinity (the early ecumenical creeds), original sin (Augustine) and the Person of Christ (especially the Creed of Chalcedon).
>
> Viewing man as a rational creature, in the light of the great obligations placed upon him, Anselm sees man as hopelessly lost, in his heinous dishonouring of the infinite honour of God. Thus it grounds the absolute necessity of the Atonement in the very being of God himself. As Shedd puts it, in Anselm's *Cur Deus Homo*, we have the first systematic and scientific "metaphysique" of the Christian Doctrine of the atonement."
>
> Anselm ably disposes of the old Ransom-to-Satan Theory. Also, to those who seek to resurrect the Example Theory of the Atonement, his words still ring out through the centuries. "You have not as yet estimated the great burden of sin". As we read the Heidelberg Catechism's Lord's Days 5 and 6, we can almost hear the great Archbishop ask, *Cur Deus Homo*?

As we have seen, *Cur Deus Homo?* has its faults, but, with James Ore we must put this down to "the necessary defects of first great attempts." Smeaton's analysis bears repeating: Anselm, "laid the foundation for all the subsequent groundings of the doctrine; and the advances made at the Reformation did not subvert the foundation laid, but fitted into it without incongruity." As the name of Athanasius is recorded in connection with the deity of Christ, and Augustine is forever associated with the doctrines of efficacious grace, and Luther is synonymous with justification by faith alone, so it is only fitting to connect Anselm's name with the necessity of our Lord's glorious atonement.

Bibliography

Cur Deus Homo?, Translated, Rose Corbert (Edinburgh: John Grant, 1909)

Frank N. Magill, *Masterpieces of Christian Literature* (Harper and Row, 1966)

History of the Christian Church, vol. 5 (Hendrickson, 1996)

Arthur Pollard, "Anselm's Doctrine of the Atonement", *The Churchman*, Internet

"Anselm's *Cur Deus Homo?*", article by Angus Steward, Internet

9. *Magna Carta* 1215

At the turn of the 12th century a remarkable transformation was being worked out in England. We were less than 150 years after the Norman Conquest, but already, primarily through the influence of Christianity, Celt and Saxon, Jute and Angle, Viking and Norman were beginning to find their identity as a united compacted nation.

> At this time there went out a new force in the land which king and barons had to reckon with: that of national opinion. It was hard to define, but easy to feel. It was based on Christianity and the love of liberty and open speaking, which the English had inherited from their remote ancestry. It was fostered by a common subordination to the law and of thankfulness for its blessing. At its core lay a strong belief in justice, of fair dealing between lord and vassal, prince and subject, neighbour and neighbour, of a rough working balance in keeping with the Divine law and human conscience. "Take away justice," Augustine had written, "and what are kingdoms but dens of thieves?" The English felt this in their bones.
>
> Arthur Bryant, *Makers of the Realm* (1953), p.278

The year 1205 saw the death of a remarkable Archbishop of Canterbury, Hubert Walter, a godly, wise and sagacious individual. He was held in such respect that he could, as was often needful at the time, admonish and even resist King John himself. On his death John set out to make sure that the next Archbishop would be more to his liking.

King John and his controversy with Innocent III

King John by all accounts was a cruel and unpleasant man. It is true that he was an excellent administrator and took an interest in, and went on to develop, a personal expertise in the workings of government and the running of the Royal household. Foxe in his *Acts and Monuments* sees something of the better side of King John, but it seems to be an undisputed fact that his overall character was one of a slippery and faithless individual.

On the death of Hubert Walter, John nominated John de Gray, Bishop of Norwich, as his successor. This was opposed however by Pope Innocent III, who nominated Stephen Langton. John was furious and thus began a long contest with the Pope, that led to the excommunication of John and the placing of England under an interdict.

John retaliated and remained stubborn until the Pope threatened him with invasion from Philip, King of France. John submitted to the Pope and only remained King as the Pope's vassal, paying a sum of 1000 marks per annum for the privilege. He was also forced to agree to accept Stephen Langton as the Archbishop of Canterbury.

Stephen Langton

Stephen Langton was an Englishman who had excelled in his studies at the University of Paris. He was an exceedingly godly man and Biblical scholar. He was responsible for giving us the chapter divisions in Holy Scripture.

One of his particular areas of study was the application of scriptural principles to the area of law and civil government. It is said that he justified his opposition to the misrule of King John, and the subsequent action he took in supporting the barons, from the Biblical example of the chief priest, Jehoida, (2 Chronicles 22:23) who covenanted with the military commanders and the Levites to restore the legitimate Davidic line of the kingdom of Judah against the actions of Queen Athaliah of the house of Ahab.

The Barons Revolt

Meanwhile because of John's misrule, the barons rose in revolt, and when in 1213, Stephen Langton was finally able to come to England, he assumed the constitutional position as Primate and champion of the old English customs and laws against the personal despotism of the King.

At a Council held in St Paul's Cathedral, he brought before the barons, and explained, the Charter of Henry I, which the barons who were present swore to maintain and fight for. Two years later, at Runnymede, John signed the Great Charter (Magna Carta). Langton signed first for the barons. "The church had led the way and the liberty on which we pride ourselves is the gift of the church to the nation." (Cecil, p. 59).

The Pope refused to accept the Magna Carta, and excommunicated the barons which had signed it, and suspended Stephen Langton from his archbishopric. It was only later in 1216 that he was able to returned to take up his post after the death of John and Innocent III.

Langton clearly saw from the beginning that the problem was that the King's will governed the law. What was needed was that the law should govern the will of the King and his subjects alike. It is said that Henry I (1154–1189) gave England "the concept of administration by law. Stephen Langton gave to England good law to administer."

The Magna Carta

Its preamble reflects the dignified and reverential language of an era dominated by a Christian worldview.

> John by the Grace of God, King of England, Lord of Ireland, Duke of Normandy and Aquitaine, and count of Anjou, to the archbishops, bishops, abbots, earls, barons, justiciaries, foresters, sheriffs, stewards, servants and to all his bailiffs and liege subjects, greetings. Knowing that having regard to God and for the salvation of our soul, and those of all our ancestors and heirs, and to the honour of God and the advancement of his holy Church for the rectifying of our realm, we have granted as the underwritten by advice of our venerable fathers, Stephen Archbishop of Canterbury etc. etc.

This was more than simple religious rhetoric of a bygone era. The preamble itself reflects Christian theological principles about the nature of law and the purpose of the state in the economy of God.

Firstly, it acknowledges that the King reigns by God's grace, as his servant, to foster a commonwealth that regards God and the salvation of souls as preeminent values of the state.

The assumption is that there is a law that is higher than the state. It is God's law, and the implication is that the King is accountable to a rule of law that transcends the state. He is therefore limited in his powers by God himself. As Henry de Bracton expressed it "The King is under no man, but he is under God and the Law."

Secondly the preamble acknowledges the priority of honouring God principally through the advancing of his "holy church" in its redemptive task of evangelism. It is towards this end that the first article of the Magna Carta points.

> Firstly, we have granted to God and confirmed by this, our present charter, for us and our heirs in perpetuity, that the English Church

shall be free, and shall have its rights in full and its liberties intact; and we wish this to be observed …

Great principles of the Magna Carta

1. The Church shall be free from state control or unwarranted interference.

2. No free man shall be taken or imprisoned, or be dispossessed of his freehold, or liberties, or free customs, or be out-lawed, or exiled, or any otherwise destroyed; nor will we not pass upon him, nor condemn him, but by lawful judgment of his peers, or by the law of the land. To no man will we sell or deny or defer to any man either justice or right.

3. Magna Carta established an elected assembly whose duty it was to hold the monarchy to its side of the bargain. Here enshrined was that great balance between the power of the monarch, and the power of Parliament which was to be further established in the Act of Settlement of 1688–89.

Lord Denning, the most celebrated of all 20th century English jurists, declared:"Magna Carta is the greatest constitutional document all times—the foundation of the freedom of the individual against the opportune authority of the despot."

Sir Thomas Fairfax in the days of Cromwell came forward clutching a piece of parchment, its Latin script barely legible, and said "This is that which we have fought for and by God's help we must maintain."

And still when mob or monarch lays
Too rude a hand on English ways,
To whisper wakes, the shudder plays,
Across the reeds at Runnymede,
And Thames, that knows the moods of Kings,
And crowds and priests and suchlike things,
Rolls deep and dreadful as he brings
Their warning down from Runnymede!

Rudyard Kipling

Bibliography

Magna Carta, with commentary by David Carpenter (Penguin Classics, 2015)

J. C. Dickinson, *The Great Charter* (Historical Association, 1955)

Ewen Stewart, *Magna Carta Today* (The Hampden Trust, 2015)
Caroline Cox, Philip Quenby, Paul Diamond, R. S. Harris, Lynda Rose, John Scriven, Michael Nazir-Ali, Roger Trigg, *Magna Carta Unravelled* (Wilberforce Publications, 2015)
Magna Carta (The Christian Institute, 2015)
Arthur Bryant, *Makers of the Realm* (Collins, 1953)
Rudyard Kipling's *Works* (London: Hodder and Stoughton Ltd, 1933)

10. Henry de Bracton—*A Treatise on the Laws and Customs of England De Legibus et Consuetudinibus* (c. 1250)

HENRY DE BRACTON (1210–1268) WAS A LONG-SERVING BRITISH JUDGE who wrote the seminal work on mediaeval English common law. Bracton's treatise, *On the Laws and Customs of England*, remained the main interpretation of British law until the mid-1700s. He also served as a clergyman and ended his career as Chancellor of Exeter Cathedral. He is buried under the aisle of that cathedral.

Bracton was born in Devon, possibly Bideford, studied law at Oxford, and became a judge under Henry III. By the time he entered the legal profession *curia regis*, or king's court, had evolved into a distinct legal forum. By 1245, Bracton had become a justice in Devon. He served on the court that became known as the King's Bench from 1247–50 and from 1253–57. During his tenure, he gained renown for his legal acumen and received a number of royal favours. In spite of the struggles between the Monarchy and the nobility, Bracton emerged as a non-partisan jurist, who was respected by both sides. He served as an early model for the non-biased judiciary. He collected some 2000 decisions in a casebook, or law report, that pioneered the use of precedents and *stare decis* ("Let the decision stand" of lower courts). Bracton's casebook would be emulated from 1291 to 1535 in the publication of an annual legal yearbook. After his retirement from the court, Bracton continued to serve on judicial commissions and as a legal adviser to the monarchy.

Bracton's opus *On the Laws and Customs of England* was the first systematic attempt to codify the common law of Great Britain. Although it is now accepted that much of the work was done previously and that Bracton's main contribution was to edit those earlier pieces, many of the latter sections were authored by the jurists. Bracton sought to provide guidance for lesser judges because English common law was not codified or written down; instead, common law was based on accepted customs and traditions. Judges needed guidance because customs and traditions varied from locality to locality. In addition, Bracton understood that justices often misapplied the law as a result of their own ignorance or inexperience, or applied the law according to their own purposes.

The work contends that justice comes from God, and that laws are accepted restraints on offences against the community or individuals. Bracton asserted that the English legal system was a combination of accepted traditional law and church law, thereby merging justice and law. Nonetheless, Bracton argued for the existence of both judges and the church. Judges or magistrates are needed to interpret and administer the law, and priests to interpret and administer the will of God.

An important point in *The Laws and Customs of England* further reaffirms the supremacy of the monarch but maintains that the monarch must be subject to God and law. Without the supremacy of law, Bracton proclaims that the monarch's rule would be based solely on personal will. The leaders of the Puritan revolution of the 17th century used Bracton's arguments on the supremacy of law to support their rebellion against the unjust rule of Charles I.

A further aspect of Bracton's insistence that the king ought to be under the law, is that Bracton uses an analogy drawn from Christ's death on the cross to emphasise the fact that Christ's death for the sins of the world reveals that God prefers to use justice to regulate the world before the use of power.

> And that he (the King) ought to be under the law appears clearly in the analogy of Jesus Christ, whose vice-regent on earth he is, for though many ways were open to him for his ineffable redemption of the human race, the true mercy of God chose this most powerful way to destroy the devil's work; he would not use the power of force but the reason of justice.

The political and constitutional implications of this are clear: society should be ruled by laws and not by men to prevent the formation of tyranny or a "governmental elite". God's choosing to reconcile humankind to himself through the instrument of justice, as opposed to brute force, serves as a model for the construction of human societies governed by laws, and not elite prerogative.

Justice is embodied in a legal code, that is God's written Law, traced back through the New Testament to Moses' written Law and so to him who is the final authority.

Francis Schaeffer adds:

"In other words, God in his sheer power could have crushed Satan in his revolt by the use of that sufficient power. But because of God's character, justice came before the use of power alone. Therefore, Christ died that justice, rooted in what God is, would be the solution. Bracton codified this: Christ's example, because of who he is, is our standard, our rule, our measure. Therefore, power is not first, but justice is first in society and law. The prince may have the power to control and to rule, but he does not have the right to do so without justice. This was the basis of English Common Law. The Magna Carta (1215) was written within 35 years or so after Bracton's *De Legibus* and in the midst of the same universal thinking in England at that time.

The Reformation (300 years after Bracton) refined and clarified this further. It got rid of the encrustations that have been added to the Judaeo-Christian worldview and clarified the point of authority—with authority resting on the Scripture rather than church and Scripture, or state and Scripture. This not only had meaning in regard to doctrine but clarified the base for law.

The humanists push for "freedom," but having no Christia consensus to contain it, that "freedom" leads to chaos or to slave under the state (or an elite). Secular humanism, with its lack of a final base for values or law, always leads to chaos. It then natura leads to some form of authoritarianism to control the chaos. Havi produced the sickness, secular humanism gives more of the sa kind of medicine for a cure. With its mistaken concept of fi reality, it has no intrinsic reason to be interested in the individual, human being. Its natural interest is the two collectives: the state society."

Francis A. Schaeffer, *A Christian Manifesto*, pp. 2

Bibliography

Francis Schaeffer, *A Christian Manifesto* (Wheaton, IL: C Books, 1981)

Henry de Bracton, *Laws and Customs of England*, online Thor

Legibus et Consuetudinibus, Sir Travers Twiss, ed. (London: and Co. 1882)

11. John Wycliffe—The English Bible

JOHN WYCLIFFE (C. 1329–1384) KNOWN AS THE MORNING STAR OF THE Reformation, was born in Yorkshire, and attended Oxford University; supported by John of Gaunt, he exercised considerable influence in the England of his day. He was a prolific writer, producing a *Summa Theologica,* at least six other known works and numerous pamphlets and writings, many of which it is said lie un-researched in some of the major university libraries of Europe.

Wycliffe set himself to rethink the whole question of the basis of society, with special reference to the status of the Church. The organisation of the Church as a feudal hierarchy seemed to him to be a great mistake, as also did the rich endowments which it enjoyed, a condition of affairs for which he could find no New Testament precedent. Wycliffe went on to propound the theory of "Dominion by Grace", by this he believed that each man was God's direct tenant–in–chief, immediately responsible to God, and immediately responsible to obey his law. For God's law was not canon law, which he repudiated, but God's law is the Bible. The Bible for Wycliffe was the rule of faith and practice, including ecclesiastical practice, and he did not conceive that the Bible's guidance on questions of Church order and organisation could be ambiguous.

So it can be seen that Wycliffe's desire to translate the Bible into English grew out of his concern to find a better pattern for the organising of society, and out of his growing awareness that the doctrines of the Mediaeval Church did not conform to the apostolic tradition.

If men and women were to live by the pattern of God's Word, they needed to know God's Word. And if men and women were to follow after true doctrine again they needed to know the Word of God. It was therefore necessary to translate and make available the whole Bible and that it should be accessible to the common man. Earlier Bible translations had concentrated on those parts of the Bible which were liturgically relevant or had some specific religious value in the narrower sense of the word. Wycliffe's theory of Dominion however meant that the Bible as a whole was applicable to the whole of human life, and therefore should be wholly available in the common tongue.

It is generally believed that it was Purvey who carried much of the

weight of the translation. He has left on record this paragraph on the task and discipline required in the translator of Scripture.

> A translator has great need to study well the sense both before and after, and then also he hath need to live a clean life and be full devout in prayers, and have not his wit occupied about worldly things, that the Holy Spirit, author of all wisdom and knowledge and truth, dress him for his work and suffer him not to err. By this manner, with good living and great travail, men can come to true and clear translating, and true understanding of holy writ, seem it never so hard at the beginning. God grant to us all grace to know well and to keep well holy writ, and to suffer joyfully some pain for it at the last.
>
> F.F. Bruce, *The English Bible*, p. 20.

Both Purvey and Nicholas of Hereford were imprisoned for their allegiance to the teaching of Wycliffe and their association with the Lollards. Some of their associates died at the stake in accordance with the statute *de heretic comburendo* passed in 1401. A synod of clergy meeting at Oxford in 1408 summoned by Thomas Aaron the Archbishop of Canterbury, forbade anyone to translate, or even to read, a vernacular version of the Bible in whole or in part without the approval of his diocesan bishop or other provincial council: this was known as the *Constitutions of Oxford.*

Wycliffe's Bible however made such an appeal to the hearts and minds of the English people that it could not be suppressed, and in spite of the severe penalties attached to its circulation it was widely received and read. Sad to say both Purvey and Nicholas of Hereford abjured their evangelical faith under threat of the stake.

F.F. Bruce gives us the following interesting observation on this subject, he says:

> "There was nothing in Purvey's revision in itself to indicate that it was the product of a movement that had been condemned as heretical. This evidence was contained in the General Prologue, in the prologues to individual books of the Bible, and in the marginal glosses. Copies of the version were made without these additions, and in spite of the Constitutions of Oxford such copies were acquired and read with impunity in many English homes. In due course the Wycliffe origin of the version was forgotten and it was looked upon as a perfectly orthodox work.

> In 1528 Sir Thomas More, Lord Chancellor of England, published *A Dialogue Concerning Heresies* in which he launched a fierce attack upon the English version of the New Testament lately completed by William Tyndale. In the course of this attack he refers to the "great arch-heretic Wycliffe", who undertook "of a malicious purpose" and translated the Bible into English and "purposely corrupted the holy text". It was Wycliffe's activity, he says, that led to the ban on unauthorised versions of the Bible in the Constitutions of Oxford. But it was by no means intended that all Bible versions should be indiscriminately banned for, he goes on," myself have seen, and can show you, Bibles fair and old written in English, which have been known and seen by the Bishop of the dioceses, and left in layman's hands, and women's too, such as he knew for good and catholic folk. But of truth, all such as are found in the hands of heretics, they used to take away."

Now it is almost certain that these Bibles, which Sir Thomas More had seen—probably in nobleman's houses and the like, were copies of the latter Wycliffite version. There was nothing in them that smacked of Lollardy either to himself, to the owners, or to the bishops who sanctioned their use. If the owners were orthodox and practising Catholics, no one would forbid them to read these books.

By the time that Sir Thomas More wrote his Dialogue a new situation had begun to develop in the history of the English Bible, which rendered all the Wycliffe and other early versions obsolete. This was the production of the first printed English Bibles, which were translated not from the Latin but from the original tongues.

Yet it is held by some, when the citizens of London welcomed the first Queen Elizabeth in 1588 and presented her with "The Word of Truth", the volume which she so gratefully received was a copy of Wycliffe's Gospels. We cannot be sure of this, but that would indeed have been a fitting climax to the history of the first English Bible.

Bibliography

F.F. Bruce, *The English Bible*, pp. 22–23, Lutterworth Press, 1961

12. John Wycliffe—The Apostles Creed

As we have seen in the previous chapter, John Wycliffe is best known for the work he and others accomplished in translating the Latin Vulgate into English. He came to be known as the Morning Star of the Reformation and his exposition of the Apostle's Creed demonstrates how his doctrine clearly anticipated that of the Reformers. For notes on The Apostle's Creed and its authorship see chapter three of this work.

The following are Wycliffe's notes on this ancient creed.

The ground of all goodness is steadfast faith, or belief. This, through grace and mercy, is obtained of God. Faith was the principal ground that enabled the woman of Canaan to obtain health of soul and body of Christ for her daughter, who was evil treated of the devil, as the Gospel witnesseth. And the centurion was much praised of Christ for the steadfast belief that he had in the power of his Godhead. Faith is likened to the lodestar, for it showeth the haven of grace to men rowing in the sea of this world. Faith is the Eastern Star, that leads spiritual Kings to worship Jesus Christ, though withstanding of sin, as the East star led the three Kings when Christ was born.

Faith or belief is a stone lying in the foundation of a strong building, that beareth up all the work. For as the buildings standeth stiffly that is well grounded upon this stone, so each virtuous deed is strong when it is grounded upon the solidarity of belief. For upon this stone, that is, solid faith, Christ said that he would build his Church, that is, man's soul. A man that hath lost his right eye is unable to defend himself in battle, for his shield hides his left eye, and so he has no sight to defend himself from his enemy; even so, he that has lost the right eye of true faith is unable to withstand or fight against his spiritual enemy, the devil. Saints, as St Paul saith, through steadfastness and true faith overcame kingdoms. (Hebrews 11). They overcame the kingdom of their flesh through holiness of soul and body; and the kingdom of the world by setting nought riches; and the kingdom of the fiend through patience and meekness.

The want of steadfast faith is the chief cause why men fall into deadly sin. For if a man truly believed that soon after he committed a sin, he should lose one of his limbs, he would, through that belief, keep himself, and flee from that sin. How much more if you believe that

God would punish in body and soul for ever more, if he died in that sin? If man's belief and trust were firmly set in God, all fear of man, fantasies, and fear of this world, would grieve him but little, or not at all. Christ said to his disciples, that if their faith were as great as the seed of mustard and they should say to this hill, pass hence, it should pass; and nothing should be impossible to them. St Jerome saith that faith is likened to the corn seed. If the corn of seed be not broken, the virtue thereof is not known; but the more it is pounded, even the stronger it smelleth; even so, a man who is firmly grounded in the faith, the more he is pounded by persecution, the greater and the more fervent is his belief. Thus if a man's faith were as great as the mustard seed, he should remove from himself the hill of pride, and all other false deceits of the fiend.

This faith maketh our souls so able to receive heavenly gifts, that we may get whatever we desire of the faithful Lord. Oh, blessed is the soul that believeth right and liveth well, and in well living keepeth true faith. While Peter had true faith, he went upon the sea as upon dry land; but when the firmness of his faith failed, he began to sink, and therefore, Christ reproveth him as of little faith. Thus it fares with us, who are staggering and un-steadfast with the wind of each temptation of fear. Therefore, brethren, let us set all our belief and full trust on him, who is Almighty, and not in any vain thing that may fail at any time. Trust we steadfastly that nothing may grieve us farther than he will suffer it, and all things which he sendeth come for the best. And let no wealth of this failing world, neither tribulation, draw our hearts from firm belief in God. Let us not put our belief, or trust in charms, or in dreams, or any other fantasies; but only in Almighty God. For it is full perilous, as the holy doctors say, to scatter man's belief about any such. And let each man and woman take heed to themselves, for good living makes man to have firm belief and trust in God and evil works draw him into despair, as John Chrysostom saith.

After the Ascension of Christ, the Holy Ghost taught his apostles all truth needful to the soul; and by His teaching they twelve settled together twelve articles, which all that will be saved must believe.

(This account of the Twelve Apostles having united to compose the Creed, which goes by their name, is given by Ambrose, also by Ruffinus, and other ancient ecclesiastical historians. The ascribing of each article to a particular apostle is mentioned in a sermon attributed to Augustine. The tradition has been justly questioned, and although this symbol of Christian doctrine was of high antiquity in the Primitive Church, it received additions and alterations at different periods. See Lord King's history of the Apostles Creed, and Bishop Pearson on the Creed. This legend, however, does not involve any erroneous doctrine.)

The first article of belief St Peter put into the Creed, saying,"I believe in God, Father Almighty, Maker of heaven and earth." To believe to God, is one thing; to believe in God is another. The first both evil men and good men have, but the second none but good men have. The fiends believe in God, that is, that he is true, and that his words are truth; and yet some men and women fail of this point! For if they truly believe that the words of God are true, which he speaketh in Holy Writ, against their sinful living, they would amend their defaults, either for dread or for love. To believe in God, as St Augustine saith is, in belief, to cleave to God through love, and to seek busily to fulfil his will; for no man truly believeth in God, but he that loveth God, and by his good living believeth to have bliss of God, as a great doctor saith. And no man, sinneth against God but he fails in belief, which is the ground of all good works: as the same doctors saith, in that he is Father, he will mildly do mercy to men forsaking sin; and in that he is Almighty, He is ready and has the power to punish all those who will not leave their sin. We should believe that God the Father, being Almighty, without beginning and ending, made heaven, earth and all creatures of nought, through his Word.

St Andrew said, "I believe in Jesus Christ, his only Son, our Lord". This article pertains to the Godhead of the Son, the Second Person in the Holy Trinity. We should believe that Jesus Christ, the Son, is equal with the Father, without beginning and ending, equal in might, and all one in might, equal in goodness, and all one in goodness; and that the Son doeth nothing without the Father; and these two Persons are One Almighty God, without beginning and ending. Jesus Christ, God's Son, and in like manner mighty with God the Father, is said plainly to be our Lord by double right; for he bought us with his precious blood, and because he shall be our Judge, and pronounce our sentence.

St James, the son of Zebedee, said, "I believe that he is conceived of the Holy Ghost, and born of the virgin Mary." This is the first article belonging to the manhood of Christ. We should believe that Christ, the Son of God, the Second Person of the Holy Trinity, took flesh and blood truly of the virgin by the Holy Ghost, and came into this world, very God and man, together.

St John, the Evangelist, said, "I believe that he suffered pain under Pontius Pilate, upon the cross, died and was buried." Here we should believe that the same Jesus Christ, very God and man, in the same flesh that he took of the virgin Mary, endured hard pain and sufferings, and even bodily death, by the doom of Pilate, Judge of that province, without impairing of his Godhead. Christ bodily suffered hard pain, for we should have sufferance or patience in our adversities and tribulations. He suffered meekly and never trespassed, for we should suffer willingly, who have much trespassed. Christ was crucified, or we should chastise our flesh by penance (Penance is often used to express repentance. It is evident the reformer here means true repentance, and not bodily penances of the Church of Rome, as he refers to mental operations), withstanding sins and unlawful lusts; Christ died on the cross bodily, that we should endure the cross of penance, withstanding sin to our life's end.

The cross of penance hath four parts. The first is sorrow for losing the love of God; the second is sorrow for losing the joy of heaven; the third is sorrow for deserving the pain of hell; and the fourth is sorrow for serving the fiend and sin. Christ was buried; let this remind us that we hide our good deeds from the favour and estimation of the world, and remember that the earth is naturally the inheritor of our mortal flesh, that our thoughts may be closed from the lusts of this world, steadfastly having in mind the dreadful pains and death of Christ.

St Thomas of India said,"I believe that he went down to hell and the third day he rose from death to life." Here we should believe that Christ's body lay dead in the sepulchre, without the soul, till the third day; that he rose from death to life, but the Godhead departed not from the body, neither from the soul, and after that the soul was departed from the body, it went down to hell; and delivered the holy souls that were there, through virtue of the Godhead. Christ went down into hell, giving as an example that we go thither by inward thought while we live; having mind upon the bitter pains which are there, that we come not thither after this life. Also, he rose the third day, in body and soul together, very God and very Man, everlasting. He would not rise before the third day, to show the time that he was verily dead in body. For if he had risen quickly, it had not been believed that he was verily dead. And as each word of true witnessing is confirmed by the mouth of two or three, so that Christ was verily dead in the body, may be known by his lying in the tomb till the third day. On the third day he rose from death, in token that the light of his death had destroyed our double death, both of Adam and ourselves; and that we should rise from spiritual death by three manner of medicines; by contrition or sorrow of heart, by confession and satisfaction.

St James, the son of Alpheus, said,"I believe that he ascended to heaven, and there sitteth on the right hand of God, the Father Almighty". Here we should believe that Jesus Christ, very God and very Man, everlasting, appeared to his disciples after his rising from the dead, teaching them of the kingdom of heaven, and eating and drinking with them to show that he was very Man, as before his death, ascending into heaven raised mankind above all orders of angels. He ascended to open the gate of heaven, he ascended to show the way to men, and to lead man with him, he ascended to pray the Father for mankind.

St Philip said,*"I believe that he is to come, to doom the quick and the dead."* Here we should believe that the same Jesus Christ, very God and very Man, shall come to the judgement in the same manner, and with the same wounds that he suffered and bore with him to heaven, and shall doom (judge) all mankind, both good and evil, according to their deeds.

That shall be a dreadful doom, and a fearful doomsman. For Christ, who shall be Judge there, is now meek as a lamb, and ready to bow to mercy; but there he will be as stern as a lion to all that are damnable, and doom according to righteousness. Before the stern Doomsman, beholding all saints, angels and fiends, as John Chrysostom saith, all men and women shall yield reckoning of all their living in earth; of all the deeds that they have done; for what intent and to whose worship they wrought them; and not only great trespasses, but also of those that seem much small. For each idle word man shall account there, as Christ saith himself. For as Isadore saith, "Each word that edifies not the hearer turns into peril to the speaker." That is an idle word, as Jerome saith, which profits not the speaker, neither the hearer. And since reckoning shall be holden of such, much more, and without comparison, harder reckoning shall be of sinful speech, as of backbiting, slandering, scorning, false accusing, lying, swearing, cursing, and licentious speech.

Also man shall yield reckoning of all the thoughts of his heart that inclineth to any sin, as God saith, by his prophet. And not only we shall account for deeds done, which we should not have done, but also deeds left undone, which we should have done. As those that have not done works of mercy to poor needy folk, nor given to them, nor lent to them, nor helped them in their suffering, as Christ shall rehearse at the doom as he himself saith.

Also the time man hath in earth, he shall yield reckoning, how he has spent it, as it is written in the book of mourning (Lamentations), and therefore saith Bernard, "All the time given to man, God shall see how he had spent it." And of misspending time, Anslem speaks, saying to man, "O thou unprofitable and dry tree, worthy everlasting fire, what shall thou answer in that day when all the time given to thee shall be asked how thou hast spent it?" Also man shall account there of all his worldly goods. How he has gotten them, kept, spent and lent them. As Christ meaneth by the spiritual understanding of ten pieces of money, and the five talents. Also of all powers of body, as strength, comeliness, swiftness, skill of body—in whose service these have been spent.

Also, each man shall yield reckoning of the keeping of his own soul. For if a King had a daughter like to himself, to whom he thought to give great dignity and worship, and took her to any of his realm to keep; the more negligent that man were about keeping, the stricter reckoning, the King would ask of him for her. What then shall the King of heaven do to him, to whom he has committed a daughter most like to himself, that is to say, man's soul; the much-loved daughter of this King, and ordained to great honour in the bliss of heaven, if this man keep her recklessly? Therefore, God commandeth in the book of his law, that each man carefully keep his own soul. The father and mother also shall account for their children whom they chastised not; as is expressed in Holy Writ, how Eli was punished by his sons, because he chastised them not, as he should have done. Also, the prelate of the curate shall account for his subjects, how he taught them by living and by word; as God saith, by his prophet, a great dread shall be at his doom.

Of the multitude of accusers, man's own conscience, which is defiled with sin and not amended, shall accuse him, not privily, but openly. Also, a man's sins, which he would not leave, shall accuse him. As a stolen thing tied to a thief's neck, accuses him, so shall sins not amended in this life accuse sinful wretches. Also Holy Writ shall accuse them that knew it, and heard it, and lived not thereafter. Such shall bear with them the sentence of condemnation, as Uriah bear with him the sentence of his own death. And in example hereof, Christ said, that

Moses's law shall accuse the Jews. Also, God's creatures, which man has used out of measure and in sin, shall accuse him there, and be as ready to take vengeance upon him, as they were before to serve him. The fiends also shall be ready there accusing sinful men and women, for they, as traitors, enticed to the sin, and whether sin is done they will accuse man thereof. And therefore in the Book of Revelation, the fiend is called the accuser of Christian men. And as Augustine saith, then shall the adversary say, "Thou righteous Judge, doom these to be mine for sin which they have wrought, who would not be Thine by grace. Thine they were by nature, for Thou madest them of nought, but mine they are now, through sin and wretchedness, which they have wrought. Thine they were, for by Thy passion Thou has bought them; mine they are now, for they did the sin that I put into their thought. To Thee they were disobedient, to me they were obedient, and to my enticing. Of Thee they took of the garment of holiness, of me they have taken this coat of sin and filth. Thy garment, they have lost, and with mine they have come hither. Righteous Judge, doom these to be mine, and to be damned with me." Alas! Where shall that wretch abide who is so hard beset?"

Also the benefits which men have received of God, who did not worship him with due service for them, shall accuse them, and be alleged against them. And it is shown in Holy Writ, where the angel came to the place of weeping (by which place is understood the doom, for there shall be weeping and wailing, as John saith in the Book of Revelation). And there he rehearsed the benefits which God hath done to the people, and reproved the people, for they had not them in mind, and worship him not for them. And the torment which Christ suffered in time of his passion, both wounds, cross, nails, and spear, shall accuse sinful men, as Bernard saith.

Therefore, all Christian people have steadfast minds upon this sentence, and flee the unlawful lusts of your flesh, and covetings, and deceits of this deceivable world; and believe ye and have ye steadfastly in mind that Christ shall appear in the judgement, stern as a lion to wicked men's sight, and doom both quick and dead. Of the great dread of that day God speaks by the prophet Joel. The day of the Lord shall be as a day of deliverance, the day of wrath, and the day of vengeance, of misery, of bitterness, the day of complaining and of accusing, the day of dread and of trembling, the day of crying and of sorrow, the day of darkness and of mourning, the day of calamity and of bitterness; a dreadful day of parting from God forever, as Anselm rehearses.

St Bartholomew said,"I believe in the Holy Ghost." Here we should believe that the Holy Ghost, the third Person in the Holy Trinity, is very God, without beginning and ending, and equal in wisdom, might and goodness, with the Father and the Son, and that these three Persons of the Holy Trinity are One Almighty God; and each one mighty, and all one might; and endless good, and all one goodness; and endless truth, and endless wisdom, and endless love, and endless righteous, and endless merciful; all are one truth, one wisdom, one beauty, one Love, one righteousness, and one mercy.

St Matthew said, "I believe in the holy church, and communion of Saints." We should believe the communion of saints, that is, that each of the three parts of the holy church takes part of the others goodness, and helps the other. The part that is in heaven helps the other two parts, praying for them, as Bernard saith; and the other two parts are said to help them that are in heaven, when their bliss and joy is increased by the fellowship of the others. For the more, there are, the more is their bliss, and thus each of these three party's communes with the other.

St Simon said, "I believe in forgiveness of sins." Here we should believe that they who amend their life, doing true penance (repentance) with leaving of sin and keeping God's commandments, and ending in love, shall have forgiveness of all their sins, and Christ, through His passion and death, got for us of His Father forgiveness of our sins.

St Jude said," I believe in the rising of the body." Here we should believe that all mankind shall rise at the day of doom, from death to life, in body and soul together, each in his own kind, and in his own body, incorruptible and immortal. And though the body were burned with fire, and the powder thereof thrown into the four seas that go about the world, yet the soul and it shall come together again, and rise from death to life, at the dreadful doom, and from that day forward, never after depart. And they that have evil lived, and ended in deadly sin, shall go in body and soul to pain for evermore, and they that have lived well in the commands of God, and fulfilled the deeds of mercy after their power, and ended in charity to God and man, shall go, body and soul together, to bliss for evermore.

Of which bliss and life, St Matthias spake in the last article, where he saith, "And I believe in everlasting life." In that everlasting life of joy and bliss, good men and women that ended well, shall dwell in body and soul, world without end.

That life may he to us grant, who bought us with his lifeblood.

Amen

Bibliography

David Ottis Fuller, *Treasury of Evangelical Writings* (Grand Rapids, MI: Kregal Publications, 1971)

13. Thomas à Kempis—*The Imitation of Christ*

THOMAS À KEMPIS WAS BORN IN KEMPEN NEAR KOLN, GERMANY, IN 1380 and died in Zwolle, 1471. His surname was actually "Hemerken" or "Hammerlein" but he is better known by the place of his birth.

He was educated in the school at Deventer, run by the Brethren of the Common Life. Later he entered the Augustinian Convent of Mount St Agnes, near Zwolle, which was a daughter house of the convent of Windesheim, of which his brother was prior. Ordained priest in 1430, he became a sub-prior in 1429 spending the rest of his life in this convent house. He worked as a copyist and is said to have copied out the entire Bible at least four times. Gerard Groote (1340–1384) was one of the founding members of the Brethren of the Common Life, and was one that profoundly influenced the early life of Thomas à Kempis. This movement was part of a wider movement advocating reform which became known as the *Devotio Moderna*.

Adherents of this movement fostered a practical sort of devotion, which sought a close relationship with Christ and the imitation of him in everyday life. Regularity in prayer and in the reading of Scripture was specified, as were activities that would reach out to benefit the surrounding communities and to be helpful to society at large.

Kenneth A. Strand, *John Calvin and the Brethren of the Common Life*, p.68, Internet

The Brethren placed emphasis on the use of the vernacular in order that the common people may understand. One of their leaders, Gerard Zerbolt, wrote a treatise advocating the importance and necessity of such an approach. Groote, Zerbolt and other early leaders of the movement produced a large amount of devotional works in the common tongue. As well as encouraging reading the Brethren also encouraged the keeping of notebooks (excerpt books, or as they were called *raplaria*) in which statements helpful for the living of the Christian life could be jotted down. It is said that the *Imitation of Christ*, had its origin in such a *raplaria*.

One of the further points to be noted about this movement was that it was a reaction to the scholasticism of that day. À Kempis protested strongly against an over speculative approach to the Christian life, which he maintained rested primarily on the need to obey Christ rather than indulge in flights of intellectual fancy. Speculative concern regarding the nature of the Trinity was singled out by him as a case in point.

> What good does it do you if you dispute loftily about the Trinity, but lack humility and therefore displease the Trinity? It is not lofty words that make you righteous or holy or dear to God, but the virtuous life. I would much rather experience contrition than be able to give a definition of it. If you knew the whole of the Bible by heart, along with all the definitions of the philosophers, what good would this be without grace and love? "Vanity of vanities, all is vanity"—except, that is, loving God and serving him alone. For this is supreme wisdom: to draw nearer to the heavenly kingdom through contempt for the world …
>
> Naturally, everyone wants knowledge. But what use is that knowledge without the fear of God? A humble peasant who serves God is much more pleasing to him than an arrogant academic who neglects his own soul to consider the course of the stars … If I were to possess all the knowledge in the world, and yet lacked love, what good would this be in the sight of God, who would judge me by what I have done? So restrain an extravagant longing for knowledge, which leads to considerable anxiety and deception. Learned people always want their wisdom to be noticed and recognised. But there are many things, knowledge of which leads to little or no benefit to the soul. In fact, people are foolish if they concern themselves with anything other than those things which lead to their salvation."
>
> *Imitation of Christ*, quoted by Alister McGrath, *The Christian Theology Reader*, p.114

A concern some Protestants have had in regard to this book is that, it's title *The Imitation of Christ*, gives the impression that it is advocating a Gospel of salvation by works. One typical advocate of this view is that of F. Scott Spencer in his article on "Imitation of Jesus," in Baker's *Dictionary of Scripture, and Ethics*, where he says:

> Luther and other Protestants worried The Imitation of Christ promoted a "works righteousness" path to salvation inimical to faith alone. Calvin noted that "the Lord did many things which he did not intend as examples for us." (*Institutes* 4.19.29), and that "it is not right to take all his actions indiscriminately as objects of imitation (Commentary on John 13:14)—in particular, our Lord's one time, forty-day fast in the wilderness, his healing the paralysed and raising the dead, his imparting the Spirit to his followers, his sacrificial death on the cross.
>
> Jimmy Agan, *Departing from—and Recovering—Tradition: John Calvin and the Imitation of Christ*, Internet.p.803

This article gives the impression that Calvin's outlook on the *Imitation* was primarily negative. This however is not the case and we discover some of these self-same emphases in his writings.

Joseph Milner, the renowned Church historian, is more balanced in his comments on Thomas à Kempis. He wrote:

> It would be impertinent in me to enter into any detail of a performance, so familiar to religious readers: and let it suffice to say that it abounds with the most pious and devotional sentiments, and could not have been written, but by one well-versed in Christian experience, though it partakes of the common defect of monastic writers; that is to say, it does not sufficiently illustrate the doctrine of justification by faith.
>
> Joseph Milner, *Milner's Church History*, Vol IV, p. 290 (London: T. Cadell and W. Davies, 1819)

Whilst it is undoubtedly true that both Luther and Calvin warned against considering the *Imitation of Christ* as a method of salvation by works, they, and particularly Calvin, did not reject the call to imitate Christ as a vital part of the work of sanctification. It must not be forgotten that during Calvin's early university life, at the College de Montaigu in Paris, he became acquainted with the ideals and practices of *The Brethren of the Common Life*, or as it was also known,

The Devotio Moderna. (Not to be confused with the *Via Moderna Movement*), Jacques Lefevre (1455–1536) often known as a "pioneer of French Protestantism" (*A Dictionary of the Christian Church*, J.D. Douglas) was one of Calvin's tutors. Though he never left the Church of Rome his commentary on the Epistles of Paul (1512), is regarded by E. Doumergue as "the First Protestant Book". Lefevre's commentary on the Psalms was also a primary influence on Martin Luther. Lefevre certainly had important links with the *Devotio Moderna* Movement and C. Louise Salley in her work. *The Dawn of Modern Civilisation* identifies extensive comparisons between Lefevre's *Commentary on the Four Gospels* and *The Imitation of Christ* and other works from representatives of the *Devotio Moderna* Movement. (Quoted by Kenneth A. Strand, *Calvin and his Brethren*, p. 76).

Though modern writers have pointed out some of Calvin's warnings about the misuse of the *Imitation of Christ*, it remains an indisputed fact that Calvin on numerous occasions used the term and the concept positively.

For example:

> And to wake us more effectively, Scripture shows that God the Father, as he has reconciled us to himself in his Christ, has in him stamped for us the likeness (imaginem), to which he would have us conform … Christ, through whom we return into favour with God, has been set before us as an example, whose pattern we ought to express in our life. What more effective thing can you require than this one thing? Nay, what can you require beyond this one thing? For we have been adopted as sons by the Lord with this one condition: that our life express Christ, the bond of our adoption."
>
> *Institutes* 3.6.3

> "We have in Christ, the most perfect example of all the graces which God bestows on his children."
>
> *Institutes* 4.16.18

Ronald S. Wallace in his *Calvin's Doctrine of the Christian Life* gives a very helpful chapter on this aspect of Calvin's teaching, for example, in chapter 5 of his book, he writes:

> "Calvin in his introductory remarks to the section on the Christian life in the Institutes, giving the Scriptural exhortations thereto and showing their superiority to any that the schools of philosophy could

> bring forth, Calvin writes, "Scripture … After showing us that we have degenerated from our true origin, viz. the law of our Creator, adds that Christ, through whom we have returned to favour with God, is set before us as a model, the image of which our lives should express." Throughout his Sermons he frequently refers to Christ as the "patron" after which the children of God must be modelled or to which they must be conformed. It is true that this word "patron" can in some contexts be used to signify "patron saint" or "champion," but it's frequent use, along with such words as "mirror" and "image" and "example" shows that Calvin more often means by the use of it to uphold Jesus Christ in his human life as the pattern of true Christian living. The purpose of Christ in making us his disciples is that he might conform us to the imitation of himself."
>
> Ronald Wallace, *Calvin's Doctrine of the Christian Life* (Edinburgh: Oliver Boyd, London, 1959), p.41.

The footnotes of this particular page in Wallace give numerous references to Calvin's commentaries, where these examples can be found.

We might also add to these references Calvin's notes on the Lord's Supper where he essentially regards the imitation of Christ as a summary for the entirety of the Christian life. Before the Supper, a communicant should ponder:

> Whether he rests with inward assurance of heart upon the salvation purchased by Christ. Whether he acknowledges it by confession of mouth; then, whether he aspires to the imitation of Christ with the zeal of innocence and holiness, whether, after Christ's example, he is prepared to give himself for his brethren, and to communicate himself to those with whom he shares Christ in common; whether, as he is counted a member by Christ, he in turn so holds all his brethren as members of his body; whether he desires to cherish, protect, and help them as his own members.
>
> *Institutes* 4.17.40 also "Short Treatise on the Lord's Supper," in *Tracts and Treatise on the Doctrine and Worship of the Church.*
>
> Quoted by Jimmy Agan, *Departing from—and Recovering—Tradition: John Calvin and the Imitation of Christ*, p. 811.

In the same vein, we may add the following quotations:

> It is the holiness of God as he is in Christ, and as in Christ

> represented unto us, that gives us both the necessity and motive unto ours with God." Jesus Christ is morally considered, "the most perfect absolute, glorious pattern of all grace, holiness, virtue, obedience, to be chosen and preferred above all others, but he only is so; there is no other complete example of it.
>
> John Owen

> Those that lay claim to a relation to God, without imitation of him, are not children, but bastards. They may be of his family by instruction, but not by descent. There is no implantation in Christ, without an imitation, both of the Creator and Redeemer.
>
> Stephen Charnock

> To deny the imitation of Christ is "evil and pernicious." So long as we insist on the fact that Christ our Redeemer is the principal focus of our faith. But after Christ our Redeemer, the most precious words to a Christian, are "Christ our example".
>
> B.B. Warfield
>
> Quotations taken from an article by Mark Jones, www.Reformation21.org

The Imitation of Christ in Literature and Hymnody

It is well-known that the Imitation played a part in the conversion of John Newton.

In the Memoirs of the Rev. John Newton, we read of Newton before his conversion on board ship taking up à Kempis's *Imitation of Christ:*

> Among the few books that they had on board was Stanhope's Thomas à Kempis. Mr Newton carelessly took it up, as he had often done before, to pass away the time, but which he had read with the same indifference as if it were a romance. But, in reading it this time, the thought occurred, "What if these things should be true?" He could not bear the force of the inference, and therefore shut the book, concluding that, true or false, he must abide the consequences of his own choice, and put an end to these reflections by joining in the vain conversation, which came in his way.
>
> "But now," says he, "the Lord's time was come, and the conviction

> I was so unwilling to receive was deeply impressed upon me by an awful dispensation..."
>
> *Memoirs of the Rev. John Newton* (Edinburgh: Thomas Nelson Publishers, 1838), p.20

We note also that it came to be a book that John Wesley recommended to his converts, though at first, before his conversion, it doesn't seem as if he thought very much of it. He recorded his first impression of it after being encouraged to read it, by Betty Kirkham in 1725.

> I cannot think that when God sent us into the world, he had irreversibly decreed that we should be perpetually miserable in it. If our taking up of the cross implies our bidding adieu to all joy and satisfaction how is it reconcilable with what Solomon affirms of religion; that her ways are ways of pleasantness, and all her powers of peace.

However, he later wrote an abridgement of the Latin text for his Kingswood Schools in 1748. This edition came to be known as *The Christian Pattern*, and further editions were issued between 1741 and 1788. John Wesley eventually came to recommend that a copy of it should be in every Methodist household.

Zinzendorf wrote three hymns based on passages from *The Imitation* though as far as I am aware, none of these have been translated into English.

One of à Kempis's hymns however, though adapted and somewhat altered by John Mason Neale, (who is sometimes recorded as its author), is the hymn *Lights abode, celestial Salem.*

> Lights abode, celestial Salem,
> Vision whence true peace doth spring,
> Brighter than the heart can fancy,
> Mansion of the Highest King;
> Oh, how glorious are the praises
> Which of thee the prophets sing!
>
> There for ever and for ever
> Alleluia is out-pour'd;
> For unending, for unbroken
> Is the feast-day of the Lord;

All is pure and all is holy
That within thy walls is stored.

There no cloud nor passing vapour
Dims the brightness of the air;
Endless noon-day, glorious noon-day,
From the Sun of suns is there;
There no night brings rest from labour,
For unknown are toil and care.

Oh, how glorious and resplendent,
Fragile body, shalt thou be,
When endued with so much beauty,
Full of health, and strong, and free,
Full of vigour, full of pleasure
That shall last eternally!

Now with gladness, now with courage
Bear the burden on thee laid,
That hereafter these thy labours
May, with endless gifts be paid;
And in everlasting glory
Thou with brightness be array'd.

Laud and honour to the FATHER,
Laud and honour to the SON,
Laud and honour to the SPIRIT,
Ever THREE and ever ONE,
Consubstantial, Co-eternal,
While unending ages run.

Hymns Ancient and Modern 232, 1904 edition
(William Clowes and Sons Ltd)

It is said that General Gordon carried a copy of *The Imitation of Christ* with him into the battlefield.

George Eliot in *The Mill on the Floss* (though no friend of true religion) wrote concerning *The Imitation of Christ:*

> The small old-fashioned book … works miracles to this day, turning bitter waters into sweetness. It was written down by a hand that waited for the heart's prompting; it is the chronicle of a solitary,

hidden anguish, struggle, trust, and triumph … It remains to all times a lasting record of human needs and human consolations.

Bibliography

Thomas à Kempis, *The Imitation of Christ.* ed. Henry Froude (Oxford University Press, 1909)

Alistair E. McGrath, *The Christian Theology Reader* (Blackwell, 1998)

Joseph Milner, *Milner's Church History* (London: T. Cadell and W. Davies, 1819)

Francois Wendel, *Calvin* (Fontana Library, 1965)

Frank N. Magill, *Masterpieces of Christian Literature* (Harper Row, 1966)

Hymns Ancient and Modern (William Clowes and Sons Ltd, 1904)

Ronald S. Wallace, *Calvin's doctrine of the Christian Life* (Oliver and Boyd, 1959)

Kenneth A. Strand, *John Calvin and the Brethren of the Common Life* (Internet)

Jimmy Agan, *Departing from—and Recovering—Tradition: John Calvin and the Imitation of Christ* (Internet)

John Julian, *Julian's Dictionary of Hymnology* (London: John Murray, 1892)

14. Sir Thomas Malory—*Le Morte d'Arthur*

Le Morte D'Arthur was completed in 1469 or 1470 and printed by Caxton in abridged form in 1485. It is the first major work of prose fiction in English and remains today one of the greatest. It is the carefully constructed story of the rise and fall of a powerful kingdom in ancient Britain but generally understood to represent the kingdom of England, which in Malory's day seemed as surely doomed by its own corruption as the ancient realm of King Arthur.

According to Leyland, Sir Thomas Malory was a Welshman, and the story of King Arthur is believed to draw on the Celtic tradition of the Welsh and Bretons. Others have suggested that the figure of King Arthur was adopted by the anglicised Normans in place of the Emperor Charlemagne, the French national hero. Caxton tells us that *Le Morte D'Arthur* was translated chiefly from the French. "Sir Thomas Malory did take out of certain books of French, and reduce it into English" (Caxton's Original Preface p.3).

> *Le Morte D'Arthur* (original spelling *le Morte Darthur*), Middle French for "the death of Arthur" is a compilation by Sir Thomas Malory of romance tales about the legendary King Arthur, Guinevere, Lancelot, and the Knights of the Round Table. The book interprets existing French and English stories about these figures, with some of Malory's own original material (the Gareth story)."
>
> Wikipedia.

The work also draws inspiration from Geoffrey of Monmouth's Chronicle, *Historia Regum Britanniae.*

The following is a further extract from Caxton's original preface to this work.

> After that I had accomplished and finished diverse histories, as well as contemplation, as of other historical and worldly acts of great conquerors and princes, and also certain books of examples and doctrine, many noble and divers gentlemen of this realm of England came and demanded me, many and oft times, where for that I have not made and imprinted the noble history of the Sangreal, and of the most renowned Christian king, first and chief of the three best Christian and worthy, King Arthur, which ought to be remembered among us English men before all other Christian kings."

(These three best worthies, being King Arthur, Charlemagne or Charles the Great, and Godfrey of Bouillon.)

… Divers men hold the opinion that there was no such Arthur, and that all such books as be made of him being feigned and fables, by cause that some chronicles make of him no mention nor remember him nothing, nor his knights. Whereunto they answered and one in special said, that in him that should say or think that there was never such a king called Arthur, might well be credited with great folly and blindness; for he said that there were many evidences of the contrary: first, ye may see his sepulchre in the monastery of Glastonbury. Also in Polichronicon, in the fifth book in the sixth chapter, and in the seventh book, the twenty third chapter, where his body was buried and after found and translated into the said monastery. Ye shall see also in the history of Bochas, in his book De Cassu Principum, part of his noble acts, but also of his fall. Also Galfridus in his British book recounteth his life; and in divers places in England, many remembrances be yet of him, and shall remain perpetually, and also his Knights. First in the Abbey of Westminster, at St Edward's Shrine, remaineth the print of his seal in red wax closed in beryl, in which is written Patricus Athurus Britannie, Gallie, Germanie, Dacie, Imperator. In the castle of Dover, ye may see Gawaine's skull and Caradoc's mantel: at Winchester the Round Table: and at other places, Lancelot's sword and many other things. When all these things be considered, there can no man reasonably gainsay, but there was a king of this land named Arthur. For in all places, Christian and heathen, he is reputed and taken for one of the nine worthy, and the first of the three Christian men. And also, he is more spoken of beyond the sea, more books made of his noble acts than there be in England, as well as in Dutch, Italian, Spanish, and Greek, as in French. And yet records remain in witness of him in Wales, in the town of Camelot, the great stones and marvellous works of iron, lying under the ground, and royal vaults, which divers now living have seen. Wherefore it is a marvel, why he is no more renowned in his own country, save only it accordeth to the Word of God, which say that no man is accepted for a prophet save in his own country … Noble Arthur first and chief of the Christian men.

Caxton then goes on to describe how Sir Thomas Malory had

prepared his work taken out of certain books of French and translated them into English and given him to print.

Caxton goes on to say:

> Wherein they shall find many joyous and pleasant histories, and noble and renowned acts of humanity, gentleness, and chivalries. For herein may be seen noble chivalry, courtesy, humanity, friendliness, hardiness, love, friendship, cowardice, murder, hate, virtue, and sin. Do after the good and leave the evil, and it shall bring you to good fame and renown. And for to pass the time this book shall be pleasant to read in; but for to give faith and believe that all is true that is contained herein, ye be at your liberty; but all is written for our doctrine, and for to beware we fall, not into vice, nor sin; but to exercise and follow virtue; by which we may come and attain to good fame and renown in this life, and after this short and transitory life, to come into everlasting bliss in heaven, the which he grant us that reigneth in heaven, the blessed of Trinity. Amen.
>
> Sir Thomas Malory, *Le Morte D Arthur* (Everyman Library), p.2–3

The claim that the legendary Arthur is based on an actual person is supported by the fact that "Arthur" is a Welsh name derived from the Roman family named Artorious. The figure of Ambrosius Aurelianus, it is argued, could have had the given name Artorious. Roman names had become common in Britain since the conquest under Claudius in AD 43.

Rome began withdrawing troops in the third century AD to protect the Empire from invading barbarians. These difficulties had been increasing in severity for around 200 years but by the time of the fifth century Rome had been steadily decreasing its garrisons in Britain as troops were needed on the Continent. By AD 410, the same year the Goths sacked Rome, all the Roman garrisons had been withdrawn from Britain.

Rome's decision to remove the troops left the people of Britain helpless against invaders. The Roman army stationed along Hadrian's Wall had been Britain's protectors for over 300 years by this time. With the power of Rome withdrawn, the Northern Picts and Scots saw their opportunity and commenced raids on British farms and villages.

About this time, the Saxon Confederacy broke apart on the Continent and Saxon immigrants and raiders began appearing on the South-East coast of Britain.

When no help came from Rome, a British king named Vortigern invited the Saxons to bring a military force to repel the Picts and Scots. The Saxons agreed but, once they had defeated the invaders, decided to stay. According to the historian, Gildas (c.500–570), Bede (672–735) and Nennius ((9th. Cent) as well as many others, Saxon immigration was an immigration in which Britain was sacked and looted continually.

At this time a great British leader appeared, rallied the people around him, and defeated the Saxons at the Battle of Badon Hill. This hero is called Ambrosius Aurelianus, by Gildas and Bede, and Arthur by Nennius, who is the first historian to mention his name. Arthur already seems to have been well known before Nennius' work. The Welsh poem *Y Goddodin,* an elegy for the warriors who fell at the Battle of Catraeth in AD 600, refers to him by name as a great hero. Although extant manuscripts date only from the 13th century, the work is thought to have been composed shortly after the battle. (*Ancient History Encyclopaedia*, King Arthur, internet)

The Identity of Thomas Malory

The true identity of Thomas Malory is still unknown. Some have maliciously tried to identify him with a Thomas Malory of Newbold Revel, who was charged with crimes of murder and violence, theft and rape at some time around 1450. Others that he was a Welsh monk. The fact that he wrote this work whilst imprisoned and translated part of the work from the French has further led to his being identified as a hostage held in France during the French Wars. Arthur Mee believes him to have been a Warwickshire knight, who in the Wars of the Roses, supported the Lancastrian side, and when the Yorkists were triumphant, was not forgiven, but suffered imprisonment and illness while he was in confinement. For he turns aside in the story of Sir Tristram to say that sickness is "*the greatest pain a prisoner may have.*" And, again in the closing sentence of his book, he says:

> "I pray you all gentlemen and gentlewomen, that read this book of Arthur and his Knights, pray for me while I am alive that God send me good deliverance, and when I am dead, I pray you all pray for my soul."

Whether Malory died in prison is not known. It is clear he had no opportunity of revising his book and removing contradictions and blemishes. Caxton received the manuscript from an unmentioned source, it seems, after Malory's death, and himself prepared it roughly for publication.

The Oxford Companion to English Literature says, his identity remains a matter of conjecture. It does seem highly unlikely and extremely far-fetched, to suggest that a man of such culture and spiritual insight should have been a murderer and rapist.

The background to Le Morte d' Arthur

The setting of this work is against the ever increasing and expanding influence of Christian teaching in the West, which had taken hold in the first millennium, and was predominant to some degree at every level of Mediaeval society.

> No other available set of ideas about man and his condition could rival Christian theology and morality in comprehensiveness, sophistication, or profundity. And this message was relevant to the knight as to the priest or the peasant. The most successful of fighting men would take no pride in his finite strength, skill, and virtues, if he began to set them against the infinite perfections of God, seeing them as gifts only kept in being by God's providence, or reflected that pride was the deadliest of sins, a ridiculous assertion of self-sufficiency that invited disaster in this world and damnation in the next. He would not mistreat the weak if he thought that their ultimate worth came, like this, from God's love and an eternal destiny, two infinities that dwarfed all the differences between them, in which they might exceed him, and in which his success might depend on how he treated them. This theory could not be refuted: it could only be ignored. The violence, robbery, and lust of the sixth to the eleventh centuries, show how often and how much it was ignored; but in time, part of the practical implication of this teaching became incorporated in the specifically knightly code of ideals. The knight was obliged to treat all his fellow men, not as a social or political equals—that would have seemed ludicrous—but as beings of infinite worth in the eyes of God. He could make an exception only (if at all) of himself. The ideal has left its mark even on the language in use centuries later: the gentleman was obliged to gentleness and generosity to all. Failing this was not only unchristian; it was also unknightly.
>
> Internet Article

Perhaps this concept is best described in Chaucer's Canterbury Tales, where it is taken for granted that Knights should love and practice the five feudal chivalric virtues of:

> "Chivalrye, trouthe, (loyalty) and honour, freedom and curteisye."
>
> *Canterbury Tales* A 45

It is to be noted that in the fifteenth century chivalry had sunk to a low level. It has been truthfully said that "never had England an aristocracy more-proud and privileged, nor, it would seem, more corrupt, than in the fifteenth century."

This also was the period of the bitter conflicts of the Wars of the Roses, as it was the time of the Black Death, and an increasing awareness of the corruption of the Mediaeval Roman Church.

It is against this background, and as a protest against this decline that the *Morte d' Arthur* was written. Written originally it is said, for the "pleasure of Edward IV."

Malory wrote:

> "O ye knights of England, where is the custom and usage of noble chivalry that was used in these days? What do ye now but go to the baynes* and play at dice? And some not well advised, use not honest and good rule, against all order of knighthood. Leave this, leave it! and read the noble volumes of St Graal, of Launcelot of Galahad, of Tristram, of Perseforest, of Perceval, of Gawain, and many more. There shall ye see manhood, courtesy and gentleness. And look in latter days of the noble acts since the Conquest, in King Richard's days Coer de Lion, Edward First and the Third and his noble sons, Sir Walter Manny; read Froissart, and also behold that victorious and noble King Harry the Fifth, the captains under him, his noble brethren, the Earls of Salisbury, Montagu, and many others whose names shine gloriously by their virtuous noblesse and acts that they did in the honour of the order of chivalry. Alas! What do ye but sleep and take ease, and are all disordered from chivalry?"
>
> Edgar Prestage, *Chivalry*, p. 180

(*Baynes, possible meaning, ballad singers)

Malory's story has as its aim to explore the forces which bring kingdoms into being and the forces internal, and external, which destroyed them. Malory's vision has relevance for any kingdom or civilisation in identifying that which builds up and that which destroys.

In the 19th century, Alfred Lord Tennyson drew on the account of King Arthur and the Knights of the Round Table in his poetic work, *Idylls of the King*. He presented the poem to Queen Victoria, who at that time was ruler over the world's greatest empire, an empire on which the sun never set. There is implicit in Tennyson's poem as in Malory's work that even the perfect King and the perfect kingdom cannot survive the loss of true faith. The unity of the Round Table broke down under the evil influences of the character Mordred and whether the tale is fact or fiction the moral of the story cannot be denied.

> "Righteousness exalteth a nation, sin is a reproach to any people."
>
> "Blessed are the people whose God is the Lord."

End Notes.

Caxton records in regard to Sir Thomas Malory… "He was the servant of Jesu both by day and night."

> Malory groups the legends around the central idea of the search for the Holy Grail. Though many of the stories, like Tristram and Isolde, are purely pagan, Malory treats them all in such a way as to preserve the whole spirit of mediaeval Christianity as it has been preserved in no other work. It was to Malory rather than to Layamon or to the early French writers that Shakespeare and his contemporaries turned for their material; and in our own age, he supplied Tennyson and Matthew Arnold and Swinburne and Morris with the inspiration for the "Idylls of the King," and the "Death of Tristram" and the other exquisite poems, which centre about Arthur and the Knights of the Round Table.
>
> In subject-matter the book belongs to the mediaeval age; but Malory himself, with his desire to preserve the literary monuments of the past, belongs to the Renaissance; and he deserves our lasting gratitude for attempting to preserve the legends of poetry in Britain at a time when scholars were chiefly busy with the classics of Greece and Rome. As the Arthurian legends are one of the great recurring motives of English literature, Malory's work should be better known. The stories may be and should be told to every child as part of his

> literary inheritance. Then Malory may be read for his style and his English prose and his expression of the mediaeval spirit. And then the stories may be read again, in Tennyson's "Idylls," to show how those exquisite old fancies appeal to the minds of modern poets.
>
> William J. Long, *English Literature, Its History and Significance for the Life of the English-Speaking World*, 1909

Bibliography

English Literature, Its History and Significance for the Life of the English Speaking World (William J. Long, 1909)

Edgar Prestage, *Chivalry* (London: Kegan Paul Trench, Trubner and Co. Ltd. 1928)

Sir Paul Harvey, *Oxford Companion to English Literature* (Oxford: Clarendon Press, 1958)

Sir Thomas Malory, *Le Morte d' Arthur* (Everyman Library)

15. William Tyndale—
The Obedience of the Christian Man

THIS WORK, WE MIGHT SAY, IS THE LARGEST AND MOST SIGNIFICANT of Tyndale's writings, next to his translation of the Bible. It was the book by which he was best known to his contemporaries, and which, the Scriptures apart, exerted the greatest influence on those friendly toward the Reformation. At the same time, it provoked deep resentment and hostility amongst his opponents. In it, others have remarked, the mind of Tyndale is most fully revealed. (Robert Demaus, *Tyndale*, p.222)

It was first published in 1528 and the book was a protest against the ever growing power and all pervasive influence of the now corrupt and worldly Roman Church. The papacy at this time exercised a super–national jurisdiction over Europe and beyond. Rome now claimed the right to act as a tax gatherer of nations, and to control the awarding of benefices within each of the national churches. At the same time, a system known as the "benefit of clergy," operated in which clergy could secure immunity from prosecution in the ordinary courts of law. The overweening wealth and power of the Church, coupled with the luxurious lifestyles of many of its leading figures and representatives, was viewed with an ever increasing dissatisfaction and contempt by many. On top of this there was a growing reaction against interference and intrigues perpetrated by Rome in the affairs of the various sovereign states.

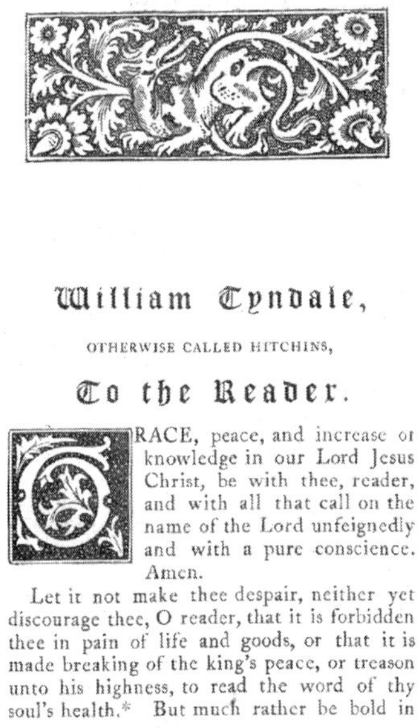
William Tyndale,

OTHERWISE CALLED HITCHINS,

To the Reader.

GRACE, peace, and increase of knowledge in our Lord Jesus Christ, be with thee, reader, and with all that call on the name of the Lord unfeignedly and with a pure conscience. Amen.

Let it not make thee despair, neither yet discourage thee, O reader, that it is forbidden thee in pain of life and goods, or that it is made breaking of the king's peace, or treason unto his highness, to read the word of thy soul's health.* But much rather be bold in

In the Lutheran states of Germany debate had begun on the concept of "worldly authority". Melanchthon had written an important essay on the subject. Meanwhile in England, Barnes had written on the theme, "What the Church is," i.e., what is the true nature of the Church and what are the true bounds of its authority? These works propounded the belief that God has providentially ordered the world, and set in place various authorities to act for the maintenance, well-being and protection of men and women in society. These authorities could be identified as, the Church, the State, and the Home.

Tyndale followed on with this theme in the opening part of his *Obedience.* He argues that the social structure created by God, begins with the child's obedience to its parents, involves wives' obedience to their husbands, servants to their masters, and the subjects' obedience to their kings, princes and rulers. From this he moves on to discuss the duties and responsibilities of parents, masters, landlords, and then at large to that of kings, judges and officers. After this he discusses the place of the Church in relation to the state in society. He quaintly describes the difference between the role of the Church and the state as follows:

> To preach God's Word is too much for half a man.
>
> To administer a temporal kingdom is too much for half a man.

Therefore, one man cannot do both. There are responsibilities and roles for pastors and teachers, and there are roles for kings and rulers. No man can fulfil both duties and responsibilities adequately.

He concludes that the Pope in Rome, and all the officials and prelates of the Roman Church, cannot preach God's Word, and pastor Christ's flock, whilst at the same time seeking to rule in states. The true unity and harmony of God's ordering of life on earth is broken and spoiled when the Church usurps the role of kings and princes. Scripture teaches that the powers that be are ordained by God and therefore nations should wake up to the fact, and resist the incursions of Papal authority into the everyday working of its affairs.

David Daniell observes and comments:

> Nations should be aware of the thoroughness with which the Bible's teaching on the order of things has been set aside and the message of the Gospel distorted in this matter.
>
> Tyndale's *Obedience* does both these things. Explaining that the Pope does the work of an "Antichrist", Tyndale analyses at length the falsehoods that control the Church's teaching on the sacraments and other practices, and ends with a long attack on the source of all

> the distortions: the authorised, and by then traditional, misreading and misrepresenting of Scripture by seeing everything as an allegory, making it mean whatever you want."
>
> *The Obedience of the Christian Man*, Preface, p. xi

Daniell goes on to add:

> While Scripture was entirely in Latin, few could object. Now, however, the Bible was arriving printed in English, and eagerly, indeed desperately, being read and heard. That changed everything. Tyndale did not write from himself. His *Obedience* is made of Scripture. The Bible is everywhere, in the words and the phrases, in the stories quoted and the references made. Sometimes, as in the first paragraphs of the book, and elsewhere, they are very thick on the page, but they are never far away. Scripture, in English, abundantly known and quoted, is the authority by which Tyndale refutes error, whether the widespread corruptions of popes, bishops or clergy, or even the sermon by the Bishop of Rochester, Fisher, who by an error of Latin grammar reversed the New Testament doctrine of faith before works, in the ordo salutis.
>
> Tyndale understood his authority: he was an outstanding scholar of the original Greek New Testament, and by 1528 it seemed he was already reading the Hebrew Scriptures in the original, almost the only Englishman to do so at that time.
>
> Ibid.

Also at this point we need to remind ourselves that Tyndale's writings were at this time being attacked by his Roman Catholic opponents on the grounds that they were seditious.

A year after the work's publication, (1529), Sir Thomas More in his *Dialogue* argued that Tyndale was arguing in favour of treason and rebellion. This charge was in every degree unfair. Tyndale, it might be argued, had overemphasised the then Lutheran teaching that under no circumstances should a believer resist the God appointed kings and rulers. His emphasis went so far as to say that this obedience even extended to non-resistance of even tyrannical princes.

Not only was the charge of Sir Thomas More unfair, and indeed a complete distortion of Tyndale's teaching, but others in more recent times have also wrongly interpreted Tyndale's teaching from the opposite point of view to Sir Thomas More. Tyndale has wrongly been accused of advocating the doctrine of the Divine Right of Kings. J.N. Figgis writing in 1914, accused Luther of the same and went so far as to say, "Had there been no Luther there could never have been a Louis XIV." Though this remark has been refuted as unhistoric, mention of it prompts us to clarify the meaning of Tyndale's doctrine of non-resistance to tyrants here in the *Obedience.*

Tyndale, as we have said was writing to refute the charge that Reformed teachings were undermining the foundations of society and creating disorder and anarchy. One of the principal aims Tyndale had in writing this work was to refute these accusations. On the other hand, it is right to say that Tyndale was influenced by Wycliffe's doctrine of Dominion. Wycliffe taught that the gift of Dominion was given by God to those appointed to rule. The giving of the gift at the same time laid upon the receivers the duty and responsibility of ruling in a righteous and godly way. If a ruler did not fulfil this responsibility and became tyrannical then they had lost the right to rule, and could be opposed.

Robert Demaus adds:

> The *Obedience* was intended as a defence of the Reformers from the imputations made against them that "they caused insurrection and taught the people to disobey their heads and governors, and to rise against their princes, and to make all common, and to make havoc of other men's goods." Such was the common accusation of the day against the doctrine of the Reformers, who were often charged with having instigated all the excesses of the unfortunate peasants in Germany, although in truth, no one had condemned them more severely than Luther. The Reformers are still sometimes spoken of as if they had been apostles of sedition and instigators of rebellion; and, unfortunately, some of them cannot be entirely freed from this charge; but to allege it against Tyndale or any of those who are usually esteemed as the leaders of the English Reformation, is simply to exhibit unaccountable and inexcusable ignorance. Against the usurped authority of the Pope and the clergy, who claimed exemption from the jurisdiction of the civil power, and lorded it over the persons and property of all subjects, Tyndale protests in the strongest terms; but to the lawful sovereign, he acknowledges himself bound to show an entire and implicit submission of the most absolute kind, as far removed from anything seditious as can well be imagined. It would, in fact, be much nearer to the truth to charge Tyndale, Latimer, and Cranmer with inculcating an almost

kingdom of life, the comfort of the Scriptures is man's best stay and help. The promises sustain us. Our care should be to go where God will lead us.

Tyndale then shows how God has dealt with those who despise or who are unfaithful to Christ's Word. His prophets warned the fathers; Gildas preached to the Ancient Britons. Those who wilfully forsake Christ are in the greatest danger; those who ignorantly resist Him may be, like Paul, restored.

He then sets forth the following reasons why the Scriptures should be published in English.

1. God gave His Word to the Hebrews in their mother tongue. Why, then, cannot the English have it?

2. The Bible commands those who read to teach its precepts to their children. How can they unless they are able to read and understand it? Common objections such as 'the lay-man, cumbered with worldly business cannot understand it,' 'lay-people would understand it every man after his own ways,' refuted by the express teaching of Christ, and by the fact that the priest and religious are not so good as they profess to be. The non-residence of the clergy is scathingly exposed, also their rapacity.

3. Apostolic sermons were preached in the vernacular. Jerome translated the Scriptures. The objection that Hebrew and Greek cannot be well translated into English met by showing that English is much nearer to these languages than is Latin.

4. When doctors differ—as they always did—who is to decide except he who can read the Scriptures?

5. The objection that only doctors can interpret Scripture shown to be 'measuring the mete-yard by the cloth.'

6. The absurdity of the view that Scripture cannot be explained except by 'philosophy falsely so-called' exposed.

7. The objection that if every man reads the Scriptures there will be no one to teach, shown to be groundless. It is because those who profess to teach have not and cannot do so, that the people must have the Word of Life. The folly of sixteenth-century ministerial training described. The hair-splitting of the schoolmen exposed.

8. Though the ecclesiastics forbid the reading of the Scriptures, they allow and even commend the reading of foolish and even vicious books.

The preface closes with a reference of the reader to the *Paraclesis Erasmi*.

II. The Prologue unto the Book (pages 69–76).

The book owes its existence to the way in which prelates and priests have attacked God's Word. This is no new thing; it was done in Jeremiah's day, it was done to our Lord. If the Word preached is not received, God sends tribulation, to punish the wicked, to purify the good. It is not the Word of God but the wickedness of the pope, prelates, and priests, that has caused so much mischief, trouble, and war in the earth. Tyndale wishes his work to be tested by the all-sufficient standard of Scripture.

* III. The obedience of all degrees proved by God's Word: and first of children unto their elders (pages 77–81).

God has placed us all in subjection to our parents, and His blessing follows obedience to them. The special question of marriage considered, and the wickedness of the ecclesiastical customs exposed.

IV. The obedience of wives unto their husbands (pages 82, 83).

Proved by Genesis iii.; 1 Peter iii.; and Ephesians v.

V. The obedience of servants unto their masters (pages 83–85).

Scripture teaching on this subject compared with the custom that an ecclesiastic is superior to all save spiritual control.

VI. The obedience of subjects unto kings, princes, and rulers (pages 85–105).

This is one of the most characteristic sections of the book, Tyndale developing the doctrine of passive obedience in a very extreme form. He bases his view upon Romans xii., and holds that those in authority are placed there by God, and that He requires obedience to them. If kings offend, God, and God only, must punish them. The case of David refusing to take vengeance upon Saul quoted. Our Lord's words, in Luke xiii. 1–3, interpreted in a similar sense. Hence the king is 'in this world without law,' accountable to God only. Hence it follows that no one, not even pope, bishop, monks, priests, &c., are exempt from obedience, and by exempting themselves from the temporal law they violated the law of God. The king is the 'minister of God' to defend his people, to secure their rights, to punish evil-doers.

There are three 'natures of men,' (1) those who are always ready to rebel against their rulers; (2) those who keep the law, but only from hope of benefit; (3) those who keep it because they 'have the law written in their hearts by the Spirit of God.' A beautiful exposition of the character of these last is given on pages 95 and 96.

'Natural blindness' is the great evil under which men labour. Hence come false judgments and evil deeds. Until God's Spirit comes to him a man's deeds must be evil. Lucrece and the Greek philosophers instanced as examples. To the same source is traced the evil conduct of 'our most holy religious' (page 99). They turn miracles away from the glory of God to the glory of the human instrument through whom they seem to be done. Their asceticism shown to be folly.

Further, kings are ordained to rule, not to fight one with another, nor on behalf of pope and bishop. This principle Tyndale illustrates by the crooked political policy of his time (pages 102 to 105), and this leads him to

VII. An argument 'Against the Pope's False Power' (pages 105–120).

He shows that Christ refused to rely upon the sword, that He paid tribute; and passes on to severely criticise a sermon by Fisher, Bishop of Rochester, based upon Matt. xvii. 27, in which he tries to prove that because Peter paid tribute he was the chief of the apostles! He contrasts the conduct of the 'spiritualty,' all eager after lucre, with the obedience enjoined by the New Testament. He charges them as being everywhere the cause of discord, rebellion, and injustice. He reiterates his fundamental position, 'The law is spiritual, and requireth the heart; and is never fulfilled with the deed, in the sight of God.' From *faith* springs love, which fulfils the law, and by faith are men justified. The highest test is 'to patiently obey evil rulers in all thing that is not to the dishonour of God, and when thou hurtest not thy neighbours, then art thou sure that God's Spirit worketh in thee, and that thy faith is no dream nor any false imagination.'

The law was given as a witness against sin and to express God's abhorrence of it. Governors are ordained of God. If they are evil, it is because of our sins, and a sign of God's anger. The wickedness of spiritual rulers is a measure of how far the true Gospel has been departed from. All things are to be received from the hand of God with humility. Resistance to evil rulers only deepens the bondage to sin; submission will lead God to deliver His children. The view that 'A Christian man, in respect of God, is but a passive thing' set forth in pages 118 to 120.

VIII. The Office of a Father and how he should Rule (pages 120–122) is tested by Scripture. They should train their children in the knowledge of the Lord; keep them from the motions of 'worldly wisdom'; lead their children to consult them about marriage; and not exact 'the utmost of their authority.'

IX. The Office of a Husband, and how he ought to Rule (pages 121, 123) briefly explained by reference to Ephesians v. and Colossians iii.

28 **Analysis of the**

X. The Office of a Master, and how he ought to Rule (pages 123, 124), illustrated briefly by references to Ephesians v. and Colossians iv.

XI. The Duty of Landlords (pages 124, 125).

A brief but most interesting section, showing that Tyndale on this question was more than three centuries in advance of his age. He teaches that the discharge of the *responsibilities* of property should be a greater object of concern than the enforcement of legal *rights*.

XII. The Duty of Kings, and of the Judges and Officers (pages 125–163).

The king should devote himself to the service of his people, the meanest of whom is 'equal with him in the kingdom of God.' Judges and all officers warned by Moses (Deut. xvii.) as to their respective duties. Kings should defend their people from wrongs, but maintain peace wherever possible, and keep faith with all men, even with the Turk and the infidel. They should be wholly given up to their work. 'To preach God's Word is too much for half a man; and to minister a temporal kingdom is too much for half a man also.' Hence bishops, &c., should not concern themselves with temporal power. The Bishop of Rochester's 'Sermon of the Condemnation of Martin Luther' further criticized (pages 126–145), with reference to the falseness of its reasoning as to the civil power of the pope. Tyndale then closes this long section by showing that laymen can not now rule well, 'because antichrist with the mist of his juggling hath beguiled our eyes, and hath cast a superstitious fear upon the world of Christian men, and hath taught them not to dread God and His Word, . . . but his own laws and ordinances.' Foolish traditions and ceremonies have replaced the Gospel. This leads him to an elaborate attack upon—

XIII. Antichrist (pages 163–192).

In this section Tyndale exposes the whole policy and

Obedience of a Christian Man. 29

conduct of the Papacy in England, and shows how utterly contrary to Scripture it is, both in spirit and in practice. From the oppression of this spiritual tyranny kings ought to set their subjects free.

XIV. Of the Sacraments (pages 193–195).

Brief references to (1) The Sacrament of the Body and Blood of Christ; and (2) Baptism; and then the Romish view of the following combatted:

(1) Wedlock (page 195) not a sacrament.

(2) Order (pages 195–202) not a sacrament. On philological grounds Tyndale shows the true meaning of the words 'priest' and 'elder,' and rebuts the view that there is in the New Testament anything of sacerdotalism in the office of priest or elder.

(3) Penance (pages 203–205) shown to be 'a word of their own forging, to deceive us withal,' it being repentance, not penance, that is needful.

(4) Confession (pages 205–210). True confession set forth, but 'shrift in the ear' shown to be 'verily a work of Satan.'

(5) Contrition (pages 210–212) shown to be repentance. The popish doctrine of *attrition* exposed.

(6) Satisfaction (pages 212, 213). Christ is the only satisfaction God-ward. He, and not the Romish sacrament, falsely so called, of contrition, confession, and satisfaction, restores the penitent sinner.

(7) Absolution (pages 213–221) as practised by the Romish Church is of no avail to forgive sins. The true meaning of Matt. xvi. 19 set forth. The saints were saved not by their own, but by Christ's merits; and Christ's merits alone avail for the salvation of all who

30 **Analysis of the**

repent. Good deeds are of no avail. The pope can neither forgive sin, nor can he cut a man off from the blessings of the Gospel.

(8) Confirmation (pages 221–224) cannot bestow the Spirit of God; He enters the heart only 'through the preaching of faith.'

(9) Anoiling (pages 224–235), that is, extreme unction. There is no authority for this practice in Scripture, and no authority for many of the current superstitious customs of the Romish Church.

Sacraments, Tyndale holds in summing up (pages 235–240), are nothing but holy signs, preaching God's Word and ministering the Spirit to them that believe. Moreover 'Christ's signs speak, and antichrist's be dumb.'

XV. Of Miracles and Worshipping of Saints (pages 240–254). Tyndale's principle here is, 'Take Christ from the saints, and what are they?' Having Christ, we have all we need.

XVI. Prayer (pages 254–264). The corruption of the Romish Church on this point indicated, and the contrast drawn between a church that prays only for its benefactors, and a love that springs from Christ. Our prayers are heard not for what we do, but for what Christ has done for us.

XVII. The Four Senses of Scripture (pages 265–302). In this section Tyndale severely condemns the current scholastic division of Scripture into four classes of meanings, viz., literal, tropological, allegorical, and anagogical. By this method the literal sense had 'become nothing at all.' He maintains, on the other hand, that the Scripture hath but one sense, viz., the literal. It uses, of course, as all literature does, proverb, allegory, &c., but all these have a literal meaning, which must be diligently sought out. He shows how the current habit of interpretation had made Scripture a dead letter, and closes his great work with a beautiful passage

Obedience of a Christian Man. 31

(page 301) on 'Christ is the end of all things. He only is our resting-place and our peace.'

XVIII. A Compendious Rehearsal of that which goeth before (pages 302–320) occupies the last eighteen pages of the volume.

> slavish obedience to Kings than to insinuate that they justly exposed themselves to punishment by abetting treason and sedition.
>
> *William Tyndale, A Biography*, p.226

Whilst this is clear it is also evident by Tyndale's life that he did not advocate a total blanket obedience to civil authorities, as he himself disobeyed in the translation of the Scriptures and having them printed.

Robert Sheehan wrote:

> Tyndale's actions had an immense influence over Protestant thinking and practice. Tudor and Stuart monarchs longed to ruler as absolute monarchs, they were to be unquestionably obeyed, supreme in both Church and state. Tyndale's disobedience began a shift in Protestant thinking. Monarchs could be disobeyed. Rebellion could be legitimate. When the state sets itself to oppose what God commands, we must obey God rather than men.
>
> The momentous events of the Puritan Age, and the Great Rebellion or English Civil War are rooted in the rejection of Tyndale's teaching of total obedience to the state and an acceptance of his practice of disobeying the state where the state opposes God. Tyndale's practice is needed again in the modern world. We need to remember that the state has no authority to control our consciences, nor to interfere in our churches, nor to require us to acquiesce in its legislation of sin. If Tyndale had waited for the permission of the King and the clergy to do his work, the English Reformation would never have happened.
>
> www.christianstudylibrary.org/article/william-tyndale's-legacy p.6.

The Obedience can be divided up into the following sections.

The Prologue:

Here Tyndale defends the translating and preaching of God's Word in English.

Disobedience lives not in the teaching of God's Word, but in the Church's ignorance of and neglect of God's Word.

The true nature of obedience is described in God's Word and how God has set degrees, and established order in all his glorious works.

The Prologue is followed by the three main sections of the work.

pp. 31–59 describes God's law of obedience from whom no-one is exempt.

This is illustrated through the requirement of children to obey their parents, wives their husbands, servants their masters, and subjects to kings, princes and magistrates and rulers.

This is followed by a section illustrating the error of believing that the Pope is Christ's appointed successor to Peter, followed by a section illustrating the Pope's wrongful use of power.

The second main section of the work runs from pp. 59–108.

It sets out directions and principles of how to rule as a father, husband, master, landlord, king or judge.

The third main section of the book runs from pp.108–191.

This section deals with those which are true biblical sacraments, i.e. baptism and the Lord's Supper and those sacraments which have no biblical foundation and are falsely called sacraments, i.e. wedlock, various offices in the Church, penance, confession, contrition, satisfaction, absolution, confirmation, and anointing.

This is followed by a section on false signs, which can come under the form of what Tyndale calls *lying miracles* and the worship of the saints.

This section also includes comments on the real nature of prayer and the right interpretation of Scripture. This includes a plea for the interpreting of Scripture in its literal sense and moves to a criticism of the mediaeval practice of interpreting Scripture in a *Four-Fold Sense,* i.e. literal, tropological, allegorical, and anagogical sense.

The final section of the book from page 180 is a summary of the book's contents, or as Tyndale calls it, "a compendious rehearsal of that which goeth before."

This section also includes what Tyndale calls *a table of the book,* which is a very useful index of the main subjects touched upon and pages on which to find these references.

Bibliography

William Tyndale, *The Obedience of a Christian Man*, ed. David Daniell (Penguin Classics, 2000)

David Daniell, *William Tyndale, A Biography* (New Haven: Yale University Press, 1994)

R. Demaus, *William Tyndale* (London: The Religious Tract Society, 1886)

C.D. Bone, *The Work of William Tyndale* (London: Blackie and Son Ltd, 1938)

www. christianstudylibrary.org/ article/william-tyndale-legacy, p.6

16. Martin Luther—Commentaries on Romans and Galatians

LUTHER IS WELL KNOWN FOR THE FACT THAT HE TRANSLATED THE whole of the Bible into German and produced in the region of 600 titles, including theological writings, biblical expositions, sermons, lectures, polemic writings, political writings and not forgetting his great Reformation hymns.

His two renowned commentaries on Romans and Galatians are highly prized and stand in the front rank of writings that have had far-reaching effect.

It is most significant that Paul's Epistle to the Romans, stands first amongst the Epistles of the New Testament. It was not the first Epistle which the apostle wrote, neither does it stand first because it is the longest, but rather it stands first because it is of first importance.

> "Now, surely this is something that we can well emphasise. It has been the universal opinion of the Christian church throughout all the centuries that Romans is the Epistle above all, which deals with fundamentals, and if you look at the history of the church, I think you will see that it has been borne out time and time again. There is a sense in which we can say quite truthfully that the Epistle to the Romans has, possibly, played a more important and more crucial part in the history of the church than any other single book in the whole of the Bible: that is a matter of great significance. We are to read and study the whole Bible—Yes! Though it is evident from the history of the church that one particular book seems thus to have been used in

an exceptional manner, surely it behoves us to give it exceptional attention."

Dr Martyn Lloyd Jones, *Romans*, p. 3

It is well-known that this great book of Scripture was used to bring Augustine of Hippo to a true and saving faith. One afternoon, he heard a child saying, or singing, "Tolle Lege, Tolle Lege", take up and read, take up and read, and he went home and took up the Epistle to the Romans and read it, and the light of truth pierced the darkness of his soul and he was brought to a true faith in Christ. The conversion of Augustine was one of the most significant and far reaching in the influential conversions of Christian history.

It was through the ministry of Augustine that one of the most, if not the most dangerous heresies ever to afflict the churches was exposed. That is the heresy of Pelagianism, which if it had taken root and if it had been universally accepted, would have brought about the ruin and end of the Christian church.

This same Epistle was turned to by Martin Luther whilst he was still not truly a converted man but lecturing in the University of Wittenberg. While studying this very Epistle the truth of justification by faith, and by faith alone dawned upon his mind, entered his heart, and he truly trusted Christ for his salvation. Luther's conversion, in a very real sense brought about the Protestant Reformation.

It was the same Epistle, and Martin Luther's commentary on it, that had such a profound effect on the life of John Wesley. The story is well known that on 24th of May, 1738, he went to a meeting that evening in Aldersgate Street, London, where a man was reading the preface of Luther's Commentary on the Epistle to the Romans. "It was about a quarter to nine", when he felt his heart "strangely warmed" and he knew that God had forgiven his sins—"even mine." There and then he was given a certain assurance that it was well with his soul, and from thence he began his great work that contributed so much to the 18th-century revival.

In regard to Luther's commentary on the Epistle to the Galatians, again there is much that could be said of its far-reaching effects.

John Bunyan was given and greatly prized Luther's Commentary on the Galatians. He wrote:

"The God in whose hands are all our days and ways, did cast into my hand, one day, a book of Martin Luther: it was his commentary on

> the Galatians which, when I had but a little way perused, I found my condition, in his experience, so largely and profoundly handled, as if his book had been written out of mine own heart. I do prefer this book of Martin Luther on the Galatians, excepting the Holy Bible, before all books that ever I have seen, as most fit for a wounded conscience."

In the same way that Luther's commentary on Romans was so instrumental in the conversion of John Wesley, was Luther's commentary on Galatians in the conversion of Charles Wesley.

On May 17, 1738 Charles Wesley wrote in his Journal for that day:

> I spent some hours this evening in private with Martin Luther, who was greatly blessed to me, especially the conclusion of the 2nd chapter of Galatians. I laboured, waited and prayed to feel "who loved me, and gave himself for me".

On May 21, four days later, an assurance of true faith flooded the heart of Charles Wesley. He expressed his conversion experience in the following lines.

> Where shall my wondering soul begin?
> How shall I all to heaven aspire?
> A slave redeemed from death and sin,
> A brand plucked from eternal fire,
> How shall I equal triumphs raise,
> Or sing my great Deliverer's praise?
>
> O how shall I, the goodness tell
> Father, which thou to me hast showed?
> That I, the child of wrath and hell,
> I should be called the child of God,
> Should know, should feel my sins forgiven,
> Blessed with this antipast of heaven!
>
> And shall I slight my Father's love?
> Or basely fear his gifts to own?
> Unmindful of his favours prove?
> Shall I, the hallowed Cross to shun,
> Refuse his righteousness to impart,
> By hiding it within my heart?
>
> Outcast of men, to you I call,

Harlots, and publicans, and thieves!
He spreads his arms to embrace you all;
Sinners alone, his grace receives:
No need of him the righteous have;
He came the lost to seek and save.

Come, O my guilty brethren, come,
Groaning beneath your load of sin?
His bleeding heart shall make you room,
His open side shall take you in:
He calls you now, invites you home:
Come, O my guilty brethren, come!

361 *Methodist Hymnal*, 1933

Commenting on the last phrase of Galatians chapter 2, verse 20, Martin Luther wrote: "Who loved me and gave himself for me." In these words, the Apostle Paul shows us the true way of justification and gives us a perfect example of the assurance of faith. Anyone who can with a firm and constant faith say with the apostle, "I live by faith in the Son of God, who loved me and gave himself for me," is blessed indeed.

Edward Sandys, Bishop of London, in 1575, wrote a foreword to the First English edition of Luther on Galatians, He wrote:

> This book being brought unto me to peruse and to consider of, I thought it my part, not only to allow of it to the print, but also to commend it to the reader, as a treatise most comfortable to all afflicted consciences exercised in the school of Christ. The author felt what he spake, and had experience of what he wrote, and therefore able more likely to express both the assaults and the failings, the order of the battle, and the means of victory. Satan is the enemy, the victory is by faith alone in Christ, as John recordeth. If Christ justifies, who can condemn, saith St Paul. This most necessary doctrine the author has most substantially cleared, in this his commentary; which being written in the Latin tongue, certain godly, learned men have most sincerely translated into our language, to the great benefit of all such who with humble hearts will diligently read the same. Some began it according to such skill as they had. Others godly, affected, not suffering so good a matter, in handling, to be marred, put to their helping hands for the better framing and furthering of so worthy a work. They refused to be named, seeking neither their own gain

nor glory, but thinking it their happiness, if by any means they may relieve afflicted minds, and do good to the church of Christ, yielding all glory unto God, to whom all glory is due.

Edwinus, London April 28, 1575

Bibliography

Martin Luther, *Commentary on Romans* (Grand Rapids, MI: Kregel Publications, 1979)

Martin Luther, *Commentary on Galatians* (London: J.Saunders, 1833)

Methodist Hymn Book (London: Methodist Conference Office, 1933)

D. Martyn Lloyd-Jones, *Romans* (Edinburgh: The Banner of Truth Trust, 1985)

17. Thomas More—*Utopia*

UTOPIA IS REGARDED AS THE PRINCIPAL LITERARY WORK OF SIR Thomas More. It was originally written in Latin and first published in Louvain in 1516, then successively at Paris, Basle and Vienna. After this it was translated into German, French and Italian, before it ever saw the light of day in English. It is regarded as being inspired by the narrative of the voyages of Vespucci, printed in 1507. The subject is the search for the best possible form of government. The narrative runs along the lines of More meeting at Antwerp a traveller named Raphael Hythloday, who had discovered "Utopia", "Nowhere land".

The laws and customs of Utopia seem to have reached a high level of perfection. Its laws included such precepts as, everybody should work, that nobody should work to excess, that there should be no wars except for very serious and grievous wrongs, that kings and princes should be forbidden to hoard, that there should be no monopolies.

Some have considered the outline of More's views to be bordering on communism, though others reject this idea. Amongst his other descriptions of Utopia, we find a national system of education, extended to both men and women alike, the freest toleration of religion upheld by law. Moreover, the official Utopian faith allowed priests to marry and forbade images of God.

In the work More is continually holding up the example of his Utopians to his countryman and at the same time censuring the social inequalities and injustices which he perceives that abound.

The irony of the work is that when he himself had become something of a power in the State, he practically repudiated every feature and aspect of his utopian vision.

The amiability of More's character has been noted by many, as has the diligence and the integrity that he showed as a servant to King Henry VIII, and particularly in his role as Lord Chancellor of England. Like Erasmus he was a man of pacific and contemplative nature and at the first friendly to a moderate reform of the abuses in the Church.

T.M. Lindsay in his *History of the Reformation* comments that More, like Tyndale his contemporary knew and concurred with Erasmus' desire "that the weakest woman should be able to read the Gospels and the Epistles of St Paul; and the husbandman should sing portions of them to himself as he followed the plough; that the weaver should hum them to the tune of his shuttle; and that the traveller should beguile the tedium of the road by repeating their stories." Sad it was that More, unlike Tyndale, should turn his back on the ennobling enthusiasms of his youth.

As the Reformation unfolded, More became bitterly opposed to the Reformers. He became opposed also to so many of the precepts that he himself advocated in his famous Utopia. Nick Needham comments, "that the Utopia was a strange book for so devout a Roman Catholic as More to write; his 'perfect society' tolerated all religions, whereas More himself went on to become a fierce persecutor of Protestants."

At the time when Henry VIII opposed the Papal Supremacy and declared himself Head of the Church of England, More resigned from his position and sometime after this was sent to the Tower of London.

He was beheaded on July 5, 1535.

Bibliography

T.M. Lindsay, *History of the Reformation* (Edinburgh: T.T. Clark, 1907)

Nick Needham, *2000 years of Christ's Power, Renaissance and Reformation* (Fearn, Tain: Christian Focus Publications, 2016)

Richard Marius, *Thomas More* (Fount Paperbacks, 1977)

Sir Thomas More, *Utopia*, Norton Critical Edition, ed. Robert M. Adams (New York: Norton and Co, 1992)

18. Calvin's *Institutes of the Christian Religion*

"One of the ten books that shook the world." Will Durant

To rightly understand the writings of John Calvin we must briefly glance at his background. He was born 10th of July 1509 at Noyon in Picardy, the fourth son of the first wife of his father, Gerard Calvinus, a minor legal official in the service of the clergy and magistrates.

His father intended him for the priesthood, but after some disagreement with the local clergy, and perhaps some reflection on the economic prospects of such a calling, he entered his son on a course of legal studies at the College de Montaigue in Paris, 1521. He studied rhetoric, logic and arts—common topics for the day—and received a classical education. He came under the influence of the leading Roman Catholic progressive, John Major, sometimes known as John Mair, who had published a commentary on the Four Gospels in which he sought to counter the teachings of Wycliffe, Huss and Luther. It was certainly John Major who familiarised Calvin with the teaching of Augustine and William of Ockham. Though he was personally against the teaching of the Reformation, John Major taught Calvin what it stood for.

In the area of biblical interpretation Calvin seems to have been deeply influenced by John Major's hostility to the Medieval allegorical method and embraced his advocacy of literal interpretation. Also, during his time at the College de la Marche Calvin came under the influence of Mathurin Cordier. Cordier, who proved to be a good and lifelong friend to Calvin, not long after their friendship began, was moved towards the teachings of the Reformation and became a preacher of the Gospel at Neuchatel, and later at Lausanne and Geneva. Calvin never forgot Cordier, and out of respect, dedicated his commentary on First Thessalonians to him.

Calvin now transferred to the flourishing legal faculties of the universities of Orleans and Bourges. At first he studied under the famous Italian jurist Alciati. Many consider Calvin's great clarity of expression is due to the training and influence of Alciati. T.H.L. Parker comments that "Calvin was a man of encyclopedic mind, born like Dr Johnson, to grapple with libraries. Whatever subject he undertook to study, he mastered." Later, when his father died he again returned to Paris, this time to pursue classical studies, which by this time was attracting more and more of his interest and attention.

In Paris, he began to associate with a group of young enlightened humanists, gathered around the aged Jacques Lefevre: a group which included such figures as Bishop Briconnet, and the King's sister, Margaret of Angouleme.

Calvin's conversion

Calvin was not a man to lay bare his soul, his innate reserve as well as his objective outlook kept him from it. He left behind no spiritual autobiography, no Confessions or Grace Abounding to the Chief of Sinners. He confessed that Jesus Christ was his Saviour and his Lord, but he did not say how he arrived at that confession.

Later in life when writing to Cardinal Sadoleto (Sadoleto had written to the Genevans inviting them to return to Roman Catholicism) he puts into the mouth of an anonymous convert this confession; he is almost certainly drawing on his own conversion story.

> I, O Lord always professed the same Christian faith in which I had been brought up as a boy. But at first I had no other reason for my faith than that which was then everywhere prevalent. Thy Word, which ought to have shone on all thy people like a lamp, was taken away, or at least was hidden from us. And in case anyone should long for a greater light, an idea had been instilled in everyone's mind that the investigation of that hidden heavenly philosophy was best in the hands of a few whom the others might consult as oracles, and that the highest knowledge fit for plebeian minds was to subdue themselves to obedience to the Church. Again, the elements in which I had been instructed were such as could neither properly train me to the

> right and true worship of Thy divine majesty, nor pave the way for me to a sure hope of salvation, nor train me aright for the duties of the Christian life. I had indeed learned to worship Thee alone as my God; but since the true reason of worship was altogether unknown to me, I stumbled at the very threshold. I believe, as I had been taught, that I was redeemed by the death of Thy Son from condemnation to eternal death, but the redemption I envisaged was one whose efficacy could never reach to me. I looked for a future resurrection, but hated to think of it, as being an event most terrible. And this was not simply my own personal feeling, but was genuinely derived from the doctrine which was then uniformly preached to the people by their Christian teachers. They certainly preached of Thy mercy towards men, but confined it to those who could show that they deserved it. What is more, they placed this deserving in the righteousness of works, so that he alone was received into Thy favour who reconciled himself to Thee by works.
>
> *Portrait of Calvin*, pp.20–22

Calvin's sudden conversion is referred to in the preface to his *Commentary on the Psalms* where he makes one of the very rare statements about his personal history. "By a sudden conversion God subdued and brought my heart to docility which was more hardened against such matters than was to be expected of my youthful age." (Basil Hall, *John Calvin*, p.14). On another occasion he wrote, "God subdued my stubborn heart and pulled me out of the mire."

His first endeavours on behalf of the Reformation

The precise order of Calvin's movements at this time are also subject to some speculation and difference of opinion. We may presume for arguments sake that by 1532, Calvin is 23 years old, and that he is converted and a true Christian.

He is lodging at the home of a merchant, Etienne de la Forge, a true believer who died at the stake in 1535. Whilst in his home Calvin was visited by many inquirers after Gospel truth, at first Nicodemus-like and then openly.

At this time Calvin's first major literary work was published: it was a commentary on Seneca's treatise *On Clemency* (April 1532). This work showed a remarkable command of the whole mass of classical literature, his fine intelligence and serious interest in the higher moralities. A great career as a humanist scholar lay open before him. Some have suggested that Calvin wrote this book on clemency in order to influence the French king to exercise less severity against the Protestants and more clemency towards the Gospel. (Wileman, p. 34) Others have seen it in the providence of God as establishing him as a man of letters, great learning and scholarship which paved the way for many to read his commentaries when they later were to appear. His conversion at this time, however caused him as Theodore Beza remarked, "to renounce all other studies and devote himself to God."

Also at about this time he made up his mind to give up his curacy and chaplaincy, from which he had derived his principal means of living. His conscience now would not allow him any longer to receive support from a church whose doctrines and practices he believed to be unscriptural.

Certainly during this period in Paris Calvin became increasingly sympathetic to the reforming ideas which were then gaining a popular hearing in the city. Those persecuted for Christ's sake found in Calvin genuine sympathy. Remembering those that were in bonds as bound up with them, he visited prisoners within his reach and wrote letters of encouragement and consolation to those at a distance, being, as we are told, "never lacking in messengers to whom the prison doors were open in spite of all the efforts of the jailers to prevent it." (*John Calvin for Young Persons*—Anon)

One of those whom Calvin influenced at this time was Nicholas Cop, Director of the University of Paris, who, having shortly to deliver a speech in public, asked the young John Calvin, to write it for him. He did so, and the day came for its delivery. To the astonishment and consternation of the listeners, the doctrine of justification by works was set aside, and salvation by faith in Christ enthusiastically stated. Cop was effectively preaching Martin Luther's doctrine of justification by faith taught to him by John Calvin. A copy of this paper in Calvin's own handwriting is still in existence. The University and city authorities, however, were becoming increasingly hostile to Luther's ideas. The Sorbonne, in alarm, ordered Cop to be arrested, but he fled to Basle.

On the second of November 1533 Calvin himself was obliged also to hastily leave Paris as it had become known that he was the author of the speech. It is said that Calvin left Paris disguised as a workman, some say a vine dresser. The famous detective Jean Morin was put on this case and he searched Calvin's private papers, looking for the names of his contacts.

We might just add an important detail here. After leaving Paris on the day after the famous oration (some suggest he fled at first to Noyon and then returned briefly to Paris and finding he was still in danger fled to the court of Marguerite de Valois, Queen of Navarre, who had interested herself on his behalf). However, before he reached the court of Margaret of Navarre he spent a period of time at a place called Angoulême at the home of one of his friends, Louis du Tillet. It was here that du Tillet made the three or four thousand volumes of his father's library available to him, and in this place of enforced hiding, taking the opportunity to pursue his theological studies, he laid the foundation of his famous *Institutes*.

An incident that gave this work added urgency took place on the night of October 18th 1534. That night, placards against the Mass were put up all over Paris, one apparently fixed to the King's chamber door. These strongly worded and provocative notices were put up by Antoine Marcourt, minister of Neuchâtel. The result was a strong reaction and Protestants were arrested, and some burnt at the stake. Protestants were denigrated as enemies of the state and dangerous insurrectionists. This incident colours the first edition of the *Institutes*, addressed to Francis I, King of France. It was intended to demonstrate what Protestants really believed and to refute the false charge that they were enemies of the state and public order.

After the effects of these disturbances had subsided, another danger arose, and that was the fanatical Anabaptist rebellion in Munster, which was ruthlessly put down in 1536. Anxious again to disassociate the Reformation from such fanaticism, the 1536 Latin edition of the *Institutes* was produced. This took the form of a manual of instruction, a kind of catechism on the lines of Luther's Catechism. The name "Institutes" denotes a manual or summary of instruction. The intent of this second edition of the *Institutes* was for the purpose of disassociating the Reformation from the extremes of the Anabaptist movement.

The general plan of the 1536 version, was followed in successive versions of 1537, 1539 and 1541, the book was gradually gaining in length and content. Various other editions, and usually translations, followed until the definitive 1559 edition. As the book expanded the influence of other Reformers was beginning to be found in its contents.

Calvin states in the preface to the 1539 edition:

> My object in this work was to prepare and train students of theology for the study of the sacred volume, so that they might both have an easy introduction to it, and be able to proceed in it, with unfaltering step. I have endeavoured to give such a summary of religion in all its parts. I have digested it into such an order as to make it easier for anyone who is rightly acquainted with it to discover both what he ought principally to look for in Scripture, and also to what head he ought to refer whatever is contained in it. Having thus paved the way, I shall not feel it necessary in any subsequent commentaries on Scripture to enter into long discussions of doctrine, or dilate on commonplaces. I will therefore always compress them. In this way, the pious reader will be saved much trouble and weariness, so long as he comes furnished with a knowledge of the present work as an essential prerequisite.

Duffield adds these points based on the preface of the 1539 Edition.

> This passage is important for several reasons.
>
> 1. It shows that Calvin's intended readership, in his Latin editions at any rate, was students of the Bible and of theology.
>
> 2. It shows the relationship between the *Institutes* and the commentaries, which is important both for any general study of Calvin and to correct certain current misrepresentations of Calvin, which are almost always built up mainly, if not exclusively, from his commentaries. We must interpret Calvinism as Calvin intended us!
>
> 3. It shows pastoral wisdom in guiding people to Bible study and in helping them use commentaries. (Read Calvin's preface to his Commentary on Romans for more of this.) Bucer's commentaries, excellent though they are in many ways, are full of long-winded digressions. Luther's are, if anything, worse. No wonder Calvin's have stood the test of time better. They are shorter. They keep to the point. They avoid interminable topical digressions which are so many in otherwise excellent Reformation commentaries."
>
> *Able Ministers of the New Testament* (Puritan and Reformed Studies Conference, 1964), p. 60–61

Calvin's Fourth Edition of 1559

In the preface to the definitive and final edition of the *Institutes* Calvin states his purpose as follows:

> Though I do not regret the labour previously expended, I never felt satisfied until the work was arranged in the order in which it now appears. As a clear proof of the diligence with which I have laboured to perform this service to the Church of God, I may be permitted to mention, that last winter, when I thought I was dying of quartan ague, the more the disorder increased, the less I spared myself, in order that I might leave this book behind, and thus make some return to the pious, for their kind urgency. I could have wished to give it sooner, but it is soon enough if good enough. I shall think it has appeared in good time, when I see it more productive of benefit than formally to the Church of God. This is my only wish…
>
> I may further observe, that my object in this work has been, so to prepare and train candidates for the sacred office, for the study of the sacred volume, that they may both have an easy introduction to it, and be able to prosecute it with unfaltering step; for, if I mistake not, I have given a summary of religion in all its parts, and digested it in an order which will make it easy for any one, who rightly comprehends it, to ascertain both what he ought chiefly to look for in Scripture, and also to what head he ought to refer whatever is contained in it. … The system here followed being set forth as in a mirror in all my Commentaries, I think it better to let it speak for itself than to give any verbal explanation of it."

Gaspar Olivianus in the introductory section of this work further describes its plan and purpose as follows:

> The subject handled by the author of these Christian Institutes is twofold: the former, the knowledge of God, which leads to a blessed immortality; and the latter (which is subordinate to the former), a knowledge of ourselves. With this view the author simply adopts the arrangement of the Apostles' Creed, as that with which all Christians are most familiar. For as the Creed consists of four parts, the first relating to God the Father, the second to the Son, the third to the Holy Spirit, and the fourth to the Church, so the author, in fulfilment of this task, divides his Institutes into four parts, corresponding to those of the Creed.

This massive work, roughly equal in size to the Old Testament plus the Four Gospels can be divided up as follows:

Book 1: The Knowledge of God, the Creator
Twofold knowledge of God
Scripture
Trinity
Creation
Providence

Book 2: The Knowledge of God, the Redeemer
The Fall, human sinfulness
The Law
The Old and New Testaments
Christ the Mediator: His Person (Prophet, Priest, King) and work (Atonement)

Book 3: The Way in which we Receive the Grace of Christ, its Benefits and Effects
Faith and Regeneration
Repentance
Christian life
Justification
Predestination
The Final Resurrection

Book 4: The External Means by which God Invites Us into the Society of Christ
Church
Sacraments
Civil Government

The Fundamental principles of Calvinism

What is the chief focus of the Calvinistic system? What is the heart and core of this way of looking at life?

1. Some in the 19th century saw it was the principle of democracy or liberty. They maintain that it arose in the Swiss city of Geneva amongst a people who loved liberty and hence the core of the theology of Calvin is liberty.

2. Others, noting that Calvin, (as we have seen), had a legal training;

claim that authority is the chief characteristic and focus of Calvin's system.

3. Alister McGrath reminds us that Calvin's greatest contribution to Protestantism lay in his demonstration of how the Bible can serve as the foundation of a stable understanding of Christian beliefs and structures. That a consistent and coherent theological system can be derived and defended on the basis of the Bible. Calvin addressed head-on what was perceived to be by its enemies the central weakness of Protestantism up to this point: that is, how can one speak of the Bible as having any authority when it is so clearly at the mercy of its interpreters? Calvin presented his *Institutes* as the authoritative guide to the correct interpretation of Scripture. "My object in this book", he wrote, "is to so prepare and train students of sacred theology for the study of the Word of God that they might have an easy access into it, and be able to proceed in it without hindrance." (Alister McGrath, *Christianity's Dangerous Idea*, p.94)

4. Others observe that Calvin was a Frenchman and that the French have a capacity and love of organisation, and delight in arranging vast arrays of facts into colossal systems of thought and philosophy. Hence they argue, Calvinism is essentially an attempt to create a vast all-comprehensive theological system. "Calvinism is the name applied to the system of thought which has come down to us from John Calvin. He is recognized as the chief exponent of this system, although he is not the originator of the ideas set forth in it, for theological views of Calvin, together with those of the other great leaders of the Protestant Reformation, are known to be a revival of Augustinianism, which in its son was only a revival of the teachings of St Paul centuries previously. But it was Calvin who, for modern times presented these views in systematic form and with the specific application, which since his day has become known to us as Calvinism. These teachings constitute a unity. Calvinism is not the mere aggregate of opinions, the sum total of ideas, held by Calvin and Calvinists but it is an organic whole with one fundamental principle as the common root. It is not always necessarily the case that the views of a group constitute a unity. The views of the Roman Catholic church prior to the time of their great organizer Thomas Aquinas (1227–1274), or officially prior to the Council of Trent (1545–1563), did not form a unity but lay scattered among the declarations of church councils and papal decrees, and

contained numerous conflicting elements. Likewise, the political views of the Republican party or of the Democratic party do not comprise a unity. However, the system derived from John Calvin can claim such distinction.

Calvinism does not restrict itself to theology: it is an all comprehensive system of thought; including views on politics, society, science, art, as well as theology. It presents a view of life and of the universe as a whole, a world and life view. In fact, it has even been described as one of the few basic systems of thought that have ever been offered to man. James Ore limits the basic philosophic systems of the world to twelve, and considers all other philosophic systems to be modifications of these. Abraham Kuyper reduces the number of basic systems of thought to only four of which Calvinism is one. (i.e. Romanism, Islam, Modernism, Calvinism)." (Meeter p. 15–16)

5. Whilst there is an element of truth in all these points they fail to observe that the great driving force in John Calvin's life was his evangelical Christianity. We can safely say without any fear of challenge or contradiction, that the great fundamental thought and heart of Calvin's life is the doctrine of God. God is at the centre of Calvin's thought. The Calvinist does not start out with some interest of man, for example, his conversion or his justification, vitally important though these are. The Calvinist places always in the foreground the thought of God.

The absolute sovereignty of God and life lived to the glory of God are the fundamental principles of Calvinism.

Speaking of the sovereignty of God, B. B. Warfield says:

> The Calvinist is the man who sees God behind all phenomena and in all that occurs recognizes the hand of God, working out his will; who makes the attitude of the soul to God in prayer its permanent attitude in all its life-activities; and who casts himself on the grace of God alone, excluding every trace of dependence on self from the whole work of his salvation.
>
> Quoted in: H. Henry Meeter, *The Basic Ideas of Calvinism*, p. 19

In another place Warfield says:

> "The Calvinist is the man who has seen God, and who, having seen God in his glory, is filled on the one hand with a sense of his own unworthiness to stand in God's sight as a creature, and much

> more as a sinner, and on the other hand with adoring wonder that nevertheless this is a God who receives sinners. He who believes in God without reserve, and is determined that God shall be God to him, in all his thinking, feeling, willing in the entire compass of his life activities, intellectual, moral, spiritual—throughout all his individual, social, religious relations—is by the force of the strictest of all logic which presides over the outworking of principles into thought and life, by the very necessity of the case, a Calvinist."
>
> Ibid p.20

6. Closely related to the above point is Calvin's teaching that the true purpose of life is to live life to the glory of God.

J. H. Merle D' Aubigne in his classic *Let Christ to be Magnified, Calvin's Teaching for Today* puts it like this:

> We have sought for the characteristic feature of this great Christian personality. It is the recognition of the sovereignty of God, absolute submission to his will in the organization of the church and of all things. The first of these features is the most prominent; and yet we must mount still higher to find the key of his doctrine and of his life. Excelsior! Higher and higher still! This was Calvin's motto: his soul perpetually soared towards heaven. The glory of God the glory of Christ; this was the overruling idea, the principle of his activity, the aim of his whole life.
>
> From time to time when Paul said, "Christ shall be magnified in my body, whether it be by life or by death", no man, perhaps, has been able to repeat these words with more truth than our Reformer. Let Christ be magnified! This is what he requires of churches, believers, and martyrs. When he wrote to the imprisoned ladies of Paris, who were about to die at the stake, he said to them, almost literally repeating the apostle's words. "For this we were brought into the world, and enlightened by God's grace, that we should magnify him in our life and in our death."
>
> All Calvin's life proclaimed, glory, glory, glory to Christ, and to self-confusion of face. Glory to his Word, glory to his Person, glory to his Grace, glory to his Life; these are the four "glories" which both the Apostle and the Reformer invite you to render to the Lord.
>
> *Let Christ be Magnified*, p.9

Another great writer on Calvinism, Abraham Kuyper, sets out what he sees to be the essential elements of Calvinism as far as doctrine is concerned as follows.

1. The Sovereignty of God

Abraham Kuyper asks the question; "does religion exist for the sake of God or for man?"

He answers the question saying that true religion exists primarily for God, adding that Scripture teaches us that he has created all things for himself.

> "Of course, religion, as such, produces a blessing also for men, but it does not exist for the sake of man. It is not God who exists for the sake of His creation;—the creation exists for the sake of God."
>
> Abraham Kuyper, *Calvinism*, p. 52

The Scriptures teach that the whole creation echoes this truth.

> The whole earth is full of Thy glory.
>
> How excellent is Thy Name, in all the earth?
>
> The heavens declare the glory of God and the firmament showeth his handiwork.
>
> Frost and hail, snow and vapour fulfilling Thy will.

As the hymn writer puts it:

> All things praise Thee Lord most high;
> Heaven and earth and sea and sky
> All were for Thy glory made,
> That Thy greatness thus displayed
> Should all worship bring to Thee;
> All things praise Thee: Lord may we.
>
> George William Conder, 1821–74

But just as the created order reaches its highest points in man, so religion finds its clearest expression in man who is made in the image and likeness of God. God has implanted in man's nature "the seed of religion", as Calvin calls it.

> "God himself makes man religious by means of the sensus divinatis, i.e., the sense of the Divine, which He causes to strike on the harp of his soul. A sound of need interrupts the pure harmony of this divine melody, but only in consequence of sin. In its original form, in its

> natural condition, religion is exclusively a sentiment of admiration and adoration, which elevates and unites not a feeling of dependence which severs and depresses. Just as the anthem of the Seraphim around the throne is one uninterrupted cry of "Holy, Holy, Holy"! So also the religion of man upon this earth should consist in one echoing of God's glory, as our Creator and Inspirer.
>
> The starting point of every motive in religion is God and not man. Man is the instrument and means, God alone is here the goal from the point of departure to the point of arrival, the fountain from which the waters flow, and at the same time, the ocean into which they finally return.
>
> To be irreligious is to forsake the highest aim of our existence, and on the other hand to covet no other existence than for the sake of God, to long for nothing but for the will of God, and to be wholly absorbed in the glory of the name of the Lord, such is the pith and kernel of all true religion. "Hallowed be Thy Name. Thy will be done," is the twofold petition which gives utterance to all true religion.
>
> Our watchword must be, "seek first the kingdom of God," and after that think of your own need.
>
> First stands the confession of the absolute sovereignty of the Triune God; for of Him, through Him, and unto Him are all things."
>
> *Calvinism*, p. 53

2. Christ is the one Mediator between God and Man

Calvinism emphasizes man's union with God through Christ.

One of the great questions which Calvin addressed himself to was that which asks, must our relationship with God, be direct or mediate?

It is a question, whether the church, or a priest, or some kind of dispenser of sacred mysteries is necessary to facilitate or enable us to have access to God?

Now of course the Bible teaches us that we all need the mediatorial work of our Lord Jesus Christ, the Divine Son of God. He is the God-Man appointed by the Father to be the one Mediator between God and man.

But truth is, however, that we find in all non-Christian religions without any exception that human mediators and human intercessors are necessary.

Even amongst those who name themselves Christians there are some who claim that the Virgin Mary, or the angels, or the saints or the martyrs of old, or a priestly hierarchy of clergy all in some way serve as mediators between God and man.

In the face of this Calvinism emphasizes that there is but one mediator between God and man, the man Christ Jesus. Calvin speaks of religion as being without any created intercessors and the fact that the believer through Christ has direct communion with God. The believer's union and fellowship with God is one of the great emphases of Calvinism.

> Religion for the sake of man carries with it the position that man has to act as a mediator for his fellow–man. Religion for the sake of God inexorably excludes every form of human mediatorship. As long as it remains the chief purpose of religion to help man, and as long as man is understood to deserve grace by his devotion, it is perfectly natural that the man of inferior piety should invoke the mediation of the holier man. Another must procure for him what he cannot procure for himself. The fruit on the branches hangs too high, and, therefore, the higher-reaching man has to pluck it, and hand it down to his helpless comrade.
>
> If on the other hand the demand of religion is that every human heart must give glory to God, no fallen man can appear before God on behalf of another.

The importance of this point, emphasizing as it does our own personal election and our own personal access to God through Christ is of incalculable value. One of the effects of true religion is to make man free: free that is to express that general religious impression stamped by God Himself upon our unconscious nature. Free to be the people God intended us to be.

> On the other hand, every appearance of an interposing priest or enchanter in the domain of religion fetters the human spirit, in a chain which presses the more woefully the more the piety increases in fervour. In the Church of Rome, even at the present day, the best Catholics are most closely confined in the fetters of the clerics …
>
> Only he who personally stands before God on his own account, and enjoys an uninterrupted communion with God, can properly display the glorious wings of liberty. And both in Holland and in France, in

> England as well as in America, the historic result affords the most undeniable evidence of the fact that despotism has found no more invincible antagonists, and liberty of conscience no braver, no more resolute champions than the followers of Calvin.
>
> In the last analysis, the cause of this phenomenon lies in the fact that the effect of every clerical interposition invariably was, and must be, to make religion external and to smother it with sacerdotal forms. Only where all priestly intervention disappears, where God's sovereign election from all eternity binds the soul directly to God himself, and where the ray of divine light enters straightway into the depth of our heart—only then does religion, in its most absolute sense gain its ideal realization.

3. This leads to the third proposition in seeking to describe the essence of Calvinism i.e. a true religion involves the whole of our lives. Every aspect of it is to be dedicated to God.

> Thou shalt love God, not only with all thy heart and with all thy strength, but also with all thy mind.

Calvin emphasized the fact that we use our mind in religion and not only our feelings or our will, and thus opened up the fact that our religious life is not to be excluded from the realm of science, or art, or literature or commerce, or any legitimate area of public life and service.

> A religion confined to the closet, the cell, or the church, therefore, Calvin abhors. With the Psalmist, he calls upon heaven and earth; he calls upon all peoples and nations to give glory to God. God is present in all life, with the influence of His omnipresent and almighty power, and no sphere of human life is conceivable in which religion does not maintain its demands that God shall be praised, that God's ordinances shall be observed and that all our lives shall be permeated with fervent and ceaseless prayer. Wherever man may stand, whatever he may do, to whatever he may apply his hand, in agriculture, in commerce, and in industry, or his mind in the world of art, and science, in whatsoever it may be, constantly standing before the face of his God, he is employed in the service of his God, he has strictly to obey his God, and above all, he has to aim at the glory of God. Consequently, it is impossible for Calvinists to confine

> religion to a single group, or to some circles among men. Religion concerns the whole of our human race.
>
> *Calvinism*, p. 63

To see how Calvin spent his whole life glorifying Christ in a practical way we may add this note from J.H. Merle d'Aubigne:

> Here is his furniture: three bedsteads, three tables, a desk, a high backed chair, and a dozen stools, "some good, some bad", says the inventory. His policy and disinterestedness glorified Christ. Knock at his door of the first gleam of daylight, and you will find him at work; return at midnight, and he is still there. His unceasing labour glorified Christ.
>
> Listen to his preaching, his conferences, his lessons, his conversations with his colleagues, with the members of his flock and with the numerous refugees continually arriving; look at his letters, and his books, which are circulated throughout Christendom thy all glorified Christ.
>
> Ibid. p.44

4. Another great aspect of Calvinism is its soteriological emphasis.

Modern day religion often starts with the assumption that man is normal. Calvin starts as the Scriptures start with the fact that man is a fallen creature. Modernism teaches that man began with a low and imperfect form of religion and is gradually moving to a higher and more sophisticated form of religion. The Bible as Calvin rightly taught sees these lower forms of religion as degenerations from true religion. Man will never gradually improve by his own efforts.

Buckle in his *History of Civilization in England*, has demonstrated that the forms in which sin makes its appearance may show us a gradual refinement, but that the moral condition of the human heart has remained the same throughout all the centuries.

Man can only be saved by grace. Calvin's heart burned with wonder and adoration at the thought of the saving grace of God. We often call the doctrines so much associated with Calvin i.e. the five points of Calvinism, the doctrines of grace. Calvin emphasizes the great Pauline truth that salvation is by grace alone.

> He ascribes no part of his conversion to himself; he claims no merit. To him belongs the hardness of heart, to God alone the power and

> the love that breaks it. He is now inflamed for grace. Adoration of Christ, on account of his free salvation, is at all times and in all places the fundamental note of all the harmonies he constructs.
>
> Calvin was not slow to see that, according to the teaching of the Popes, the natural powers of man had not been corrupted by the Fall, but only weakened, so that man might still have some power to save himself. He saw that from this Pelagianism or semi-pelagianism preceded all the errors of Popery-good works, meritorious penances, human expiations, indulgences, the merits of the saints, all (in short) that is substituted for the fullness of grace. And against these errors and many others he set up the great truth: all salvation comes by the grace of Christ.
>
> D'Aubigne, p.30

It is sometimes forgotten that the teaching of Calvin and the other Reformers is that Scripture reveals that Christ has, irrespective of anything in man, fulfilled the demands of the Law on his people's behalf. That it is to him that we must look for salvation and not within ourselves. This was a truth not only of unspeakable benefit to the individual soul but it also brought with it wide sociological implications.

> "Once the subjectivism of the medieval Church was eliminated in Protestant countries, the energy consumed by desperately seeking and "earning" salvation was turned outward, and a thousand years of intellectual, political, social and economic and religious stagnation ended."
>
> John W. Robbins, *Civilization and the Protestant Reformation*, p.4

Further note on the Doctrine of Predestination

Election and Reprobation stated

It is in the third Book of the *Institutes* that Calvin deals with election and reprobation, and then only as deductions from a consideration of the extent of the Spirit's work in regeneration. Since the work of Christ is not efficacious for all men, although Christ is freely offered to them in the Gospel, the reason for this must be in the predestination of God. This is different from foreordination. The predestination of God is his eternal decree by which he has determined in himself what he would have become of every individual of mankind. All are not created for the same destiny. Some are predestinated to eternal life, some to eternal death. The election of the one class leads to eternal life by the effectual calling and saving work of the Holy Spirit, the destruction of the other classes secured by their own wickedness. By their faith, the one class make evident their election; by unbelief, the other class make evident their reprobation. Here we have the clearest application of the divine sovereignty.

Election and Reprobation contrasted

> Salvation entails on the part of God the full choice of the objects of his mercy, and this choice is an eternal election from God's side. That means that what God does in time in the salvation of souls, he willed to do in eternity. This is really a tracing of the experience of salvation back to its roots in the sovereignty of divine grace. In this connection it is interesting to note that the term elect is applied to none in the Scripture, except those who are in Christ, and Calvin himself, as already indicated, places his exposition of this doctrine in Book III, after he had dealt with the doctrine of salvation in Christ. Election is thus viewed and interpreted in the light of an experience of salvation, the context in which it becomes meaningful. It is in light of the fact that all are not put in possession of salvation that Calvin expounds the corollary of election, reprobation. On both he is equally emphatic as disclosures of the will of God given in Scripture. "The predestination by which God accepts some to the hope of life, and adjudges others to eternal death, no man who would be thought pious ventures to deny", he affirms with perhaps a confidence that not all the pious nowadays share. Notwithstanding, he makes an essential difference between election and reprobation. While "unconditional" is a term applied to both, since both proceed from the free and sovereign will of God, the distinction lies in the fact that while men are saved by an act of absolutely free and unmerited grace, without regard to faith or good works, men are condemned on the ground of their own sin. This is in line with Paul's argument that while the vessels of mercy were afore prepared by God unto glory, vessels of wrath were fitted for destruction, fitted not by God, but by their own character and conduct. While it is clear that Calvin attributes their reprobation to the decree of God, he does not suggest that the decree

> is the ground of condemnation, or the cause of their corrupt state. He indeed teaches a positive decree of reprobation involving more than mere preterition, involving a foreordination to damnation, but it must be remembered that Calvin does not represent foreordination as the cause of acts in the sphere of human responsibility, even when the decree makes their occurrence certain. In other words, the judicial reprobation need not be viewed as merely a purpose formed in eternity, and therefore unconditional, but as having its termination in time as the inescapable sequel to a career of impenitence and sin.
>
> In short, we do not know why the elect are chosen, but we know why the reprobate are condemned, and Calvin would have us rest there.
>
> "Wherefore", he says, "let us in the corruption of human nature, contemplate the evident cause of condemnation rather than enquire into a cause hidden and almost incomprehensible in the predestination of God".
>
> *Able Ministers of the New Testament* (Puritan and Reformed Studies Conference, 1964), article by R. A. Finlayson pp. 12, 13

5. A final and indeed vital and fundamental emphasis of Calvinism is on the absolute necessity of a Revelation from heaven and the supreme authority of Holy Scripture. To undermine the authority of Scripture is to destroy Christianity itself.

> Calvin held to the absolute inspiration of the Word. And the grand unity resulting therefrom. "The principle which distinguishes our religion from all of us", he said (and modern Protestants should listen attentively to his words) "is the knowledge we possess that God has spoken to us."
>
> Ibid. p.14

Calvin like Luther before him believed that the Word of God worked powerfully but secretly in men's hearts, bringing repentance, faith and new life. The preacher can get to the ears of his listeners but not to their hearts. It is God alone that speaks to the conscience and moves the innermost will. The preacher preaches the Word but must leave the results to God.

Other important doctrines, space only enables us to briefly mention at this point

Firstly: in defining the conscience as belonging to God's dominion Calvin and the Reformers established the right of liberty of conscience and protected conscience from the power of the state.

Secondly: he taught that there must be no mediation by any creature between God and the soul. This mediation is the work of Christ the Son of God alone and is further seen to be solely the work of God through the doctrine of election.

Thirdly: religion is not partial but universal, it touches the whole of our life, and indeed through the doctrine of common grace touches the whole of human life.

Fourthly: in our sinful condition, religion cannot treat man as normal, but has to be soteriological i.e. saving. This salvation is salvation by grace alone.

Fifthly: the human mind could never have conceived of these doctrines and hence the necessity of Revelation. This revelation becomes the source of all authority in the Church.

Calvin also emphasized many other doctrines, principally, the doctrine of the Trinity, the doctrine of the work of the Holy Spirit, the doctrine of prayer (the longest chapter in the *Institutes* of 1559 is devoted to prayer which Calvin called the exercise of faith, and the means by which we daily receive God's benefits), and of course the doctrine of Providence.

Predestination and Election

Again, space only permits a brief mention of this subject, which many wrongly would believe to be the main and chief emphasis of Calvin's teaching. We may note firstly:

> If we examine the Calvinistic confessions, especially the earlier ones drafted by Calvin or under his influence, or the *Institutes* of Calvin, we shall soon discover that predestination is not the fundamental principle. In some of these confessions the thought of predestination is not even as much as mentioned; in others it is cited only in passing. In the *Institutes* the doctrine of predestination is treated not as the basis of the system, but as a conclusion rather than as a premise in the soteriological section.
>
> Meeter, p.21

Alexandre Schweitzer in 1844 and Ferdinand Christian in 1847 had claimed that predestination was the central doctrine of Calvin's theology and that all of the originality of his teaching proceeded from it. Historians and dogmaticians went on for three quarters of a century repeating that affirmation like an article of faith which did not even need to be verified.

See pp. 263–264, Calvin, Francois Wendel.

> "It is notable too, that in his children's Catechism there is no mention of predestination, and in his Church Catechism eleven sections (or one fifth of the whole) are devoted to prayer. There spoke the real heart of the man."
>
> A. Mitchell Hunter, *The Teaching of Calvin*, p.297

It needs to be reiterated that these doctrines with which Calvinism is popularly identified did not originate with Calvin at all.

> He inherited them and much else, from Augustine, echoed by Aquinas, just as Luther's owed much to Occam. But he was not the man to take them over from Augustine, however much he revered him if he did not find them in Scripture for himself. That they are there was no belated discovery of the Church, even so late as Augustine. Controversy had busily concerned itself with them since the dawning of the day of dogmatic thought. In the second century, for example, the Letters of Octavius proved that the same complexities were felt about the election of God and same vehement objections made to the doctrine as in latter ages, when in the cyclic revolution of emphasis, it came once again over controversy's underlining stroke.
>
> Ibid. p. 297–298

> One of the central functions of the doctrine is to emphasize the graciousness of God. For Luther, God's graciousness is reflected in the fact that he justifies sinners, men and women, who are totally unworthy of such a privilege. For Calvin, God's graciousness is demonstrated in his decision to redeem individuals irrespective of their merits: the decision to redeem an individual is made without reference to how worthy that individual might be. For Luther, God's graciousness is demonstrated in that he saves sinners despite their demerits. For Calvin, that graciousness is demonstrated in that he saves individuals *irrespective* of their merits. Although Luther

> and Calvin defend the graciousness of God in somewhat different manners, the same principle is affirmed by their respective views on justification and predestination.
>
> A E. McGrath, *Reformation Thought*, p. 125

Calvin said:

> we shall never be clearly convinced ... that our salvation flows from the fountain of God's free mercy till we are acquainted with his eternal election, which illustrates the grace of God by this comparison, that he adopts not all promiscuously to the hope of salvation but gives to some what he refuses to others.
>
> Quoted by P. Tillich, *A History of Christian Thought*, p.268

When we think of God not choosing, all this introduces us to an absolute mystery. We cannot call God to account. We cannot go beyond the divine will, we can only rest in the fact that the Judge of all the earth will do right.

It was Calvin and not John Wesley who originated the reference to the *awful* or the *horrible* decree. Calvin did not like the thought of God passing by some but he was not prepared to speculate beyond what Scripture revealed. This leads us to another aspect of Calvin's teaching i.e. his principle of not going beyond what Scripture revealed. Calvin recognized the paradoxes sometimes described as the antinomies of Scripture (two parallel truths that as yet cannot be reconciled by our finite minds) one of the greatest being divine predestination and human responsibility. When pressed about the matter of the lostness of the lost he replied. "Their perdition depends on the divine predestination, in such a manner that the cause and matter of it are found in themselves." Ibid p.268. (See *Reformation Thought*, p. 126–127 and principally p. 125 one of the central functions of the doctrine is to emphasise the graciousness of God.)

Further note on Predestination

Alexander Hodge in the 19th century who was quick to see that the concept of freedom, and with it the concept of responsibility, was under threat because of Darwinian deterministic thinking. People were beginning to say that human beings could not help the way they behaved. Their behaviour was the result of various glands and other biological factors. The historian Paul Johnson has also commented on this saying; "Marxist and Freudian analysis combine to undermine in their different ways, the highly developed sense of personal responsibility, and of duty towards a settled and objective true moral code, which was at the centre of nineteenth-century civilisation. Sociology, criminology, penology and psychology are largely based on the assumption that environment, education and genetic inheritance not only influence, but determine human behaviour, and that individuals are therefore only minimally answerable for their own conduct." In the light of this, it is of paramount importance for us to grasp this synthesis that we find in A.A. Hodge, in William Cunningham and in "Rabbi" Duncan between fore-ordination on the one hand and freedom and responsibility on the other. Fore-ordination, says the Westminster Confession, does not destroy liberty. I am free because God fore-ordained my freedom. I am not the play-thing of pressure and circumstance or even of internal and endocrinological factors. I am free. I make my own decisions. I am the cause, the ultimate answering cause, the responsible cause, of my own decisions. (Based on Donald Macleod, *A Faith to Live By*, p.44)

The Practical Aspects of Calvinism

Calvin's doctrine of predestination might well have issued in a fatalism which induced a paralysis of ethical endeavour. It actually did the very reverse; it braced men's wills; it saturated them with aspiration; it inspired them to a strenuous and heroic activity which brought about a very miracle of moral revolution in all spheres of life in all quarters of the world.

Calvinism indeed worked as a moral purgative and stimulant wherever it gained any influence at all—and that is its greatest glory. It cleansed the Augean stables of Geneva. It entered licentious courts and touched reckless cheeks there to a strange, unwanted shame. Everywhere it awakened and made sensitive lethargic consciences. It created a refined, if vehement, piety, which blossomed into a strength and frequent beauty of high character that has since been the world's most valuable asset. Calvin's religion was reflected in his crest—a hand with a burning heart, and the words, "I give Thee all." That is what it meant to him, and what it meant to him he taught to others. Calvinism in a word stood for consecration, a consecration that found its ideal and example in the Christ whose tired feet climbed Mount Olivet to pray and the hill Calvary to die.

It is this fundamental and ultimate aim of Calvinism to moralize life by religion which interprets and explains the character of Calvin's own activities. It instructed his legislation. It determined his views on the relation between Church and State. The Church should be the conscience of the State, the State the organ of an evangelized conscience. As a reminder of the spirit that should infuse all life, private and public, Calvin had the letters I. H. S. carved or stamped on all public buildings, coins, and standards in Geneva. (*Iesus Hominum Salvator—Jesus Saviour of Men, sometimes interpreted to stand for, I have suffered or, In His Service*)

It is notable how closely Calvin keeps to everyday life in his commentaries. That is one of the reasons why these expositions still retain their value. They are instinct with a constant concern for the attunement of life to the divine precepts. The fundamental principle, too, explicates his attitude to heresy. He was wonderfully patient for those days and for one in his position with all kinds of creedal vagaries around him. It was only when these threatened (in his view) the foundations of morality and orderly government, and therefore of society, he became severe. But (excepting in the case of Servetus) his severity limited itself to expulsion of the offender from Geneva as a threat to the public peace, as a discordant element in the community whose continuance there might be fraught with insidious and perilous potencies of evil.

A. Mitchell Hunter, p. 300

Calvin's teaching on the Providence of God

The doctrine of Providence teaches us that all things are under the control of a good and wise God and that all things work together for good to them that love Him. This teaching creates a tremendous impetus towards a life that is noble, good and self-sacrificing.

Huxley, the Victorian evolutionist, claimed that belief in God's providence was a kind of opiate that bred fatalism and sapped the strength out of human endeavour. He wrote,

> The release of God from the anthropomorphic disguise of personality also produces release from another vice that we may term "Providentialism". God provides for the sparrow we are told; how much more for man? And so this beneficent Power will always provide. Divine providence is an excuse for the poor whom we will

> always have with us; for the human improvidence which produces whole broods of children without reflection or care as to how they shall live; for not taking action when we are lazy; or, more rarely, for justifying the action we do take when we are energetic. From the point of view of the future destiny of man, the present is a time of clash between the idea of Providentialism and the idea of Humanism—human control by human effort in accordance with human ideals. If Providentialism wins, even if it wins only in the dominion of the soul and religious life, humanity is doomed to stagnation or to destruction.
>
> *Religion Without Revelation*, p18

If Huxley is correct it is reasonable to expect it to be borne out and confirmed by the history of Calvinism. The question is, does that story bear out the thesis that faith in God's providence paralyzes man's vital energies in seeking that which is good, or Marx's theory that *religion is the opiate of the people.* It is manifestly clear that it does not. We may use as an illustration the great Calvin Memorial in Geneva. The idea of that monument is that out of the faith of Calvin were born all the free governments of the modem world. Right and left the figure of John Calvin are the figures of William the Silent of Holland, Coligne of France, John Knox of Scotland, a Pilgrim Father of New England and Oliver Cromwell, Calvinists all.

When we think of such men we do not think of pietistic acquiescence, or of their faith as *an opiate of the people*, we think of firm endurance on the very edge of despair against overwhelming odds and of their Herculean activity for the City of God.

> So far is Calvinism from producing slackness of will and feebleness of character that Calvinists have been the most strenuous of men. The true Calvinist feels himself to be an instrument of the Divine Will and bends to whatever toil he undertakes in the unshakable conviction that he is on the side of God. How copious a spring of moral energy lies in this thought I need not tell you. Calvinism was the form of faith in the strength of which the Dutch Republic was sustained, and the American Republic founded, to propagate which Tyndale gave the English people the Bible in their own tongue and with it his life; which formed the Royal intellect of Cromwell and inspired the majestic verse of Milton.
>
> Beard's Hibbert *Lectures on The Reformation*, pp. 257 and 261

Calvinism and Politics

A.M. Fairbairn the famous Congregationalist writing in *The Cambridge Modern History* series commented:

> Calvin's chief title to place in history rests upon his success as a legislator. As a theologian he was a follower, as a legislator he was a pioneer. His system of doctrine was derived, while his political economy broke new ground and based the social edifice on new principles. Certainly he is entitled to the credit of having established a political and legal system on a model of its own, which has profoundly influenced, directly or indirectly, all subsequent democratic institutions.
>
> Quoted by Meeter p. 72

It is true to say that Calvinism is a much greater influence upon modern political history that is commonly supposed. Calvin himself never developed a theory of the State, but future Calvinists did and those who, while not Calvinists in theology were profoundly influenced by his Democratic ideas, such as Hugo Grotius and John Locke. As far as Britain is concerned, the work of the various Puritan groups at the time of the Civil War were deeply influenced by Calvin's teachings. Cromwell's influence on the Mother of Parliaments, the Glorious Revolution of 1688 and the Act of Settlement of 1703 all bear the marks of that influence.

> "We have an important and vexing problem to consider in determining the task of the state: the extent of the territory over which the state has jurisdiction and in which it must administer justice. In the solution which it offers to this problem, the Calvinist system occupies the middle ground between all theories which advocate state absolutism and the theories which advocate consistent individualism, as those of the old-time liberals.
>
> The tendency of state absolutism is to bring everything under the domination of the totalitarian state. According to this view the state's task would be to govern everything within the territorial limits of the state—a man's personal life, his home, his religion, and the internal affairs of all groups in society would then only have as much liberty as the state would allow them. There never existed a thoroughly totalitarian state. But the various forms of state absolutism hold that,

if the state should choose, it would have the right to direct all matters of all citizens residing within its territory.

The individualistic view of liberals goes to the opposite extreme. The ideal condition under this system would be reached if the state could almost cease to exist and leave the individual himself to run things as he might choose.

In opposition to the first of these two propositions, the Calvinist maintains that there are very definite limits to the state's authority. The state is not absolute; it cannot do anything it pleases. First of all, its territory is limited to the province of the natural common good. It may not presume to regulate such spiritual matters as the religion of a man's heart, sometimes defined as his conscience. In this area, conscience has not improperly been termed the limit of the state's authority.

A second boundary of the state's authority arises from the nature of the individuals who inhabit the state. The individual is not the mere creature of the state, existing only by and for the state. As God's image-bearer he has duties and responsibilities in his private life beyond the duties he owes to the state for which he must be allowed the necessary freedom and upon which the State may make no encroachment.

A third boundary limiting the state's authority lies in such natural spheres in society as the home, the school, the church, and economic and social organizations, which do not owe their origin or mode of existence to the state, and have their own task entrusted to them by God. These are sovereign within their own boundaries. Only insofar as any of these should overstep its limits, or endanger the welfare of other spheres, or of individuals, or the state, or insofar as by neglect of its duty it should endanger the well-being of the state, has the state here a duty to perform.

A case in point would occur when parents neglect the proper training of their children, or when the husband abuses his wife, or one group in society tyrannizes another group."

H. Henry Meeter, *The Basic Ideas of Calvinism*, p.101

Calvinism and the Virtues—Holiness and Reverence

The virtue of reverence was emphasized by Calvin and this carried with it a horror of all kinds of profanity. This meant also the obligation to go to church regularly and remember the Sabbath day and to keep it holy.

> "The supreme virtue, Calvin says is holiness. This means that above all else, God's honour must be exalted and God's will obeyed. To break in any least detail one of God's commandments is to offend God. To defraud one's neighbour of his rightful due is to offend God. To give rein to one's natural impulses towards pride or avarice or lewdness is to offend God. Any deviation whatsoever from the strict path of model rectitude is a direct affront to the Almighty."
>
> Georgia Harkness, *John Calvin the Man and his Ethics*, p. 78

Sobriety

When Calvin referred to sobriety he meant by the term both moderation in the use of intoxicants and a general simplicity of living. To live soberly meant to avoid excess of any kind. Following Paul, he summarized the virtues of a well-regulated life as sobriety, righteousness and Godliness. (Titus 2: 11–14)

Sobriety undoubtedly denotes chastity and temperance, as well as a pure and frugal use of temporal blessings, and patience under poverty. Righteousness includes all the duties of equity, that every man may receive what is due. Godliness separates us from the pollutions of the world and by true holiness unites us to God. When these virtues are indissolubly connected, they produce absolute perfection. (III, v II, 3 quoted by Harkness p. 160)

Frugality

Calvin noted that the sins of the drunkard, the spendthrift and the adulterer are often closely intertwined. The pure and frugal use of goods is constantly enjoined. Economy was the dominant trait of the Calvinist conscience. Calvin lived simply and frugally himself, and laid on his followers an aversion to extravagance, the effects of which still persist, for example, among the Scots and many others of Calvinistic lineage. Calvin had a deep insight into the perils of prosperity. We cannot blame God for sending scarcity and wants, he said, for when he sends us plenty we misuse his gifts.

Industry

The question of whether Calvin was the originator of the capitalist system (as Max Weber maintained) I think must be answered in the negative. Calvin however worked very hard himself and took it for granted that people ought to work hard.

It is taught by the Scripture and recognized even by the heathen that man was created to do something. Paul's principle is wholly reasonable, that idleness is not to be encouraged by supplying the lazy with food. Calvin elsewhere enjoins almsgiving as a religious duty, but never the feeding of the shiftless. "For idle bellies that chirp sweetly in the shade", he had no sympathy. (Harkness p. 172)

Honesty

Among the Florentine traders, where arguably capitalism had its rise, the virtue of honesty came as early as the 14th century to be highly prized. Calvin certainly contributed to an emphasis on the virtue of honesty but he was not the first to give it religious or popular sanction in general, but the Puritans and other early Calvinists accepted this view of the sinfulness of chicanery and avarice. Fair dealing toward master, servant, or peer was a virtue highly prized. Honesty of spirit, not simply the appearance of honesty was an economic asset—characterized by the Puritan conscience. Though covetousness existed, it was condemned. It was not respectable to be avaricious or to defraud one's neighbour.

Calvinism: a bastion against the spread of Islam

It is often forgotten that Islam made massive progress putting her to the forefront of human civilization during the Middle Ages. John W. Robbins writes:

> As the greatest political, military, economic, and religious power on earth, Islam's global triumph seemed inevitable. The battles in Europe that the Europeans thought so decisive, such as Charles Martel's victory at Tours in Northern France in 732, only a century after Muhammad's death, were regarded as minor setbacks by the Muslim. Rather, they saw their inexorable advance reflected in the ignominious expulsion of the Catholic Crusaders from the Levant in the 13th century, the capture of Constantinople in 1453, and their

> triumphant march through the Balkans towards that end in the early 17th century.
>
> Quoted by Robert L. Raymond, *John Calvin His Life and Influence*, p.141

But for some reason Islam did not absorb these backward peoples of the West. And the answer to why that was the case is that God revived his church at the Reformation and humanly speaking the man foremost in being responsible for that revitalization of the West was John Calvin.

Calvin has left a massive legacy to the western world, though few today seem to be aware of it. David Hill in a recent work on Calvin lists ten areas on which this outstanding Christian man has made a lasting impact.

1. He was one of the forerunners of modern public education. He was the only Reformer to found a university that would last for centuries i.e. The Academy of Geneva.
2. He contended for the freedom of the church from state interference.
3. He opposed the idea of totalitarian government, arguing that the powers of government should be limited.
4. He began a system of social welfare which provided for the needs of the deserving poor.
5. He maintained that the 10 Commandments were the foundation of public morality.
6. He established in Geneva one of the earliest forms of democratic society.
7. He believed that one could serve God in every legitimate area of life. He dignified work and said that whether we eat or drink we are to do all to the glory of God.
8. He encouraged enterprise in business, but warned against the danger of riches and mere materialism. He warned against the squandering of money and said that all work should be done without fraud or deception.
9. He introduced congregational singing into public worship.
10. He encouraged the printing of Christian literature and the widespread reading of good Christian books.

"There are people", remarks Paul Wernle, "who are certainly under the influence of no glamour for Calvin or Calvinism":

> There are people who have been told at school that Servetus was burned through Calvin's fault, and are therefore done with this man. They ought to remember that had they lived at the time, they would in all probability have joined in burning him. It is not so easy to be done with the man who was the most luminous and penetrating theologian of his time and the source from which flowed that power which Protestantism showed in Scotland, France, England and Holland. We are all glad, no doubt, that we did not live under his rod; but who knows what we would all be had not this divine ardour possessed him? Concentrated, well-directed enthusiasm—that is his essence; it was himself, first of all whom he consumed in his zeal; his rule at Geneva was no more rigorous than the heroism was glorious with which he compacted half the Protestantism of Europe into a power which nothing could break. Calvin was in very truth the soul of the battling and conquering Reformed world; it was he who fought on the battlefields of the Huguenots and the Dutch and in the hosts of the Puritans. In scarcely another of the Reformers is there to be seen such thoroughness, absoluteness. And yet what moderation, what real dread of every kind of excess; with what deference and tact did he know how to speak to the great! If you would know the man, how he lived with and for God in the world, read first of all in the *Institutes* the section "On the Life of the Christian Man". It is the portrait of himself. And then for his religious individuality add the sections "On Justification" and "On Predestination", where will be found what is most profound, most moving in his life of faith.
>
> Benjamin B. Warfield, *Calvin and Calvinism*, pp. 25, 26

Such a man was John Calvin; and such was the work he did for God and his kingdom on earth. Adolf Harnack has said that between Paul the Apostle and Luther the Reformer, Augustine was the greatest man God gave to his Church. We may surely add that from Luther the Reformer to our day God has given his Church no greater man than John Calvin. Central to the influence of Calvin, and his continued relevance in our day was this great work, *The Institutes of the Christian Religion*, as stated at the beginning of this chapter, "One of the ten books that shook the world."

Bibliography

John Calvin, *Institutes of the Christian Religion*, Henry Beveridge ed. (Eerdmans, 1975)

Able Ministers of the New Testament (Puritan and Reformed Studies Conference, 1964)

T.H.L. Parker, *A Portrait of Calvin* (Lion Publishing, 1977)

Francois Wedel, *Calvin* (Collins Fontana Library, 1965)

Timothy George, *Theology of the Reformers* (Broadman and Holman Publishers, 1988)

Basil Hall, *John Calvin* (Historical Association, 1956)

Alister McGrath, *Christianity's Dangerous Idea* (S.P.C.K., 2007)

Robert L. Raymond, *John Calvin his Life and Influence* (Fearn, Tain: Christian Focus, 2004)

Georgia Harkness, *John Calvin the Man and his Ethics* (H. Holt, 1931)

H. Henry Meeter, *The Basic Ideas of Calvinism* (Baker Book House).

J.H. Merle D' Aubigne, *Let Christ be Magnified* (Edinburgh: The Banner of Truth Trust, 2007)

Abraham Kuyper, *Calvinism* (Sovereign Grace Union, 1932)

A. Mitchell Hunter, *The Teaching of Calvin* (James Clark and Co. Ltd, 1950)

Benjamin B. Warfield, *Calvin and Calvinism* (Baker Book House, 1981)

William Wileman, *John Calvin* (Robert Banks and Son)

Charles Beard, *The Reformation of the Sixteenth Century in its Relation to Modern Thought and Knowledge* (The Hibbert Lecture for 1883; Williams and Norgate, 1883).

P. Tillich, *A History of Christian Thought* (S.C.M. Press Ltd, 1968)

John W. Robbins, *Civilization and the Protestant Reformation* (Trinity Foundation, 1994)

19. John Foxe—Foxe's *Book of Martyrs*

John Foxe was born in 1516, the same year in which Luther affixed his famous 95 Theses to the door of the Cathedral in Wittenberg. The year of his death, 1587, was the year of the execution of Mary Queen of Scots.

He was one of the great figures of the English Reformation. A quiet and scholarly man, though exceedingly well known and respected, entering into correspondence with John Calvin in Geneva and an associate of John Knox of Scotland, amongst many others. He enjoyed the friendship of Francis Drake, Sir Thomas Gresham and Lord Burleigh, Queen Elizabeth I's trusted advisor as well as the Queen, herself who always called him, Father Foxe.

He played no small part in the matters of State at that time, and though, as noted, naturally retiring, literary and academic by nature, he was at the same time a popular and likable individual.

Professor Trevelyan, the noted historian, puts Foxe's *Martyrology* alongside Hakulyt's *Voyages* as being the most influential books of the age of Shakespeare. (That is of course the Bible apart.)

Queen Elizabeth I gave order that Foxe's *Martyrs* be set up and chained next to the Great Bible of 1540, in every parish church, halls of hospitals, colleges, schools and other public institutions. In some parish churches it remains to this day. The incumbent of Holy Trinity Old Hill, Near Dudley is presented with a copy of Foxe's *Martyrs* on the day of his induction.

In 1613 it was one of the source books used by William Shakespeare for his *Life of King Henry VIII*.

John Foxe was born in Boston, Lincolnshire. The biography written by his son, Simeon, states that Foxe's father and mother …

> Were of the commonality of the town, well reported and of good estate.

According to the old traditions of the town of Boston, Foxe was born in a house at the end of the marketplace, within a stone's throw of the parish church with its famous *Boston Stump* tower. Later this house was turned into *The Bell Inn.* This was subsequently demolished in the 19th century, and replaced by another rather unsightly building still a public house, which now stands on the same site, and was known as *The Rum Puncheon* but has now been renamed *The Stump & Candle.* A tablet on its wall records it as the birthplace John Foxe the Martyrologist.

The tablet states that Foxe's family: "was both ancient and renowned, though latterly obscured, and that it's number formerly included bishops Richard and Edward Foxe amongst its scions."

In an earlier note by Foxe's son Simeon, he had written that whilst his father was of the plebeian class, his mother was of higher rank.

We also know that while John Foxe was still very young his father died and his mother married again. The family went to live in the house of the new husband. Foxe tells us that his stepfather's name was Richard Melton, this is recorded in a tract dedicated to him by Foxe about 1548.

The second edition of this tract (1579) gives the following further detail. It says "For a dear father of mine, one Richard Melton …, to recompense him with some fruit of my studies for the charge which he, more like a natural than stepfather, bestowed upon me in sending me to school".

Further we know that Foxe was a studious child from his earliest years. Whilst others went out to play he could not be found amongst them, but either spent his time in the church at his prayers or deep in a book. His character and his intelligence won him wide approval and admiration and in due course, when he had scarce past boyhood, he was sent to Oxford.

This was not done without outside help. It is certain that John Hawarden, originally from Lancashire, who was also sometimes referred to as John Harding, a fellow and afterwards principle of Brazenose College, Oxford, paved the way for him to enter university.

In later life Foxe wrote to John Hawarden, whom he calls his patron, these words of appreciation:

> I shall never forget how much I owe to the Lord through you, and to you in the Lord, for your old services to me. Nor do I think it fitting that when as a boy I was first drawn to these university studies by divine providence, through you and by your influence with my father in law [this is often thought to be Foxe's way of describing his

> stepfather], I should, now that I am grown up, be slower in thanking than I seemed in accepting the benefit.

John Hawarden before becoming principal of Brasenose College, was the incumbent of Coningsby, a large village near Boston, Lincolnshire. Incidentally John Hawarden was something of a pluralist, because the record show that he remained Rector of Coningsby all the time he was principal of Brasenose, and not only so but that he also held the living of Steeple Aston, and the living of Tackley both in Oxfordshire, at the same time.

Foxe later married Agnes Randal of Coventry. Because Foxe often use the term "father-in-law" to describe his stepfather, there is still some historical confusion as to whether his stepfather Richard Melton, or his father-in-law Mr Randall of Coventry paid for his early university education.

However, John Foxe went to the University of Oxford, first it seems to Brasenose College at 16 years of age and then to Magdalen College. Here he became friendly with Alexander Nowell who afterwards became Dean of St Paul's, and a strong adherent of the Reformed faith.

In 1539 Foxe was elected a Fellow of Magdalene College—a distinction which sufficiently proved the high reputation for scholarship which he had already gained.

The nine or ten years between Foxe's matriculation and his election to the Fellowship were among the most eventful years in the history of the Reformation. In 1534 the Parliament of England renounced the Papal Supremacy. In the years following the first complete English Bible was published by Myles Coverdale, followed two years later by a further revision of Coverdale's work, *The Great Bible*, the use of which was made available to all English churches, the famous Chained Bible, referred to earlier.

This was a complex period in English Church history, whilst Henry VIII was severing the ties with Rome, he was also seeking to follow the course of an independent English church still embracing Roman Catholic doctrine. In 1539 the Act of the Six Articles was passed which made the denial of Transubstantiation an offense punishable by death at the stake. At this time to affirm the papal supremacy was treason, whilst to deny papal doctrines was heresy. Such contradictions could not but help to stir to reflection the minds of many serious and thoughtful individuals. One of these undoubtedly was John Foxe. It led him to look into the history of the church both ancient and modern and to understand what it believed and practiced at the beginning. Such was the seriousness and diligence with which he undertook this task that by the time he was 30 years of age he had read through all the writings of the Greek and Latin Fathers, together with all the writings of the Medieval Schoolmen and on top of this he had mastered the Hebrew language.

These studies engrossed the days and nights of the future writer of the *Martyrology*. In the grounds of Magdalene College, he would spend many evenings pacing to and fro, kneeling in prayer and pouring out his soul to God. His fellow students marvelled at his desire to find out the truth.

It was also noted that at this time he failed to attend the services of the Church. He was soon called to account by the authorities of the college and directed to attend the services. He confessed that in many things he was not of one mind with the teaching; the authorities could have disciplined him for this breach of what was required, and for his challenge to the teachings of the Roman Church. Perhaps because he had already achieved such distinction as a scholar or because of his excellent character or because they had some sympathy with his views he was not called to account, but voluntarily resigned from his Fellowship in 1545.

Leaving Oxford, he became tutor to the children of Sir Thomas Lucy, at Charlecote, Warwickshire.

S.G. Green writes;

> His eldest pupil would no doubt be the Thomas Lucy whom Shakespeare (who was born 19 years after Foxe became tutor at Charlecote) has depicted for the laughter of all time as Mr Justice Shallow. The fact is that this country Knight was a sturdy, inflexible Puritan, with little mercy on the poet's youthful escapades; and Shakespeare revenged himself by the caricature.

Something of the stern Protestantism of the Warwickshire Squire may have been traceable to the influence of his old tutor Foxe. Foxe only remained at Charlecote for about one year. However, it was here that he met his future wife Agnes Randall who was visiting from Coventry and for a short time after this he lived in Coventry with his wife's family.

As an indication of the fact that he was now a marked man, we can note that he wrote to his stepfather in Boston proposing to visit and spend some time in the town. The answer was a grudging permission, warning Foxe that he had committed a capital offence, i.e. in his criticism of Roman Catholic doctrine, and should be aware of the hazards he was exposing himself and his family to in returning to a small town such as Boston, where everyone knew each other's movements and opinions. He did return to Boston for a short time but soon moved to London where he considered himself to be safer—more easy to become anonymous in a bustling city.

His financial situation at this time was exceedingly difficult as, because of his opinions it was difficult to get work. One day he was sitting despondent in St Paul's Cathedral. His resources were so exhausted that he couldn't even buy food. Suddenly an unknown person took a seat by his side and told him to be of good cheer, at the same time thrusting a purse of gold into his hand and then disappearing. Who this benefactor was Foxe never learned. But, three days later he was sent for by the Duchess of Richmond, and requested to take up the post of tutor to three children, to whom as their aunt, she was guardian.

The father of these children, the Earl of Surrey, was in prison in the Tower of London, with his father the old Duke of Norfolk, and was soon after beheaded on a charge of high treason, the Duke being detained in captivity for some years longer. The young Howard's, that is the children to whom Foxe was tutor, were Thomas Howard, afterwards Duke of Norfolk, Henry Howard who became the Earl of Northampton, and Jane Howard who afterwards became the Countess of Westmoreland.

When Henry VIII died in January 1547 and was succeeded by his son the young Edward VI, life became much easier for Protestants, and Foxe was now safe. He moved with his young wife to the Surrey village of Reigate and continued instructing his young pupils. Lady Jane Howard, became the friend of the renowned Lady Jane Grey. Of both these young women it was said that they were "not unworthy of comparison with the most learned men of that time for the praise of elegance in learning."

Whilst at Reigate Foxe was ordained deacon by Bishop Nicholas Ridley. Foxe began to preach against the idolatrous symbols of Rome. He was busy in writing, including a treatise on church discipline, and also a paper called, *An Address to Parliament*, warning of the dangers of a return to the doctrines of the Church of Rome.

Part of the irony of this situation in which Foxe now found himself is that he was the tutor to the grand children of the Duke of Norfolk who was a devout Roman Catholic. On the accession of Queen Mary, the imprisoned Duke was released from the tower, who promptly dismissed Foxe as the tutor of his grandchildren. However, Foxe remained close to the Howard children, and one of them, Thomas Howard in the later years of Foxe's life granted him a pension.

Foxe was now being closely watched, and found it necessary to flee to the Continent. He crossed the country to Ipswich, where he immediately set sail for Antwerp. Unfortunately, the ship encountered bad weather in the North Sea (the German Ocean as it was called in those days) and had to put back into the shelter of the River Orwell. Unknown to Foxe, Bishop Gardiner had sent his commissioners to apprehend and arrest Foxe and take him to Winchester for trial. They arrived in Ipswich but a few hours after the ship had re-embarked. After the stormy passage the vessel reached Nieuport in Holland where Foxe and his wife were now safe.

He eventually met up with Edmund Grindal, later to become Archbishop of Canterbury in Elizabeth's reign, in Strasburg. It was here that the first draft of the famous *Book of Martyrs* was written. It was about 400 pages long and bore the title, *Commentaries on the affairs of the church and an account of the chief persecutions in all Europe from the days of Wycliffe to the present time. First Book, by John Foxe, Englishman.*

Soon after the publication of this book we find Foxe at Frankfurt, where a small company of refugees from Great Britain gathered, including John Knox and William Whittingham, brother-in-law to Calvin, and afterwards Dean of Durham, with William Kethe, to whom English-speaking Christians are under lasting obligation for his version of the Hundredth Psalm, *All people that on earth do dwell.*

Here they formed a little Protestant English congregation, and worshiped harmoniously together, until troubles arose when Dr Cox arrived from England and insisted on the exclusive use of the Prayer Book of Edward VI.

A division and separation arose, and some say this incident characterized the subsequent difference between Anglicans and Puritan's in the succeeding century.

After this John Knox moved to Geneva and John Foxe and others found employment in Basle, Switzerland. Foxe worked for the famous printer Oporinus, as a corrector of the press and general editor of his publications. Though the pay was scanty it allowed him time to continue his work on the *Martyrology.*

Accounts of the fierce persecutions taking place back at home in England under Queen Mary were passed on via Grindal, still at Strasburg, to Foxe in Basle, and carefully recorded.

Foxe was extremely well-informed on the state of affairs back at home. So much so that one Sunday morning whilst preaching to the English exiles he suddenly encouraged them to be of good cheer, adding, "for now was the time come for their return to England." He was reproved by the most sober amongst them for his outrageous, unfounded and dangerous comments. However, it was later found that Queen Mary had died the day before the sermon was preached and that Queen Elizabeth had now been designated as a successor. Foxes intelligence gathering network was second to none.

Foxe was not quick to return to England. He now had two children, a boy and a girl to support, he needed to continue in his livelihood He was also keen to see the next phase of his book through the press.

He did however write to the Queen, and again proving how well-known and respected he was, was so bold as to offer her some advice on how she should proceed as Queen. As it had come from her old friend "Father Foxe, " she received it in a good spirit.

On his return to England he was looked after by his old pupil Thomas Howard, now the Duke of Norfolk. He received various benefices in the Church of England. He was invited to speak at St Paul's Cross but was somewhat apprehensive.

He said to Grindal;

> Who could have instigated you thus to think of crucifying me at Paul's Cross? There never was an ass or mule so weighed down by burdens as I have been by literary labours. I am almost worn out by that toil, and by my ill health. Yet I am summoned to the celebrated pulpit, where, like an ape among Cardinals, I shall be received with derision or driven away by the hisses of the auditory!

To which Grindal replied

> Forget self and preach Christ and Him crucified.

At this time in order to complete his great work Foxe left the mansion of the now Duke of Norfolk, (Thomas Howard) and took up lodgings in Grub Street, near Cripplegate, at that time the favourite residence of authors, in order to finish his great work. He laboured unremittingly and brought out his first English edition in 1563. Further editions followed in 1570, in 1576 and 1583. The first two editions of the *Acts and Monuments* were produced in Latin on the Continent whilst he was in exile during Queen Mary's reign, the Strasbourg Edition 1554 and the Basle Edition of 1559. Many further editions of *The Book of Martyrs* were produced by others, some with extra information and others severely cut down in size in the subsequent centuries to the present day. The 1550 edition was dedicated to his former pupil Henry Howard, Duke of Norfolk.

We might try to picture him week by week walking to the printing offices of John Day, a man like-minded with Foxe, in Aldersgate Street. Many would know him and greet him on his journey, a well-known figure with a faraway look, an emaciated form, sunken cheeks and neglected garb. Carrying his precious manuscripts under his arm.

The Book of Martyrs was very well received by the public, many of the accounts in it had been witnessed by people that were still living. Others had ties of family or friendship to those who were described in its pages.

Queen Elizabeth gave command after the second edition to place a copy in all the parish churches and public institutions.

Turning now to consider what was John Foxe's purpose and aim in producing the *Martyrology*...

Firstly, we may need to note that the 16th century was a period when educated people were acutely aware of the past. This was partly because of the Renaissance or the revival of learning. The motto *Ad Fontes,* back to the sources, was of vital impact on all areas of study.

A second a very important reason for this interest in the past, was to refute the charge that the Reformation was a new thing, an innovation, and novelty. What Foxe and other set out to do was to prove that the Reformation in England was a return to the purer church of the past: the church that had existed in these islands before Papal dominance, and the accretions and distortions of medieval Catholicism had engulfed it like the ivy on an ancient building.

This same spirit prevailed in some of the Protestant countries on the continent. Foxe's work was to some extent paralleled by similar works produced on the Continent such as, *The Magdeburg Centuries* or Jean Crispins' *Martyrology.*

Foxe himself sets out his purpose in the various prefaces to the various editions of his work.

1. His first preface is addressed to our Saviour in the form of a thanksgiving that the work is done, and an acknowledgment that it is only through his strength that it has been achieved and completed.

2. The second preface is dedicated:

> "To the right virtuous, most excellent, and noble Princess Elizabeth, our peaceful Salome." He apologizes to the Queen that he has written in English, but explains that he has not had her and learned people in mind, but the unlearned. For they have lived in ignorance, especially of God's Word, but also of Church history, with the result that they have in the past been imposed upon by the Papists with their biased and fraudulent histories. The knowledge of the Gospel is necessary to any nation and this is why he has written his Church history, which is, after all, not something separate from the Gospel.

3.The third preface is addressed to: *The Persecutors of God's Truth*, reminding them that on the Last Day they will be charged with the blood of so many martyrs.

4. The fourth preface is addressed to: *The true and faithful congregation*. Here he explains his purpose in writing the *Acts and Monuments* in this way:

> "First, to see the simple flock of Christ, especially the unlearned sort, so miserably abused and all for ignorance of history, not knowing the course of times and true descent of the Church, it pitied me that part of diligence so long to have been unsupplied in this my country's Church of England.
>
> What makes it worse is that the multitude of Chronicles and story writers were monks, who have handled the stories partially. This partial dealing and corrupt handling of histories, when I considered, I thought with myself nothing more lacking in the church than a full and complete story… That all studious readers, beholding as in a glass the state, course, and alterations of religion, decay of doctrine, and the controversies of the Church, might discern the better between antiquity and novelty."

It is certain that Foxe saw all history as under the control of divine Providence. He looked on the Reformation as the ending of a period comparable to the 70 years of the Babylonian captivity.

5. Similar statements are made in the fifth preface.

6. In the sixth preface he relates another important purpose of his work.

He says:

> The martyrs deserve to be remembered. What is more that it is great usefulness in reading about them for they not only serve as examples and encouragements, but their history shows God at work: by reading thereof we may learn a lively testimony of God's mighty working in the life of man, contrary to the opinion of atheists, and all the whole nest of Epicureans.

He didn't believe it seemly that those who sacrificed so much in the cause of God and truth should be easily forgotten. The blood of the martyrs is the seed of the church. This book was intended to serve as an inspiration and example to his own and future generations.

Continuing to consider the purpose of the *Book of Martyrs* ...

J.F. Mosley in his, *John Foxe and his Book*, rightly draws attention to Foxe's humanitarianism. Foxe strongly protests against men and women being put to death for their beliefs, and especially the practice of burning alive. This is seen in his endeavours to save Joan Boucher, the Anabaptist, in 1550, and the Flemish Anabaptists in 1575. When he wrote to the Queen on their behalf, he told her that even to pass a butcher's slaughter-house he found upsetting. We shall not be fanciful if we see the *Acts and Monuments* as a manifesto directed against brutal forms of punishment directed against those who may hold beliefs contrary to ours. There is evidence that Foxe even sought to save the life of the Roman Catholic, Edmund Campion and his fellow conspirators in 1581.

T.H.L. Parker in his *English Reformers* gives us four points he believes that Foxe was trying to emphasise in the production of this great work.

Firstly, concerned the matter of the Reformation being described by its opponents as an innovation, this is a point we have already touched on, but we look at in further detail here.

> "It was a belief, of the Reformers that they had on their side, not only the Bible but also, on the major dogmas at issue, the Church Fathers. It was not they who were the innovators; it was the Roman Catholics. Unfortunately, they had a difficult battle to fight here, for all the evidence seemed to the contrary. And in England they had the stubborn conservatism of their countrymen to contend against

> (and that meant the majority of Englishmen). Innovation covered anything that had not been done "in my time, or my father's time, or my grandfather's time"—in other words since about 1490. For the learned Reformers, however, "modern" meant the Lateran Council of 1215.
>
> It was precisely this problem that Foxe had in mind. The "ignorant folk" had been accustomed to late medieval Christianity. No-one could point to a great upheaval when this brand of religion had come about, because it had very slowly evolved. For them this was Christianity and they could imagine no other sort. The history books themselves had sprung from this religion and naturally treated it as the true faith.
>
> Foxe knew that the first need was for Bibles; but he believed that the second need was for history books that would put a different slant on things. To the Queen he speaks of the "ignorant flock of Christ committed to your government in this realm of England; who, as they have been long led in ignorance, and wrapped in blindness, for lack especially of God's Word, and partly also for wanting the light of history, I thought pity but that such should be helped, and their ignorance relieved, and simplicity instructed. What was needed was a full and complete story."

Secondly, the purpose of Foxe's *Acts and Monuments* is to trace out the pedigree of the Church of England or the English Church.

The Reformation Church was no new-fangled invention; nor was it simply the resurrection of the Church of former centuries, but in fact God had never left himself without a Church in England, though very often this Church was hard to discern. There was a Church before 1517. Foxe is concerned to show the continuity of the Reformed Church with the past, and to this end provides a pedigree for the Church of England.

This pedigree traces back by way of "faithful witnesses" in the 15th century—Wyckliffe, Thorp, White, Lord Cobham, even including Geoffrey Chaucer in the list.

He then traces these "faithful witnesses" back through the centuries to the Venerable Bede, and right back to the saints of Roman Britain.

He says, in those times the doctrine of faith without men's traditions was sincerely preached as it had been received from the Apostles and Christ. He even makes use of the early stories of Joseph of Arimathea bringing the Gospel to Glastonbury, and those stories which suggest that the Apostle Paul and other of the Apostles, perhaps Peter visited these islands. Foxe proclaims that the Church of England stands in the line of *Apostolic Succession* and was joined, not by manual ordination, but by the transmission of the apostolic doctrine.

Thirdly, Foxe's *Martyrs* as set out by Parker is to show the mighty works of God in history.

The Reformers were faced with a practical atheism of some of the Renaissance teachers: i.e. teaching that God is not concerned with the affairs of man. The Reformation teachers opposed this with the Biblical doctrine of the Providence of God. That is the teaching that God continues to work in the world to the same purpose and in the same spirit as he created the world, preserving, upholding, guiding, overruling in the lives of men and of nations.

Foxe traces the hand of Divine providence in bringing the Reformation and preserving his church through the centuries.

Fourthly, Foxe's purpose is to communicate an apocalyptic understanding of time. Foxe interprets history in the light of Biblical apocalyptic. *The Acts and Monuments* divides church history into five periods: the age of persecution, lasting for about 300 years, and followed by "the flourishing time of the church" for another 300 years. Then came the "declining and backsliding of the church" over yet another 300 years. Fourthly, followed the "time of Antichrist", (which he calculated to have been about the year 1000) or the loosing of Satan and the desolation of the church, which occupied 400 years—and this brings us to the 14th century and the time of Wyckliffe. Finally, there has come "the time of the Reformation and purging, while Antichrist is being unmasked and has steadily lost ground to the true church." So far this age has lasted around 280 years, and how long it shall continue more, "the Lord and Governor of all times, he alone knoweth."

What we mean by all this is that Foxe understood history in terms of the final coming in all its glory, of the kingdom of God. Professor Haller's thesis that Foxe's *Martyrs* was simply trying to convey the idea that England was the chosen nation of God above all the others, does not bear close scrutiny. It is true that Foxe emphasized God's favour over many years to these Islands and he could not fail to wonder at the glories and blessings God poured upon this nation during the reign of the Virgin Queen Elizabeth and all the blessings which flow out of the Reformation.

But his eye was chiefly set on the Second coming of Christ. He believed that the time of the Reformation, the time in which he and his countrymen were living, was decisive in bringing about this glorious Second Coming and therefore his purpose was to urge his readers to a sense of the significance and urgency of their lives in this world, to live by the help of God's grace to the glory of the coming kingdom.

Enemies of Foxe's Book of Martyrs

It was natural that such a book should have awakened fierce opposition. Roman Catholics called it *Master Foxe's Golden Legend*, and denounced it as a mass of inventions and inaccuracies.

Others have spoken of Foxe as a one-sided, and inaccurate historian. Modern writers have come to the conclusion that Foxe was an historian of high integrity.

In the wake of the Oxford Movement of the early 19th century several learned articles were published criticizing the accuracy of Foxe's accounts. The first of these was from the pen of S. R. Maitland, the librarian of Lambeth Palace, who attacked the integrity, truthfulness and reliability of Foxe. It had great initial success and at the same time exposed the fact that many who claimed to admire Foxe's work had read little of it and had limited appreciation of its true meaning.

An anti-Foxe tradition once launched had a long run, and other critics included J. S. Brewer and James Gardiner, all highly respected Victorian historians, who joined in the criticism.

The High Anglican historian R. W. Dixon, however, was the first to challenge these attacks on Foxe and subsequently the tide began to turn once again in support of Foxes accuracy and integrity.

The mid-20th century brought the invaluable study by Mr J.F. Mosley which still remains the standard textbook on Foxe, and throws considerable light on the greatness of this most excellent individual.

Two other classic testimonies to the integrity of Foxe might appropriately be mentioned at this point. The first is from the great 17th century historian Bishop Francis Burnet:

> "In some private passages which were brought to him upon flying reports, Foxe made a few mistakes, being too credulous; but in the account he gives from records or papers he is a most exact and faithful writer; so that I could never find him in any prevarication or so much as a designed concealment. He tells the good and the bad,

the weakness and the passion, as well as the constancy and patience, of those good men who sealed their faith with their blood."

The second is from the famous Bishop of Lincoln, Dr Christopher Wordsworth:

> I am not ignorant of what has been said by critics of Foxe, but neither his writings nor theirs have proved, and it never will be proved, that John Foxe is not one of the most faithful and authentic of all historians. All the many researches and discoveries of latter times in regard to historical documents have only contributed to place the general fidelity and truth of Foxe's narrative, on a rock which cannot be shaken.
>
> Taken from *Champions of the Truth*, ed. A. R. Buckland p.150

Some further insights into the character of Foxe

In 1572, Foxe's long-standing benefactor and former pupil, Thomas Howard, now the Duke of Norfolk was brought to trial for being part of a conspiracy to put Mary Queen of Scots on the throne of England. He was tried for high treason and condemned to be hanged. Foxe did not desert him but went so far as to accompany him to the scaffold together with Dean Nowell (his old friend Alexander Nowell). The two sought to comfort the Duke and later bore testimony to the fact that he had died penitent and in the Protestant faith. The Duke of Norfolk left Foxe a small pension in his will, which in fact put Foxe beyond the reach of want for of the rest of his life.

Another fact that we may note is that though Foxe was ordained an Anglican minister in 1560, soon after he returned from Switzerland, he nevertheless later refused all church offices because of his increasing Puritan views. He did, however continue to preach and publish sermons.

Although, as we noted earlier, he had the nature of a recluse, and the vast amount of study and literary work he undertook required him more so to be alone with his books, nevertheless, the company and wise council of Foxe were continually sought after.

It was said of him:

> There repaired unto him both citizens and strangers, noblemen and

> common people of all degrees, and almost all for the same cause, to seek some salve for a wounded conscience.
>
> *Champions of Truth*, p.155

Many of his letters of spiritual counsel have been preserved—some of them dealing with very personal matters. Among his correspondence preserved in the British Museum is a letter to him "from one on the temptation to blaspheme, requesting counsel." Several letters to "persons in concern about their spiritual state", whom with loving council he exhorts to seek their rest in Christ. One of them is to a young lady whom he advises to marry a certain youth. Whether she took his advice we do not know.

He had a kind sense of humour and occasionally a caustic tongue. On one occasion he met a woman that he knew, who pulled a book from under her arm, waved it at him and said, "See I'm going to hear a sermon". He replied: "If you will be ruled by me, go home, you will do little good in church today." And when she asked, "At what time did he counsel her to go to church?" He replied: "When you tell nobody before-hand."

Foxe's good heartedness is illustrated by the fact that when in 1563 plague broke out in London he was amongst the few ministers who remained in the city to support and care for the beleaguered population. Not only so, but he wrote to those ministers who had fled, appealing to them to at least send money to help the bereaved and pennyless.

Foxe's death

Foxe died, worn out by incessant labour at the age of 70. In the year of his death the great Armada was threatening England. To the last, though he never claimed to be a prophet, he was constantly reassuring his friends that the attempt would result in failure.

He was buried in the chancel of St Giles Church, Cripplegate on April 18th, 1587. It is said that the whole City turned out to lament him.

His monument in St Giles Church bears an inscription in Latin written by his son Samuel. It reads in English: To John Foxe, most faithful martyrologist of the English Church, most sagacious explorer of historical antiquity, most valiant defender of evangelical truth, and admirable thaumaturge, who has brought again as living from their ashes like the Phoenixes, the Marion martyrs: Samuel Foxe his first born has, with dutiful affection and tears, erected this monument. He died, April 18th AD 1587, at the age of 70. "*Life's duration is mortal, it's hope immortal.*"

J. F. Mosley in his book quoted above, *John Foxe and his Book* concludes with these words:

> In reading Foxe's Book, then, we learn, or should learn, to respect and admire him. We respect him for his zeal and earnestness for his enormous pains-taking. We thank him for the historic knowledge which he has preserved from destruction. We are touched by his devotion to the Martyrs, by his championship of the poor and downtrodden, by his hatred of cruelty. If he was a partisan he was no more so than Sir Thomas More, whom the present day finds no difficulty in taking to its bosom. And then there's this to be said, Foxe's fierce words spring not from attachment to a set of theological dogmas or ecclesiastical systems, but from deep and spontaneous human sympathy; he sees men suffer, and his soul rebels.

The great humanity and sympathy of Foxe is an important aspect of his attractive character and must not be overlooked.

However, we must not forget his great love for the doctrines of the Reformation, and beyond that of course, his love for Christ.

Neither must we forget the inspirational and soul strengthening value of the reading of this volume with understanding. Sir Francis Drake read it aloud to his little company at sea as they nosed their anxious way into unknown waters on that desperate adventure of sailing around the world. John Wesley chose it is the first of the Christian Classics, to be woven into his famous *Christian Library*, to be foremost in the preparation and edification of his Preachers, because it set before their eyes the noble army of martyrs, and the need to continue the blessed warfare of the Church militant here on earth, in the anticipation of the glories of the City of God beyond this scene.

Let me close with the words of John Foxe himself, taken from the end of his book, *To the True and Faithful Congregation*, the work that really formed the introduction to his *Martyrology*.

He concluded by saying:

> The God of peace, who hath power both of land and sea, reach forth his merciful hand to help them up that sink, to keep up them that stand... that we, professing one Christ, may, in one unity of doctrine, gather ourselves into one Ark of the true Church together;

where we, continuing steadfast in faith, may at the last, prosperously be conducted to the joyful port of our desired landing place, by his heavenly grace. To whom, both in heaven and earth, be all power and glory, with his Father and the Holy Ghost, forever. Amen.

From T.H.L Parker, *English Reformers*, p.86

Wherefore seeing we also are compassed about with so great a cloud of witnesses, let us lay aside every weight, and the sin which doth so easily beset us, and let us run with patience the race that is set before us,

Looking unto Jesus the author and finisher of our faith; who for the joy that was set before him endured the cross, despising the shame, and is set down at the right hand of the throne of God.

Hebrews 12:1–2.

The noble Army, men and boys,
The matron and the maid,
Around the Saviour's throne rejoice,
In robes of lights arrayed;
They climbed the steep ascent of heaven,
Through peril, toil, and pain:
O God, to us may grace be given
To follow in that train.

Reginald Heber, 1783–1826

(from the hymn 'The Son of God goes forth to war', *Methodist Hymn Book*, 816)

Bibliography

John Foxe, *Book of Martyrs*, ed. Adam Clarke (Ward, Lock, Bowdon and Co., n.d)

J.F. Mosley, *John Foxe and his Book* (London: SPCK, 1940)

A.G. Dickens, *The English Reformation* (Fontana Paperbacks, 1981)

T.H.L. Parker, *The English Reformers* (Westminster Press, 1966)

A. R. Buckland, *Champions of the Truth* (London: Religious Tract Society, 1903)

20. Edmund Spencer—*The Faerie Queene* (Edmund Spencer c. 1552–1599)

SPENCER'S *FAERIE QUEENE* IS AN OUTSTANDING LITERARY masterpiece, the purpose of which is to portray the demands and struggles of those seeking to live out the Christian life amidst the trials, obstructions, temptations and tumults, warfare and worries of everyday life in this world. Another helpful way to describe this poem is to see it as portraying the spiritual and moral power of Protestant Reformed religion to enable an individual to live life nobly and well.

By way of background it is helpful to remember that the poet spent a considerable part of his early life (18 years) in Ireland as secretary to Lord Grey D'Wilton, at that time Lord Deputy of Ireland. The bulk of *The Faerie Queene* was composed there in what have been described as, "the wild and desolate wastes of barbarous Ireland." To English eyes of that time, "a place of universal conspiracy, of fraud against righteousness, a universal battle going on between error and religion, between justice and the most insolent selfishness." Dean Richard William Church comments that, "they found there every type of what was cruel, brutal, and loathsome. The aim of the poem was to challenge men to rise above this and to live lives of noble generosity, gentle strength, knightly sweetness and courtesy."

The poem brings out the difficulties of living life in this fallen world, the partial successes and failures encountered on the way, the constant frustrations, the dragons that need to be fought, the feeling that we are always on the verge of defeat, but at the same time constantly sustained by the certain promise of triumph and victory at the last.

The plan of the poem is described in Spencer's preparatory letter to Sir Walter Raleigh. The twelve books were

> to tell the warfare of twelve knights, in whom twelve virtues are represented. They are sent forth from the court of Gloriana, Queen of Fairy-land, and their warfare is against the vices and errors, impersonated, which opposed those virtues. In Arthur, the Prince, the Magnificence of the whole of virtue is represented, and he was at last to unite himself in marriage to the Faerie Queene, that divine glory of God to which all human acts and thought aspired.
>
> Six books of this plan were finished, setting forth the virtues and legends of Holiness, Temperance, Chastity, Friendship, Justice and Courtesy.
>
> Alongside the spiritual allegory is the historical one, in which Elizabeth is Gloriana and other figures and movements of the day are represented.
>
> Stopford A. Brooke, *English Literature*, p.76

The framework of the poem is based on the exploits of Gloriana's twelve knights. The one constantly recurring knight, however, is King Arthur, the great historical/mythical figure of Britain's epic history. Nearly every time Arthur appears in the poem it is to save another knight. Some have speculated on whether Spencer's portrayal of Arthur draws on Geoffrey of Monmouth's portrayal of him in his *The History of the Kings of Britain*, or whether he has taken his picture of him from Thomas Mallory's *Le Mort D'Arthur*. Both of these sources depict Arthur as intent on conquering Rome. Geoffrey of Monmouth's account portrays Arthur as ruthless in his conquering zeal. Mallory's account of him portrays him as rather less brutal, but Spencer's account, while still portraying him as one set on the conquest of Rome removes the harshness of his zeal and portrays him as a man with a mission to defend the needy and conquer for the right.

The unfolding structure of the work is based on the exploits of twelve of the *Faerie Queene's* knights, each of these in turn portraying examples of the twelve virtues mentioned above.

First we read of the adventures of the Red Cross Knight, or the real St George. He represents holiness, and he is the protector of the Virgin Una who represents truth or true religion, against the wiles of Archimago and Duessa, the former of these refers to the image worship of the Roman Church and the latter refers to the false doctrine of the same.

The second knight is Sir Guyon who represents Temperance. This second section, Canto X, contains a chronicle of British rulers from Brutus to Elizabeth I.

In the third section Chastity is exemplified by Britomart and Belphoebe.

The fourth section portrays two figures exemplifying friendship, Triamond and Campbell.

In the fifth section we read of the adventures of Artegail, the Knight of Justice, in which allegorical references are made to various historical events in the reign of Queen Elizabeth: the defeat of the Spaniards in the Netherlands, the defeat of the Spanish Armada, the recantation of Henry IV of France, the execution of Mary Queen of Scots, and the administration of Ireland by Lord Grey D' Wilton.

The sixth section portrays the adventures of Sir Calidore, who exemplifies Courtesy.

There is also an addition to the sixth section of the original work which was published after Spencer's death in 1599 and known as the Mutabilitie Cantos.

This section has been described as portraying Spencer's worldview, indeed we might call it the Reformation worldview, or better still the biblical worldview.

> "Here is portrayed a benign Creator, a Creation whose plenitude exhausted possibility; this plenitude ordered in hierarchies and analogies of being—then the grand design thrown into confusion by the Fall with the Divine original veiled behind the mutability of a fallen world and a corresponding disorder in human faculties, which now only Grace could alleviate."
>
> *The Mutabilitie Cantos*, Introduction p.4

In this work the seventh virtue is added, that being the virtue of Constancy.

It seems that from Spencer's explanatory letter to Sir Walter Raleigh the work originally was to fall into twelve parts. The Mutabilitie Cantos are but a small fragment of the seventh part, the rest are either lost or were never completed.

> "The Faerie Queene was designed to set forth Spencer's conception

of a gentleman or noble person. Upon the first view the poem seems a labyrinth of flowery glades, through which for mere delight the imagination may wander without end or aim; but Spencer had planned it with a purpose, and that purpose had the high seriousness of the time. He would exhibit all the chief elements which go to form a heroic character, all the chief dangers to which such a character is exposed in the warfare of this world, and would incite men towards the attainment of that magnanimity, or, as he terms it, "magnificence," which sums up all the virtues of our fully developed manhood. Poetry, as it was then conceived, was to be like a trumpet–call summoning men to action, as was also history on the one hand and moral philosophy on the other to be the auxiliaries and subordinate allies of poetry. Such was Spencer's design. He thinks of life as a warfare against the principalities and powers of evil; he represents godliness, self-control, and chastity as the foundational virtues on which a complete and beautiful humanity is to be erected; he is at once a son of the Renaissance and the son of the Reformation; a cosmopolitan in his culture, and a patriot in his passion. Enamoured of all beauty appealing to the senses and to the spirit, yet no wanton lover of sensual delights; rather, indeed, with a certain sternness at his heart, honouring as much as any Puritan, the girt loins and the lit lamp. Ariosto and Tasso, Aristotle and Plato, St Paul and the writer of the Apocalypse alike contribute to the structure of the adornment of The Faerie Queen."

International Library of Famous Literature vol. 6, Edward Dowden on *Characteristics of Elizabethan Literature*, p. xxi

For Spencer's extensive use of Scripture texts and passages, see Naseeb Shaheen's work, Biblical References in *The Faerie Queene*

For Edmund Spencer's letter to Sir Walter Raleigh explaining the plan of the poem, see R.W. Church on Spencer, in the *English Men of Letters* series, pages 122–123.

See also Sir Paul Harvey, *The Oxford Companion to English literature*, p.277.

Arthur Mee, *The Children's Encyclopaedia*, volume 8, p. 5919. gives us this summary.

In the allegory as used by Spencer the characters represent good or bad qualities. *The Faerie Queene*, is a poetic allegory of the moral virtues, first printed in the year 1590. It takes us to Fairyland at the

> time of the annual festival, lasting twelve days, and on each of these days a brave knight has to go forth on some adventure to fight against evils. Gloriana, the Faerie Queene, stands for Glory; Prince Arthur for the Spirit of Chivalry, St George for Christianity, Sir Guyon for Temperance, Britomart for True Love, Sir Calidore for Courtesy, and so forth. The deeds of these and many other champions in overcoming the forces of evil are all told in the "The Faerie Queene," which is the old way of spelling "Fairy Queen." Only six books of this great poem exist. The original plan of the work was probably not carried out to completion but, as it stands, it is an enduring monument.

Milton called Spencer "Our sage and serious Spencer."

Incidentally some lines from part 1 of *The Faerie Queene* are inscribed on the monument to Admiral Robert Blake the commander of Cromwell's navies, in his home town of Bridgwater, Somerset.

> He there does now enjoy eternal rest
> And happy ease, which thou dost want and crave,
> And further from it daily wanderest:
> What if some little pain the passage have,
> That makes frail flesh to fear the bitter wave?
> Is not short pain well borne, that brings long ease,
> And lays the soul to sleep in quiet grave?
> Sleep after toil, port after stormy seas,
> Ease after war, death after life does greatly please."

The last two lines of this verse are inscribed on the monument.

These lines may well have been the inspiration for Frances Ridley Havergal's hymn;

> Light after darkness, gain after loss
> Strength after weakness, crown after cross;
> Sweet after bitter, hope after fears
> Home after wandering, praise after tears.
> Sheaves after sowing, sun after rain
> Sight after mystery, peace after pain;
> Joy after sorrow, calm after blast,
> Rest after weariness; sweet rest at last.

Bibliography

Arthur Mee, *The Children's Encyclopaedia* (The Educational Book Company Ltd, n.d.)

R.W. Church, *English Men of Letters* (Macmillan and Co., n.d.)

International Library of Famous Literature, Vol. 6, ed. Ernest Barker, (International University Society, n.d)

Sir Paul Harvey, *The Oxford Companion to English Literature* (Oxford: Clarendon Press, 1958)

Stopford A. Brooke, *English Literature* (Macmillan and Co., 1896)

Edmund Spencer, *The Mutability Cantos*, ed. S.P. Zitner (Nelson's Mediaeval and Renaissance Library, 1968)

Naseeb Shaheen, *Biblical References in the Faerie Queen* (Memphis State University Press, 1976)

The Political Works of Edmund Spencer, with critical notes by J.C. Smith and E. De Selincourt (Oxford University Press, 1912)

21. Francis Bacon—*The Novum Organum*

Sir Francis Bacon was born in London in 1561 after the recent accession of Elizabeth I, when English society was taking a dramatic upturn. He was a contemporary of Galileo, Shakespeare, Sir Walter Raleigh and Sir Francis Drake. Bacon worked not as a scientist, but as a lawyer and politician, becoming a barrister in 1582 and a member of the House of Commons in 1584. He was knighted in 1603 under the newly-crowned King James I, and advanced to Solicitor General, Attorney General, and by 1618, Lord Chancellor.

Although not a practising scientist, Bacon is considered by many historians to be the "founder of modern science." His philosophy and writings were largely responsible for igniting the scientific revolution of the 17th century. Numerous intellectuals such as Robert Boyle and Isaac Newton developed the "new philosophy" of Bacon that emphasised empiricism and induction. Casting aside dependence on authorities like Aristotle, the new science yielded a wealth of discoveries and inventions that has continued unabated to this day. As has been said, however, this new philosophy was really nothing new; it was but a return to the principles of the Bible. We cannot emphasise too strongly that the "founder of modern science" was a Bible-believing Christian, and Christian doctrine was the foundation and basis of his thinking.

Bacon firmly believed that he was living in the era in which the Scriptures predicted that knowledge would increase beyond all recognition. After all, had not the past decades seen crucial advances in learning, warfare and navigation, in the invention of the printing-press, gunpowder and the magnetic compass? Like a spark to a fuse, the Bible ignited in Bacon's mind a dream of a new instrument, a *Novum Organum* (new instrument) that could lead to an increase of knowledge, just as the Bible predicted for the last days.

The essence of Baconian philosophy is induction: instead of deducing the nature of Nature from authorities like Aristotle and Galen, scientists should build from the ground up. Gather facts. Measure things. Collect and organise observational evidence, then build a hypothesis to explain them. Test all hypotheses against the facts. Bacon was convinced this method would provide a more certain path to truth than trust in fallible human reason, and would issue in a golden age of discovery.

Later philosophers from David Hume onward would question the reliability of the method of induction. Those issues aside, the value of Bacon's method was seen in its fruits: for example, major new discoveries in chemistry, physics, biology and astronomy; the founding of new branches of science; the overturning of long–held false beliefs, and the establishing of new institutions like the Royal Society. Interestingly three and a half centuries earlier than this time, another Bacon, in this case the monk Roger Bacon had promoted the same value of experimental science; however, it was to take another three and a half centuries for these ideas to really take hold.

The question might be asked, did not the rejection of authority shoot down Bacon's own belief in the authority of the Bible? Sceptics sometimes portray the early Christian founders of science as closet doubters who made a show of Christian piety to keep out of trouble. According to this view, Bacon sugar-coated his scientific philosophy with biblical words to make it more palatable to the religious authorities. If that were so, Bacon would not have written elegant poetry, apparently from the depths of his soul, praising God and the Bible. There is no evidence that Bacon was a hypocrite in this matter. Bacon built his scientific philosophy on the foundation of his biblical view of the world.

To Francis Bacon, the Bible provided a view of God, the world, and man that made science a noble duty. Nature was God's finely crafted machine, and God had given man the aptitude and duty to discover its workings. Human reason alone was insufficient; it needed to be guided by Bible doctrine on the nature of God and the world, and by observation of the Creator's laws. The very belief in natural laws was a legacy of the Scriptures. Bacon believed that, in fulfilment of Daniel's prophecy, man would increase in knowledge in the last days by casting off unbiblical authorities like Aristotle and investigating God's natural revelation (Creation) with minds that had been created in his image.

Two modern writers on Bacon and his work *Novum Organum*, that is John Henry and Alan Stewart, have identified three foundational principles of Bacon's philosophy i.e.

1. *Religious belief*, which Stewart calls "a profound underpinning" of Bacon's philosophy.

2. *Government*, underscoring the God-given responsibility of governments to work for the good of the people.
3. *Apocalyptic vision*, the belief that Daniel's prophecy should inspire us to advance knowledge for the good of mankind.

While the Bible does not propose a scientific method, it provides the fundamental view of God, man, and the world that makes scientific progress both possible and desirable. "The works of the Lord are great," writes the author of Psalm 111:2, "sought out by all them that have pleasure in them."

Frances Bacon was not only a pioneer of modern science but he was also an occasional poet, he wrote the following hymn of praise to the Creator.

> O sing a new song, to our God above,
> Avoid profane ones,' tis for holy choir:
> Let Israel sing songs of holy love
> To him that made them, with their hearts on fire:
> Let Zion's sons lift up their voice, and sing
> Carols and anthems to their heavenly King.
> Let not your voice alone his praise forth tell,
> But move withal, and praise him in the dance;
> Cymbals and hearts, let them be tuned well,
> 'Tis he that doth the poor estate advance:
> Do this not only on the solemn days,
> But on your secret beds your spirits raise.
> O let the Saints bear in their mouth his praise,
> And a two edged sword drawn in their hand,
> Therewith to revenge the former days,
> Upon all nations, that their zeal withstand;
> To bind their kings in chains of iron strong,
> And manacle their nobles for their wrong.
> Expect the time, for 'tis decreed in heaven,
> Such honour shall unto his saints be given.

Bibliography

Adapted from David F Coppedge, Internet, https://crev.info/scientists/sir-francis-bacon/

Sir Paul Harvey, *The Oxford Companion to English Literature* (Oxford: 1958)

Francis Bacon, *Novum Organum*, Preface and translation by Rev. Andrew Johnson (Bell and Dowdy, Fleet Street, 1859)
The Works of Francis Bacon (Cambridge University Press, Internet, 2013)

22. Francis Bacon—*The Wisdom of the Ancients*

BACON PUBLISHED *WISDOM OF THE ANCIENTS* IN 1609. IT WAS written at the time when there was renewed interest in classical mythology. Bacon was strongly influenced by Comes's book *Mythologia* written in 1551. Bacon was persuaded that many of the ancient fables contained useful philosophical insights into the difficulties of life and the secrets of science. Over the centuries however, the true meaning of the fables had been lost or distorted. These fables therefore needed to be reinterpreted. With the renewed interest and new translations of these ancient works by the scholars of the Renaissance, there was now, he believed, the opportunity to recover their original meaning.

> This recovery of ancient learning was complemented by Bacon's advances in natural philosophy. So while Bacon's interpretations sometimes depart from the predominant understanding of individual fables, he did not regard his interpretations as arbitrary. He believed he was re-establishing their true meaning, which had been lost. *Wisdom of the Ancients* is therefore, a project of instauration. It is a recovery of ancient truth that had been lost or obscured, and it is an advancement of learning through Bacon's own epistemological efforts.
>
> Stephen A. McKnight, *The Religious Foundations of Bacon's Thought*, p. 121.

The Wisdom of the Ancients deals with thirty-one fables, covering ethics, politics, human nature, and the sciences. These include the fables of Orpheus, Prometheus, Pentheus, Pan etc.

Bacon said of these fables:

That they "must be regarded as neither being the inventions nor belonging to the age of the poets themselves, but as sacred relics and light airs breathing out of better times, that were caught from the traditions of more ancient nations and so received into the flutes and trumpets of the Greeks." What he meant was that their true meaning has been lost, obscured, or distorted over time; and previous generations have been unqualified to interpret them. Bacon's purpose, therefore, is to re-present the fables and give them their proper interpretation.

For example, we might consider the fable of Orpheus, which is for Bacon the story of the decline of philosophy, as it descends from the natural philosophy of the ancient wise man to moral and civil philosophy and finally to a state of almost total disintegration. In its pristine state, according to Bacon, "natural philosophy proposes to itself, as its noblest work of all, nothing less than the restitution and renovation of things corruptible, and (what is indeed the same thing in a lower degree) the conservation of bodies in the state in which they are, and the retardation of dissolution and putrefaction." The effort at retardation however, means arduous labour, and failure leads to frustration and to the adoption of the easier task—the management of human affairs through moral and civil philosophy.

This stage of philosophy remains stable for a while, but declines with the passage of time, and moral and civil laws are put to silence.

And if such troubles last, Bacon warns, "it is not long before letters also and philosophy are so torn to pieces that no traces of them can be found but a few fragments, scattered here and there." When philosophy and civilisation reach this low point, barbarism sets in and disorder prevails "until, according to the appointed vicissitude of things, they break out and issue forth again, perhaps among other nations, and not in the places where they were before."

By the expression "the appointed vicissitude of things", Bacon means the Providential intervention of God.

As a further illustration we may take the fable of Prometheus. A great deal can be said of this fable, and it will serve as a full introduction to the way these writings, in the hands of Bacon, were interpreted and might be applied with Christian insight to the modern world. (Prometheus here represents the Providence of God, and the special work of Providence was the creation of Man.)

Prometheus is a fable about the human condition. Today he is often portrayed as a secular hero who provided humanity with fire out of Mount Olympus, in order for man to become more self-sufficient and therefore, less dependent on the gods. The gist of the story is that Zeus employed Prometheus to make men out of mud and water, and then, in pity for their state, he stole fire from heaven, and gave it to them. (Fire in this case, being a great help to mankind, the instrument of instruments, the help of helps, and the means of means). For this he was chained by Zeus to Mount Caucasus, where an eagle by day preyed upon his liver, the liver being renewed at night, thus his suffering never ended. He was eventually released by Hercules, who slew the eagle. It was to counterbalance the gift of fire to mankind that Zeus later sent Pandora to earth with her box of evils.

In order to follow Bacon's reinterpretation, we need to see his own summary of the fable:

> "Tradition says that Man was made by Prometheus, and made of clay; only that Prometheus took particles from different animals and mixed them in. Desiring to benefit and protect his own work, and to be regarded not as the founder only, but also as the amplifier and enlarger of the human race, he stole up to heaven … and brought fire to the earth and presented it to mankind."
>
> Stephen A. McKnight, p. 123.

However, humans were not full of gratitude to Prometheus for what he had done, and instead, conspired against him and his invention before Jupiter. Because they had rejected Prometheus and turned again to Jupiter, the gods were pleased, and presented humanity with a new gift, this being the gift of perpetual youth. However, humanity in its folly lost this gift by loading it onto the back of an ass.

The ass, as it made its way, was overcome with extreme thirst, and seeing a fountain moved towards it to drink. It discovered that a serpent was set to guard the fountain and would not let him drink unless he gave in payment whatever it was that he carried on his back. The ass for a mere mouthful of water accepted the conditions and exchanged, the power of man's renewing youth was transferred to the serpent.

After this tragic setback, Prometheus made his peace with human beings, but retained his animosity towards Jupiter and offered a deceitful sacrifice.

> "Having slain two bulls he stuffed the hide of one of them with the flesh and fat of both, and bringing them to the altar, with an air of devotion and benignity offered Jupiter his choice. "
>
> ibid p.133

Jupiter, however, was not deceived and decided to punish the human race. This he did by requiring Vulcan to make a lovely woman, who was given gifts by each of the gods, and became known as Pandora. They gave her a beautiful vase, which contained Hope at the very bottom, and the rest was filled with trouble and misfortune. Pandora offered her gift to Prometheus, but he refused it. She then offered it to Prometheus's brother Epimetheus who opened it without thought or hesitation. When he realised his mistake, he tried to close the jar, but only succeeded in trapping Hope inside. Jupiter then seized hold of Prometheus, charged him with stealing fire, making a deceitful sacrifice, and attempting to rape Minerva. It was at that point that Jupiter bound Prometheus to a column on Mount Caucasus and had an eagle tear at his liver by day. Each night the liver was renewed, meaning that the torture would never end. However, it did end when Hercules sailed across the ocean in a cup that was given to him by the sun, who killed the eagle and set Prometheus at liberty. The memory of this was kept alive by some nations in games called torch races, in which the runners carried lighted torches in their hands; and if any went out the bearers stood aside, leaving the victory to those that followed; and the first to reach the finishing line with his torch still burning received a prize.

Bacon's exposition of this fable is as follows:

He explains that Prometheus "clearly and expressly signifies Providence; and the one thing singled out by the ancients as the special peculiar work of Providence was the creation and constitution of man."

He further notes that one of the reasons that Providence was associated with human nature is that "the nature of man includes mind and intellect, which is the seat of providence;" (providence here with a small p refers to the gift to mankind of foresight, provident management, timely preparation, seeing beforehand). And since there is not a logical way to derive the unique properties of the mind and reason, "from principles brutal and irrational… it follows almost necessarily that the human spirit was endued with providence, not without the precedent and intention and warrant of the greater providence." Bacon therefore maintains that humanity is a unique product of divine Creation, and the human mind is evidence of divine Providence.

Bacon says that the "chief aim of the parable" is to affirm that humanity is the centre of the world and "in so much that if man were taken away from the world, the rest would seem to be all astray, without aim or purpose… For the whole world works together in the service of man and there is nothing from which he does not derive use and fruit."

Bacon's view of the cosmos is grounded in the conviction that humanity's place in nature is providentially designed. The benefits that can be derived from creation are put there by divine Providence and are of two kinds: those that are obvious gifts and those that have to be drawn out through human providence or ingenuity. Bacon then interprets the section of the fable, which states that Prometheus made man from clay and from "particles of different animals." He explains this by saying that humanity's powers and faculties to understand and draw benefits from nature are reflected in his composite nature which joins the material world with aspects of the divine intellect.

Bacon then goes on to interpret that part of the fable, which he says is the most remarkable part, in that humanity instead of being grateful to Prometheus for the gift of fire, complains to Jupiter; and Jupiter in response provides humanity with the new gift that is eternal youth. The meaning of this section of the fable, according to Bacon, is that human beings have to resist the temptation to assume that the discoveries made by foresight (the literal meaning of Prometheus) are full and complete discoveries of all the benefits to be founded in nature. This attitude springs from human laziness, and it is ultimately blasphemous, because it turns humanity's devotion towards his own discoveries and to the work of a few men rather than towards the true giver who is God, and to the pious study of other benefits placed in nature, by God. According to Bacon, humanity's complaint and Jupiter's response can only be understood when it is recognised that the complaint reflects the realisation by humanity that its own insight and its own practical gifts are both limited and flawed, and that God is the only source of the goodness that humanity derives from nature.

When man becomes proud of his own achievements and fails to recognise the great benevolence of God, he becomes complacent and his powers decline. Bacon says, "let them know that conceit of plenty is one of the principal causes of want."

Bacon then turns to the gift of perpetual youth and its subsequent loss. He says that this part of the allegory "seems to show that methods and medicines for the retardation of age and the prolongation of life were by the ancients not despaired of, but reckoned rather among those things which men once had and by sloth and negligence let slip, than among those which were wholly denied or never offered."

Bacon then begins to consider how this loss occurred. He attributes it to the slow pace of empirical investigation and human impatience. Experience, represented as an ass, "seems stupid and full of delay… this gave birth to the ancient complaint that life is short and art is long." Bacon criticises the retreat from experience into sterile philosophical speculation, no doubt referring to the scholastics of the Middle Ages. As a result of this little progress has been made through the course of history. He goes on to make a call for collaborative research that can accelerate the pace with which discoveries can be made.

Moving on, he interprets the deceitful sacrifice by Prometheus as a parable on religion. The sacrifice of the meat and the fat of two bulls represents the true religious attitude on the part of man, and the offering of the empty skin represents hypocrisy. The godly man offers God his proper due, that is faith and devotion, and true love of God which will manifest itself in charitable deeds towards our fellow men. Hypocrites on the contrary, produce no good fruit only "dry and barebones, with which the skin is stuffed out till it looks like a fair and noble victim: whereby are signified those external and empty rites and ceremonies with which men overload and inflate the service of religion: things rather got up for ostentation than conducive to piety."

The reference to Pandora is a parable touching on the theme of "morals and the conditions of human life." While Pandora represents "pleasure and sensual appetite; which, after the introduction of civil arts, culture and luxury, is kindled up as it were by the gift of fire" the material benefits gained through the work of divine and human providence become sources of complacency, and even become the standard for measuring the quality of a society or civilisation. The materialism that this attitude produces, which begins as pleasure, soon deteriorates into all kinds of misfortune and trouble, such as "wars and civil disturbances and tyrannies." The part played by Epimetheus stands for those humans who are "improvident, who take no care for the future but think only of what is pleasant at the time…, they indulge their genius and amuse their minds moreover, as their ignorance allows them to do, with many empty hopes, in which they take delight as in pleasant dreams, and so sweeten the miseries of life." On the other hand, Prometheus represents "the wise and fore-thoughtful class of men" who succeed in avoiding many of the misfortunes in life, but in doing so, "they stint themselves of many pleasures and of the various agreeableness of life, and cross their genius, and what is worst torment and wear themselves away with care, loneliness and inward fears. Few humans are able to escape from these conditions. Very few therefore, are they to whom the benefit of both portions falls,—to retain the advantages of providence, and yet free themselves from the evils of solicitude and perturbation." The only way a right balance can be attained is through external help. This is represented by Hercules. He represents "fortitude and constancy of mind, which being prepared for all events and equal to any fortune, foresees without fear, enjoys without fastidiousness, and bears without impatience." This "harmonious inborn or natural fortitude", Bacon maintains, is something that is "adventitious" a word Bacon uses to refer to divine Providence or grace, a point that Bacon returns to toward the end of his analysis, where he makes an association with Hercules and Christ." p.128

Bacon also comments on the meaning of the chastity of Minerva, whom he sees as representing divine wisdom. This section of the fable Bacon interprets as a wrongful effort by man to "bring the divine Wisdom itself under the dominion of sense and reason".

McKnight comments: "Bacon carefully distinguishes between divine and human knowledge and is careful to limit the pursuit of knowledge to the natural world. Divine truth is not accessible to man except through the Scriptures and through divine revelation. Man must, therefore, "soberly and modestly" distinguish between things divine and human, between the oracles of sense and of faith unless they mean to have at once a heretical religion and a fabulous philosophy." He makes at this point, a plea for the study of the arts and science, lamenting the stagnation that has arisen from the constant going over the works of ancient thinkers such as Aristotle, Galen, Euclid, and Ptolemy.

> For science to advance and for the human condition to improve, the pursuit of arts and sciences must be revived, and for real progress to be made, the efforts must be collaborative. "Therefore men should be advised to rouse themselves, and try each his own strength and the chance of his own term, and not to stake the whole venture upon the spirits and brains of a few persons."
>
> Ibid p. 129

In the last paragraph of the work Bacon seeks to interpret the account of the rescue by Hercules.

"The voyage of Hercules, especially sailing in a pitcher to set Prometheus free, seems to represent an image of God the Word hastening in the frail vessel of the flesh to redeem the human race.". Bacon does not pursue this analogy further, however. To do so would violate caution against attempting to use human reason to explore the mysteries of the divine. Such an effort is likely to produce blasphemy and insult God. Bacon concludes by saying, "I purposely refrained myself from all licence of speculation in this kind, lest per adventure. I bring strange fire to the altar of the Lord." (Quoted by Stephen A. McKnight, p. 129.)

Stephen A. McKnight, on whom the above is based, gives us a useful summary of Bacon's interpretation of the fable of Prometheus as follows:

> "Bacon regards the myth of Prometheus as being primarily about the interplay of divine Providence and human action. Bacon also contrasts humanity's pre-lapsarian condition to its fallen state. Prior to the Fall, there was a coincidence between divine and human providence; humanity was placed by God at the centre of the world, and nature was intended for humanity's use. Because of pride and laziness, humanity lost this direct correspondence and has had to struggle to obtain the few benefits acquired over the course of history. Deliverance from this disordered state is possible, and has been possible from the outset. God intends humanity to be at the centre of the universe and for nature to provide for all of humanity's needs. The defect is in humanity, which has lost sight of its divine vocation. As a result, it has created idols and worshipped them, rather than God. The remedy, however, can now be recognised *through faith in the all atoning sacrifice of our Saviour Jesus Christ, who has died for our sins according to the Scriptures through whom* (emphasis mine) humanity can resume its proper relation with God, and rapid success will be possible, if humanity joins in the collaborative effort to advance the true philosophy of nature."
>
> *The Religious Foundation of Francis Bacon's Thought*, p. 129.

Bibliography

E. Cobham Brewer, *Brewer's Dictionary of Phrase and Fable* (Odhams Press Ltd)

Stephen A. McKnight, *The Religious Foundations of Francis Bacon's Thought* (University of Missouri Press, 2006).
Sir Francis Bacon, *Wisdom of the Ancients and New Atlantis*, ed. Henry Morley (Cassell and Co. Ltd, 1892)
The Works of Francis Bacon (Cambridge University Press, 2013, Internet)

23. Francis Bacon—*The New Atlantis*

THE KEY NOTE OF *THE NEW ATLANTIS* IS THE PURSUIT OF knowledge, which in Bacon's view is a religious duty. In one sense the work is a plea for the founding of a College of Scientific Research. It is generally regarded that Bacon started a movement that led to the foundation of our Royal Society in 1660. He has been described as a bell-ringer awakening men and women to thought and worship. Cowley, the 17th century poet, compared him with Moses on Pisgah, surveying the Promised Land, but not entering into possession.

We may briefly outline the story line of *The New Atlantis* as follows:

A ship has been driven off course in the Pacific and, when supplies begin to run out and there were many sick on board, the crew sight an island, which as they later discover, bears the Hebrew name of Bensalem, meaning, Son of Peace. This island utopia turns out to be very much a home from home. Its customs are not unfamiliar to the new arrivals; they are simply better. As James Spedding put it; "simply our own world as it might be made if we did our duty by it." (1808–1881).

A boat puts out from shore to contact the ship and brings back a document couched in four languages; ancient Hebrew, ancient Greek, good Latin, and contemporary Spanish. The culture of the island, therefore, is not different from that of England; nor is its religion. The scroll is stamped with the sign of the cross, which is taken as a certain presage of good. "God is manifested in this land," they exclaim soon after they come ashore. "We have come here among a Christian people of piety and humanity." Of the first important official they meet they enquire who was the apostle of the island. "Ye knit my heart to you," he cries "by asking this question in the first place; for it shows that ye seek first the kingdom of heaven". He then explains the miraculous circumstances in which, not long after the Ascension, the islanders became possessed of a small ark of cedar wood containing all the canonical books of the Old and New Testaments. For in Bensalem, as in Bacon's ideal for England, the Bible is the treasure, the Church only the ark that contains it. There is a Hebrew element in the population living in great mutual amity and respect with their neighbours—a point of some curiosity, since the Jews had been expelled from England in the 13th century and not allowed to return until after Bacon's time, that is the time of Oliver Cromwell. It is owing to their presence that the scientific works of Solomon, lost to Europe, have survived in Bensalem. The central institution of the island, though its main business is science and technology, is called Solomon's House, or the College of the Six Day's Works. Its chiefs are designated Fathers, and their spokesman explains:

> We have certain hymns and services we say daily, of laud and thanks to God for his marvellous works; and forms of prayer imploring his aid and blessing for the illumination of our labours, and the turning of them into good and holy uses.

Such is the setting Bacon provides for his brilliant sketch of the scientific wonders of Bensalem, which so strikingly anticipate the achievements of the last four centuries. Bacon was probably about fifty years old when he composed it. We may take it that it represents, in its deeply religious and consistently Biblical colouring, a permanent and lifelong characteristic of his thought.

Bacon was a man with a vision, and taken as a whole the New Atlantis presents us with a twofold view or description of "*instauration*". Instauration meaning Paradise Reinstated. One is represented by Bensalem and involves a spiritual rejuvenation, a return to Scripture and a return to the Gospel of Jesus Christ. The second is the recovery of natural philosophy, represented by the work of Solomon's House. This program envisioned by Bacon is clearly not a secular humanistic program, nor is it a prototype for a modern scientific think-tank. The aim is to rebuild man's relationship to God through the Gospel and to recover the benefits God has placed in nature for human beings to enjoy. Bacon clearly sees man's spiritual well-being as the prerequisite to his physical well-being. The reverent study of nature also guards against humanity's pride and its effort to create its own fantasy world. The Solomonic wisdom alluded to in Solomon's House is wisdom of the workings of nature and the ability to use that knowledge for the benefit of humankind. We must emphasise that in Bacon's thought the work of Solomon's House is not a substitute for the work of the Temple; it is the compliment to it. Atlantis provides an object lesson regarding the need for right religion to guard and guide the efforts of natural philosophy. If pride replaces piety, science and technology will become sterile or self-destructive.

In the end, *The New Atlantis* offers a multi-layered analysis of the disorder of the European sailors' society and then prescribes the necessary cure. The contrast between European nations and Bensalem points to the sources of order and disorder. Both Bensalem and Europe have the benefit of the Christian religion. Bensalem's Christianity is a pure form of Gospel Christianity uncorrupted by human ignorance and error. Europe's Christianity, by contrast, has been distorted and is plagued by philosophical and theological squabbling. Bensalem and Europe also have schools of natural philosophy. The Bensalem School of natural philosophy is the House of Solomon, which investigates nature in the reverent attempt to discover the benefits placed in creation by a loving God. Europe's natural philosophy has been marginalised and corrupted by scholastic and philosophical bickering and is dominated by competing schools of thought no longer grounded in empirical investigation of nature. England, nevertheless, has at its disposal the necessary means for utopian reform: a reformed and purified religion and, through Bacon's efforts, a reformed and revitalised natural philosophy. The two are complementary and each is indispensable for the restitution of humanity to its prelapsarian condition.

Bibliography

Sir Francis Bacon, *Wisdom of the Ancients and New Atlantis*, with notes by Henry Morley (Cassell's National Library, 1892)

Bacon's New Atlantis, ed. Harold Osborne (London: University Tutorial Press Ltd)

John Pringal Nicol, *The Imperial Dictionary of Universal Biography* (Glasgow: William Mackenzie, n.d.)

24. Francis Bacon—His Character

In regard to Bacon's personal moral principles he has been much maligned. Alexander Pope said of him that he was "the wisest, brightest, meanest of mankind". Macauley in his work seems to have followed the same line. Thanks to the work of Spedding, these false impressions have been corrected. The Universal Biographical Dictionary records:

> Let it be stated briefly, that Lord Macauley's brilliant essay is a very false one. Bacon never crouched to the Cecil's or to the court, although he used the language common in times when the "divine right" had not been questioned. He was the truest of friends to Essex—in truth, his only real friend. But he performed, also, his duty to the Commonwealth of England. As to his integrity as a judge, we must speak more in detail. Macauley tells us that he had "jackals" hunting for bribes. No charge more unfounded was ever before written down. He tells us further, that this was necessary to sustain Bacon's ostentatious extravagance; and in his quotations it would appear, that having been seen once riding in state, it must rightly be inferred that so Bacon rode always. Did Bacon take bribes—was he in fact a corrupt judge? It is necessary, in the first place, to clear away one cause of misunderstanding very powerful in these our modern days. In the times we are treating of, it had not become a matter of delicacy that one should not take money from a friend, but only an "acceptance," or a present of china or a title, or a gold snuffbox. Elizabeth herself received presents in money, but she was not bribed thereby. Bacon did receive presents of money from two suitors, but neither was he bribed. Nor was any charge of false or partial movements in his high capacity as a judge ever laid against him.
>
> Nineteen twentieths of the statements, and—worse than direct statements—the insinuations which deface Lord Macaulay's essay on Bacon, are sheerest romance. It seems strange that a writer, himself so brilliant, should have been inspired by such an animus. But antithesis is not always truth; nor is blinded hero worship in one direction inconsistent with the most irreverent iconoclasm in others. Lord Campbell appeals in self-defence to the "impartial severity of history." May God forgive us all! Is it meant by "impartial history," that the

> conduct and acts of immortal men are not to be interpreted in so far by their characters; that the brilliancy of the sun shall be measured by his spots; or that the history of his spots shall be produced as the history of his vast cosmical influences? Thanks to the Universal Parent, it is not by such "impartiality of history," that the mighty assembly of all men and tribes and nations, and of all the ages, even the meanest of us shall ultimately be judged!"

Bibliography

John Pringle Nicol, *The Imperial Dictionary of Universal Biography* (William Mackenzie, Glasgow, undated), Vol. 1, p.330

Chambers Biographical Dictionary, Ed. J.O. Thorne, T. C. Colocott (Chambers, 1986)

James Spedding *An Account of the Life and Times of Francis Bacon*, (Hathi Trust, Internet)

Stephen A. McKnight, *The Religious Foundations of Francis Bacon's Thought* (University of Missouri Press, 2006).

25. Sir Philip Sidney—Writings

'One who espoused and dedicated his life to the cause of Protestant freedom with a wholehearted zeal.' (John Drinkwater, the poems of Sir Philip Sidney p. 15)

Sir Philip Sidney was regarded as the ideal of an English gentleman in the Elizabethan age, born in Penshurst, Kent, on 29th November, 1554. He was the son of Sir Henry Sidney, described as one of the most upright, energetic and ill-requited of Queen Elizabeth I servants, whose responsibilities included a period of being Lord Deputy of Ireland and later the Lord President of Wales. His mother was the daughter of the Duke of Northumberland, father-in-law of Lady Jane Grey.

At the age of 10 he was sent to Shrewsbury School: his father was Lord President of Wales then living at Ludlow Castle. At school he met his life-long friend and biographer Fulke Greville.

Fulke was later to write of him,

> I will report no other wonder but this, though I lived with him and knew him from a child, yet I never knew him other than a man; with such staidness of mind, lovely and familiar gravity, as carried grace and reverence above greater years; his talk ever of knowledge, and his very play tending to enrich his mind, so as even his teachers found something in him to observe and learn above that which they had usually read or taught.

From Shrewsbury School he went up to Christchurch, Oxford in 1568, where he seems to have remained until 1571. Through the influence of his uncle, the Earl of Leicester he was able to spend two years travelling on the continent. He spent time in Paris at the invitation of the Earl of Lincoln, and at the time of the Huguenot massacres he found refuge in the house of Sir Francis Walsingham, then serving as the English envoy in Paris. The outrage of the St Bartholomew's Day massacre strengthened his Protestant sympathies. After this he toured Germany and Italy. He studied, he saw the world and took a keen interest in continental politics, a study which made him very much aware of the growing power of Spain and the apathy of the European princes to this danger. This led him to consider the part that England might play in the protection of European Protestants. One important personal result of this continental tour was that he made acquaintance with Hubert Languet who had been converted from Catholicism to true faith by Melanchthon, who further introduced him into the circle of the Protestant champion, Du Plessis Mornay. At this time Sidney was 18 years old and Du Plessis Mornay 54 years old: in spite of the age difference they became great friends and entered into a lifelong correspondence.

On his return to England he became a courtier, and fell in love with Penelope, the young daughter of the Earl of Essex. The Earl of Essex encouraged this match, but he died in 1576, and four years later she was married by her guardians against her will to Sir Robert Rich, the wealthy heir of Lord Chancellor Rich. This loss Philip Sidney felt for the rest of his life.

At the age of 22, Sidney was sent abroad on a diplomatic mission to Vienna and Heidelberg, the purpose of his mission being to promote union among the reformed states of Germany where there had been tensions between Lutherans and Calvinists. At this time, he made acquaintance with William of Orange, who formed a very high opinion of him and was impressed by his grasp of continental politics.

Queen Elizabeth I was impressed by his diplomatic skills and his general demeanour. He was growing to be a favourite of the Queen's, and the first of his known literary compositions was a masque, *The Lady of the May*, performed in honour of the Queen during her visit to Lord Leicester's home in Wanstead, May, 1578.

Court life however with its empty round of sycophancy and ceremony, was very distasteful to Sidney. His heart was really set on action on the continent, his great desire was to do something to further the Protestant cause in that region. However, such bold continental enterprises were not favoured by the court of that time.

Unable to pursue the course he desired, he once again turned his attention to literature, and it was at this time that Edmund Spencer dedicated his *Shepherd's Calendar* to Sidney. In this period also came Sidney's *Defence of Poesy* and his *Astrophel and Stella*.

Sir Philip Sidney sat in the Parliament of 1581, and in 1582 he was among the courtiers, Sir Walter Raleigh being another, deputed by the Queen to escort the Duke of Anjou to the continent. In January, 1583 he was knighted and at about the same time received from Queen Elizabeth a grant of 3 million acres of land in the unknown parts of

America. Schemes of colonisation in the west greatly interested him, and such was his enthusiasm in this direction that Hakluyt dedicated the first edition of his *Voyages* (London: 1582), to Sidney.

He married in the spring of 1583, Frances, daughter of his old friend Sir Francis Walsingham, Queen Elizabeth's famous Secretary of State.

William the Silent of Holland died in the summer of 1585, and this was followed by the surrender of town after town in the Netherlands to the occupying forces of the Duke of Parma. Sir Philip Sidney pressed upon the Queen and her councillors the necessity for active support for the Protestant cause on the continent, and for strenuous resistance to the formidable power of Spain. However, though he was supported by his father-in-law Walsingham, he was baffled by the influence of Burleigh, whose do-nothing policy recommended itself for the time to the Queen. By this time also Sidney was very active in parliamentary life. He played a significant part in strengthening the ordinance department of public service.

In the midst of these pressing duties his mind was still upon the danger threatened by Spain. He used all his influence to promote Drake's famous expedition to the West Indies of 1585, which he himself was resolved to join. He actually got so far as Plymouth and was waiting secretly to sail with Drake when the Queen discovered his plan. She immediately sent word to him threatening him with disgrace if he sailed; and promising him, if he returned, a command in the Low Countries.

The policy of action previously recommended by Sidney had prevailed, and Queen Elizabeth was about to send to the Netherlands an auxiliary force under the command of Leicester. With the appointment of Governor of Flushing, Sidney set sail on 16th November, 1585 and took up his office on the 21st. In the following February he led a successful expedition against Axel, and received high praise for his gallantry and skill. In September, 1586 he joined the force under his uncle, Leicester, attempting to capture Zutphen, which was vital in order to take control of the Yssel. Zutphen was surrounded on 13th September, and Sidney was one of three superior officers commissioned to watch it by land, while Leicester guarded the water.

On the 21st, Leicester received information that a large supply of provisions was collected at Deventer, a few miles up the river, and that an attempt was planned to get them into Zutphen at daybreak on the following morning. Arrangements were made on both sides for a battle. The morning of the 22nd came, and dense mist covered the whole area. Sidney led a party of horsemen 200 strong right up to the walls of the town. When he reached them with his men, the fog suddenly broke, and they saw before them the enemy's cavalry twice their own strength, while the canon from the ramparts and the musketeers in the trenches began to fire upon them. Three charges were made by the English; Sidney was in all of them, and in the first his horse was killed under him. He had gone into the field, it is said, properly armed; but meeting Sir William Pelham, the Lord Marshal of the camp, whom he saw to be poorly defended, with reckless chivalry he threw off his own armour.

In the last charge, accordingly, he was wounded severely in the thigh, and his new and untrained horse took fright and galloped off the field with him. As he was being carried wounded and in pain, there occurred the well-known incident later chronicled by Fulke Greville: "In the which sad progress, passing along by the rest of the army, where his uncle the general was, and being thirsty with excess bleeding, he called for some drink, which was presently brought him; but as he was putting the bottle to his mouth he saw a poor soldier carried along who had eaten his last at the same feast, gasping and casting up his eyes at the bottle. When Sir Philip perceiving, took it from his head before he drank, and delivered it to the poor man with these words, "Thy necessity is yet greater than mine." The wound was to prove a fatal one, as from almost the first Sidney is said to have felt. Removed to Arnheim, he lingered on for 25 days under the care of the surgeons, and nursed by his wife, who had joined him previously at Flushing.

Such was the anxiety respecting him that even Queen Elizabeth sent a messenger "with comforting letters" and enquiries as to his condition. During his closing days he spoke much of spiritual matters, the immortality of the soul among them. His last words were a valediction addressed to his gallant young brother, Robert, who watched by his bedside: "Love my memory, cherish my friends; their faith to me may assure you they are honest. But above all, govern your will and affections by the will and word of your Creator; in me beholding the end of the world with all her vanities."

He died in the afternoon of Monday, 17th October, 1586, a few weeks before completing his thirty-second year. His body was conveyed to England, and on 16th February, 1587, it was brought through the City of London to its resting place in the churchyard of St Paul's.

Brave, adventurous, spirited, accomplished, affectionate, generous—poet, scholar, patriot and soldier—Sir. Philip Sidney united in his own person all the excellences which we are accustomed to regard as rife in his time and country, and the circumstances of his death enhanced the lustre of his character and life. (Adapted from *The Imperial Dictionary of Universal Biography*, Vol. 16.)

The Oxford Companion to English Literature adds the following:

> Sidney exercised extraordinary influence on the poets of his own and the following generations, heightened, perhaps, by the romantic character of his personal history. None of his works appeared in his lifetime; the *Arcadia* included his *Apology for Poetry* and *Astrophel and Stella* of which an unauthorised edition appeared in 1591. Sidney's version of the Psalms was published in 1823 and repeat printed as *Rock Honeycomb* in Ruskin's *Bibliotheca Pastorum*. His collective political works were edited by Dr Grosart in 1873.

Patrick Collinson, commenting on Sidney's connection with Phlippe du Plessis Mornay and Hubert Languet reminds us that after the St Bartholomew Day Massacre there developed in France the doctrine of resistance. Theodore Beza wrote his *Du droit desmagistrates* in 1573 in which he went beyond Calvin in sanctioning resistance by inferior magistrates. But it was Plessis Mornay, seemingly influenced by Hubert Languet who went further in his *Vidiciae*, arguing that both king and subjects are in a contractual relationship with God. If the king fails in his duty, the inferior magistrates, and even the least of the people, must honour their contract by removing him. These theories help us to understand something more of Philip Sidney's involvement in the Dutch Wars. (Patrick Collinson, *The Reformation*, p. 138.)

Further we may note, as Preserved Smith points out, that Philip Sidney's maxim was that it was the highest wisdom of statesmanship never to separate religion from politics. Church and state were practically in his mind one and the same body, and opinions repugnant to established religion naturally resulted in acts inimical to the civil order. (Preserved Smith, *The Age of the Reformation*, p. 336)

Philip Du Plessis Morney was the founder of the Huguenots College of Saumur which became famous for its Amyraldianism sometimes known as hypothetical universalism.

Du Plessis Mornay also published, *La verite de la religon chrestienne* in Antwerp in 1579–80: in which he sought to prove the truth of

Christianity by natural reason, and so convert "atheists, Epicureans, pagans, Jews, Mohammedans and other infidels". Sidney began an English translation completed after Sidney's death, by Arthur Golding.

Bibliography

Hugh Trevor Roper, *Catholics, Anglicans and Puritans* (London: Secker & Warburg, 1987), p. 191

Preserved Smith, *The Age of the Reformation* (London: Jonathan Cape, 1960).

Sir Paul Harvey, *The Oxford Companion to English Literature* (Oxford: Clarendon Press, 1958).

Patrick Collinson, *The Reformation* (London: Weidenfeld and Nicolson, 2003).

The Imperial Dictionary of Universal Biography (Glasgow: William Mackenzie, 1876), vol. 16.

Sir Philip Sidney, edited and introduced by John Drinkwater (London: George Routledge & Sons Ltd, 1934).

26. Shakespeare and Christianity

THE 19TH CENTURY HISTORIAN HALLAM CALLED SHAKESPEARE "THE greatest name in our literature. The glory of his age, and the glory of the present age". Henry Irving, the actor described him as "the noblest literary man of all time, the finest and yet most prolific writer—the greatest student of man, and the greatest master of man's highest gift,—of language—surely it is treason to humanity to speak of such an one as in any sense a commonplace being."

The question is sometimes asked, was Shakespeare a professing Christian?

In regard to Shakespeare's Christianity, Archbishop Trench in his sermon preached at Stratford-upon-Avon on the occasion of the tercentenary of Shakespeare's birth on Sunday, 24 April 1864, from James 1:17 included the following comments:

> "Every good gift and every perfect gift is from above, and cometh down from the Father of lights, with whom is no variableness, neither shadow of turning."
>
> Shakespeare was the child of England—of the Reformation. He was born of its spirit …
>
> As we read his works we feel that justice walks the world, delaying, it may be but not forgetting; as is ever the manner of the Divine Avenger…
>
> He who towers above every other is memorable by all which we know him for, the equable and harmonious developments of his whole being… The dear heir of a memory which the world would never let die…
>
> Men attain heaven, not soaring on wings of genius, but patiently climbing up the stairs of faith, and love, and obedience. The brightest crowns are doomed to wither; there is but one amaranthine crown—even that which Christ gives to them, be they high or low, wise or simple, emperors or clowns, who have loved, and served, and obeyed him…
>
> For myself, I am strong in my belief, that from one so gentle so tender, so just, so true as Shakespeare, the grace to make this highest

> consecration was not withholden; that we might have the right to number him with Dante, with Spencer, with Milton, and with all that august company of poets, "who sing and are ever singing in their (the) glory." His intimate, nay in one sense, profound acquaintance with the Scriptures, no-one can doubt, or the strong grasp which he had on their central truth. He knew the corruption of our fallen nature—the desperate wickedness of the heart of man; else he could never have put into the mouth of a Prince of stainless life such a confession as this; "I am myself indifferent honest; but yet I could accuse me of such things, that it were better my mother had not borne me. I am very proud, revengeful, ambitious; with more offences at my beck, than I have thoughts to put them in, imagination to give them shape or time to act them in." (Hamlet Act III, scene 1)
>
> He has set forth the scheme of our redemption in words as lovely as have ever proceeded from any uninspired pen."
>
> Richard Chenevix Trench *Shakespeare and the Bible,* p. 40

George H. Morrison in his classic, *Christ in Shakespeare*, comments:

> It has been said that men should be divided into those who see and those who do not see. Shakespeare is the lord of those who see. It is therefore a matter of profoundest interest to discover what human life revealed to him of the power that lies behind all human action.

Morrison remarks that in Shakespeare we do not find what we call poetic justice. If we did, the plays would not be tragedies. He points out that novels almost without exception have happy endings to the story. Evil is punished and virtue is rewarded. This we know in the ultimate is true, but often in the experience of life this is not immediately revealed. Shakespeare brings this out for example in Macbeth, there the villain Macbeth attains the apex of his hopes, and the mild, good Duncan is murdered in the night.

Iago accomplishes his villainy, and the virtuous Desdemona dies. And yet it is true that what Shakespeare shows us about the mysterious facts of life, is not the moral indifference of heaven. Shakespeare takes us deeper into life's moral problems. When it comes to the problem of suffering in Shakespeare we can see how sin reacts on the soul of Macbeth, and how suffering on the soul of Lear. In the case of the latter the suffering purifies his soul, quickens his vision; deepens and extends its sympathies; drives him to his knees in prayer.

Further, Shakespeare reveals to us that the consequences of evil are not always exhausted in the experience of the evildoer. This also is so true to life, Lady Macduff and her innocent son suffer for the evil in Macbeth. Pure and beautiful souls like Desdemona have to die because Iago is a villain. In these things Shakespeare is showing the solidarity of man. The embracing woe that evil brings is but the other side of the great fact on which the richness of society depends.

In reading Shakespeare, claims Morrison, we see that Satan is altogether hateful; he is mean and cowardly and evil and the heart protests against him at all times.

Goodness may appear to be vanquished, but our heart remains upon the side of goodness: evil may be victorious, but we loath it even in its victories. Shakespeare does not leave us sullen and despairing, we are not tempted to flee for refuge to the gods of pessimism. Shakespeare leaves us with a glowing certainty that the good of the real victors, though they perish, and that heaven, though dark with cloud, is on our side.

Shakespeare's view of mankind

Scripture teaches us that man is made in the image and likeness of God. In Shakespeare we discover the corresponding estimate. Man in Shakespeare is never a poor creature. He may be hardened, cruel, wicked; he may be set on deeds of villainy, but nobody ever closes one of Shakespeare's tragedies with the depressing sense of the littleness of man. Shakespeare never makes anyone a pessimist, though villainy may seem to walk triumphant. He leaves us with a consciousness of the larger world, and of mighty forces moving in the darkness, and of man a little lower than the angels.

For Shakespeare the greatest of all troubles was not the battle of a man with circumstances. It was the unseen battle that is waged on the field of his own heart, and nobody can study Shakespeare without discovering in his tragedies a like stern insistence on the inward.

Hamlet is torn asunder inwardly, and that inward division is the tragedy. The deadliest combat of Othello was not with Iago but with himself. Shakespeare conveys the fact, just as our Lord conveyed it, that the determinative field is inward.

No pain from a sword-cut of Macduff is comparable to Macbeth's interior agonies. Cordelia dies for loving, but who does not feel the radiance of her soul? Faithful to fact Shakespeare recognises the infinite significance of what is inward, and that is just what our blessed Saviour the Lord Jesus Christ did.

Shakespeare on the fact of temptation

Temptation is one of the universal elements in human life; it is an experience which nobody escapes. One may escape the experience of illness, and never know the perils of poverty or wealth: but temptation is a fact in everyday life, never to be eluded.

Character depends, in no small measure, on a man's reaction to temptation. There are no issues in life so determinative as the issues of conflict with temptation. This conflict is one of the constant elements in all the great tragedies of life, as it is in the greater tragedies of literature.

No writer equals Shakespeare in profound and penetrating studies of temptation. Of these there is none more absorbing than Macbeth.

Shakespeare on the peril of delay

Shakespeare illustrates this perhaps most profoundly in the character of Hamlet. Hamlet recognises the duty of revenge and yet postpones the execution of it. He procrastinates; *he lets the week's slip by with nothing done.* Macbeth is not a tragedy of passion like Othello. His is the tragedy of delayed obedience. Shakespeare through this character explores what lay at the back of his delays, and secondly with what effects it produced.

Hamlet is not an active wrongdoer. His criminality is doing nothing. Hamlet has a noble heart and loves all noble things—there is a world between him and Macbeth, yet his inaction, his negative resistance to the moral order of the world, is as fatal as the most daring criminality.

Time fails us to tell of Shakespeare's insights into the power of choice through the character of the Merchant of Venice, or we might mention his insight into the passion of jealousy through the character of Othello, or again looking at Iago the tragedy of egoism. Morrison however closes his survey on Shakespeare on the theme of the sovereignty of love.

This he finds portrayed in the play, Romeo and Juliet. The great message of this glorious drama is the sovereignty of love.

Morrison comments that for Shakespeare all love was in its essence one. The Greeks had different names for different kinds of love; but it is a question if Shakespeare, who knew little Latin and less Greek, would have tolerated any such sharp cleavages.

Nothing could be more lofty or spiritual than the love of Juliet. The dullest must feel that it is dazzlingly pure.

With Shakespeare there are not different kinds of love but different proportions in the various elements of which all love is compounded.

The love which is heavenly and holy is not the love which despises or ignores the sensuous, as though it had its being in a different world; but that which subdues and radiates the sensuous in the sovereignty of what is spiritual.

In such books as the Song of Solomon (for all who read it mystically), and the Letters of Samuel Rutherford, and many of the sermons of Murray McCheyne, there is that fearless and frank acceptance of the facts of life, inherent in and transmuted by the highest, which, in the sphere of drama, is the characteristic attitude of Shakespeare.

For Shakespeare love is the most absorbing of all passions. Love is stronger than everything that separates; love breaks every barrier down, every wall of partition is removed; true love liberates character, intellect awakes, imagination deepens and expands, and the will becomes steady and strong.

And finally Shakespeare would have us learn that love is the great reconciler, for the play closes, not with death alone, but with the reconciliation of the divided houses. The feud is laid aside; the old enmities buried; the estrangement ends; the alienation is removed; and all this through a love that was so deep and true that it brought the hearts which cherished it to death.

Love was the mediator; love that did not count the cost; love for the joy that was set before it went down into the darkness of the grave.

And though Shakespeare does not point us to the road that leads to the place called Calvary, do we not catch a glimpse of the way of sorrows; and here on it, far off, the footfall of one who loved unto the uttermost, and loving died, and thereby achieved a mightier reconciliation than any that Verona ever knew.

These above remarks are summarised from George H. Morrison's work referred to above. I believe they give us an insight into a way to read Shakespeare which reveals something of the innermost faith of his heart.

R.E. Prothero in his classic *The Psalms in Human Life* adds the following note on Shakespeare and the Psalms. (Note all Psalm references are taken from the Prayer Book version.)

> Whether Shakespeare, for example, was indeed "untutored in the lore of Greece and Rome," may be open to dispute; but none can doubt his familiarity with the Psalms. "Death," as the Psalmist saith, "is certain to all: all shall die." So says Justice Shallow to Silence, alluding to Psalm 89:47, "What man is he that liveth, and shall not see death?" When Queen Margaret asks, in the second part of *Henry the Sixth*.
>
> "What! Art thou, like the adder, waxen deaf?
> Be poisonous too, and kill their forlorn Queen";
>
> or when Hector tells Paris, in *Troilus and Cressida*,
>
> "Pleasure and revenge
> Have ears more deaf than adders to the voice
> of any true decision,"

The allusion is to Psalm 58:4, "even like the deaf adder that stoppeth her ears."

Buckingham's words in *King Henry the Eighth* refer to Psalm 141:2,

> Let the lifting up of my hands be an evening sacrifice:
> And, as the long divorce of steel falls on me,
> Make of your prayers one sweet sacrifice,
> And lift my soul to heaven.

Antony's prayer in *Antony and Cleopatra*,

> Oh, that I were
> Upon the hill of Basan, to outroar
> The horned herd! for I have savage cause.

plainly refers to the Psalmist's "Hill of Basan" in Psalm 68:15, and the "fat bulls of Basan" in Psalm 22:12. The prayer of Adam in *As You Like it*.

> He that doth the ravens feed,
> Yea, providentially caters for the sparrow,
> The comfort to my age!

is partly founded on Psalm 147:9, "He feedeth the young ravens that call upon him." In *King Henry the Fifth*, where the king sings his *Non-nobis, Domine*, in thanksgiving for his victory at Agincourt,

> O God, thy arm was here;
> And not to us, but to Thy arm alone
> Ascribe we all,

he only paraphrases the "Not unto us, O Lord, not unto us, but unto Thy Name give the praise," of Psalm 115:1," as the "Widow's champion and defence." is taken from the Psalmist's "Father of the fatherless and defendeth the cause of the widow." (Psalm 68:5)

When the King in *Hamlet* asks,

> "What if this cursed hand
> Were thicker than itself, with brother's blood,
> Is there not rain enough in the sweet heavens
> To wash it white as snow?"

He refers to Psalm 51:7, "Thou shalt wash me, and I shall be whiter than snow."

The description of the approach of Alcibiades in *Timon of Athens*:

> Who, like a boar too savage, doth root up
> His country's peace

suggests Psalm 80:13, "The wild boar out of the wood doth root it up."

The address of Romeo to Juliet, where he compares her to "a winged messenger of Heaven,"—

> When he bestrides the lazy—pacing clouds
> And sails upon the bosom of the air,

recall such sentences in the Psalms as "Magnify him that rideth upon the Heavens, as it were upon an horse," Psalm 68:4; or "Who maketh the clouds his chariot, and walketh upon the wings of the wind," Psalm 104:3; or, "He came flying upon the wings of the wind," Psalm 18:10.

> See how the morning opes her golden gates,
> And takes her farewell of the glorious sun!
> How well it resembles it, the pride of youth,
> Trimmed like a younker, prancing to his love,

is a reminiscence of Psalm 19:5, where the sun rejoices "as a giant to run his course."

Finally, in the speech from the second part of *King Henry the Sixth*, addressed by the King to Humphrey, Duke of Gloucester,

> Stay, Humphrey, Duke of Gloucester; ere thou go
> Give up thy staff; Henry will to himself
> Protector be: and God shall be my hope,
> My stay, my guide, and lantern to my feet;
> And going in peace, Humphrey.

> Shakespeare makes use of such passages as "Truly, my hope is even in thee," Psalm 39:8; "but the Lord was my upholder," Psalm 18:18; "our guide unto death," Psalm 48:13; and, "a lantern unto my feet, and a light unto my paths," Psalm 119:105.
>
> Rowland E. Prothero, *Psalms in Human Life* (London, John Murray, 1904) pp. 172–175.

Finally, a man's last will and testament reveals something of a man's life.

We might note, Shakespeare's last will and testament begins as follows:

> "In the name of God, Amen. I, William Shakespeare. In perfect health and memory, God be praised, do make and ordain this my last will and testament in manner and form following. That is to say, First, I commend my soul into the hands of God my Creator, hoping and assuredly believing, through the only merits of Jesus Christ my Saviour, to be made partaker of life everlasting, and my body to the earth whereof it is made." 25th March 1616

Bibliography

George H. Morrison, *Christ in Shakespeare* (James Clark and Co., Limited, 1928).

R.E. Prothero, *The Psalms in Human Life* (London: John Murray, 1904).

Charles Ellis, *The Christ in Shakespeare* (London: George Stoneman, 1902).

Henry Hallam, *The Constitutional History of Britain*, Vol 1–2 (London: Ward, Lock, and Co., n.d.).

27. John Amos Comenius—*Orbis Pictus*
The Father of Modern Western Education

John Amos Comenius was born on March 28 1592. His parents, who were members of the Moravian Brethren or the *Unitas Fratrum*, died when he was but a small boy and relatives sent him to the Moravian Brethren's boarding school. When he later announced his desire to become a minister, he was sent to a theological institute and later to the University of Heidelberg. In 1616 he was appointed headmaster of the Moravian Brethren High School in Fulneck, Moravia.

The importance of Comenius in the educational world is apparent from the fact that his name is among those engraved upon the American Library of Congress. It appears also on the main building of Teachers' College at Columbia University. Also in the United States when Harvard University was being established, the then governor John Winthrop invited Comenius to join the faculty and indeed become its president.

We may sum up the educational achievements of Comenius by saying that it was he who first introduced pictures into schoolbooks. His *Orbis Pictus*, for instance, consists of pictures illustrating various trades. One page of the book has a picture of a shoemaker at his work. Every object in the picture was numbered. Beneath the picture were two columns, Latin on the right, and the child's own language on the left.

With this kind of book children easily learned not only words, but their meanings as well. Comenius' books were translated into many languages and his theories of teaching found wide acceptance.

One of his principles was "The teacher must be kind and fatherly, must distribute praise and reward, and must always where it is possible give the children something to look at." When we consider what most schools were like in the days of Comenius, we see what great new ideas a simple statement like this contained. Comenius believed that children belonged to God and that it was a teacher's privilege to help and instruct them in the knowledge of Jesus Christ.

For just over two years Comenius contentedly fulfilled his position as headmaster of the school at Fulneck. By this time, he was happily married with a small family. The Thirty Years War broke out in 1618; the Emperor Rudolf died and was succeeded by a fanatical Roman Catholic, Ferdinand, Archduke of Styria. In 1620 the Emperor's troops attacked the town of Fulneck dispersing the citizens and destroying their properties.

Comenius lost his home and all his possessions. His little family went into hiding and during this time his wife and one of his small children died. In his sorrow he wrote a little book called *The Labyrinth of the World*. This book was similar in style to the *Pilgrims Progress* (which had not yet been written) and told the story of a pilgrim wandering through the world, mistreated and abused by Mr Nolittle, Mr Lovestrife, Mr NoGod, and others. At last the pilgrim finds happiness in the church in which good men and women endeavour to follow Christ.

Eventually the Moravian Brethren escaped to Poland where they received a warm welcome. A small city named Lissa became their headquarters. In 1636 Comenius was made head of the college of the Moravian Brethren in that town and for about 20 years they remained in peace.

After this, in 1652, the Catholic Bishop of Posen confiscated their church and college properties. They remained in that town until 1655 when the King of Sweden, King Charles invaded Poland. Charles was a Protestant and many people hoped that he would conquer. However, his invasion failed and the backlash against the Protestants once more forced the Moravian Brethren into exile. Comenius had worked for 40 years on a Latin—Bohemian dictionary. The soldiers snatched it from him and burned it along with many of his other possessions.

Again after a period in hiding he was offered refuge in Amsterdam and this Comenius was happy to accept.

Whilst in Holland Comenius, through his contacts in England, raised many thousands of pounds to help the suffering Moravian Church. Whilst in Holland he published another work entitled *Ratio Disiplinae;* this was a Latin work containing the history of the Moravian Brethren and an explanation of their teachings. He dedicated the work to the Church of England praying that the English Church would be a support and help to the suffering Moravian Church.

Comenius died in Amsterdam in 1670, at the age of 78. His work was carried on by Peter Jablonski, his son-in-law.

The Moravian Brethren continued to be persecuted until 1722 when a godly Saxon nobleman Nicholas Louis von Zinzendorf heard of their plight and offered them refuge and sanctuary on his large estate at Herrnhut. After this the Moravians became the first missionaries of the modern era. It was the Moravian missionary Peter Bohler that was used of God in the conversion of John Wesley. The influence of Wesley's later visit to Herrnhut has influenced English Methodism even to the present day.

Bibliography

John Amos Comenius, *Orbis Pictus*, introduction by John E. Sadler (Oxford University Press, 1968).

28. Cromwell's Letters and Speeches

Thomas Carlyle in his foreword to Cromwell's Letters and Speeches praised him "as a Puritan hero, God–sent to save England, grappling "like a giant, face-to-face, heart-to-heart, with the naked truth of things". (*The Oxford Companion to English Literature*, p. 242)

Further, as he explains his purpose in making these letters available to the general reader he says:

> I have ventured to believe that, to serve patient earnest readers, these old dear Letters of a noble English Man might, as they had done to myself, become dimly legible. Again might dimly present, better than all other evidence, the noble figure of the Man himself again. Certainly there is Historical instruction in these Letters:—Historical, and perhaps other and better, at least, it is with Heroes and God-inspired men that I, for my part, would far rather converse, in what dialect soever they speak! Great, ever fruitful; profitable for reproof, for encouragement, for building up in manful purposes and works, are the words of those that in their day were men. I will advise serious persons, interested in England, past or present, to try if they can read a little in these Letters of Oliver Cromwell, a man once deeply interested in the same object.
>
> Thomas Carlyle, *The Life of Oliver Cromwell* (London: Hutchinson and Co. 1905), p. 22

A further reason for the re-publication of these letters, Carlyle states is as follows:

His purpose he says:

> is to discredit the wide–spread report that these 17th—century Puritans were superstitious, cracked brained persons; given up to enthusiasm, the most part of them; the minor ruling part being cunning men, who knew how to assume the dialect of the

> others, and thereby, as skilful Machiavels, to dupe them. This is a wide-spread report; but an untrue one.
>
> I advise my readers to try precisely the opposite hypothesis. To consider that his Fathers, who had thought about this World very seriously indeed, and with very considerable thinking faculty indeed, were not quite so far behind in their conclusions respecting it. That actually their "enthusiasms," if well seen into, were not foolish but wise. That Machiavellism, Cant, Official Jargon, whereby a man speaks openly what he does not mean, were, surprising as it may seem, much rarer then than they have ever been. Really and truly, it may, in a manner be said, Cant, Parliamentary and other Jargon, were still to invent in this world. O, heavens, one could weep at the contrast! Cant was not fashionable at all; that stupendous invention of "Speech for the purpose of concealing Thought" was not yet made. A man wagging the tongue of him, as if it were the clapper of a bell to be rung for economic purposes, and not so much as attempting to convey any inner thought, if thought we have, of the matter talked of, would at that date have awakened all the horror in men's minds, which at all dates, and at this date, is due to him. The accursed thing! No man as yet dared to do it; all men believing that God would judge them.
>
> Thomas Carlyle, *Life of Oliver Cromwell*, p. 25

Oliver Cromwell (1599–1658) is one of the outstanding men of English history, his letters give us a remarkable insight into his complex character, and his deeply Christian outlook on life. Cromwell was a country gentleman of modest means, a silent backbencher in the House of Commons who never sought greatness, and yet had greatness thrust upon him. He had never studied the arts of war yet became an outstanding soldier. Not a mere soldier but a general. It is said that in the early 20th century, the German Imperial General Staff used to cite him as one of the most notable examples of a great cavalry leader. It is doubtful that Cromwell ever spoke as a backbencher, and it is certain that no-one at that time would have ever predicted that he would achieve supreme political power in the land.

In reading his letters we can see how this obscure country squire was raised up by God to meet the desperate spiritual, moral, and political needs of his day.

The earliest letters show him rising to the challenge of forming an army. He is responding to urgent needs, the situation facing him complex and confused. His commands are clear and explicit as we see him mobilising the resources of the eastern counties to serve the Parliamentary cause.

He is quick to realise that the quality of the army depends on the character of its soldiers. He immediately grasped that mounted soldiers will be far more effective than foot soldiers.

> A troop of horse, which indeed will by God's blessing, far more advantage the cause than two or three companies of foot; especially if your men be honest, and godly, which by all means, I desire.

Later he writes:

> be careful what captains of horse you are forced to choose, what men be mounted: a few honest men are better than numbers … If you choose godly honest men to be captains of horse, honest men will follow them … I had rather have a plain russet-coated captain that knows what he fights for, and loves what he knows, than that which you call "a gentleman" and is nothing else. I honour gentleman that are so indeed!

Cromwell wanted men fighting in his army as he wanted men in his parliament who believed in God, and who believed in the cause they were fighting for, or serving; genuine men, honest men, men like those described in our last quotation.

Also in these early letters we see the tender side of Cromwell. The letter sent after the Battle of Marston Moor (1644) was a letter of sympathy, to Colonel Valentine, whose son had been killed in the fight. The letter begins with a vivid description of the encounter, and how the Parliamentary forces had scattered Prince Rupert's troop of horse, and also his foot soldiers: "God made them as stubble to our swords … Give glory, all the glory, to God." He then expresses himself with great sympathy feeling his friend's loss, and goes on to add, "let this public mercy to the Church of God make you to forget your private sorrow." (Letter XXI in Thomas Carlyle, *Cromwell's Letters and Speeches*, vol. 1., p.152)

Cromwell's sincere patriotism and the awareness of God's providential governance of all things, appears in many of these early letters. For example: after the Battle of Naseby (1645) he writes to the Speaker of the House of Commons, the honourable William Lenthall:

> Sir, this is not other but the hand of God; and to him alone belongs the glory, wherein none can share with him.

Here on the one hand, he acknowledges God's mercy in granting victory. On the other hand, he realises those who would serve faithfully need encouragement and so he goes on,

> The general served you with all faithfulness and honour: and the best commendation I can give him is, that I daresay he attributes all to God, and would rather perish than assume to himself. Which is an honest and thriving way: and yet as much for bravery may be given to him, in this action, as to a man. Honest men served you faithfully in this action. Sir, they are trusty; I beseech you, in the name of God, do not discourage them. I wish this action may beget thankfulness and humility in all that are concerned in it. He that ventures his life for the liberty of his country, I wish he trust God for the liberty of his conscience, and you for the liberty he fights for.
>
> Letter XXIX *Cromwell's Letters and Speeches*, vol. 1 p. 174

Another concern that we see emerging in the letters is Cromwell's desire for a common unity between those of differing denominational persuasions. In a long letter that was appointed to be read in the several Congregations in and around about London after the storming of Bristol, he makes this plain in the following words:

> Thus I have given you a true, but not a full account of this great business; wherein he that runs may read, that all this is none other than the work of God. He must be a very atheist that does not acknowledge it.
>
> It may be thought that some praises are due to those gallant men, of whose valour so much mention is made: their humble suit to you and all that have an interest in this blessing, is, that in the remembrance of God's praises they be forgotten. It's their joy, they are instruments of God's glory, and their country's good. It's their honour that God vouchsafes to use them. Sir, they that have been employed in this service know, that faith and prayer obtained this city for you: I do not say ours only, but the people of God with you and all England over, who have wrestled with God for a blessing in this very thing. Our desires are, that God may be glorified by the same spirit of faith by which we ask all our sufficiency, and have received it. It is meet that He have all the praise. Presbyterians, Independents, all have here

> the same spirit of faith and prayer; the same presence and answer; they agree here, have no names of difference: pity it is it should be otherwise anywhere! All that believe, have the real unity, which is most glorious; because inward, and spiritual, in the Body, and to the Head. For being united in forms, commonly called Uniformity, every Christian will for peace-sake study and do, as far as conscience will permit. And for brethren, in things of the mind, we look for no compulsion, but that of light and reason. In other things, God hath put the sword in the Parliament's hand—for the terror of evildoers, and the praise of them that do well. If any plead exemption from that, he knows not the Gospel: if any, would wring that out of your hands, or steal it from you under what pretence soever, I hope they shall do it without effect. That God may maintain it in your hands, and direct you in the use thereof, is our prayer.
>
> Letter XXI *Cromwell's Letters and Speeches*, vol. 1 p.185

Beside these graphic accounts of Cromwell's military activity, we find as the letters progress much evidence of the many trials and troubles Cromwell endured in seeking to establish ordered government in the face of many conflicting factions and the duplicity and cunning of those who sought to challenge his vision. Not least was the duplicity of King Charles I which time and again betrayed Cromwell's trust. There were the demands of the Presbyterians who wanted to establish a national Presbyterian Church. There was the difficulty of trying to find a just and equitable pattern of governance in the face of the demands of the Fifth Monarchists, Levellers, and Diggers, etc.

The following letter is an example written at the time when there was tension between the Presbyterian Parliament, the City of London and the Army. The following letter was written in the town of Royston, Herts on 10th of June 1647.

> As for the things we insist upon as Englishmen—and surely our being soldiers hath not stripped us of that interest, although our malicious enemies would have it so,—we desire a settlement of the peace of the Kingdom, and of the liberties of the subject, according to the votes and declarations of Parliament, which, before we took arms, were, by the Parliament, used as arguments and inducements to invite us and divers of our dear friends out; some of whom have lost their lives in this war. Which, being now, by God's blessing, finished, we think we have as much right to demand, and desire to see, a

> happy settlement, as we have to our money and to the other common interests of soldiers, which we have insisted upon. We find also the ingenious and honest people, in almost all parts of the Kingdom where we come, full of the sense of ruin and misery if the Army should be disbanded before the peace of the kingdom, and those other things before mentioned, have a full and perfect settlement.
>
> We have said before, and profess it now, we desire no alteration of the Civil Government. As little we do desire to interrupt, or in the least to intermeddle with, the settling of the Presbyterian government. Nor did we seek to open the way for licentious liberty, under pretence of obtaining ease for tender consciences. We profess, as ever in these things, when once the state has made a settlement, we have nothing to say but to submit or suffer. Only we could wish that every good citizen, and every man who walks peaceably in a blameless conversation and is beneficial to the Commonwealth, might have liberty and encouragement; this being according to the true policy of all states, and even to justice itself.
>
> To the Right Honourable, the Lord Mayor, Aldermen, and Common Council of the City of London:
>
> Signed by,
>
> Thomas Fairfax, Oliver Cromwell, Robert Hammond, Thomas Hammond, Hardress Waller, Nathaniel Rich, Thomas Pride, Henry Ireton, Robert Lilburn, John Desborow, Thomas Rainborow, John Lambert, Thomas Harrison.
>
> Letter XXIX *Army Manifesto*, ibid p. 224

In seeking to deal with unnecessary divisions among Christians, Cromwell wrote the following in regard to the activities of the more violent Fifth Monarchists and Levellers.

> Fifth Monarchy I think pretending more spirituality than anything else. A notion I hope we all honour, and wait and hope for "the fulfilment of" that Jesus Christ will have a time to set up His reign in our hearts by subduing these corruptions, and lusts, and evils that are there; which now reign more in the world than, in due time, they shall do. And when more fullness of the Spirit is poured forth to subdue iniquity and bring in everlasting righteousness, then will the approach of that glory be.

> The carnal divisions and contentions among Christians, so common, are not the symptoms of that kingdom! But for men, on this principle, to belittle themselves, that they are the only men to rule kingdoms, govern nations, and give laws to people, and determine of property and liberty and everything else: upon such a pretension as this is:—truly they had need to give clear manifestations of God's presence with them, before wise men will receive or submit to their conclusions! Nevertheless, as many of these men have good meanings, which I hope in my soul they have, it will be the wisdom of all knowing and experienced Christians to do as Jude saith when he reckoned up those horrible things done upon pretences, and happily by some upon mistakes: "of some," says he, "have compassion, making a difference; others save with fear, pulling them out of the fire." I fear they will give too often opportunity for this exercise! But I hope the same will be for their good. If men do, but so much as pretend for justice and righteousness, and be of peaceable spirits, and will manifest this, let them be the subjects of the magistrate's encouragement. And if the magistrate, by punishing visible miscarriages, save them by that discipline, God having ordained him for that end, I hope it will evidence love, not hatred, so to punish where there is cause.
>
> Indeed, this is that which doth most declare the danger of that spirit. For if these were but notions—I mean these instances I have given you of dangerous doctrines, both in civil things and in spiritual; if, I say, they were but notions, they will best let alone. Notions will hurt none but those that have them. But when they come to such practices as telling us, for instance, that liberty and property are not the badges of the Kingdom of Christ; when they tell us, not that we are to regulate law, but that the law is to be abrogated, indeed, subverted; and perhaps wish to bring in the Judaic Law.
>
> Speech II, September 3rd, 1654 after the sermon preached by Thomas Goodwin in the Abbey Church at Westminster, Cromwell gave the speech in the Painted Chamber. *Letters and Speeches*, vol. 3 p.24

Summing up

The Letters and Speeches of Oliver Cromwell are a source of primary importance for the history of the English Civil Wars, the Commonwealth, and the Protectorate. Here we see events through the eyes of one of the chief participants in them; a man, moreover, who had an amazing gift for direct and vivid narrative. We can share in the turmoil of battle and we can appreciate the mounting perplexities which made government so difficult.

These letters are a Christian classic because it is a clear and moving revelation of the character of one of the greatest of the Puritans. We do not see in them, of course, the whole of Cromwell's very complex nature. However, from other sources, we know that when faced with a difficult problem he often suffered agonies of indecision, but when he acted, he did so with swift and irresistible force. We can sense a little of the former quality in some of the political letters and speeches from the latter years of his life. We can see the decisive figure clearly enough in the early letters describing his activities during the initial stages of the First Civil War. When he felt that he was fighting the Lord's battles his characteristic qualities appear most clearly; then his sense of God's presence and his submission to God's will find humble expression. Events become the stage on which the divine purpose is being accomplished, and it is his high privilege to be a fellow labourer in this great task. This is what makes his battle dispatches among the great documents of militant Puritanism.

But there is a less public side to Cromwell's religious life. He can write to friends and relatives with a directness which makes his Christian convictions both clear and contagious. He can write, too, with a simplicity largely free from the dogmatism which sometimes defaces the expression of Puritan beliefs. And he can deal wisely with the spiritual perplexities of others. His letter on the spirit of fear and the spirit of love is still one of the most perceptive statements on an important theme.

> "Fear", he says, "is the natural result of a bondage spirit," and is the antithesis of love: "The voice of fear is: if I had done this; if I had avoided that, how well it had been with me! … Love argueth in this wise: what Christ have I; what a Father in and through him! What a name hath my Father: merciful, gracious, long-suffering, abundant in goodness and truth; forgiving iniquity, transgression and sin. What a nature hath my Father: He is LOVE: free in it, unchangeable, infinite … This commends the love of God: it's Christ dying for men without strength, for men whilst sinners, whilst enemies. And, shall we seek for the root of our comforts within us—what God hath done, what He is to us in Christ is the root of our comfort: in this is stability,

in us is weakness. Acts of obedience are not perfect, and therefore yield not perfect grace. Faith, as an act, yields it not; but only as it carries us unto him, who is our perfect rest and peace in whom we are accounted of, and received by the Father,—even as Christ himself. This is our high calling. Rest we here, and here only."

Letter CLXXXVII, Vol.2 p.305

Frank N. Magill, *Masterpieces of Christian Literature* (Harper Row, 1966) p.496–7

Bibliography

F.R. Magill, *Masterpieces of Christian Literature* (Harper Row, 1996)

Thomas Carlyle, *Cromwell's Letters and Speeches* (London: Hutchinson and Co., 1905)

Life of Oliver Cromwell (London: Hutcheson and Co., 1905)

29. Samuel Rutherford—*Lex Rex*

Samuel Rutherford (1600–1661) was a Scottish theologian and Covenanter. He was ejected from his parish on the Solway by the then ruling Episcopalian party and exiled to Aberdeen (1636). He became a professor of divinity at St Andrew's University, attended the Westminster Assembly and after the Restoration of the Stuart monarchs would almost certainly have been numbered amongst the martyrs had he not at the time been fatally ill. Richard Baxter held him in high regard and C. H. Spurgeon regarded his *Letters* as the nearest thing to inspiration after the Bible.

Lex Rex (Law is King), is the title and theme of Samuel Rutherford's great volume on political philosophy. This work was written primarily to counter the claim of the Stuart monarchs of the 17th century to be above the law—the question of whether the monarch ruled with the authority of God (Rex Lex—the king is law)—or whether the king together with his subjects was ultimately under the Law of God. Rutherford was arguing against the concept that maintained that as the king was appointed by God he was above the law and effectively was the law.

The concept that kings and queens, together with all their subjects, lie under the Law of God can be traced back to the Old Testament. In the Old Testament, we read that the Hebrew people were defined as, the people who lived under the Law of God. In Deuteronomy 17:18–19, Moses writes concerning the time when the people of Israel would be ruled by a king, he instructed that the king when he sitteth upon the throne of his kingdom, "shall write him a copy of this law in a book out of that which is before the priests, the Levites; And it shall be with him, and he shall read therein all the days of his life: that he may learn to fear the Lord his God, to keep all the words of this law and these statutes, to do them…"

This same concept was also enshrined in the Law Codes of the Saxon kings, notably those of Alfred the Great, and later by Edward the Confessor. Alfred began his dooms, (laws) by reciting the 10 Commandments, and then as they were summarised by our Lord himself. By putting God's Law first he and other Saxon kings were recognising that law is not simply what we make it, but is answerable to a higher moral standard based on and derived from the Bible.

This same principle was enshrined in the Magna Carta 1215, and shortly after in the writings of the great English ecclesiastic and jurist, Henry de Bracton (d. 1268).

Rutherford argues for constitutionalism, meaning that the government should not be an absolute monarchy or an oligarchy or a dictatorship, in which the nation is ruled by an individual or an elite few. Rutherford argued that the rule of law is what is best for the people. The book was published in 1644 at the time of the Puritan Revolution.

Rutherford concedes that God in his providence appoints rulers, but this is done, not directly, but through the will of the people.

> "If government is in the form of a monarchy, it is not because monarchy is the immediate appointment of God, for other forms could also have divine approbation. Mediately, however, a monarch may be from God as he guides his people to choose a form of magistracy. Actually, the power of government is in the people, for every man has the right to preserve himself from violence; and consequently the people appoint as many officers for government as their safety and peace warrant."
>
> *Masterpieces of Christian Literature* p. 463–4

The whole work is set out in the form of questions, and answers, and question 9 asks whether the people have the right to depose a corrupt and despotic ruler, should the case arise? To this Rutherford replies in the affirmative, that the community retains the right to reform in cases of flagrant abuse of power, though they "are to suffer much before they resume their power."

This great work of Rutherford had been preceded in Scotland by the celebrated treatise *De jure regni apud Scota,* of George Buchanan (1506–1582), a scholar and humanist of international fame and tutor to James VI of Scotland, to whom Buchanan dedicated his book in 1579. James VI became James I of the United Kingdoms of Scotland and England, and his son Charles I, was the monarch about whom Rutherford was concerned.

John Knox (c.1505–1572), in his *History of the Reformation in Scotland* had faced the same issue with Mary Queen of Scots, the grandmother of Charles I. The core of the solution to the constitutional question is the same in these three works by Scotsmen; namely, that monarchs are responsible to God and the people and cannot place themselves above the public good. The authority of a king is relative to his use of it. "I desire," wrote Buchanan, "that the people from whom he derived his power, should have the liberty of prescribing its bounds; and I require that he should exercise over the people only those rights which he has received from their hands."

In the light of these sentiments, it is not surprising that Buchanan's book met with the same fate as that of Rutherford's and was banned in Scotland.

Rutherford was a distinguished theologian in his time, a member of the Westminster Assembly and over the course of his career in the Church and seminary travelled all over Scotland and contributed much of lasting value through his writings.

He was born in 1600 and died in 1661. He studied at the University of Edinburgh and was installed as minister in Anwoth, a congregation that would remain close to his heart throughout his life. Under the Kings James I and Charles I, during the attempts to force the Scottish Church to adopt more Anglican practices, Rutherford opposed the changes and found himself exiled from his beloved pulpit.

In 1638, with the signing of the National Covenant, Presbyterianism was restored in Scotland and Rutherford was installed as a Professor of Divinity at the historic University of St Andrews. But he always deeply loved and longed for his congregation back at Anwoth.

One of the striking things about Rutherford is the letters he wrote. In our era, most people just don't write letters any more. Rutherford lived in an era when writing letters was how people kept in touch. Rutherford's letters to his friends and former congregation are full and extremely rich in pastoral encouragement, discipleship, guidance in living the Christian life, understanding how God's Word is lived out, and how to engage the culture of that time. These letters from Samuel Rutherford are treasures for us as we look back over the pages of Church history.

Another thing about Rutherford is his love for Christ. His book entitled of *The Loveliness of Christ* is a worthy Christian Classic which in recent years has been re-published by the Banner of Truth. Those who heard Rutherford preach would say that this was a man who preached the Gospel, this was a man who preached Christ. Rutherford in all his preaching and writing sought to bring his hearers, or readers, to see the beauty and excellence of Jesus Christ.

Bibliography

Samuel Rutherford, *Lex Rex* (Pantianos Classics)
Frank N. Magill, *Masterpieces of Christian Literature* (Harper Row, 1966), p.463
John Knox, *History of the Reformation in Scotland* (London: Andrew Melrose, 1905)

30. John Bunyan and his Bible

When first we come face-to-face with Pilgrim in *The Pilgrim's Progress* we see him described as follows:

> A man clothed with rags (Isaiah 64:6) standing in a certain place, with his face from his own house, a book in his hand, and a great burden upon his back.

The book in Pilgrim's hand we are intended to recognise was the Bible, Bunyan's Bible.

Likewise, as we read in *Grace Abounding*, Bunyan's autobiography, we are again brought face to face with Bunyan's Bible. Bunyan describes his conversion experience and early Christian life as follows: an emphasis is laid on the hearing and reading of Scripture, he records:

> That there was a great bending of my mind toward the truth I had heard spoken or read in the Scriptures.

He goes on to say, "I began to look into the Bible with new eyes, and I read as I never did before". *Grace Abounding*, pp. 17–18.

Likewise returning to the opening chapters of *The Pilgrim's Progress* when the distressed Pilgrim meets Evangelist for the first time he says to Evangelist:

> I perceived by the book in my hand, I am condemned to die and after that the judgement; and I feel that I am not willing to do the first, and not able to do the second.

The book in his hand, is again the Bible and we are intended to see that the Bible was to be in Bunyan's hand, heart and mind for the rest of his life, guiding every thought and step of his pilgrimage through the wilderness of this world. It was this book that was to change his life from a rough and ready, fiery tempered, cursing and swearing country tinker, to a private under Fairfax, to a warm-hearted, struggling family man, a minister of God, a man of unbending courage, a preacher, a writer, and teacher of enormous depth and vitality, one of the foremost Christians of all time.

It is significant to note that in 1660, at the time of the Restoration of the Stuart Monarchy, the authorities issued a warrant for Bunyan's arrest for breaking the old Elizabethan Conventicle Act.

One evening in November 1660, Bunyan was opening his Bible and about to preach in a farmhouse, in the hamlet of Lower Samsell (Bedfordshire), when officers of the law burst in, broke up the meeting and arrested him, and conveyed him to Bedford, where eventually he was incarcerated in the County Gaol where he remained until 1672. During that twelve–year imprisonment, Bunyan wrote the following *Christian Behaviour* (1663), *The Holy City* (1665), and *Grace Abounding* (1666, the year of the Great Fire of London).

It has been rightly said of Bunyan that, "Throughout Bunyan's works is a Biblical theology." From his first published work, *Some Gospel Truths Opened* (1656), he carefully builds up his arguments on the basis of Scripture texts, rather as Milton was doing at the same time in the *De Doctrina Christiana.* Bunyan believed and taught that a Christian must rely on his own experience, but this experience must be carefully checked against the Bible. The full title of this work, his first work, was *Some Gospel Truths opened, According to the Scriptures.*

Throughout his life, as Christopher Hill has remarked, "The Bible is Bunyan's sheet anchor, his defence against despair and atheism. He would have been lost if he had abandoned it". (Christopher Hill, *A Turbulent, Seditious and Factious People, John Bunyan and his Church*, p.169.)

The question is sometimes asked in regard to the Bible version Bunyan used

The answer is that he used both the *Geneva Bible (*1560) and the *Authorized Version* (1611).

He seems to have quoted the Puritan *Geneva Bible* equally with the *Authorised Version* throughout his career. Of some thirty instances which George Offor noted in which he cited a text from the *Geneva Bible*, twenty came after 1672 half-way through his publishing career.

Offor also claimes Bunyan seems to quote from Tyndale's Version in his work, *The Acceptable Sacrifice* (1689).

> Bunyan could read no language other than English, and his Bible had of necessity to be an English Bible. It is not entirely clear which English translation Bunyan used as the problem has not attracted scholarly investigation. My impression is that in his early works he relied on the sixteenth century translation probably the Geneva version; departures from that translation may be due to Bunyan's habit of quoting from memory, or he may have used one of the related translations.
>
> Translations from memory sometimes contain echoes of the Authorised Version which he would have heard read in church. Later in life he seems to have turned to the Authorised Version; sectarian misgivings about the Authorised Version had receded, and the new enemy was the Book of Common Prayer.
>
> Gordon Campbell, *John Bunyan: Conventicle and Parnassus*. p.138.

The Geneva Bible was commonly known as the *Breaches Bible* from its rendering of Genesis 3:7 "They made themselves breaches" (AV "aprons"). It was translated in Geneva by a committee of Protestant exiles which probably included William Whittingham and John Knox. The Geneva Bible's Calvinistic annotations greatly irritated James I of England, but delighted and instructed his increasingly Puritan subjects. It was however gradually laid aside as the confidence and popularity of Authorised Version increased, the last Geneva Bible was published in 1644.

The Authorised Version arose out of the Hampton Court Conference convened by James I of England in 1604. A suggestion by John Reynolds, President of Corpus Christi College, Oxford, and a puritan that a new translation of the Bible be undertaken, was eagerly seized on by the King. The work was entrusted to six panels of scholars; some forty-seven translators in all.

King James directed that the entire text of the Bible was to be divided into six sections, with roughly the same number of men allocated to the translation of each section. Two were assigned to meet at Westminster, two at Oxford University, and two at Cambridge University. The first group of three companies were assigned the Old Testament, a second group to the New Testament. A sixth group was entrusted with the apocryphal works. When each section had completed its tasks, twelve delegates were to be chosen (two from each company from the entire body of translators). These would meet together to review and revise the entire work.

It was intended originally to have fifty-four translators, but this was not achieved. Gilbert Burnett in his *The History of the Reformation of the Church of England* (1643–1715) only identifies 47 names. Other lists allow up to 51 to be identified. The traditional explanation for the inconsistency may well be correct: it is suggested that early deaths led to the number of translators being reduced from the original intention of the King. Another explanation is offered by the fifteenth of Bancroft's translation rules, which allowed for "three or four additional persons to be allocated as required to the translation teams"; this suggests that a translation team of fifty or fifty-one was appointed, on the assumption that three or four others would be called upon as required. (Alister McGrath, *In the Beginning, The Story of the King James Bible*, p. 178.)

Alongside the Bible Bunyan had his Concordance

He notes in his work, *Solomon's Temple Spiritualised* (1688). "My Bible and concordance are my only library in my writings".

Again we do not know which concordance he used in his earlier life. However, we know that in his later life he used the concordance compiled by Vavasor Powell the fiery Welsh preacher. This is confirmed by the fact that we actually have preserved the 1673 edition of this work with Bunyan's signature in the frontispiece, the book is now in the hands of the Baptist College in Bristol. Ibid p.140.

We may also add Bunyan's own words at this point:

> I do not presume to say that I know I have hit right in everything; but this I can say, I have endeavoured so to do. True, I have not for these things fished in other men's waters; my Bible and Concordance are my only library in my writings. Wherefore, courteous reader, if thou findest anything, either in word or matter, that thou shalt judge doth vary from God's truth that it be counted no man's else mine.
>
> *Works* volume 3, p.464.

John Bunyan took Scripture seriously, as the lamp and guide of his life and actions.

As mentioned above Bunyan had accepted an invitation to preach at a cottage in the village of Samsell, Bedfordshire. (A village about thirteen miles south of Bedford, beyond Ampthill). The meeting had been widely publicised, and a large gathering was anticipated. News of this however had reached a rich country squire who was also a commissioner of the peace. He communicated the information to his fellow justices and they determined to take this opportunity to arrest and silence John Bunyan. Their plans became known to the believers in the village, and Bunyan was warned not to attend. However, he was resolved to keep his appointment. He arrived at the cottage mounted the pulpit steps, prayed and read his text; "Dost thou believe on the Son of God?"

At that point the constable entered the meeting-house, and began to mount the pulpit steps, at the same time ordering Bunyan to come down. Bunyan pointed to the open Bible; and, for an instant, the man was stopped in his tracks. However, in a moment he had recovered his composure and again ordered Bunyan to come down in the name of the King. Bunyan complied and he was taken off to the house of Justice Wingate. He was not at home; and Bunyan was released, his friends pledging and giving their word that he would appear before the justice the next morning.

Bunyan, it is said, complied with the authorities and accepted his arrest believing that it might prove an awakening to the saints in the country.

There is a full account of this on page 109 of the *Grace Abounding*.

> Had I been minded to play the coward, I could have escaped and kept out of his hands. When I was come to my friend's house, there was a whispering that that day I should be taken, for there was a warrant out to take me; which when my friend heard, he being somewhat timorous, questioned whether we had best have our meeting: and whether it might not be better for me to depart, lest they should take me and have me before the Justice, and after that send me to prison, (for he knew better than I what spirit they were of, living by them) to whom I said, No: by no means, I will not stir, neither will I have the meeting dismissed for this. Come, be of good cheer, let us not be daunted, our cause is good, we need not be ashamed of it, to preach

> God's word, it is so good a work, that we shall be well rewarded, if we suffer for that: to this purpose … After this I walked into the close, where I somewhat seriously considering the matter, this came into my mind: That I had showed myself hearty and courageous in my preaching, and had, blessed be Grace, made it my business to encourage others; therefore, thought I, if I should now run, and make an escape, it will be of a very ill savour in the country. For what will my weak and newly converted brethren think of it? But that I was not so strong indeed, as I was in word. Also I fear that if I should run now there was a warrant out for me, I might by so doing make them afraid to stand, when great words only should be spoken to them. Besides I thought, that seeing God of his mercy should choose me to go upon the forlorn hope in this country; that is, to be the first, that should be opposed for the Gospel; if I should fly, it might be a discouragement to the whole body that might follow after.

Brought before the authorities and wondering how he should answer them he became very conscious of the Lord's help. At one point during his examination he felt God sending him the appropriate text to respond to the interrogating justice, as he said as if the Scripture had said, "take me, take me." (*Grace Abounding* p.119. See also John Bunyan, *Conventicle and Parnassus*, p.154.)

At this trial the justices were trying to force Bunyan to accept the usage of the Book of Common Prayer and to give up preaching. Again we find him using Scriptural texts to explain why he can accept neither of these propositions.

He took the biblical exhortations "to pray with the Spirit" as making it impossible for him to accept the set forms of the Book of Common Prayer being urged upon him.

His accusers argued that the Book of Common Prayer teaches us how to pray. Bunyan replied again quoting Scripture: "for we know not what we should pray for as we aught: but the Spirit itself maketh intercession for us with sighs and groanings which cannot be uttered. Mark," said I, "it does not say the Common Prayer Book teacheth us how to pray, but the Spirit. And it is the Spirit that helpeth our infirmities, saith the Apostle; he does not say it is the Common Prayer Book."

In relation to his being required to cease from preaching he took the biblical exhortations to minister "according to one's gift" as a command to preach the Gospel, rather than, as his chief examiner patronisingly suggested, to follow his calling as a tinker.

Bunyan replied,

> Truly Sir, I do not desire to commend myself, but to think meanly of myself; yet when I do most despise myself, taking notice of that small measure of light which God hath given me, also that the people of the Lord by their own saying are edified thereby: besides, when I see that the Lord, through grace, hath in some measure blessed my labour, I dare not but exercise that gift which God hath given me, for the good of the people.
>
> *Grace Abounding*, p.126.

If John Bunyan had yielded to these demands he would have been released immediately. This however he would not do. Except for a few brief periods of parole, he remained in Bedford County jail until 1672. Here Bunyan is following the biblical example of brave believers such as Daniel, and Shadrach, Meshach and Abednego.

There have been those like the poets Robert Southey, Alfred Noyes and Robert Bridges who have maintained that Bunyan's sufferings were self-inflicted, and for the sake of his family he should have not have gone to jail. In response to this we must affirm that Bunyan knew that he was fighting for the spiritual integrity of his fellow Independents, his fellow Free Churchmen. Many were looking to him to defend the right of the Christian to decide without interference from the State, the character of his relationship to God. Bunyan is one of the long line of men who stood for the religious liberties of our land and indeed all those in other nations who stood for the same principles.

In his Ode to Oliver Cromwell, *To the Lord Chief General,* Milton has the line:

> Help us to save free conscience from the paw, of hireling wolves whose Gospel is their maw. [Maw, meaning stomach, or as we might say self-interest].

This Bunyan was doing when he refused to stop preaching or holding conventicles.

It was the same principle that many face under political oppression across the world even today. "You have only to say you will join the Party, and we will not send you to a concentration camp."

Many of us would succumb to this sort of pressure to save our wives or families or whatever, but not the John Bunyan's of this world. Not the Shadrach, Meshach and Abednego's of this world who will not bow down to the image set up by Nebuchadnezzar or anybody else.

In that prison Bunyan had the Bible, as one described it, "The rarest and richest in all departments of thought or imagination which exists." Also he had with him a copy of *Foxe's Book of Martyrs*, that is the complete edition, which would have given him a very rich, complete and adequate knowledge of history, or we may say the providence of God in history. With these two books he had no cause to complain of intellectual or spiritual destitution. Some claim that he had other books for in his works we find shades of influence from *Robert Langland's Piers Ploughman*, *George Herbert*, perhaps *Spencer's Faerie Queene*, and inklings of *Paradise Lost*. These however he may have read before his incarceration.

As we have noted above, it was in these prison years that Bunyan wrote some of his most useful and lasting works.

It is sometimes remarked that in the providence of God Bunyan's imprisonment was not so severe as many suffered at that time.

Two examples could be used to illustrate the sufferings of some taken from Neil's *History of the Puritans*, vol. 4, p. 486.

> Mr Banfield, educated at Wadham College, Oxford, and Minister of Sherborne, in Dorset. Having ventured to preach in private, after the Act of Uniformity had been passed, he was apprehended, and cast into prison, with twenty-five of his hearers. There was but one room, and one bed, for all. Having been released, after a few days, from this imprisonment, he was again apprehended, and lay nine years in Dorchester jail, from which he was only liberated to be seized again, and thrown into Newgate, where he lingered some time, and then died.
>
> A second Mr Delaune, the author of a Plea for Nonconformists, being finde to an amount of money which he could not meet, was sent to Newgate. His wife, and two little children, homeless and penniless, went with him. The unhappy family struggled with their wretchedness for fifteen months, when father, mother, and children all died within the prison walls.

Bunyan's imprisonment was not so bad as this but we get some idea of how difficult it was for him when we read of the extent of his wife's effort and torment to get him released. We must not forget that at first sentencing, Bunyan was to be detained in prison for three months and then transported. That would have been the last he would ever see of his family or they of him.

His wife journeyed to London to plead for him, only to be fobbed off time and again. She later went before the assizes in Bedford during the visit of no less a figure than Sir Matthew Hale himself. There is no doubt that Sir Matthew Hale was one of the wisest and godliest judges of all time in this country. Though he showed enormous sympathy towards Bunyan's case, yet declared himself powerless to bring about Bunyan's release. The sentence of deportation however was never executed, and his wife continued to petition assize court after assize court for his release. Bunyan was not however released until Charles II made his famous *Declaration of Indulgence* 1672. This however was chiefly directed towards the benefit of Roman Catholics, but to conceal his main intention he had to grant the same indulgence to Nonconformists.

James Antony Froude in the *English Men of Letters* Series gives a fairly lengthy description of Bunyan's imprisonment showing that in many ways Bunyan's imprisonment was in no way so severe as others at that time had suffered.

Some have said that Bunyan's twelve-year imprisonment from 1660 to 1672 was briefly interrupted after six years with Charles II's declaration of indulgence. Others maintain Bunyan was released but almost immediately rearrested because he returned to his preaching.

> His condition during his long confinement has furnished the subject for pictures which if correct would be extremely affecting. It is true that, being unable to attend to his usual business, he spent his unoccupied hours in making tags for bootlaces. With this one fact to build on, and with the assumption that the scene of his sufferings was the Bridge Lockhouse, Nonconformist imagination has drawn a "den" for us, "where there was not a yard or a court to walk in for daily exercise;" "a damp and dreary cell; a narrow chink which admits a few scanty rays of light to render visible the abode of woe; the prisoner, pale and emaciated, seated on the humid earth, pursuing his daily task, to earn the morsel which prolongs his existence and his confinement together. Near him, reclining in pensive sadness, his blind daughter, five other distressed children, and an affectionate wife, whom pinching want and grief have worn down to the gate of death. Ten summers have rolled over

> the mansion of his misery whose reviving rays have never once penetrated his sad abode."
>
> English prisons in the seventeenth century were not models of good management. But prisoners, whose friends could pay for them, were not consigned to damp and dreary cells; and in default of evidence of which not a particle exists, I cannot charge so reputable a community with a neglect so scandalous. The entire story is in itself incredible. Bunyan was prosperous in his business. He was respected and looked up to by a large and growing body of citizens, including persons of wealth and position in London. He was a representative sufferer fighting the battle of all the Nonconformists in England. He had active supporters in the town of Bedford and among the gentlemen of the county. The authorities, so far as can be inferred from their actions, tried from the first to deal as gently with him as he would allow them to do. Is it conceivable that the Baptists would have left his family to suffer; that his own confinement would have been made so absurdly and needlessly cruel? Is it not far more likely that he found all the indulgences which money could buy and the rules of the prison would allow? Bunyan is not himself responsible for these wild legends. Their real character appears more clearly when we observe how he was occupied during these years."
>
> pp.79–80

Froude quotes a description by one Charles Doe, a distinguished Nonconformist, who visited Bunyan in his confinement, and left the following account of what he saw:

> When I was there, [he writes] there were about sixty Dissenters beside himself taken but a little before at a religious meeting at Kaistor, in the County of Bedford, besides two eminent dissenting ministers, Mr Wheeler and Mr Dun, by which means the prison was much crowded. Yet, in the midst of all that hurry, I heard Mr Bunyan both preach and pray with that mighty spirit of faith and plerophory of divine assistance, that he made me stand and wonder. Here they could sing without fear of being overheard, no informers prowling round, and the world shut out."
>
> Ibid p.83

There is clearly an element of truth in Froude's description, it is certainly the case that there was a lot of anti-establishment feeling in the town of Bedford. There was a riot in the town at that time against government policies, and the local officers refused to assist in quelling it. Yet we also know that it was local officials who had put Bunyan in prison and these local officials and landowners had considerable power. It is also true that there were times when Bunyan seems to have been out of the prison preaching in nearby woods. Again a local magistrate got to know this and reported it to the constable who came to the prison to investigate, only to find Bunyan was in the prison. As the story goes the jailer is supposed to have said "You may go out when ye please, for you know better than I went to return." Ibid p. 83

Certainly towards the end of his imprisonment Bunyan was appointed elder in the Bedford congregation and later on its pastor, and neither of these appointments could have been made unless he was available to carry out their duties. There must have been some laxity developing in the rules of the prison and the area generally towards the end of Charles II reign as the Bedford church reopened before the Declaration of Indulgence was passed.

Bunyan certainly worked during his imprisonment, and employed many hours of the day making tagged laces, (according to his biographer John Brown he made literally many hundred gross of these laces p. 169) to assist the maintenance of his family. He certainly did everything that he could to mitigate their suffering family.

Comments on some of Bunyan's Works

The Grace Abounding

The preface of *Grace Abounding* in which Bunyan writes as a minister as yet still in prison encouraging his flock, reveals Bunyan securely established in the Scripturally defined world that this same autobiography shows himself struggling to enter.

The introduction to it is like a Scripturally packed sermon. The following is a brief extract from it where he addresses his congregation in Bedford.

> Children, Grace be with you, Amen. I being taken from you in presence, and so tied up, that I cannot perform that duty which from God doth lie upon me, to you-ward, for your further edifying and building up in Faith and Holiness, yet that you may see my soul hath fatherly care and desire of your spiritual and everlasting welfare: I

> now once again, as before from the top of Shenir and Hermon, so now from the Lions Dens, and from the Mountains of the Leopards (Song of Solomon 4:8) do look yet after you all, greatly longing to see your safe arrival in the desired haven.
>
> I thank God upon every remembrance of you, and rejoice even while I stick between the teeth of the lions in the wilderness, at the grace, and mercy, and knowledge of Christ our Saviour, which God has bestowed upon you, with abundance of faith and love. Your hungerings and thirstings also after further acquaintance with the Father, and his Son; your tenderness of heart, your trembling at sin, your sober and holy deportment also, before both God and men, is a great refreshment to me: For ye are my glory and my joy (1 Thessalonians 2:20.)
>
> I have sent you here enclosed a drop of that honey, that I have taken out of the carcass of a lion (Judges 14:5–8). I have eaten thereof myself also, and am much refreshed. (Temptations when we meet them at first, are as the lion that roared upon Samson; but if we overcome them, the next time we see them, we shall find a nest of honey within them). The Philistines understand me. It is a relation of the work of God upon my own soul, even from the very first, till now; wherein you may perceive my castings down, and raisings up; for he woundeth, and his hands make whole. It is written in the Scripture (Isaiah 38:19), The father to the children shall make known the truth of God. Yea, it was for this reason I lay so long at Sinai (Deuteronomy 4:10–11), to see the fire, and the cloud, and the darkness, that I might fear the Lord all the days of my life upon earth, and tell of his wondrous works to my children, (Psalm 78:3–5).

Here we get a wonderful taste of Bunyan's preaching, full of Scripture quotations and allusions and imagery. Full of application of the Word of God. These words also revealed to us his pastoral heart.

Next we may observe Bunyan was very interested in the figurative and typical aspect of Scripture.

We see this in his sermons or short books on *The Barren Fig Tree* (1682), likewise in another sermon or we may say short book, *The Water of Life* (1688) or in what we might call a sustained piece of biblical exegesis such as *The Holy City* (1665), or a longer work,

Solomon's Temple Spiritualised (1688). All these can be found in the volumes of Bunyan's works. (See *Conventicle and Parnassus*, p.162)

Bunyan would have seen no inconsistency between a strong commitment to the literal truth of the biblical narrative, and a spiritualizing of the text. Bunyan clearly operated within the Protestant tradition that acknowledged only one literal sense but saw and acknowledged spiritual interpretations at the same time. In the words of the Elizabethan Puritan, William Whitaker, "not various senses, but various collections from one sense, or various applications and accommodations of that one meaning." Bunyan was certainly in this tradition.

Likewise, he followed the common practice of reading the Old Testament text typologically.

In his *Solomon's Temple Spiritualised,* its windows become figures of the Word of God, the Bible, the altar a type of Christ, the golden candlesticks types of the churches of the New Testament, the "net-work" ornamenting the capitals of the Temple's pillars was for Bunyan a figure of the net of the Gospel by which the Apostles caught men.

In his *The Holy City,* he allegorises the details of the New Jerusalem with its walls and gates and jewels. (Revelation 21:10–28; Revelation 22:1–4) He sees the New Jerusalem of Revelation as the fulfilment of the Old Testament prophecies, such as Jeremiah 31:10–12.

> Hear the word of the Lord, O ye nations, and declaring in the isles afar off, and say, He that scattered Israel will gather him, and keep him, as a shepherd doth his flock.
>
> For the Lord hath redeemed Jacob and ransomed him from the hand of him that was stronger than he.
>
> Therefore, they shall come and sing in the height of Zion and shall flow together to the goodness of the Lord for wheat, and for wine, and for oil, and for the young of the flock and the herd: and their soul shall be as a watered garden: and they shall not sorrow any more at all;

meaning that in the fullness of time God would gather together the scattered sheep of Israel.

This exposition covers from pages 284 to 337 of the first volume of Bunyan's works.

It ends with these words, p. 337 vol. 1

> The wolf shall dwell with the lamb, and the leopard shall lie down with the kid; and the calf and the young lion and the fatling together: and a little child shall lead them. The lion shall eat straw like the ox; And the little child shall play on the hole of the asp; and the weaned child shall put his hand on the cockatrices den. They shall not hurt nor destroy in all my holy mountain, saith the Lord.
>
> Isaiah 11:6–9.
>
> Blessed is he whose lot it will be to see this holy city descending and lighting upon the place that shall be prepared for her situation and rest!
>
> Then will be a golden world: wickedness shall then be ashamed especially that which persecutes the church; holiness, goodness, and truth shall then, with great boldness, countenance, and reverence, walk upon the face of all the earth: "From the rising of the sun, even to the going down of the same, my name shall be great among the Gentiles; and in every place incense shall be offered unto my name, and a pure offering: for my name shall be great among the heathen, saith the Lord of Hosts." (Malachi 1:11). It will be then always summer, always sunshine, always pleasant, green, fruitful, and beautiful to the sons of God; "And it shall come to pass in that day, that the mountains shall drop down new wine, and the hills shall flow with milk, and all the rivers of Judah shall flow with water: and a fountain shall come forth of the house of the Lord, and shall water the valley of Shittim; and Judah shall dwell for ever even from generation to generation." (Joel 3:18–19).
>
> "And the name of the city shall be from that day, The Lord is there." (Ezekiel 48:35).
>
> Oh, blessedness! "And he said unto me, these sayings are faithful and true: and the Lord God of the holy prophets sent his angel to show unto his servants the things which must shortly be done." (Revelation 22:6)

Bunyan's way of exposition is a good corrective to the often dry and predictable method so current today.

John R. Knott, in his essay in the collection of papers on John Bunyan, *Conventicle and Parnassus*, comments,

> "Perhaps the best example in all Bunyan's work of the nurturing and

consoling properties of Scripture occurs in *The Holy War*, in the scene of feasting that follows Emanuel's first triumphal entry into Mansoul. In a treaty that appeared the same year as *The Holy War*, i.e. *The Greatness of Soul* (1682), Bunyan drew upon several biblical metaphors in characterising the soul's experience of Scripture: the soul of a saint can taste and relish God's word, and doth oft-times find it sweeter than honey, nourishing as milk, and strengthening like to strong meat".

On their "Feasting-day" the people of Mansoul are treated by Emanuel to "outlandish food" from "his Father's court", glossed by Bunyan as "Promise after promise". Musicians play and wine flows at this marvellous banquet. Bunyan makes the scene credible and delightful by showing the naive wonder of the "townsfolk": "but still when a fresh dish was set before them, they would whispering say to each other, what is it? For they wist not what to call it". Emanuel provides appropriate entertainment by explaining the "Riddles" of Scriptural metaphors that portray him with a gesture of love removing all anxiety about the mystery of Scripture.

This scene and others celebrating the triumphs of Emanuel—with Psalm-singing, dancing, bell ringing, strewing of the streets with flowers and branches—are characterised by a holy joy that suggests Bunyan's description of Beulah in the *Pilgrim's Progress*. Yet despite a strongly Biblical colouring of the scenes, with their suggestions of Christ's entry into Jerusalem and of Old Testament celebrations, they remain rooted in this world. The most extraordinary thing about them is that Bunyan daringly brings Emanuel into the urban setting of Mansoul, dissolving the distance between human and divine. Bunyan gives his readers a dazzling preview of the heavenly bliss of the saints and, at the same time, reminds them that Diabolus and his followers remain at large in their world.

In his final speech Emanuel distinguishes this world with its dangers and anxieties from the world to come, where Mansoul will be remodelled in an altogether new way and its inhabitants will experience such communion with divinity "as is not possible here to be enjoyed". Emanuel's parting advice, "thou must live upon my Word", puts simply and powerfully the essence of Bunyan's message about Scripture. His *Relation* and *Grace Abounding* show him trying to live upon the Word, and his didactic and his imaginative works attempt in their diverse ways to persuade his readers to do the same."

Finally, in regard to Bunyan's most well-known work, *Pilgrim's Progress*, we may remember its famous opening words, *As I walked through the wilderness of this world. I lighted upon a certain place where was a Den, and I laid me down in that place to sleep; and as I slept I dreamed a dream.* John Brown goes on to say *"These words, which open for us the story of the Pilgrim, suggest to the majority of its readers the culminating point of interest in Bunyan's life."*

The *Pilgrim's Progress* was written whilst Bunyan was in prison, and this is confirmed by Bunyan's own note in the 1679 edition, in which he adds against the word Den, the marginal note, jail. It is debated whether the *Pilgrim's Progress* was written during his first imprisonment or second imprisonment. John Brown believes it to have been written after his first twelve years in prison, when he was again arrested and spent the winter and early spring of 1675–76 incarcerated in the town jail on Bedford Bridge.

Many have speculated where Bunyan got his first idea, for this arguably his most famous and most read literary work. Some have suggested he took the idea from William Langland's fourteenth century work, *The Vision of Piers Plowman*; others such as Adam Clarke suppose him to have been influenced by reading *Spencer's Faerie Queen*. Others, such as Dr Dibdin, believe his influence came from Caxton's *Pilgrimage of the Soul*. Many have been the suggestions, but Bunyan himself in his introduction to *The Holy War* tells us quite clearly that he wrote it out of his own heart and mind.

Some say the *Pilgrim's Progress* is not mine,
Insinuating as if I would shine
In name and fame, by the worth of another,
It came from mine own heart, so to my head,
And thence into my fingers trickled;
Then to my pen, from whence immediately
On paper. I didn't dribble it daintily.
Manner and matter too was all mine own,
Nor was it unto any mortal known,
'Til I had done it. Nor did any then
By books, by wits, by tongues, or hand, or pen,

Add five words to it, or write half a line
Thereof: the whole and every whit is mine.

The first edition of the *Pilgrim's Progress* was published in 1678, a second with some additions appearing in the same year, the third in 1679, and a fourth in 1680. It was estimated that in Bunyan's own day a hundred thousand copies of the English edition were sold apart from those selling in America.

Many ecclesiastical and literary figures have poured out their commendations of the book, including William Cowper, Dr Samuel Johnson, John Wesley, Samuel Taylor Coleridge, Lord Macaulay, Arnold of Rugby, Henry Martyn, Charlotte Brontë, C.S. Lewis and countless others.

Augustus M. Toplady described it as:

> A masterpiece of piety and genius; and will, we doubt not, be of standing use to the people of God, so long as the sun and moon endure.

C.H. Spurgeon remarked on Bunyan's *Pilgrim's Progress*:

> Read anything of his, and you will see that it is almost like reading the Bible itself. He had read it until his whole being was saturated with Scripture; and though his writings are charmingly full of poetry, yet he cannot give us his *Pilgrim's Progress*—without continually making us feel and say, "Why, this man is a living Bible!"

The *Pilgrim's Progress* is the most famous Christian allegory in print. It has been called, the ultimate English classic. Only the Bible itself has sold more copies, and it is estimated that it has been translated into over a hundred languages.

Bibliography

John Bunyan, *Conventicle and Parnassus*, edited by N.H. Keeble (Oxford: Clarenden Press, 1988).

Daniel Neil, *History of the Puritans* (Klock and Klock, 1979).

John Bunyan, *Grace Abounding*, ed. Roger Sharock (London: Oxford University Press, 1966)

The Works of John Bunyan, ed. Henry Stebbings (London: John Hurst, 1861).

J.A. Froude, *English Men of Letters* (London: Macmillan and Co., 1888).

John Brown, *John Bunyan* (London: Wm. Isbister Ltd, 1885).

Alister MacGrath, *In the Beginning, The Story of the King James Bible* (Hodder and Stoughton).
Christopher Hill, *A Turbulent and Seditious People* (Oxford University Press, 1989).
Curtis W. Freeman, *Undomesticated Dissent* (Baylor University Press, 2017).

31. John Milton—*Paradise Lost*

The following introduction to the life and writings of John Milton is taken from Leland Ryken's, *Christian Guide to the Classics.*

> "John Milton (1608–1674) was born into a prosperous middle-class family in London. He was a child prodigy whose father gave him the best education imaginable: St Paul's School (one of the famous grammar schools of the Renaissance, located right in Milton's neighbourhood). Private tutors, Cambridge University, and five years after college for self-education. As a result, Milton is the most learned of English writers. In addition to being a famous author, Milton spent a twenty-year interval in the prime of his life as a famous public and political figure. Near the beginning of this time, Milton became totally blind. He wrote his three major works—*Paradise Lost*, *Paradise Regained*, and *Samson Agoniste*—after his public career had ended."

The Protestant Reformation. "The Religious context into which Milton and his writings fit is the Protestant Reformation, which was a century old by the time Milton wrote. The central tenet of Protestantism is that the Bible alone is the final authority for religious belief and conduct. From this flow the main doctrines of the movement: God's creation of the world, and providence over it, the sinful state into which all people are born, and faith in the substitutionary atonement of Jesus Christ as the means of salvation. These doctrines and more formed the intellectual foundation of Milton's writings, including *Paradise Lost*."

Puritanism. "The English branch of the Protestant Reformation is known as Puritanism, which began as a church movement intended to purify (hence the name Puritan), the Church of England of its remaining Catholic vestiges. Milton is "a Puritan of Puritans". Some specific emphasis of English Puritanism within the broader context of European Protestantism, includes extraordinary immersion in the Bible and an obsession with vocation and work; affirmation of marriage and of sex within it; and the primacy of the spiritual (even though the physical is regarded as good in principle). These traits are conspicuous in Paradise Lost."

Paradise Lost, as a religious poem. "While readers with Christian sensibilities and biblical knowledge can find an abundance of Christian elements in the writings of authors such as Shakespeare and Hawthorn, non-Christian readers find it possible to read them with minimal attention to the Christian aspects. Milton stands in contrast to this. As C.S. Lewis put it, Milton's poetry does not exist apart from his theology. Milton himself said that in writing the great English and Christian ethic he intended to write a poem "doctrinal and exemplary to a nation." *Paradise Lost* is a complete repository of biblical truth and Christian doctrine. As for the claims of revisionist scholars that Milton was heretical in his thinking, any ordinary reader will be hard pressed to find any hint of heresy in *Paradise Lost.* Most of what the debunkers claim as heresy is taken straight from the Bible, such as the title "only begotten Son" for Christ". (Leland Ryken, *Milton's Paradise Lost, Christian Guide to the Classics* (Crossway, 2015), p.12)

Paradise Lost is generally regarded to be one of, if not, the greatest poems in the English language, and there is no religious epic in English which measures up to Milton's masterpiece. Those who are best suited and best equipped to confirm this, i.e. those who know poetry and true religion best, have left ample testimony to this fact and the following are some examples of their commendations.

> "Milton, by the choice of the noblest words and phrases which our tongue would afford him, has carried our language to a greater height than any of the English poets have ever done before or after him, and made the sublimity of his style equal to that of his sentiments.
>
> The *Paradise Lost* is an epic, or narrative poem, and he that looks for a hero in it, searches for that which Milton never intended; but if he will needs fix the name of an hero upon any person in it, it is certainly the Messiah, who is the hero, both in the principal action, and in the chief episodes …

Milton's sentiments and ideas were so wonderfully sublime, but it would have been impossible for him to have represented them in their full strength and beauty, without having recourse to classical/ foreign assistances. Our language sunk under him, and was unequal to the greatness of Soul, which furnished him with such glorious conceptions..."

Thomas Addison

"A reader of Milton must be always upon duty; he is surrounded with sense, it rises in every line, every word is to the purpose; there are no lazy intervals, all has been considered, and demands, and merits observation. Even in the best writers you sometimes find words and sentences which hang on so loosely you may blow them off; Milton's are all substance and weight; fewer would not have served their turn, and more would have been superfluous.

His silence has the same effect, not only that, he leaves work for the imagination when he has entertained it, and furnished it with noble materials; but he expresses himself so concisely, employs words so sparingly, but whoever will possess his ideas must dig for them, and oftentimes pretty far below the surface".

Richardson, *Explanatory Notes and Remarks on Milton's Paradise Lost*, 1734

"The characteristic quality of this poem (*Paradise Lost*) is sublimity.

In Milton every line reads sanctity of thought and purity of manners, except when the train of the narration requires the introduction of the rebellious spirits; and even they are compelled to acknowledge their subjection to God in such a manner as excites reverence and confirms piety...

... In reading *Paradise Lost*, we read a book of universal knowledge ... The reader feels himself in captivity to a higher and nobler mind, and criticism sinks in admiration".

Dr Samuel Johnson, *Life of Milton*, 1779

"I could not prevail on myself to approach the *Paradise Lost*, without impressing on your minds the conditions under which such a work was in fact producible at all, the original genius having been assumed as the immediate agent and efficient cause; and these conditions I find in the character of the times and in his own character. The age in which the foundations of his mind were laid, was congenial to it as one golden era of profound erudition and individual genius—that in which the superstructure was carried up was no less favourable to it by a sternness of discipline and a show of self-control, highly flattering to the imaginative dignity of an heir of fame, and which won Milton over from the dear-loved delights of academic groves and cathedral aisles to the anti-prelatic party.

The character of Satan is pride and sensual indulgence, and finding in himself the sole motive of action. It is the characters so often seen "in little" on the political stage. It exhibits all the restlessness, temerity, and cunning which have marked the mighty hunters of mankind from Nimrod to Napoleon. The common fascination of men is, that these great men as they are called, must act from some great motive. Milton has carefully marked in his Satan, the intense selfishness, the alcohol of egotism, which would rather reign in Hell than serve in Heaven. To place this lust of self in opposition to denial of self or duty and to show what exertions it would make, and what pains endure to accomplish its end, is Milton's particular object in the character of Satan.

In the description of Paradise itself you have Milton's sunnyside as a man; here his descriptive powers are exercised to the utmost, and he draws deep upon his Italian resources. In the description of Eve, and throughout this part of the poem, the poet is predominant over the theologian. Dress is the symbol of the Fall, but the mark of intellect; and the metaphysics of dress are, the hiding of what is not symbolic and displaying by discrimination what is. The love of Adam and Eve in Paradise is of the highest merit—not phantomatic, and yet removed from everything degrading. It is the sentiment of one rational being towards another made tender by a specific difference in that which is essentially the same in both; it is a union of opposites, giving and receiving mutually of the permanent in either, a completion of each in the other".

Samuel Taylor Coleridge

The above quotations are taken from Hugh Sykes Davies, *Poets and their Critics,* (Hutchison Educational, 1960)

An Outline of the Twelve Books that make up the Paradise Lost

Book I

Book one opens with a prayer to God for help and assistance in setting forth such an epic and exalted theme.

> "Fast by the Oracle of God; I thence
> Invoke thy aid to my adventurous song,
> That with no middle flight intends to soar
> Above the Aonian mount, while it pursues
> Things unattempted yet in prose or rhyme.
> And chiefly Thou, O Spirit, that dost prefer
> Before all temples the upright heart and pure,
> Instruct me, for Thou know'st Thou from the first
> Wast present, and with mighty wings outspread,
> Dove-like, sat'st brooding on the vast abyss,
> And madest it pregnant: what in me is dark,
> Illumine: what is low, raise and support;
> That to the height of this great argument
> I may assert Eternal Providence,
> And justify the ways of God to men."

Milton then moves to announce his subject, the Fall of mankind into sin, and the reassurance that God's Providential governance of the world will continue despite the presence of evil, now in it.

Book I is full of the drama of Satan's rebellion and fall into the burning lake. It describes with poetic licence, his rising from the lake of fire, and mustering his fallen legions, who unite with him to build the hellish city of Pandemonium from which he will launch his opposition to the purposes of God.

Book II

The main purpose of this section is to describe the demonic council in hell where the way to proceed in this opposition is discussed and planned by the fallen angels. Here Milton tries to convey Satan's demonic determination to wage all-out war against God for having defeated them, and cast them out of heaven.

Four principal Demons are identified, Moloch, Belial, Mammon. Beelzebub. Each make their defiant proposals of how this can be done. The proposals of the *first three* are rejected and Beelzebub proposes that Satan, who by now is dictator of this hellish society, is nominated to bring about the Fall of Adam with the intention of spoiling the creation of God, and bringing to nought his purposes of good.

Book III

Here we find portrayed the dialogue in heaven between the Persons of the Trinity set forth as the counterpoint to the dialogue in Hell described in Book II. The dialogue in heaven is that between the Persons of the Godhead, where God the Father, purposes to save the world and proposes the whole plan of salvation. God the Son undertakes to fulfil that plan by the Incarnation, taking flesh and dwelling amongst us, the fulfilling of all righteousness, the paying of the price of sin by his death on the cross, and satisfying the demands of justice and mercy.

The Son of God freely offers himself a ransom for man.

> Father, Thy word is pass'd, man shall find grace;
> And shall grace not find means, but finds her way
> The speediest of Thy winged messengers,
> To visit all Thy creatures, and to all
> Comes unprevented, unimplored, unsought.
> Happy for man, so coming; he her aid
> Can never seek, once dead in sins, and lost;
> Atonement for himself, or offering meet,
> Indebted and undone, hath none to bring:
> Behold me, then; me, for him life for life
> I offer; on me, let Thine anger fall;
> Account me man; I for his sake will leave
> Thy bosom, and this glory next to Thee
> Freely put off, and for him. lastly die …

We might also at this point remind ourselves of Milton's intention throughout this great poem is "to justify the ways of God to men."

Here we see Milton is seeking to show us part of the answer to the problem of suffering in the world. Here he is showing us that through Christ, suffering evil will be ultimately defeated. God permitted evil in the world but did not create it, and God will ultimately overrule it for good.

Book IV

In this section Milton seeks to describe life in Paradise. This portrayal has been described as "The greatest version of the archetypical earthly paradise in all of world literature." (Ryken, p. 34)

In this section also Milton describes Satan's first sight of Adam and Eve. When Satan sees them for the first time he wonders at their excellent form and happy state, but resolves nevertheless to bring about their fall. He listens to their conversation and ascertains the significance of "The Tree of Knowledge" and of the "forbidden fruit." He therefore plans to fashion his temptation by way of seducing them to transgress by eating the fruit and thereby to doubt and disobey God.

Also in this Fourth Book, we find set out Adam's first speech in the poem. It exalts God's wonderful provision for himself and Eve (lines 411–439). It is a tender recollection of the couple's first meeting.

Milton records Satan's expressed torment on seeing Adam and Eve's love for one another.

Further we see described the Puritan vision of true romantic love and marriage. Adam is anxious that they retire in order that they can rise early to fulfil their work and duty the next day. After singing an evening hymn of praise, they retire, experiencing sexual union before falling asleep.

Book V

In this book Milton describes the next morning when Eve relates to Adam a troubled dream that she has had that night. Adam is disturbed, but tries to comfort her. They go out to their daily tasks, and sing their morning hymn. This hymn again gives a valuable insight into their life in Paradise, the picture is of the perfect bliss and happiness of the couple and indicates the fact that they are endowed with every capacity to resist temptation.

The Angel Raphael is introduced at this point, and reminds them of their freedom and privilege, but at the same time warns them of the danger they face from Satan. A description of Satan is given and an account of his purposes to destroy the work of God.

This visit and Raphael's warning with its implications is taken up and developed in the following four books that is books 5–8.

Here also is introduced the angel *Abdiel* (*Abdiel* = the servant of God). Abdiel is described as one of the Angels who heard Satan's first rebellious speech, and unlike the others who rebelled, opposed Satan and forsook him, remaining faithful to God. He is introduced here to emphasise the virtue of resistance to evil, and comes as an example to Adam and Eve, and to all, to imitate and to follow.

So spake the seraph Abdiel faithful found,
Among the faithless, faithful only he;
Among innumerable false, unmov'd,
Unshak'n, unseduc'd, unterrifi'd
His loyalty he kept, his love, his zeal;
No number, nor example with him, wrought
To swerve from truth, or change his constant mind
Though single. From amidst them, forth he pass'd,
Long way through hostile scorn, which he sustain'd
Superior, nor of violence fear'd ought
And with retorted scorn his back he turn'd
On those proud Tow'rs to swift destruction doom'd".

Book V. 895.

Book VI

This book contains a continued exhibiting of the virtues of *Abdiel*. Abdiel is everything that Satan should have been. In this description of the virtuous angel Milton is seeking to portray the nature of truth, goodness and the character of heroic spiritual virtue.

Servant of God, well done, well has thou fought
The bitter fight, who single hast maintain'd
Against revolted multitudes the Cause
Of truth, in word. Mightier than they in arms;
And for the testimony of truth hast borne
Universal reproach, far worse to bear
Than violence: for this was all by care
To stand approv'd in sight of God, though worlds
Judg'd the perverse: the easier conquest now
Remains thee, aided by his host of friends,
Back on thy foes more glorious to return …

Book VI. 30

Also in this chapter, there begins the description of the great celestial battle, that now commences against Satan and his hosts.

Here I adapt Milton's own summary of this passage:

The angel Raphael here again speaks, relating how the angels Michael and Gabriel are sent out to battle against Satan and his hosts. After the first fight Satan and his powers retire under the cover of night, where he calls a council, at the same time inventing infernal war machines, which in the second day's conflict are successful in putting Michael and his angels into serious disarray. However, at length, "pulling up mountains" the forces of good overwhelm the force and war machines of Satan. However, the war is not so easily ended, and God on the third day sends Messiah his Son for whom is reserved the glory of total victory.

> He in the power of his Father coming to the place and causing all his legions to stand still on either side, with His chariot, and thunder driving into the midst of his enemies, pursues them unable to resist toward the wall of Heaven. Which opening, they leap down with horror and confusion into the place of punishment prepared for them in the deep. Messiah returns with triumph to his Father.

Book VII

Raphael is described here as pausing at Adam's request to explain more fully how and why this world was created, and that how, after the expulsion of Satan from Paradise, God purposed to create the world and mankind and all the creatures that inhabit it. Raphael explains how God sent his Son, attended by the glorious company of angels, to create the world in six days. Christ's return to heaven, accompanied by the angel songs of praise, is described here, this description is said to be, "one of the most exuberant passages of praise in all English literature." (Ryken, p. 58)

The reason for the inclusion of this theme at this point is to establish a foil to the destructive war in heaven. Satan's destructiveness is now countered by God's creativity. As readers we feel a great sense of relief: with Satan off the scene temporarily, we are free to luxuriate in Milton's story of God's original acts of creation.

Note also that: Here begins another dialogue in heaven, as God the Father and God the Son determined to compensate for the loss of a third of the hosts of heaven by creating earth, with Adam and Eve as its first inhabitants.

> But lest his heart exalt him in the harm
> Already done to have dispeopled Heav'n
> (My damage fondly deemed). I can repair
> That detriment (if such it be to lose
> Self-lost), and in a moment will create
> Another world, out of one man a race
> Of men innumerable there to dwell,

Not here, till by degrees of merit raised
They open to themselves at length the way
Up hither, under long obedience tried,
And Earth be changed to Heav'n and Heav'n to Earth,
One Kingdom, joy and union without end.

Book VII 150.

Book VIII

Adam expresses his great admiration for Raphael's account of the supernatural events. This is followed by Milton cautiously warning against human overmuch enquiry into the hidden knowledge of God, and stressing that it is better to know the will of God and to fulfil man's responsibilities in this world.

To ask or search I blame thee not, for Heav'n
Is as the Book of God before thee set,
Wherein to read his wondrous Works, and learn
His Seasons, Hours, or Days, or Months, or years:
This to attain, whether Heav'n move or Earth,
Imports not, if thou reck'n right; the rest.

Book VII 65.

Here in this section of the poem we have as it were, an exposition of Deuteronomy 29:29:

> The secret things belong unto the Lord our God: but those things which are revealed belong unto us and to our children for ever, that we may do all the works of this law.

Book IX

Book IX is said to be the greatest of the books of *Paradise Lost.*

In this chapter Satan has come back to Eden (having been temporarily driven out by Gabriel) and now enters into the serpent (the most subtle of all beasts) in order to disguise himself. Before actually entering into the serpent Satan utters a speech which shows how much further he has degenerated into a spiteful destroyer who finds delight only in destruction which brings him revenge; even if revenge "Bitter and long back on itself recoils". Satan here is seen as cutting off his nose to spite his face.

After a description of dawn in Eden, the text turns to a conversation between Adam and Eve, where she, presumably because of the suggestion put into her mind by Satan while she slept, suggests to Adam that they divide their labours and work in different parts of the garden that day.

Adam is reluctant to let her go, but out of love consents. She promises to return at noon. Milton uses all his powers of poetic sensitivity to enable us to feel that the Eve that has left will not be the Eve that returns.

> "O much deceiv'd much failing, hapless Eve
> Of thy presum'd return! event perverse!
> Thou never from that hour in Paradise
> Foundst either sweet repast, or sound repose;
> Such ambush hid among sweet flowers and shades
> Waited with hellish rancour imminent
> To intercept thy way, or send thee back
> Despoiled of innocence, of Faith, of Bliss".
>
> *Book IX*. 405

Milton's purpose in this section is to create a "before and after" scenario in our consciousness. So far in his epic he has set before us images of the perfections and glories of Paradise. Now, by way of absolute contrast, he is bringing before us scenes of the misery of life in a fallen world. All through this work Milton is seeking to make the good attractive, and the evil repulsive.

For example, one way that he does this is seen in lines 1004–2011 which show the perversion of appetites that had been good before the Fall, but are now corrupted.

Eating becomes gluttony; unfallen sexuality becomes lechery; consciousness of sin sets in, followed by scenes of quarrelling and mutual accusation of each other, in marked contrast to earlier scenes of marital harmony.

Book X

Book X opens with Milton reiterating, and making it absolutely clear that none of what has transpired was God's fault, even though he was and is the omnipotent and omniscient Creator of all things.

Milton himself summarises this passage as follows:

> Man's transgression known, the Guardian Angels forsake Paradise and return up to Heaven to approve their vigilance, and are approved, God declaring that the entrance of Satan could not be by them,

> prevented. He sends his Son to judge the transgressors, who descends and gives sentence accordingly; then, in pity, clothes them both and re-ascends. Sin and Death, sitting till then at the gates of Hell, by wondrous sympathy feeling the success of Satan in this new world, and the sin by man there committed, resolved to sit no longer confined in Hell, but to follow Satan their sire up to the place of Man. To make the way easier from Hell to and fro, they paved a road or bridge over chaos, according to the track, that Satan first made. Then, preparing for Earth, they meet him, proud of his success, returning to Hell pour on him their mutual congratulation. Satan arrives in Pandemonium, and in full assembly relates with boasting his success against Man; instead of applause is entertained with a general hiss by all his audience, transformed with himself also, suddenly, into serpents, according to his doom, given in Paradise. Then, deluded with the show of the Forbidden Tree springing up before them, they greedily reaching to take of the fruit, chew dust and bitter ashes, the proceedings of Sin and Death. God foretells the final victory of his Son over them, and the renewing of all things; but for the present commands his angels to make several alterations in the heavens and elements. Adam more and more, perceiving his fallen condition, heavily bewails, rejects the condolement of Eve; she persists, and at length appeases him; then to evade the curse likely to fall on their offspring, proposes to Adam violent ways which he approves not, but conceiving better hope, puts her in mind of the late promise made them that her seed should be revenged on the serpent and exhorts her with him to seek peace of the offended Deity by repentance and supplication.

Book XI

Books IX and X have presented the Fall and its immediate effects. The final two books tell the story of the effects of the Fall throughout human history. Scholars point out that it is a convention in the composition of epic stories to include near the end, a vision of future history. Milton follows this pattern by making part of the vision of the future a relentless exposure of human sinfulness.

However, the story of the future is not entirely one of discouraging negativity. We see Adam and Eve bowing in contrition and confession of the failure and sin before God. They are nevertheless put out of the garden of Eden, expelled by the angel Michael, but at the same time, it is revealed to them the promise of a coming Saviour.

"Dismiss them, not disconsolate." (line 113). Or, "So send them forth, though sorrowing, yet in peace" (line 117). On the literal level, Michael is informing Adam's mind about the facts of human history. On a more interpretive level, he is giving Adam and Eve, a survival kit for living in a fallen world, and even more a theology lesson about the Gospel.
(Ryken, p. 81)

Book XII

The words of Adam, in reply to the angel Michael beginning at line 270 of this section are a fitting final word on this immortal poem and on the eternal just and gracious purposes of God.

> "Here Adam interposed: O sent from Heav'n,
> Enlight'ner of my darkness, gracious things
> Thou hast revealed, whose chiefly, which concern
> Just Abraham and his seed. Now first, I find
> Mine eyes true op'ening and my heart much eased,
> Erewhile perplexed with thoughts what would become
> Of me and all mankind, but now I see
> His Day, in whom all nations shall be blessed,
> Favour unmerited by me who sought
> Forbidden knowledge by forbidden means.
> This yet. I apprehended not, why to those
> Among whom God will deign to dwell on Earth
> So many and so various laws are giv'n?
> So many laws argue so many sins
> Among them: how can God with such reside?"

And then follows the account of the Old Testament promises and prophecies of the coming of Christ of the House of David, followed by, commencing at line 380, a glorious depiction of the Christ who should come and the deliverance he shall bring.

> The Seed of woman: Virgin Mother, hail!
> High in the love of Heav'n, yet from my loins
> Thou shalt proceed, and from my womb, the Son
> Of God. Most High: so God with Man unites!
> Needs must the serpent now his capital bruise
> Expect with mortal pain. Say where and when
> Their fight! What stroke shall bruise the Victors heel?
> To whom thus Michael: dream not of their fight

As of a duel or the local wounds
Of head or heel. Not therefore joins the Son
Manhood to Godhead with more strength to foil
Thy enemy nor so is overcome
Satan, whose fall from heav'n—a deadlier bruise—
Disabled not to give thee thy deaths wound,
Which he who comes thy Saviour shall recure
Not by destroying Satan but his works
In thee and in thy seed. Nor can this be
But by fulfilling that which thou didst want:
Obedience to the Law of God imposed
On penalty of death, and suffering, death,
The penalty to thy transgression due,
And due to theirs, which out of thine will grow—
So only can hide justice rest apaid.
The Law of God exact He shall fulfil
Both by obedience and by love, though love
Alone fulfil the Law. By punishment
He shall endure by coming in the flesh
To a reproachful life and cursed death,
Proclaiming life to all who shall believe
In his Redemption, and that his obedience
Imputed becomes theirs by faith, his merits
To save them, not their own, through Legal works.
For this he shall live hated, be blasphemed,
Seized on by force, judged and to death condemned,
A shameful and accursed, nailed to the cross
By his own nation, slain for bringing life.
But to the cross, he nails thy enemies:
The Law that is against thee and the sins
Of all mankind with him there crucified,
Never to hurt them more who rightly trust
In this his satisfaction. So he dies
But soon revives: Death over him no pow'r
Shall long usurp. Ere the third dawning light
Return the stars of morn shall see him rise
Out of his grave, fresh as the dawning light,
Thy ransom paid which Man from death redeems,
His death for Man: as many as offered life

> Neglect not, and the benefit embrace
> By faith, not void of works. This godlike act
> Annuls thy doom, the death thou shouldst have died
> In sin forever lost from life. This act
> Shall bruise the head of Satan, crush his strength,
> Defeating Sin and Death, his two main arms,
> And fixed far deeper in his head their stings
> Then temporal death shall bruise the Victors heel
> Of theirs whom he redeems, a death like sleep,
> A gentle wafting to immortal life …

Before closing this brief account. Something needs to be said in regard to those who criticise Milton, accusing him of Arianism.

It is sometimes said that, Milton rejected Trinitarian doctrine as set out in the Nicene Creed. To understand this, we have to understand that Milton's position was that of mainstream Puritanism which believed that the true test of orthodoxy was Holy Scripture. Milton believed that the ultimate standard of orthodoxy was that of Scripture as is clearly set out in the Westminster Confession.

> The authority of the Holy Scripture … Dependeth not on the testimony of any man or Church; but wholly upon God (who is truth itself) the author thereof … Powerful persuasion and assurance of the infallible truth and divine authority thereof is from the inward work of the Holy Spirit, bearing witness, by and with the word, in our hearts… Nothing is at any time to be added—whether by new revelations of the Spirit or traditions of men—the Church is finally to prove to them—The infallible rule of interpretation of Scripture is the Scripture itself.

The sentiments expressed in the Westminster Confession were precisely those held by John Milton.

When it comes to his understanding of the nature of our salvation, his beliefs set out in *Paradise Lost* and *Paradise Regained*, are clearly that Christ died in the sinner's place to redeem us from our sins. Milton also reveals that he believes that none but one that is both God and Man could atone for the sins of mankind. Sin is that which violates God's holy Law. An infinite reparation is required from man since man has broken that Law. However, it is a price that man the sinner, and slave to sin cannot pay, nor remedy. Only one who is both God and Man can pay that price.

There was no other good enough to pay the price of sin
He only could unlock the gate of heaven and let us in.

This is orthodox Puritan theology, and the theology of John Milton, and is certainly the theology of *Paradise Lost.* What Milton believes about the Atonement is a clear indication of what he believes about the nature of Christ.

The writer C. A. Patrides has written extensively on the subject and has helpfully set out the following tenets of Arius, illustrating the wide difference between Milton's theology and that which calls itself Arianism.

> 1. Arius held that God is utterly incommunicable and absolutely isolated from his entire creation, whether physical or spiritual, animate or inanimate. Milton, on the other hand, asserted God's direct involvement in both the origin and the history of the created order." (This we may add, is manifestly displayed in the *Paradise Lost.*)
>
> 2. Before the advent of time, Arius further maintained, God "begat" the Son, of whom it must properly be said, "there was once when he was not." The Son was produced not of the Father's divine nature, but out of nothing. The two persons, in fact, are utterly dissimilar in substance or essence and totally unequal in every respect, even glory. The Son may indeed, on occasion be termed God", but this is merely a nominal concession because in reality, he is not "true" God.

In contrast, Milton rejected this scheme, he believed Christ was begotten of God, very God of very God; he was wrong however in suggesting that, in principle, there could have been a time when he was not. This may be partly accounted for by the fact of Milton's strange view that time began just prior to the creation of the world.

> 3. Arius scrupulously avoided the use of metaphorical statements which had the effect of emphasising the close relationship existing between the Father and the Son, but Milton did not.
>
> 4. Whereas Arius maintained that the Father is both invisible and ineffable to the Son, Milton took great pains to assert the extremely close communion between the two Persons.
>
> 5. According to Arius, the Son of God was expressly produced in order to create the universe and time "out of nothing". Milton

> disagreed, he did not hold that the Son was "begotten" specifically with a view to the creation of the world.
>
> 6. Whereas Arius maintained that the Son is, like all rational creatures, immutable, and indeed peccable, Milton vehemently denied that He may be regarded as in any way liable to change.
>
> 7. Whereas the Arian shattered the unity of the incarnate Son with their affirmation that He assumed the body without a soul. Milton maintained that Christ Jesus was "very man" in both body and soul.
>
> 8. Whereas Arius was of the opinion that the Holy Spirit does not partake of the Son's substance, and still less of the Father's, Milton asserted that the Third Person, though inferior to both the Father and the Son, was none the less also, "begotten" of the substance of God.
>
> C.A. Patrides, "Milton and Arianism", *Journal of the History of ideas* XXV, July–September, 1964, pp. 423–9. Quoted by Bernice M. Gerard, *Milton's Orthodoxy and its Relation to the Form of Paradise Lost*, University of British Columbia, 1967

Though we may not concur with every one of Patrides' points they are helpful in highlighting some of the differences between Milton's beliefs and those of Arias.

Milton firmly asserts his belief that Jesus Christ is God, that the Incarnation is the central event of history, marking the entrance into the world of no fantastic creature with a body but without a soul, totally alien from God, but of God himself.

> "O unexampled love,
> Love nowhere to be found less than divine!
> Hail Son of God, Saviour of Men, thy Name
> Shall be the copious matter of my Song
> Henceforth, and never shall my Harp thy praise
> Forget, nor from thy Father's praise disjoin."
>
> *Book* III, 410–5

In further considering this controverted issue it needs to be remembered that until 1825 and the discovery of a long lost work of Milton's *De Doctrina Christiana,* his orthodoxy was never doubted. Bishop Sumner, who translated this work into English and published it proclaimed it as clear evidence of Milton's Arianism. Much debate has raged over this issue ever since. Some have questioned whether this was that of Milton at all. Others question whether it does confirm his Arianism, while others are utterly convinced that it does.

Whatever we may believe about this particular document it does remind us, as its author states, that his theological views were in a constant state of revision over a period of years. Since the discovery of this work many have sought to find evidences of Arianism in *Paradise Lost.* Others however strongly reject this view. C.S. Lewis in his *Preface to Paradise Lost*, states, that "read independently, not the slightest indication of Arianism can be detected." Another critic, B. Rajan, states an interesting point, "*Paradise Lost* represents Milton's final and true position, its Scriptural references reverberate orthodoxy." An interesting comparison would be to go to Milton's early work, *Ode on Christ's Nativity*, and discover in it very clear Trinitarian doctrine. In the light of Milton's statement, quoted above, that his theological views were in a state of revision over a period of years, Milton being a very deep thinker, committed to a right understanding of Scripture, not taking for granted man-composed statements of doctrine or creeds, he needed to come to his own understanding, through the Scriptures themselves, by prayer and meditation. Taking this view, and noting the dates of his various publications, we may rightly contend that both *Paradise Lost* and *Paradise Regained*, as the critic Rajon suggests, represent his final conclusion that is a return to the orthodoxy of his earlier years.

Another writer who has examined this issue has given us the following samples of Milton's orthodox Christology in *Paradise Lost.*

We read in the *Paradise Lost* of Christ. "Christ, the image of the invisible God" (PL III. 374) and *light* (PLIII. 3), the Son is only rightly identified with the holy light of heaven as the "radiant image of his Father's glory (III., 63) in whom "the almighty Father" is "made visible" and "shines" (III, 386).

The light of "the Eternal coeternal beam" (PL. III:2), the dwelling of God. "From eternity" (III.2), and "Bright effluence of bright essence in-create." (III.6). To view the light so portrayed as anything other than God himself is tantamount to create an irreconcilable dualism between God and light: both are said to exist from eternity, and light is pronounced uncreated—as is assumed God alone is—as well as streaming from God's own essence … The light of heaven is significantly identified as "offspring of Heav'n first–born". (III.1)

In the final analysis, no better description of the Son is found in

Paradise Lost than that provided by the Nicene Creed: "light of light, very God of very God, begotten not made." All in all, the Son of the poem is nothing short of the "ineffable and everlasting love. The effluence of God's very essence, whose piercing ray descends to man in his darkness and saturates him with the Gospel, the Son is the light of the knowledge of the unknowable God communicated by the prevenient, concomitant and subservient agency of the third subsistence of Divine Infinitude, the illuminating Spirit." (Filippo Falcone, *Connotations*, vol. 27 Internet.)

This is a huge and complex subject, and I'm conscious that I've only scratched the surface. For a full and complete presentation of the above argument see: William B. Hunter, *Milton's Arianism Reconsidered*, and B. Rajan, *Paradise Lost and the 17th Century Reader.*

Bibliography

William B. Hunter, *Milton's Alleged Arianism* (n.d.)

B. Rajan, *Paradise Lost and the 17th Century Reader* (Chatto and Windus, 1947)

C.S. Lewis, *Milton's Preface to Paradise Lost* (Internet)

Filippo Falcone, *Connotations* (Internet)

The Poetical Works of John Milton (Edinburgh: W.P. Nimmo, 1865)

John Milton, *Complete Poems and Major Prose*, ed. Merrit Y. Hughes (New York: The Odyssey Press, 1957)

John Milton, *Paradise Lost*, David Daiches, Edward Arnold (n.d.)

Milton's Paradise Lost, ed. Leland Ryken (Crossway, 2013)

Hugh Sykes Davies, *The Poets and their Critics* (Hutchinson Educational, 1960)

Bernice M. Gerard, *Milton's Orthodoxy and its Relation to the Form of Paradise Lost*, M.A. Thesis, submitted for the requirements of the degree of M.A. (The University of British Colombia, 1967, Internet)

32. John Milton—*Areopagitica*

John Milton was born in London in 1608. He is considered to be the greatest writer in English after Shakespeare. A private tutor, an excellent school in London, seven years at Cambridge University, and six years of self-directed study made him an extraordinarily learned man with fluency in Latin, Greek, Hebrew, French, Spanish, and Italian. He also possessed a vast knowledge of modern writing; an intimate familiarity with the literature and thought of ancient Greece and Rome, of late antiquity, and of the Middle Ages.

A deep and sincere Christian, during the time of the English Civil War, he devoted his wide and extensive learning to the support of Cromwell and the Parliamentary cause. As an unwavering advocate of religious, civil and political liberty during this time, he became the author of many treaties and pamphlets in support of the preservation and extension of civil and religious freedom.

Principal amongst these was the *Areopagitica*, probably the greatest polemical defence of the freedom of the press ever written. The circumstance that prompted its composition was the law passed through Parliament in 1643 authorising twenty licensors, or censors, in England, to approve or reject book and pamphlet manuscripts before publication, a general policy (not always strictly enforced), dating to the mid-1500s but abolished in 1641 by the Long Parliament. There followed a brief explosion of pamphlet publishing—from 22 in 1640, to 1,966 in 1642. Milton argues that policies of prior censorship had never existed in any ancient or mediaeval society before the Catholic Inquisition, that stifling the free exchange of ideas would stunt intellectual development; that ideas should be rejected only after they have been carefully assessed by society; that truth will always prevail against falsity; that evil ideas test and fortify our discipline and ability to resist temptation; that a society cannot remain free and vigorous without a robust sphere of public disputation; that distinguishing truth from falsity is the duty of citizens and not government; and finally that a handful of censors cannot possibly be trusted to judge what is right for an entire society. Milton's powerful arguments did not convince the parliament of that time to overturn the law of 1643, and prior censorship was ended in England only in 1695, yet the pamphlet exerted a formidable impact on many subsequent political thinkers, including the Founders of the American Republic.

Milton begins his written speech for the liberty of unlicensed printing in England with a quote from *The Suppliants*, a play by the Greek tragedian, Euripides.

"This is true liberty when free-born men—having to advise the public may speak free," Milton quotes. "What can be juster in a state than this?" Milton addresses his speech to the "High Court of Parliament," which in the 1643 Licensing Order mandated that "no book, pamphlet, or paper shall be henceforth printed, unless the same be first approved and licensed by such." Milton is passionately opposed to Parliament's order—at least the part that requires pre-publication licensing. He supports the portion of the order that "preserves justly every man's copy to himself," and argues that "the utmost bound of civil liberty" is attained only when, "complaints are freely heard, deeply considered and speedily reformed." He begins with a look at censorship through the ages and asserts that the type of prepublication censorship mandated by Parliament's Licensing order was not seen until after the year 800. Until then, Milton contends, "books were ever as freely admitted into the world as any other birth: the issue of the brain was no more stifled than the issue of the womb." Here Milton is referring to the Roman Catholic Church and the Spanish Inquisition, and he is speaking directly to an overwhelmingly Protestant Parliament. The "inventors" of pre-publication censorship, Milton says, "be those whom ye will loath to own."

Books and ideas weren't censored in biblical times, to such an extent either, Milton argues, unless they were found to be heretical or defamatory. The English Parliament meant to suppress books they considered bad, or evil, and Milton asserts this is not only impossible, but an affront to God as well. "God uses not to captivate under the perpetual childhood of prescription," Milton writes, "but trusts (man) with the gift of reason to be his own chooser." Furthermore, good and evil are inextricably linked, within books and in man, so they are impossible to "sort asunder," Milton claims. "It was from the rind of one apple tasted, that the knowledge of good and evil, as two twins cleaving together, leapt forth into the world. And perhaps this is that doom which Adam fell into of knowing good and evil, that is to say, of knowing good by evil." God never intended for humankind to live a life independent of evil, which is why he gave Adam "reason," and "gave him the freedom to choose." To eliminate evil means that each Christian virtue is left untested and "is but a blank virtue, not a pure." Without evil to reject, Adam is "a mere artificial Adam, such an Adam as he is in the motions." In addition to negatively affecting the virtue of Christians, Milton maintains that Parliament's Licensing Order violates God's divine authority and plan as well.

Milton continues his argument by pointing out how inadequate Parliament's Licensing Order is, claiming that it "induces nothing to the end for which it was framed." The law means to spare citizens from evil, but it only seeks to regulate printed material. "If we think to regulate printing, thereby to rectify manners, we must regulate all recreations and pastimes, all that is delightful to man." "What about music?" Milton questions, "and the gestures and motions of dance? Surely these things can be evil as well and need regulation," he contends. There is even "household gluttony" to consider, and the "daily rioting" of gossip, which is most certainly to blame for the spread of evil. Milton argues that "whatever thing we hear or see sitting, walking, travelling, or conversing may be fittingly called our book," and to suppress books only "is far insufficient to the end which (Parliament's order) intends." One cannot "remove sin by removing the matter," Milton posits.

Books "cannot be suppressed without the fall of learning," Milton also claims, which too "hinders and retards the importation of our richest merchandise, truth." According to Milton, both "faith and knowledge thrives by exercise," and suppressing books hampers this exercise. Truth, the product of study and knowledge, "is compared in Scripture to a streaming fountain; if her waters flow, not in perpetual progression, they sicken into a muddy pool of conformity and tradition." Parliament's Licensing Order does just that, Milton claims, by controlling and mandating what is read and learned. "A man may be a heretic in the truth; and if he believes things only because his pastor says so, or the assembly so determines, without knowing other reason, though his belief be true, yet the very truth he holds," Milton warns, "becomes his heresy."

Milton contends "that truth came once into the world with the divine master, and was a perfect shape most glorious to behold." But truth did not retain its original shape, Milton claims, and the "lovely form" of "virgin truth" was "hewed" into thousands of pieces, and "scattered" from "the four winds." Pursuit of knowledge is searching for bits and pieces of scattered truth, but all the pieces are yet to be found and likely never will be, "till her Master's Second Coming," Milton says. Additionally, Milton cautions, when truth is bound, as it is by Parliament's order, "she speaks not true," but instead "turns herself into all shapes, except her own." It is not "impossible," Milton contends, that truth, "may have more shapes than one," and he implores Parliament to lend equal weight to all shapes of truth and not "fall again into a gross conforming stupidity" which "is more to the sudden degenerating of a church than many subdichotomies of petty schisms."

Of course, Milton maintains, he cannot "think well of every light separation" of the church, and while he argues for more Christian beliefs to "be tolerated, rather than compelled," he does not mean to tolerate "popery, and open superstition, which as it extirpates all religions and civil supremacies, so itself should be extirpate." While Milton argues against the pre-publication censorship of books, he supports the censorship and full eradication of the Roman Catholic Church. Milton maintains that Parliament's new practice of suppressing books "is the worst and newest opinion of all others; and is the chief cause why sects and schisms do so much abound, and true knowledge is kept at a distance from us." He claims to know that "errors in a good government and in a bad are equally almost incident," and he entreats Parliament, "to redress willingly and speedily what hath been erred" in the passing of the Licensing Order of 1643.

Bibliography

John Milton, *Areopagitica*, Foreword by John Alvis (Liberty Fund, Indianapolis, 1999)

Summary of *Areopagitica*, www.litcharts.com

33. Richard Baxter—*A Christian Directory*

Lord Macaulay once quipped that the Puritans hated bear baiting, not because it gave pain to the bear, but because it gave pleasure to the spectators". Nothing could be further from the truth. The Puritans attitude toward the world is expressed by Sibbes in his Saint's Cordials: "Worldly things are good in themselves, and given to sweeten our passage to Heaven ... This world and the things thereof are all good, and were all made by God, for the benefit of his creatures." And J. B. Marsden reminds us "that among the Puritans were found not only the greatest divines but also many of England's ablest statesman, most renowned soldiers, and not a few gifted orators and poets." Contrary to public opinion, Puritanism acted as a grand spiritual and cultural catharsis on England under Elizabeth. It was the Puritan spirit that brought about the freedom of the press, a high view of the sanctity of the marriage vow, the invocation of divorce on the ground of infidelity, a dignified view of labour, and an active and positive programme of life.

David Otis Fuller, *A Treasury of Evangelical Writings*, p. 205

Richard Baxter (1615–1691) was one of the outstanding Puritan divines of his day (1615–1691), often misunderstood and censured by many, while others down to this present day have held him in high regard. Amongst these was Sir Matthew Hale, noted judge, jurist, and Chief Justice of the King's Bench, and Bishop Burnett Historian and philosopher. Another, Bishop Wilkins, said of him, "he cultivated every subject he handled: and if he had lived in the primitive time, he had been one of the Fathers of the Church." Later figures such as Elliott the apostle to the Indians who had Baxter's, *Call to the Unconverted,* translated for his work, called it "the next book after the Bible".

Baxter was the author of a metrical version of the Psalms, published in 1692 and two volumes of poetry from which we have the hymns beginning, "Lord, it belongs not to my care", "Ye holy angels bright, and "Away distrustful care." He also wrote Latin poetry his *Poetical Fragments: Heart Imployment (Employment) with God and Itself: The Concordant Discord of a broken—healed Heart*, is dated, *London, at the*

Door of Eternity; Richard Baxter, August 7, 1681. The death of his wife, Margaret Charlton, was the occasion of its publication.

Dean Boyle, a latter incumbent of Kidderminster notes,

> The works of Lightfoot extend to thirteen volumes; Jeremy Taylor's to fifteen, Dr Owen's to twenty-eight; but Baxter's could not be comprised in less than sixty volumes.

Dr Orme calculates the number to be one hundred and sixty-eight treaties. The most well-known of these are *The Saints Everlasting Rest, The Call to the Unconverted, Gildas Salvianus* or *The Reformed Pastor* and *Reliquiæ Baxterianæ* or *Richard Baxter's Narrative of the Most Memorable Passages of his Life and Times.* (*Schaff-Hertzog Encyclopaedia of Religious Knowledge*, vol. I, p. 227)

It has also been said that probably Baxter preached more sermons, engaged in more controversies, and wrote more books than any Nonconformist of his era.

It has been commented that by his writings Baxter has bequeathed to the reading world a priceless library of books, pamphlets (some 200), and a few poetic fragments, and has left the Christian world an example of a godly life, a dedicated mind and intrepid spirit, and a character unimpeachable. (Fuller p. 206)

Added to this list of writings must be included his work *Methodus theologia Christianae* (1681), a Latin work of nine-hundred folio pages: to this the *Christian Directory* (printed 1673) was the practical part.

It was the learned James Ussher, Bible chronologist, Calvinistic theologian and first professor of theology at Trinity College, Dublin, that first conceived the idea of a *Christian Directory* as a vehicle for the advance of Christianity. What he had in mind was a full-scale academic exposition of Puritan practical divinity in Latin, which was then the language of international scholarship, for the benefit of Protestant clergy in our own and other countries. Baxter himself writes in the preface to his work:

> It is long ago, since many foreign divines subscribed a request, "that the English would give them in Latin, a Sum of our Practical Theology", which Mr Drury sent over, and twelve great divines of ours wrote to Bishop Ussher to draw them up a form or method. But it was never done among them all. And it is said, that Bishop Downame at last undertaking it, died in the attempt. Had this been

> done, it is like my labour might have been spared. But being undone, I have thus made this essay. p.4.

When Baxter was first approached to undertake this work, he refused, but later changed his mind. What he has produced is a work of tremendous thoroughness, making our modern works on practical Christianity to be seen as shallow and superficial.

Baxter, in his introduction tells us a number of basic facts about the *Directory* as a book.

It was written almost entirely in 1664–65, while Baxter was living in Acton, just outside London. He had only a few of his own books with him, and no secretarial help of any sort. Together with nearly 2000 others, Baxter was, in 1662, "forbidden by law to preach." for refusing the requirements made of clergy in the *Act of Uniformity* that restored the Church of England after the Interregnum. Thus silenced, he turned to full–time writing, and the *Directory* was an early fruit of this new focus, although it was not actually printed till 1673.

The purpose of the *Directory* is summed up in its very full title, i.e.: *A Christian Directory or A Practical Theology, and Cases of Conscience, Directing Christians How to Use Their Knowledge and Faith; How to Improve All Helps and Means, and to Perform all Duties; How to Overcome Temptations, and to Escape or Mortify Every Sin.*

The work is divided into four parts:

1. Christian Ethics (or Private Duties)
2. Christian Economics (or Family Duties)
3. Christian Ecclesiastics (or Church Duties)
4. Christian Politics (or Duties to our Rulers and Neighbours)

J.I. Packer, comments that it is the opinion of many that the *Directory* is the richest and best single counselling resort available to those who give pastoral guidance today. This no doubt may seem paradoxical until one works one's way through it; after doing so, however, one is likely to find that verdict inescapable.

He goes on to say, *A Christian Directory* may justly be described as a landmark. It is the fullest, most thorough, most profound treatment of Christian spirituality and standards that has ever been attempted by an English-speaking Evangelical author. The fact that it embraces both spirituality and standards (the principles of communion with God, plus the specifics of obedience to God) merits approving comment in itself; nowadays spirituality and ethics have become two distinct disciplines in the schools, and books written on either say virtually nothing about the other; and the teacher who recognises that you cannot have a good focus on either one unless you have also laboured to get a good focus on the other is a rare bird indeed.

The following are two extracts from the work:

A passage from the section, *What godliness is*. Directory XIII p. 51

> Know, that true godliness is the best life upon earth, and the only way to perfect happiness. Still apprehend it therefore, and use it as the best; and with great diligence resist those temptations which would make it seem to you a confounding, grievous, or unpleasant thing.
>
> There are all things concurrent in a holy life, to make it the most delectable life on earth, to a rational, purified mind, that is not captivated to the flesh, and liveth not on air or dung. The object of it is the eternal God himself, the infallible truth, the only satisfactory good; and all these condescending and appearing to us, in the mysterious, but suitable glass of a Mediator; redeeming, reconciling, teaching, governing, sanctifying, justifying, and glorifying all that are his own. The end of it is the pleasing and glorifying of our Maker, Redeemer, and Sanctifier; and the everlasting happiness of ourselves and others. The rule of it is the infallible revelation of God, delivered to the church by his prophets, and his Son, and his apostles, and comprised in the Holy Scriptures, and sealed by the miracles and operations of the Holy Ghost that did indict them. The work of godliness is a living unto God, and preparing for everlasting life, by foreseeing, foretasting, seeking, and rejoicing in that endless happiness which we shall have with God; and by walking after the Spirit, and avoiding the filthiness, delusions, and vexations of the world and the flesh. The nature of man is not capable of a more noble, profitable, and delectable life, than this which God hath called us to by his Son. And if we did but rightly know it, we should follow it with continual alacrity and delight. Be sure, therefore, to conceive of godliness as it is, and not as it is misrepresented by the devil, and the ungodly. Read what I have written of this in my "A Saint or a Brute."

Appropriately for this work I add a further section on his exhortation regarding the choice of books read.

Directory XVI.

> Make careful choice of the books which you read. Let the Holy Scriptures ever have the pre-eminence; and next to them, the solid, lively, heavenly treaties, which best expound and apply the Scriptures; and next to those, the credible histories, especially of the church, and tractates on inferior sciences and arts: but take heed of the poison of the writings of false teachers, which would corrupt your understanding; and of the vain romances, play–books, and false stories, which may bewitch your fantasies, and corrupt your hearts.
>
> As there is a more excellent appearance of the Spirit of God in the Holy Scriptures, than in any other book whatever, so it hath more power and fitness to convey the Spirit, and make us spiritual, by imprinting itself upon our hearts. As there is more of God in it, so it will acquaint us more with God, and bring us nearer to him, and make the reader more reverent, serious, and divine. Let Scripture be first and most in your hearts and hands, and other books be used as subservient to it. The endeavours of the devil and papists to keep it from you, do show that it is most necessary and desirable to you.
>
> Books are (if well chosen) domestic, present, constant, judicious, pertinent, yea, powerful sermons; are always a very great use to your salvation; but especially when vocal preaching faileth, and preachers are ignorant, ungodly, or dull or when they are persecuted, and forbidden to preach.
>
> You have need of a judicious teacher at hand, to direct you what books to use or to refuse. For among good books there are some very good that are sound and lively; and some are good but, mean, and weak, and somewhat dull: and some are very good in part, but have mixtures of error, or else of incautious, injudicious expressions, fitter to puzzle than edify the weak …
>
> *Directory*, p.56

In regard to Baxter's theology. *The Schaff-Hertzog Encyclopaedia* adds the following comments:

> In theology Baxter was an Independent, (though earlier he supported the Presbyterian Church) as he was in church polity. Characteristically, he was an eclectic. He held to Calvinism, but not in its regular form. He sought to find a common resting place for Calvinist and Arminian, Episcopalian and Presbyterian… He taught that all who from their hearts confessed that Christ was Lord belong

> to the true catholic church, which is composed of believers in every Christian denomination. It is difficult, as Orme confesses, to get a clear notion of what he really believes, because his works contains few definitions, and are, besides, so diffuse. But, speaking generally, he taught that common grace was given to all, which, however, needed special grace to render it effectual to salvation; that election and reprobation are not equally to be ascribed to God, who elects, but is not chargeable with the sin which causes the reprobation; that Christ died for all, therefore, the widest invitation can be given, but not equally for all. He taught the Calvinistic theology upon the perseverance of the saints and the will. Those who sympathised with him have been called Baxterians.
>
> p. 227

Though we may not agree in every respect with his theology, he preached the fundamentals of the Gospel. Through his work in Kidderminster, covering 19 years, by the power of his preaching and the example of his holy life, the whole community was transformed from a place of cruelty and immorality to what has been called a garden of true piety.

When George Whitefield visited Kidderminster a hundred years later, he remarked, "The Sweet Savour of good Mr Baxter's doctrine, works and discipline still lingered in the place."

It can also be noted that Richard Baxter was one of the first to condemn the West Indies slave trade.

> To go as pirates and catch up poor Negroes or people of another land… and to make them slaves, and sell them, is one of the worst kinds of thievery in the world, and they that buy them and use them as beasts, for their mere commodity… are more fitted to be called incarnate devils than Christians.
>
> *Directory*, p. 462

Richard Baxter suffered much under the later Stuart Kings, and in May 1685, he was tried by the notorious Chief Justice Jeffries, who sentenced him to pay 500 marks (an immense sum in those days), and until it was paid to lie in prison, and to be bound to his good behaviour for seven years. He endured 18 month's imprisonment; but through the exertions of Lord Powis, a Roman Catholic nobleman, the fine was remitted; and he was pardoned and released on November, 24th, 1686. His last days were his best. His evening time was light. Delivered from fear of persecution after King William of Orange entered England (1688), thoroughly respected for his courage, and, above all, for his godliness, he preached, when he was able, and continued his publications. When he died, Non-conformist England mourned her chief; Protestant England, one of her saints. (Adapted from *Schaff-Hertzog*, p. 226)

In July 1875, a statue representing Baxter in the preaching attitude, was erected in Kidderminster, bearing the following inscription.

> Between the years 1641 and 1660 this town was the scene of the labours of Richard Baxter, renowned equally for his Christian learning and his pastoral fidelity. In a stormy and divided age he advocated unity and comprehension, pointing the way to everlasting rest. Churchmen and Nonconformists united to raise this memorial AD 1875.

Bibliography

The Practical Works of Richard Baxter, A Christian Directory, vol. 1 foreword by J.I. Packer (Soli Deo Gloria Publications, 2000)

Schaff-Hertzog Encyclopaedia of Religious Knowledge vol. 1 (New York: Funk and Wagnalls Company, 1891)

David Otis Fuller, *A Treasury of Evangelical Writings* (Kregel Publications, Grand Rapids, 1971)

34. Matthew Henry's *Commentary*

C.H. Spurgeon once said:

> Every minister ought to read Matthew Henry's *Commentary* entirely and carefully through at least once.

This remark is made in the introduction to his well-known *Commenting on Commentaries* and I can introduce and emphasise the value and importance of this Commentary no better than to quote Spurgeon's introduction in full.

> First among the mighty for general usefulness we are bound to mention the man whose name is a household word, Matthew Henry. He is most pious and pithy, sound and sensible, suggestive and sober, terse and trustworthy. You will find him to be glittering with metaphors, rich in analogies, overflowing with illustrations, superabundant in reflections. He delights in apposition and alliteration; he is usually plain, quaint, and full of pith; he sees right through a text directly; apparently he is not critical, but he quietly gives the result of an accurate critical knowledge of the original fully up to the best critics of his time. He is not versed in the manners and customs of the East, for the Holy Land was not so accessible, as in our own day: but he is deeply spiritual, heavenly, and profitable; finding good matter in every text, and from all deducing, most practical and judicious lessons. His is a kind of commentary to be placed where I saw it, in the old meeting-house at Chester—chained in the vestry for anybody and everybody to read. It is the poor man's commentary, the old Christians companion, suitable to everybody, instructive to all.
>
> His own account of how he was led to write his exposition affords us an example of delighting in the law of the Lord. "If any desire to know how so mean and obscure a person as I am, who in learning, judgement, felicity of expression, and all advantages for such a service, am less than the least of all my Masters servants, came to venture upon so great a work, I can give no other account of it, but this. It has long been my practice, what little time I had to spare in my study from my constant preparations for the pulpit, to spend in drawing up expositions upon some parts of the New Testament,

not so much for my own use, as purely for my own entertainment, because I know not how to employ my thoughts and time more to my satisfaction. Trahit sua quemque voluptas; every man that studies hath some beloved study, which is his delight above any other; and this is mine. It is that learning which it was my happiness from a child to be trained up in by my ever honoured father, whose memory must always be very dear and precious to me. He often minded me, that a good textuary is a good divine; and that I should read other books with this in my eye, that I might be the better able to understand and apply the Scripture. You are aware, perhaps, that the latter part of the New Testament was completed by other hands, the good man having gone the way of all flesh. The writers were Messrs. Evans, Brown, Mayo, Bays, Rosewell, Harriss, Atkinson, Smith, Tong, Wright, Merrill, Hill, Reynolds, and Billingsley—all Dissenting ministers. They have executed their work exceedingly well, have worked in much of the matter which Henry had collected, and have done their best to follow his methods, but their combined production is far inferior to Matthew Henry himself, and any reader will soon detect the difference. Every minister ought to read Matthew Henry entirely and carefully through once at least. I should recommend you to get through it in the next twelve months after you leave college. Begin at the beginning, and resolve that you will traverse the goodly land from Dan to Beersheba.

You will acquire a vast store of sermons if you read with your notebook close at hand; and as for thoughts, they will swarm around you like twittering swallows around an old gable towards the close of autumn. If you publicly expound the chapter you have just been reading, your people will wonder at the novelty of your remarks and at the depth of your thoughts, and then you may tell them what a treasure Henry is. Mr Jay's sermons bear indubitable evidence of his having studied Matthew Henry almost daily. Many of the quaint things in Jay's sermons are either directly traceable to Matthew Henry or to his familiarity with that writer. I have thought that the style of Jay was founded upon Matthew Henry: Matthew Henry is Jay writing, Jay is Matthew Henry, preaching. What more could I say in commendation of either the preacher or the author?

C.H. Spurgeon, *Commenting and Commentaries*, p. 2–4

Matthew Henry began his commentary, November 1704. The first

> volume was published 1708. This first volume with four others appeared in uniform edition 1710. Before he died he completed volume 6, up to the Acts, and after his death, the Epistles and Revelation were prepared by thirteen Nonconformist divines,
>
> Leslie F. Church, Foreward to Matthew Henry's *Commentary* (Marshall Pickering, 1960)

Matthew Henry was born in Broad Oak, a Welsh farmhouse at Iscoid, Flintshire, on 18th October 1662. His father Philip Henry was one of the near 2000 ministers ejected from their livings by the infamous *Act of Uniformity*, August 1662. The family were moderately well-off and were therefore able to live at Broad Oak, which had been left to them, by Philip's wife, née Catherine Matthews, before Matthew Henry was born. Matthew Henry's grandfather John Henry had served in the civil service under James I and Charles I and during Charles I time was the keeper of the Orchard at Whitehall. This situation brought him into contact with several influential individuals of that day, including Archbishop Laud, who when passing through Whitehall, Water Gate, (which was under the supervision of John Henry), would leave a small gift for the keeper's son, Philip Henry.

John Henry was not seriously concerned about spiritual things, but his wife, nee Magdalen Rochdale, was a deeply pious woman who took her son to hear the best puritan preachers of that day. These included Thomas Case, Stephen Marshall, Jeremiah Burroughs, William Bridge and the like. Philip Henry was converted and entered the ministry after studying at Christ Church, Oxford. On leaving Oxford, he became minister of Worthenbury, on the English, North Wales border.

Matthew Henry, because of the family's Nonconformist views, was not allowed to study at Oxford as his father had done. He first of all studied at home under his father, and then was enrolled at Thomas Doolittle's Academy in Islington, London. Doolittle was from Kidderminster where he had been converted under the Ministry of Richard Baxter, he also entered the ministry, but was ejected in 1662 and then opened up a school for the children of Nonconformists. After this Matthew Henry entered Gray's Inn in 1685 to study law. Strangely, the ban on Nonconformists entering universities did not apply to the Inns of Court. Matthew Henry valued the education he received at this time, but increasingly felt called to the ministry. Eventually he accepted the call to be minister of the Presbyterian congregation in Chester in 1687.

> Interestingly, the church held their services so as not to compete with the Cathedral and other parish churches: in fact many of the Presbyterians attended the sermons of the Rev. Lawrence Fogg, Prebendary and later Dean of the Cathedral. Fogg was the son of the ejected minister of Bangor-is-y-Coed, but later conformed and became increasingly bigoted against his former denomination; on one occasion, he informed a Nonconformist, who told him why the Nonconformist did not have meetings at the same time as the Anglican churches, he replied that "Your meetings are schismatic at any time." Not surprisingly, Fogg managed to alienate the Dissenters who had readily attended his preaching, and service times at the Presbyterian churches were rearranged. It is pleasing to note that Fogg later regretted his words, and Matthew Henry heard him with pleasure and freely forgave the Dean.
>
> Gervase M. Charmley, *Peace and Truth Magazine*, p. 12

Matthew Henry was twice married. His first wife, Catherine Hardman died of smallpox as she gave birth to a child in 1689. He married his second wife, Mary Warburton in July 1690. Matthew Henry exercised a much blessed ministry in Chester from 1687 to 1712. The plan of his Lord's Day services was that he usually prayed for half an hour, preached for an hour, and joined in singing Psalms, from a selection he himself had made, most likely a Psalm at the beginning and at the end of the service.

In 1704 he began his Notes on the New Testament, and the entry in his diary concluded with a typical prayer: *The Lord help me to set about it with great humility.*

In 1710 he received a call from the congregation in Silver Street, Hackney, London. He was reluctant to leave Chester, but felt that his work on the Commentary would be helped by easier access to books and to Biblical scholars in London. He left Chester on 18 May 1712 and by the end of that year was very much employed, not only in Hackney but in exercising a wider ministry amongst the churches of the metropolis.

He did not however forget his flock in Chester and returned in the summer of 1713 to visit them and also some of the churches of the surrounding district. These included Whitchurch, Knutsford and Middlewich.

He promised at this time to return the following year, and on 31st May 1714, though exceedingly tired and in failing health, he again preached in his old church, and also at Whitchurch, Wrexham, Knutsford, and Chowbent near Manchester.

On his return to London he had planned to ride to Nantwich, with the intention of preaching there and joining the London coach the next day. *En route*, passing through Tarporley, Cheshire, his horse stumbled, and he suffered a serious fall. He insisted, however, on pressing on, so as not to disappoint the friends in Nantwich. He preached that day, though with great difficulty, but in the early hours of the Monday morning, he suffered a stroke, and passed to his eternal rest on Tuesday morning 22nd of June, 1714, aged 51.

Matthew Henry's *Commentary* was largely based on his preached sermons, and was the first full exposition of the entire Bible ever undertaken. It became also the forerunner of several highly useful and beneficial works which followed in the subsequent years; these included the works of John Gill, Adam Clark, Thomas Scott, and we may also include that of Albert Barnes.

George Whitfield read the *Commentary* through four times—literally reading it on his knees, and spoke always of *the great Matthew Henry*. It is also said that the hymns of William Cowper were undoubtedly inspired by the spirit, and even the words of Matthew Henry. Without Matthew Henry, we should never have had the often sung and poignant line, *O for a closer walk with God*. Nor that line so full of comfort, *God moves in a mysterious way, his wonders to perform*. Leslie Church also reminds us that Matthew Henry's comments on Leviticus 8:35 gave Charles Wesley the hymn:

> A charge to keep I have
> A God to glorify,
> A never dying soul to save,
> And fit it for the sky.

Matthew Henry wrote on this text: "They attended to keep the charge of the Lord: we have every one of us a charge to keep, an eternal God to glorify, an immortal soul to provide for, needful duty to be done, our generation to serve; and it must be our daily care to keep this charge, for it is the charge of the Lord our Master."

Leslie Church, concludes his notes on Matthew Henry and his remarkable ministry by saying:

> To have exercised so virile and continuous a ministry, to have been a pastor with such intimate insight into the problems of his people,

> and to have produced so monumental a work as his Commentary, was an astonishing achievement. For three centuries, innumerable people have been enlightened and inspired by his interpretation of the Scriptures. Its essentials have stood the test of time, as, in his own day, they stood the test of human experience. The explanation is, surely, that it had its origin in his fellowship with his Master and in his constant concern for the deepest needs of the people committed to his care.

We may also add, that, amongst his other works, Matthew Henry produced his most notable and helpful, *A Method for Prayer, with Scripture Expressions, Properly to be Used Under Each Head.*

To enable succeeding generations to understand and to live life according to the Scriptures, to know and experience its comforts and its challenges, at the same time also to teach us from the Scriptures how to pray, is a lasting legacy of great worth.

Indeed, *He being dead, yet speaketh.*

Bibliography

Charles H. Spurgeon, *Commenting and Commentaries* (Grand Rapids: Baker Book House, 1981)

Matthew Henry's *Commentary* (Marshall Pickering, 1960)

Peace and Truth Magazine, ed. Gervase Charmley, vol. 2, 2019

The Complete Works of Rev. Matthew Henry, Vol. 2 (Edinburgh, London, and Dublin: A Fullerton and Co. 1853)

Lesley F. Church, *According to Matthew Henry* (Marshall, Morgan and Scott, 1961)

35. Jonathan Edwards—*A Narrative of Surprising Conversions* and *Sinners in the Hands of an Angry God*

THE COMPLETE WORKS OF JONATHAN EDWARDS CAN BE FOUND IN THE two volume edition published by The Banner of Truth Trust. Volume 1 consists of 691 small print, double column pages, and volume 2, consists of 969 pages printed and arranged in the same way. A mere glance at these volumes show how extensive his writings were. Here we simply have space to comment on the effects of the two titles given above.

Jonathan Edwards was born in East Windsor, Connecticut, in 1703, where his father, Timothy Edwards, served as pastor of the Congregationalist Church. His mother, Esther, was the daughter of the Rev. Samuel Stoddard minister in Northampton, Massachusetts, where Edwards would eventually serve as his assistant before following his grandfather as minister of that church.

He was at first educated at home by his father, before entering what was later to become Yale University in 1716. A precocious child, who before he was thirteen gained a good knowledge of Latin, Greek, and Hebrew, and was at the same time writing papers on philosophy. It was while he was still thirteen that he entered college, and it seems that whilst he was at college he was deeply converted. After a short pastorate in New York, he was appointed tutor at Yale. It was after this short appointment that he became the assistant of his grandfather's church at Northampton, Massachusetts, serving alongside his grandfather Samuel Stoddard until the latter's death in 1729. At this point, he became sole pastor of the church. It is said that at this time he spent in the region of thirteen hours each day in his study. Under his powerful preaching, revival broke out in 1734–35, resulting in 300 people confessing faith in Christ, and this being followed by a more extensive revival in the wider area later, in 1740–41. At this time George Whitfield was journeying through New England, including Northampton. Jonathan Edwards and George Whitefield became firm friends. Through Whitefield's preaching this period came to be known as the *Great Awakening*. Over 50,000 people professed conversion, 150 new churches were established, and it was during this time of awakening that Edwards delivered his most famous sermon, *Sinners in the Hands of an Angry God.* While he was preaching men, women and young people rose to their feet weeping and begged God for mercy.

A written record of the events of these times was made by Jonathan Edwards in his works, *A Faithful Narrative of the Surprising Work of God* (1736), in *Distinguishing Marks of a Work of the Spirit of God* (1741), and in *Thoughts Concerning the Present Revival of Religion in New England* (1742)

It was the first of these, *A Faithful Narrative of the Surprising Work of God* that found an immediate and wide readership, and it has become widely acknowledged as contributing a most powerful impetus to the whole work of revival on both sides of the Atlantic. It was published in England in 1737 by Isaac Watts and John Guyse.

In their preface they note:

> The friendly correspondence which we maintain with our brethren in New England, gives us now and then the pleasure of hearing some remarkable instances of divine grace in the conversion of sinners, and some eminent examples of piety in that American part of the world. But never did we hear or read, since the first ages of Christianity, any event of this kind so surprising, as the present Narrative we have set before us. The Rev and worthy Dr Coleman, of Boston, had given us some short intimations of it in his letters; and upon our request of a more large and particular account, Mr Edwards, the happy and successful minister of Northampton, which was one of the chief scenes of these wonders, drew up this history in an epistle to Dr Coleman.
>
> First Editors, Dr Isaac Watts, and Dr John Guyse p.1

It was this edition of the *Favourable Narrative* that was read by John Wesley as he was walking from London to Oxford on 9th October, 1738. He went on to publish his own extracts from it in 1744 and this was reprinted in 1755. Publication of the *Favourable Narrative* in England by Watts and Guyse certainly was used of God to stir British believers to call upon God to revive his work in these islands.

Jonathan Edwards' sermon: *Sinners in the Hands of an Angry God,* on the text "Their foot shall slide in due time", Deuteronomy 32:35 has been criticised by some as a crude "hell-fire" sermon. This is far from the case. It is important to realise that Jonathan Edwards is widely regarded as possessing one of the most acute minds of all American thinkers. It was Jonathan Edwards who wrestled with the new issues of scientific discovery, the Enlightenment, and the Age of Reason in the light of Christian teaching and experience. It was he who faced the emerging onslaught of the so-called humanistic rationalists who were attacking the validity of the teaching of a personal and loving God against the background of a suffering world. Edwards was no crude or superficial thinker.

Vishal Mangalwadi makes the following helpful remarks on the sermon:

> Those who dislike this sermon dislike the thought that God holds human beings accountable to an absolute standard of right conduct.
>
> The principles of responsibility and accountability are but the flipside of dignity and freedom. For a person to be free to choose, she or he must accept responsibility and be judged for the choices she or he makes. Some hold that a serial rapist and murderer should not be punished, for example, because his behaviour was conditioned by the way his father treated him. This reduces a human person to the level of a fish that can make no free choices, doing only what it has learned. The atheistic countries, USSR, China, and Kampuchea demonstrate that when you exclude the spiritual dimension and abolish the fear of God, as Watson and Skinner did, you replace them with fearsome totalitarianism. Sermons such as Edwards's helped create the West's freedom because Edwards hearers knew that, like Jesus, Edwards was inviting sinners to the eternal bosom of a loving and forgiving Father.
>
> The belief in the immortality of the soul was a huge factor behind the West's respect for the inalienable rights of every individual.
>
> *The Book that Made Your World*, p.382

To understand Jonathan Edwards rightly, it is necessary for us to keep in mind his conversion experience which took place when he was about 17 years of age as he began to read 1 Timothy 1:17:

> Now unto the King eternal, immortal, invisible, the only wise God, be honour and glory, for ever and ever. Amen.

As he read these words he was overwhelmed by a sense of God's greatness and glory. This never left him, all the days of his life.

Also we need to bear in mind that as a child growing up the so-called enlightenment theories were pressing in on every hand. These influences at first caused him to recoiled at the idea of God's absolute sovereignty and justice. However, as he read these words in First Timothy, he recounts:

> As I read the words, there came into my soul, and it was, as it were, diffused throughout it, a sense of the glory of the divine Being: a sense quite different from anything I had ever experienced before.

This sense of God's glory and transcendent majesty never left him.

We also have to bear in mind that Edwards was preaching to a hard hearted congregation at Enfield, who had so far resisted the winds of revival that were being experienced elsewhere. What he achieved by this sermon was an awakening and a convicting of his hearers, bringing them to the unshakeable conclusion: only the grace of God could save them from eternal ruin and destruction.

> Edwards, on a missionary tour at Enfield, Connecticut on July 8th, 1741, preached this sermon to try to wake his complacent hearers from their spiritual torpor. By far the most famous of Edward's writing, its original delivery "caused an immediate general revival of religion throughout the place."
>
> *Memoirs of Jonathan Edwards, Sermons of Jonathan Edwards*, p.viii

Bibliography

Sermons of Jonathan Edwards (Massachusetts: Hendrickson Publishers, 2005)

The Works of Jonathan Edwards (Edinburgh: The Banner of Truth Trust, 1979)

Jonathan Edwards, *A Narrative of Surprising Conversions* (London: The Banner of Truth Trust, 1965)

David Otis Fuller, *The Treasury of Evangelical Writings* (Grand Rapids: Kregel Publications, 1971)

Christian Theology, 4th ed. Alistair E. McGrath (Blackwell Publishing, 2007)

D. Martyn Lloyd-Jones, *Romans* vol. 1 (Edinburgh: The Banner of Truth Trust, 1985)

Vishal Mangalwadi, *The Book that Made Your World* (Nashville: Thomas Nelson, 2011)

Dictionary of the Christian Church, ed. J.D. Douglas (The Paternoster Press, 1974)

36. Wesley's *Hymns*

"After the Scriptures, the Wesley Hymnbook appears to me the grandest instrument of popular religious culture that Christendom has ever produced." James Martineau

If we were to trace the origins of this book we would need to go back to 1737, the time that John Wesley was in Charleston, Savannah. He had produced for him there a Collection of Psalms and Hymns containing forty hymns for Sundays, twenty-four for Wednesdays or Fridays, and eighteen for Saturdays. Half of the contents are from Dr Isaac Watts; seven, from John Austin; and six are based on Herbert's poems.

The Watts selection includes—
Before Jehovah's awful throne
I'll praise my Maker while I've breath
Praise ye the Lord: 'tis good to raise
Awake, our souls; away, our fears
And must this body die?
Come, ye that love the Lord
O thou that hear'st when sinners cry
With joy, we meditate the grace
How sad our state by nature is!

Three of the hymns are by Samuel Wesley junior, all three being addressed to the different Persons of the Trinity, and the fourth by Samuel Wesley senior, "Behold the Saviour of mankind." Added to this are five translated from the German.

Thou Lamb of God, Thou, Prince of Peace
O God, thou bottomless abyss
My soul before Thee prostrate lies
Jesu, to thee my heart I bow
O Jesu, Source of calm repose.

Together with two hymns from Joseph Addison—

When all thy mercies, O my God
The spacious firmament on high.

Canon Ellerton in the 19th century, highlighted the importance of this hymn book, saying, John Wesley's voyage to Georgia was memorable. "as a turning-point in the history of English hymnody."

On return to England in 1738 John Wesley went on to publish, *A Collection of Psalms and Hymns* which included one hymn from the Spanish, "O God, my God, my all Thou art," and from the German;

Thou, Jesu, art our King
Shall I, for fear of feeble man
All glory to the eternal Three
Thou hidden love of God, whose height
O thou, to whose all-searching sight

The rest of the hymns were largely taken from Dr Watts and the three hymns by Bishop Ken are also included.

Up to this point Charles Wesley had not been involved in the composing of hymns. It is not until Whit-Sunday 1738, when he came to put his trust in Christ as his only Saviour, that he came to pen his magnificent conversion hymn, *Where shall my wondering soul begin?*

John Wesley together with his brother Charles published the first collection of hymns in 1739. In this book, the stream of Charles Wesley's hymnody begins to flow, there are clear signs that the Evangelical revival has begun for it contains the *Hymn for Kingswood Colliers, Glory to God, whose sovereign Grace.* and another headed, "To be sung in a Tumult"—*Earth, rejoice; the Lord is King.*

The same book also includes the beginnings of Wesley's great Festival Hymns, including:

Hark, how all the welkin rings
Sons of men, behold from far
Christ the Lord is risen today
Hail the day that sees Him rise
Granted is the Saviours prayer

The publishing of hymns continued when in 1741 the Wesley brothers John and Charles published, *A Collection of Psalms and Hymns* and two pamphlets of Hymns on *God's Everlasting Love.*

In 1742 the first Methodist tune-book was published, with forty-two tunes, "as they are commonly sung at the Foundry."

A further volume of *Hymns and Sacred Poems* was produced in 1742 and a further addition of newly composed hymns was added in 1749.

Hymns continued to flow from Charles Wesley's pen and were at first published in various pamphlets. In 1780 he produced *A Collection of Hymns for the Use of the People called Methodists.*

After Wesley's death, this book went through a succession of alterations. In the addition of 1797, twenty of the hymns he selected were omitted, and sixty-five others were inserted.

In 1831, a further supplement was added to what was then called *Wesley's Hymn Book*, and in 1875 it was revised, and a new extended supplement added. The first part of this book was still made up of the hymns Charles Wesley had included and arranged and put in order in the 1780 edition. (Note the 1780 edition bears the preface dated October 20th, 1779, when Wesley obviously prepared the preface for the book about to be published).

What is most unique and most valuable about this book, first published in 1780 and its vital part retained in the 1874 edition, is seen in its table of contents and the arrangements of the order of the hymns. The hymns are arranged in what can be called the conversion experience, conviction, repentance, coming to faith, service, the ongoing Christian life, death and glory.

It is said that Prime Minister W.E. Gladstone always kept a copy of this hymn book on his desk.

Wesley's Hymns—A collection of Hymns for the use of the People Called Methodists, with a New Supplement 1874

The following notes are based on the above hymnbook.

The structure of the first part of this book is fascinating and it has been compared in its arrangement to the unfolding story of Bunyan's *Pilgrim's Progress.* The order in which the hymns are arranged trace the course of a sinner from his unregenerate state and outside the pale of true faith, coming then under the sound of the Gospel, being convicted of his sins and turning to Christ by faith for salvation, after this, like Bunyan's Pilgrim, pursuing the heavenly pathway and finally entering into the celestial city.

The opening scene is that of Evangelist in the marketplace of the city of destruction endeavouring to get a hearing for his message.

It is represented here by the hymn, *O for a thousand tongues to sing,* which has always traditionally been the first hymn in Methodist Hymn Books.

O for a thousand tongues to sing,
My great Redeemer's praise,
The glories of my God and King,
The triumphs of his grace.
My gracious Master and my God,
Assist me to proclaim
To spread through all the earth abroad,
The honours of thy name.

By every sort of scriptural appeal and argument he seeks to plead with the sinner to repent and believe. In doing so he describes the goodness of God, the brevity of life, the certainty of judgment, the glories of heaven, the terrors of hell.

Hymn no.2

Come sinners, to the Gospel feast,
Let every soul be Jesus' guest;
Ye need not one be left behind,
For God hath bidden all mankind.
Come, all ye souls by sin oppressed,
Ye restless wanderers after rest,
Ye poor, ye maimed and halt, and blind,
In Christ a hearty welcome find.

Hymn no.3

All ye that pass by, to Jesus draw near,
He utters a cry, ye sinners, given ear!
From hell to retrieve you, he spreads out his hands;
Now, now to receive you, he graciously stands.

Hymn no. 4

Ho! every one that thirsts, draw nigh!
'Tis God invites the fallen race,
Mercy and free salvation buy;
Buy wine and milk, and Gospel grace.

In describing the goodness of God in salvation he includes his father Samuel Wesley's hymn as no. 22

> Behold the Saviour of mankind nailed to the shameful tree!
> How vast the love which him inclined to bleed and die for thee.

In describing the brevity of life, he says in hymn no. 43

> And am I born to die?
> To lay this body down?
> And must my trembling spirit fly
> Into a world unknown.

In describing the Last Judgment, he says in hymn no. 55:

> Thou Judge of quick and dead,
> Before whose bar severe,
> With holy joy, or guilty dread,
> We all shall soon appear;
> Our cautioned souls prepare,
> For that tremendous day,
> And fill us now with watchful care,
> And stir us up to pray.

In the next scene the preacher returns to the chapel to pray for a blessing on the Word preached, this is illustrated by hymns 81–91 headed, "Praying for a Blessing."

Hymn no. 82 reads:

> Shepherd of souls, with pitying eye
> The thousands of our Israel see:
> To thee in their behalf we cry,
> Ourselves but newly found in thee.
> See where o'er desert wastes they err,
> And neither food nor feeder have,
> Nor fold, nor place of refuge near,
> For no man cares their souls to save.
> Extend to these like pardoning grace,
> To these be thy salvation showed:
> O add them to thy chosen race!
> O sprinkle all their hearts with blood!

Here we may add the characteristic marks of essential Methodism, indeed essential Christianity, are seen the great work of preaching and prayer.

But whilst he is here, those who have been touched by his preaching come to the chapel to find out more of the way of salvation.

Here he warns them of the dangers of mere formal religion and describes inward religion, the way of repentance and faith. He prays with them that they might come to a true reliance on Christ. In hymns 91–95 he describes the difference between mere formal religion and inward religion.

> O oft did I the assembly join,
> And near thine altar drew;
> A form of godliness was mine,
> The power I never knew.
> I rested in the outward law,
> Nor knew its deep design;
> The length and breadth I never saw,
> And heights, of love divine.

Here John Wesley is partly reflecting on his own experience as a failed missionary in Georgia in the American colonies.

Describing true inward heartfelt religion, hymn no. 96 says:

> How can a sinner know his sins on earth forgiven?
> How can my gracious Saviour show my name inscribed in heaven?
> What we have felt and seen, with confidence we tell;
> And published to the sons of men the signs infallible.
> We who in Christ believe, that he for us hath died,
> We all his unknown peace receive, and feel his blood applied;
> Exults our rising soul, unburdened of her load,
> And swells unutterably full of glory and of God.

Then in section three of the book hymns 99–182, we hear the prayers of those who are seeking salvation, praying for repentance, mourners convinced of sin, others convinced of backsliding, backsliders seeking to return.

Hymn no. 99 verse 2 contains the line:

> Since by thy light myself I see,
> Naked and poor and void of thee.

Hymn no. 109 reads:

Wretched, helpless and distressed
Ah, wither shall I fly?
Ever grasping after rest
I cannot find it nigh:
Naked, sick, and poor and blind,
Fast bound in sin and misery,
Friend of sinners, let me find
My life, my all, in thee!

This of course is so like Bunyan's description of the "Slough of Despond."

At last, in hymn no. 189 the seeker comes in sight of the Cross and begins to sing such hymns as:

Now I have found the ground wherein
Sure my soul's anchor may remain.
Jesus thy blood and righteousness
My beauty are my glorious dress.
Arise my soul, arise,
Shake of thy guilty fear
The bleeding sacrifice
In my behalf appears:
Before the throne my surety stands;
My name is written on his hands.

There then follows the sections which describe the various aspects of the Christian life for believers: rejoicing, fighting, praying, watching, working, suffering, seeking for full redemption, saved, interceding for the world.

This section includes such hymns as:

no.216 What shall I do my God to love, my loving God to praise?

no. 205 My God I am thine, what a comfort divine,
What a blessing to know that my Jesus is mine!
In the heavenly lamb thrice happy I am,
And my heart it doth dance,
At the sound of his name.

Then follows the equipping for the war; the sections of conflict, watchfulness, prayer, suffering, intercession, in which the many incidents of the Christian pilgrimage and warfare are abundantly and vividly set forth.

The way to the land of Beulah is mapped out and described in the great section *Seeking for full redemption*, and the blessedness of dwelling there set forth in the section *For believers saved*. The peace, joy, and happy fellowship of the *House Beautiful* are reflected in the *Hymns for the Society*. The climax is reached as, watching their friends pass into the glories of the country on the other side of the river, the rest, like Bunyan, "wish themselves among them" with the characteristically Methodist assurance of hope,

Hymn no. 539

Live till the Lord in glory come,
And wait his heaven to share:
Our Saviour now prepares our home:
Go on;—we'll meet you there.

This section also contains hymn no. 478, one of Methodism's classic hymns of fellowship which was and still is sung every year at the annual Methodist Conference.

And are we yet alive
To see each other's face?
Glory and praise to Jesus give
For his redeeming grace!
Preserved by power divine
To full salvation here,
Again in Jesu's praise we join
And in his sight appear.

Having described the plan of the first part of the book we are now ready to make some further general observations.

First of all, the fact that John and Charles Wesley's original collections still constituted the main body and first half of the new publication. This is significant because what we have in the first part of the book is a clear statement of Christian orthodoxy setting out essential marks of Evangelical experiential Christianity.

The period from 1870 to the end of the century was a time of increasing departure from Christian orthodoxy within the churches. Those responsible for the compilation of the 1874 Hymn Book are to be commended. While seeking to enhance Methodist worship by adding metrical Psalms and a larger selection of hymns of adoration and worship, together with hymns expressing the central doctrines of the Christian faith, they saw clearly that it was vital in uncertain times to preserve and emphasis the need for conversion and true spiritual experience.

We may also note the very high literary standard of the hymns included in the earlier collections: The Wesleys never spoke down to their hearers nor despised the faculty of the intellect. This is illustrated by the literary influences to be found in many of the hymns. Both John and Charles Wesley were tremendously well educated men, phenomenally well read. Hence literary influences found their way into their hymns.

For example, verse three of hymn no. 276 shows the influence of Milton's *Paradise Lost.* Compare Milton's lines:

As on dry land, between two crystal wells
Awed by the Rod of Moses so to stand
Divided till his rescue gained their share.

With:

Thine arm hath safely brought us
A way no more expected,
Than when the sheep passed through the deep,
By crystal walls protected.
Thy glory was our rearward,
Thine hand our lives did cover,
And we, even we, have past the sea,
And marched triumphant over.

The line in hymn no. 67 verse 5, *Those amaranthine bowers unalienably ours* is also taken from *Milton's Paradise Lost.*

When critics protested that the ordinary man in the street would not understand these lines Wesley added foot-notes to his hymns giving brief explanations and the literary source of the expressions. No one could ever accuse Charles Wesley of dumbing down.

Those amaranthine bowers
(Unalienably ours)
Bloom our infinite reward,
Rise, our permanent abode,

From the founded world prepared;
Purchased by the blood of God.

The line in hymn no. 186 *O love divine what hast thou done, My Lord my love is crucified,* is taken from *Ignatius's commentary on the Epistle to the Romans.*

Verse five of hymn no. 44:

Nothing is worth a thought beneath
But how I may escape the death
That never, never, dies;
How make mine own election sure,
And when I fail on earth, secure
A mansion in the skies.

is said to be based on a paragraph in Law's *Christian Perfection.*

A line from the Hymn, *When, quiet in my house I sit:*

I sink in blissful dreams away, And visions of eternal day.

is thought to have been taken from Alexander Pope's, *Eloisa to Abelard.*

To sounds of heavenly harps, she dies away,
And melts in visions of eternal day.

Of course the hymns of the Wesley brothers are full of Scriptural allusions and interpretations. Wesley did not take random verses of Scripture and set them to catchy tunes, often taking them right out of context, and simply repeating them *ad nausium* as some moderns have done.

The Wesley's hymns are Scriptural expositions and applications.

Jesu lover of my soul	Song of Solomon 2:10
Let me to thy bosom fly.	Isaiah 40:11, John 13:23
While the nearer waters roll	Psalm 69:1, Isaiah 43:2
Hide me, oh my Saviour hide,	Psalm 27:5, Psalm 32:7, Luke 2:11
Till the storm of life be past	Matthew 14:32
Safe into the haven guide	Psalm 107:30, John 6:21
O receive my soul last.	Acts 7:59

The Doctrinal Content of the Hymns

The Trinity

e.g. Hymn no. 643

> Hail, co-essential three, in mystic unity!
> Father, Son and Spirit hail! God by heaven and earth adored,
> God incomprehensible; one supreme Almighty Lord.

The Creation

Hymn no. 653

> Father of earth and sky, thy name we magnify:
> O that the earth and heaven might join, thy perfections to proclaim;
> Praise the attributes divine, fear and love thy awful name!

Providence

Hymn no. 650 v.3

> Through all his mighty works amazing wisdom shines,
> Confounds the powers of hell and breaks their dark designs;
> Strong is his arm, and shall fulfil his great decrees and sovereign will.

The Incarnation

> When the fullness of the time was come, God sent forth his Son, made of a woman, made under the law, to redeem them that were under the law, that we might receive the adoption of sons. (Galatians 4:4–5)

The incarnation of God, taking flesh and dwelling amongst us here,

> And the Word was made flesh, and dwelt among us, (and we beheld his glory, the glory as of the only begotten of the Father,) full of grace and truth. (John 1:14)

The hymn *Hark the Herald Angels Sing*, has been described as one of the greatest hymns on the Incarnation ever written.

We give this sublime hymn in its original form, showing the way each of the lines in and of themselves are expositions and summaries of Scripture.

Hark how all the welkin rings,	Luke 2:13–14
Glory to the King of Kings,	Rev. 17:14, 19:16
Peace on earth, and mercy mild,	Luke 2:14, 1 Tim. 1: 2
God and sinners reconciled!	Rom.5:11, 2 Cor. 5:18–20
Joyful, all ye nations rise,	Ps. 67:4, Rom 15:9–10
Join the triumph of the skies,	Luke 2:15
Universal nature say	Rev. 5:13
Christ the Lord is born today!	Luke 2:11
Christ by highest heaven adored,	Dan. 7:13, Heb. 1:6, Rev. 5: 8
Christ, the everlasting Lord,	Isa. 63:16
Late in time behold him come,	Gal. 4:4, Heb. 1:2, 1 Pet. 1:20
Offspring of a virgin's womb.	Matt. 1:18. Lk. 1:34
Veiled in flesh, the Godhead see,	Heb. 10:20
Hail, the incarnate Deity!	John 1: 14
Pleased as Man with men t' appear	1 Cor. 15:47, 2 Tim. 1:10
Jesus, our Immanuel here!	Isa. 7:14
Hail the heavenly Prince of Peace!	Isa. 9:6
Hail the Sun of Righteousness!	Isa. 32:1, Mal. 4:2, Jer. 23: 6
Light and life to all he brings,	John 1:4, 8:12
Risen with healing in his wings.	Mal. 4:2
Mild he lays his glory by,	John 10:17–18, 17:5
Born that man no more may die,	Rom. 6:8, 1 Cor 15:22, 2 Tim. 1:10
Born to raise the sons of earth,	1 Cor. 15:47, Heb. 2:10
Born to give them second birth.	John 3:3
Come, Desire of nations, come,	Hag. 2:7
Fix in us thy humble home,	Isa. 57:15, Phil. 2:8
Rise, the woman's conquering Seed,	Gal. 3:16, Rev. 19:15–16
Bruise in us the serpent's head.	Gen. 3:15
Now display by saving power,	Rom. 1:16
Ruined nature now restore,	Gen. 3:16, Rom. 8:21, 1 Cor. 15:21–2
Now in mystic union join	
Thine to ours, and ours to thine	Eph. 5:28–32
Adam's likeness, Lord, efface,	1 Cor. 15:47, 49
Stamp thine image in its place,	
Second Adam from above	1 Cor. 15:45, 47
Reinstate us in thy love!	1 Cor. 15:22, 2 Cor. 5:18–20
Let us thee, though lost, regain,	1 Cor. 15:22, Phil. 3:7–8

Thee the Life, the inner Man;	John 14:6, Eph. 3:16, 1 Pet. 3:4
O! to all thyself, impart,	
Formed in each believing heart.	Gal.4: 19, Eph. 3:17

What we have sought to show here could be done with all the great doctrinal hymns of Charles Wesley as can be seen in two other examples below.

The Atonement

Arise, my soul, arise	Isa. 60:1, Eph. 5:14
Shake off thy guilty fears;	Ps. 51:4, 14, Heb. 10:31, 1 Jn. 4:18
The bleeding sacrifice	Lev. 16:14–16, 17:11, Rom. 3:25, Heb. 9:12–14 10:19, 13:12, 1 Pet. 1:19
In my behalf appears;	Isa. 53:4–5, 1 Cor. 15:3, Gal. 2:20
Before thy throne, my Surety stands;	Heb. 4:14, 7:22, 25, Rev. 5:6
My name is written on his hands.	Isa. 49:16

The Resurrection

Christ the Lord is risen today,	Mark 16:6, Luke 24:6
Sons of men and angels say!	Matt. 28:6, Luke 24:34, John 20:18
Raise your joys and triumphs high,	Col. 2:15
Sing ye heavens, and earth reply	Isa. 49:13
Love's redeeming work is done,	Rom. 6: 9–10
Fought the fight, the battle won:	Luke 11:22, Col. 2:15
Lo! Our Sun's eclipse is o'er,	Mal. 4:2, Luke 23:45
Lo! He sets in blood, no more.	Isa. 60:20

An excellent and fuller treatment of examples of all the great themes of Wesley's hymns, together with Scriptural references can be found in John Lawson's very helpful work *A Thousand Tongues*.

Henry Bett writing in his *The Hymns of Methodism*, comments:

> The best work of Charles Wesley abides for the universal Church in *The Collection of Hymns for the Use of the People called Methodists* of 1780.—an anthology, selected mainly from the vast mass of his brothers works by John Wesley. The supreme skill with which this selection was made has not been sufficiently recognised. It is only when you go through the original volumes of Charles Wesley's verse, and note the way in which his brother chose the best of the hymns, and then omitted from these, the weaker stanzas, until out of a long

string of verses of very varied quality there often emerges a hymn of sustained excellence, which is a complete lyric in itself—it is only after such a study that one realises the excellence of John Wesley's editorial work. Bernard L. Manning wrote of the collection of 1780: "you may think my language about the hymns extravagant: therefore, I repeat it in stronger terms. This little book ranks in Christian literature with the Psalms, the Book of Common Prayer … in its own way. It is perfect, unapproachable, elemental in its perfection. You cannot alter it, except to mar it; it is a work of supreme devotional art by a religious genius."

The hymns of Methodism stand alone, in many respects, in the religious literature of the world. They are unique in their intimate connection with one of the greatest spiritual movements of history, for the very genius of the Evangelical Revival is in their burning lines: they enshrine what has been well called "the holy, compassionate, believing spirit of the early Methodism. They constitute the greatest body of devotional verse in the English language".

Henry Bett, *The Hymns of Methodism* (Epworth Press, 1956)

Bibliography

A Collection of Hymns for the Use of the People called Methodists, 1780

John Wesley (Methodist Conference Office, City Road 1804)

Wesley's Hymns with Tunes (Wesleyan Conference Office, 2 Castle Street, City Road, London, 1877)

John Telford, *The Methodist Hymn Book Illustrated* (Epworth Press, 1922)

W.J. Townsend, H.B. Workmen, George Eayrs, *A New History of Methodism* (Hodder and Stoughton, London: 1909)

Henry Bett, *The Hymns of Methodism* (Epworth Press, 1956)

John Lawson, *A Thousand Tongues* (Exeter: The Paternoster Press, 1987)

37. Handel's *Messiah*

"My Lord, I should be sorry if I only entertained them; I wish to make them better." (Handel's reply to Lord Kinnoul, who congratulated him on the noble entertainment he had just given to the town (Dublin).)

HANDEL'S *MESSIAH* WAS COMPOSED IN 1741, BY WHICH TIME GEORGE Frederick Handel was a naturalised British subject. He was born in Halle, Saxony, Germany, in 1684, the son of a surgeon barber. This is the date found on the tombstone and monument in Westminster Abbey. Due to changes in the Gregorian Calendar there is a slight mix-up between the old and new dates, and sometimes his birth date is given as 1685.

From a very early age he displayed exceptional musical talents, but received little encouragement from his father, who had intended him for the study of Civil Law. His opposition took the practical shape of consigning to the flames all the musical toys, drums, trumpets, and so forth, with which the boy had filled his nursery. George Frederick himself was packed off to school, although he cannot very well have been more than five or six years old. However, in spite of this opposition, he was not altogether cut off from his beloved music. He contrived with the aid of his aunt, or possibly his mother, to smuggle a clavichord, no doubt one of the miniature sort, into the loft at the top of the house. There, in the dead of night he would creep and practice to his heart's content, while the rest of the household slept unawares.

When Handel was seven years old his talents came to the attention of Duke Adolf of Wiessenfels. Handel's father had taken him with him on a visit to the duke's estate where a family relative served on his staff. The young boy found his way to the household Chapel and was playing the organ when the duke discovered him. The duke was much impressed and surprised at his extraordinary talents and convinced Handel's father that he should allow him to study music. On their return back to Halle the young boy was put under the instruction of Friedrich Wilhelm Zachow, the organist at Liebfrauen.

In 1703 he went to Hamburg and played the violin in the orchestra of the Opera House. Here his first opera, *Almira,* was produced in 1705. After this he went to Italy for three years to study the methods of Italian opera composers, and it was there he produced several other operas with great success.

In 1710 Handel returned to Germany, and was appointed "Chapel-master" to the Elector of Hanover, afterwards George I of England. The same year he came to England, where, apart from a few short visits to Germany, he spent the remainder of his life. He introduced himself to English audiences with his opera *Rinaldo*, which aroused great enthusiasm. Other operas followed; also a *Te Deum* to celebrate the peace of Utrecht in 1713. For some time, he was organist to the Duke of Chandos at Canons, Edgware. In 1719, the *Royal Academy of Music* was established for the performance of opera, and Handel specially composed many operas for this society, which came to an end in 1728. After this he became interested in other operatic schemes, which, however, were unsuccessful owing to financial difficulties, quarrels between singers, and the opposition of rival composers.

He next turned to oratorios, and began a series of sacred works by which he is chiefly remembered today. Amongst these were *Saul, Israel in Egypt* composed in 1739, the *Messiah* and *Samson* in 1741, *Judas Maccabeus* in 1746, and his last oratorio, *Jepthah* in 1751.

Shortly after this he became totally blind and died on April 14, 1759.

In regard to Handel's character and faith we may note the remark of William Coxe, one of Handel's first biographers.

> It is true indeed, that the composer was not of a temper to treat singers with great respect; he considered them, perhaps too much, as mere instruments, which gave utterance to that harmony, which he was so distinguished an author. He possessed the virtuosity and inflexibility of genius... In temper he was irascible, impatient of contradiction, but not vindictive; jealous of his musical pre-eminence, and tenacious in all points which regarded his professional honour.

William Coxe, *Anecdotes of George Frederick Handel and John Christopher Smit*h, reprints of the 1799 first edition. Quoted by Edward Blakeman, Handel, p. 26, Faber and Faber, 2009

Also the following reminiscence of Charles Burney who knew him well and records an anecdote from Handel's visit to Dublin in 1742.

> One night, while Handel was in Dublin, Dubourg having a solo part in a song and a close to make, ad libitum, he wandered about in different keys a great while, and seemed indeed a little bewildered, and uncertain of his original key… But, at length, coming to the shake, which was to terminate this long close, Handel, to the great delight of the audience, and augmentation of applause, cried out loud enough to be heard in the most remote parts of the theatre: "You are welcome home, Mr Dubourg." Ibid p.26

Handel could also be very cutting in his remarks regarding other composers. Once when asked his opinion of the composer Gluck, he answered:

> He knows no more of contrapunto, as mein cook, Waltz.

This remark is only properly understood when it is remembered that Handel did have a cook, whose name was Gustavus Waltz.

Handel loved the organ and liked nothing better than to play in St Paul's Cathedral for the evening service, which began at 3pm. After the service none could coax him down from the organ loft. He often remained until eight or nine o'clock at night, remembering that the unfortunate organ blower had to remain on duty all that time.

Coming to Handel's religious beliefs Charles Burney also notes:

> Handel, though he was rough in his language at times, and in the habit of swearing, (a vice more in fashion then than later in the century), in his later life he was truly pious, constantly attending public prayers, twice a day, winter and summer, both in London and Tonbridge.
>
> Edward Blakeman, *Handel*, p. 23

Another contemporary of Handel's, John Hawkins also left testimony of Handel's later life of piety.

> For the last two or three years of his life he was used to attend divine service in his own parish church of St George, Hanover Square, where, during the prayers, the eyes that at this instant are employed,

in a faint portrayal of his excellences, have seen him on his knees, expressing by his looks and gesticulations the utmost fervour of devotion. Ibid. p.23

The same writer continues to inform us:

"In his religion he was of the Lutheran profession; in which he was not such a bigot as to decline a general conformity with that of the country which he had chosen for his residence... And he would often speak of it as one of the great felicities of his life that he was settled in a country where no man suffers any molestation or inconvenience on account of his religious principles."

To quote Coxe again:

"His great delight was derived from his attachment to his own science, and he experienced particular satisfaction from religious principles in presiding at the organ in the Cathedral Church of St Paul. He frequently declared in conversation, the high gratification enjoyed in setting the Scriptures to music, and how greatly he was edified by contemplating the sublime passages abounding in the sacred writings... His pen... is sublime, affecting, animated, and devoted, without the gloom of superstition to the service of God."

Again:

"Handel's religious disposition was not a mere display, it was amply productive of religion's best fruit, charity; and this liberal sentiment not only influenced him in the day of prosperity, but even when standing on the very brink of ruin."

Edward Blakeman, p. 24

In Handel's later life he took a particular interest in the work of Thomas Corum's *Foundling Hospital* in London. It is well-known that the premiere performance of the *Messiah* in Dublin, was devoted to the support of various charitable causes in that city.

Handel's Christian faith again is evident in his own account of the composition of the *Messiah*. He himself described his experience as follows. His diary records shutting himself away and beginning to compose *Messiah* on August 22nd. During this time, he was totally absorbed in his task and never left the house at all. His servant brought him food, but it was seldom touched when he returned to collect the plate. He completed the draft of Part 1 on August 28th. On 6th

September he completed the draft of part II. After writing out the *Hallelujah Chorus*, he is reported to have exclaimed to his servant with tears in his eyes, "I did think I did see all heaven before me, and the great God Himself seated on His throne, with his Company of Angels."

On 12 September, he completed the draft of Part III.

He further describes this time he spent, again quoting the words of St Paul:

> Whether in the body, I cannot tell; whether out of the body, I cannot tell: God, knoweth. 2 Corinthians 12:2

It is also said regarding the *Hallelujah Chorus* that it was inspired by a recollection of Handel's when he was taken to hear the great Welsh revival preacher Daniel Rowlands. Daniel Rowlands was preaching on the text from Revelation 19:6. "Hallelujah, for the Lord God omnipotent reigneth".

As Daniel Rowland thundered out his text, *The Lord God omnipotent reigneth,* the Welsh congregation echoed back "Hallelujah" "Hallelujah". The scene greatly moved Handel, and has since been forever immortalised in the *Hallelujah Chorus.*

When the Messiah was first performed in Dublin, 13 April 1742, the proceeds were shared between three Dublin charities, the chief being Mercer's Hospital but also the Charitable Infirmary and the Society for the Relief of Prisoners. It is also said that the funds raised enabled 142 people to be released from the debtor's prison.

The *Dublin Newsletter* reported:

> Mr Handel's new sacred Oratorio… far surpasses anything of that nature which has been performed in this or any other Kingdom.

This was indeed a remarkable review for a first performance. In an attempt to satisfy some of the extra demand for seating on the first night, ladies were urged to come without hoops in their dresses and gentlemen to come without swords. The extra space this created increase the capacity of the hall from 600 to 700. Handel conducted from the harpsichord and, along with all the soloists, gave his services free.

The following year King George II attended the performance and during the singing of the *Hallelujah Chorus* rose to his feet, initiating a tradition which has lasted for well over two centuries.

It is also said that in later years, on hearing the *Hallelujah Chorus* sung, he wept like a child and exclaimed … "He is the Master of us All".

It is important when looking at the life of Handel to note the growing seriousness of his character and music as time went on. When he first arrived in England he sought the patronage of the court, so-called privileged and polished society. He soon however abandoned this course, discovering that this courtly and polished society was in fact beneath the surface, coarse, selfish and sceptical.

He quickly changed to what we might call a freelance musician and composer, producing popular operas on a commercial basis. Independent of any patronage he was involved in his own publicity and promotion, organising his own publications and even selling them from his house in Brook Street.

His operas were generally well received by the rising middle classes. Amongst his works at this time was the *Beggars Opera*, a humorous, light-hearted and somewhat ribald production which filled the opera house night after night.

However, during this time a change was coming over the country. Earlier in the century Montesquieu, after a visit to England, had commented: "Everyone laughs if one talks of religion in England." Morality was out of fashion, drunkenness and obscenity were thought no disgrace to the highest in the land. At this time also William Pitt was beginning an attempt to lift the moral tone and standards in the realm of politics. Handel was turning away from the production of popular operas to the more serious oratorios that have since secured his lasting fame.

Behind these movements was of course the preaching of John Wesley, George Whitfield and others, and the increasing influence of what we today call the 18th-Century Revival.

R.A.Streatfield rightly observes:

> At this time neither Pitt nor Handel could have done what they did, had not English thought and feeling been guided to higher levels by the genius of one of the greatest men produced by the 18th-century—John Wesley. To him, the vast gradual change that came over society during the latter years of Walpole's rule was mainly due. The religious struggles of the Civil War and the political struggles of the Revolution had left in the minds of the middle-class one overpowering sentiment—a craving for peace. This craving was fostered by Walpole, who saw better than anyone what England

> wanted, became the parent of our later commercial prosperity, but with regard to the higher claims of life, it induced something very like lethargy. Of the attitude of society towards these higher claims during the first half of the century nothing positive can be stated. Under the first two Georges, the upper-class was frankly materialistic, the middle-class apathetic, and the lower class not far removed from sheer brutalisation.
>
> Doubtless, beneath this lethargic exterior England was still religious, though the old Puritan spirit seemed asleep. It was the voice of Wesley that woke it to new life. The religious revival that he inaugurated is unparalleled in the history of the English people. It penetrated every part of the kingdom and every strata of society. Its strength and importance lay in the fact that its results were not merely religious. Pitt's appeal was not religious, Handel's appeal was not religious at first, though his oratorios dealt for the most part with subjects technically termed sacred as opposed to secular. Both men appealed to the higher instincts of the nation from a wider standpoint, but without the influence of Wesley (and Whitefield) ever preaching the seriousness of life and the responsibility of the individual, they would have been the voices of men crying in the wilderness. The audience that guffawed over the *Beggar's Opera* and the audience that rose to its feet to honour the sublime strains of *The Messiah* were one and the same, but Wesley had breathed new life into dead souls, had opened blind eyes and unstopped deaf ears, had lifted England from its slough of sensual depravity, and made it capable of understanding the noblest outpourings of human genius.
>
> *Handel*, R.A. Streatfield, p.211

The same writer R.A. Streatfield does not believe Handel possessed the same depth of spirituality as did Bach, but we must maintain that Handel, certainly in later years possessed a true and genuine faith in Christ. Like Milton, blind in his later years and very much aware of his approaching demise, he expressed a desire that he might breathe his last on Good Friday, in hopes, he said, of "meeting his good God, and his sweet Lord and Saviour on the day of his Resurrection", meaning the third day, the Easter Sunday following.

In actual fact, he died on Easter Saturday at about 8 am. One of his friends, Bernard Granville who was with him at the end recorded, that he forgave all those who had injured him during life, and as he said, "let all their legacies stand."

> He died as he lived—a good Christian, with a sense of his duty to God and man, and lived in perfect charity with all the world.

His funeral service was preached in Westminster Abbey by Dr Pearce, Bishop of Rochester; and at his own expense a marble monument was erected to his memory, the work of the sculptor, Roubiliac.

The inscription being, "I know that my Redeemer liveth."

Handel's Messiah, it's important and polemic libretto—Charles Jennens Librettist

The story of Charles Jennens is a fascinating one. Jennens was a firm friend to Handel over a long period of time. He provided Handel with libretto's, for the oratorios *Saul*, *Belshazzar*, most likely *Israel in Egypt*, and *L' Allegro*. He had also helped to finance the publication of every Handel score since the mid-1720s. Handel was a frequent visitor to Jennens estate *Gopsal Hall* in Leicestershire. It was also a venue where John Wesley enjoyed hospitality. The hymn tune *Gopsal*, composed by Handel, and set to Charles Wesley's hymn, *Rejoice, the Lord is King!* reminds us of this connection. Jennens was an old-fashioned High Churchman, a genuine Christian and committed to the inspiration and inerrancy of Scripture.

We need to remember at this time, alongside the general decline in public morality so characteristic of the first part of the 18th-century there grew up the heresy of Deism. Deism was the view that our knowledge of God comes through reason rather than through revelation. Robert Boyle, founder of *The Royal Society* had sought to counter this teaching, as early as 1691, when he instituted the annual Boyle Lectures with the aim of refuting the teachings of *Atheists, Deist, Jews, and Mohammedans.* In England Deism was widely propagated by John Toland in his *Christianity, not Mysterious* (1696). Another advocate of these views was Matthew Tindal in his *Christianity*

as Old as Creation (1730). The Deists effectively dispensed with the need for faith or personal religion. The Deist also attacked the concept of the Trinity, specifically denying the personal nature of the Father and the Son. It further sought to undermine belief in the Bible as the inspired divine revelation of God, the miracles and the prophecies of Scripture, bearing the brunt of their attack. The Deist, Antony Collins, in his *A Discourse on the Grounds and Reasons of the Christian Religion* (1724) sought to prove that the fulfilment of the Old Testament prophecies was invalid as an argument for inspiration. He maintained as others did, that the Old Testament prophecies could only be applied to Jesus Christ allegorically, and as he maintained this is no proof. Further, he taught that the whole of Christian revelation is contained in the Old Testament. By this he meant that the New Testament contains nothing new, and further, the Old Testament has become corrupt in transmission and is therefore unreliable. What remains in the Bible, according to Collins, was that it merely republished the laws of nature, which had been since the beginning of time.

Bishop Butler in his renowned *Analogy of the Christian Religion, Natural and Revealed* was one who sought to refute the teachings of Deism.

What is significant for our present subject is the number of figures in Handel's circle who actively resisted and opposed the teachings of the Deists. These, included two of his librettists, Miller and Morell, both clergymen and strong opponents of Deism. Dr Patrick Delany, who had published his *Defence of Orthodoxy* in 1732. Another, Humphreys, had written a three volume commentary on the Bible, again defending and defining the inspiration and inerrancy of Scripture. Added to these was Charles Jennens, who like Miller and Morell used the librettos of Handel's oratorios to refute Deism.

There is a very useful passage in David Daniell's *The Bible in English*, where he demonstrates Jennens use of the libretto of *The Messiah*, to expose the falsity of the teachings of the Deists.

> The libretto of the Messiah clearly sets out to declare that the Jesus Christ of the Gospels, "born in the City of David, a Saviour, which is Christ the Lord", is the fulfilment of the Old Testament hopes and prophecies. Daniell states that all the passages before part 14 of the Oratorio are Old Testament prophecies. From "Glory to God" (17), which is the chorus of the angels from Luke, to the end of the Oratorio, thirty-four more numbers in all, twenty-three are either

> the words of Old Testament prophecies, or of Psalms with prophetic intent. Part 3 of Messiah begins, famously, with the single soprano upward reach of haunting beauty, "I know that my Redeemer Liveth."
>
> (45; from Job 19:25), a statement of personal faith if ever there was one, ... Towards the end of that number, the change of musical subject at "For now is Christ risen from the dead" marks the change to New Testament fulfilment, the words of all Messiah's numbers 46–51 being from Paul at the end of that 1 Corinthians chapter, 15, which also supplies the words for all those six numbers, then moving to Romans 8 and Revelation 5 for the last two numbers of the Oratorio.
>
> Jennens has sometimes been said to have been less original than might at first appear, as his Bible passages occur in those sequences in various parts of the Book of Common Prayer. He could have found the passages for Part 1 in the Christmas service, and for Part 3 in the Burial service. That is so obvious that it hardly needs saying. The Part 2 passages are more scattered, but they are all present somewhere in the Prayer Book at strong liturgical moments. The argument needs to be turned, both upside down and round. Not only does the Prayer Book naturally quote the texts that have been central to Christians since the faith began, so that any searcher after Old and New Testament statements of the Good News is going to arrive at these (as well as others, of course, not present): in that sense Jennens and the Prayer Book coincide in orthodoxy. More importantly, the very fact that these are, to state it rather gaudily, jewels of the Prayer Book, underlines Jennens's High Church orthodoxy. The future of the country, he is saying, has to lie in the daily worship in its church, and in the biblical story contained in its liturgical year, wherein is contained all the elements that call out personal faith. The Bible has a hundred thousand times the number of texts here used, and the Church Fathers a million times more: Jennens could have made a compelling libretto, still called Messiah, out of all sorts of great stuff. He chose these, the core of his church's Bible in daily use."
>
> *The Bible in English*, pp. 567–8

We might conclude by also noting that the oratorios *Belshazzar* and *Hercules,* again librettos by Charles Jennens, also contained refutations of Deism.

Handel's last two oratorios *Theodora* and *Jephtha,* both with librettos by Morell, each in their turn are attacks on Deism, refuting Deism's deterministic philosophy, and affirming the Christian teaching of Resurrection.

Bibliography

R.A. Streatfield, *Handel* (London: Methuen and Co., 1910)
Edward Blakeman, *Handel* (London: Faber and Faber, 2009)
Robert Bashford, *Focus on Jesus, a Guide to the Messiah* (The Latimer Trust, 2020)
David Daniell, *The Bible in English* (New Haven, CT: Yale University Press, 2003)
Ruth Smith, *Handel's Oratorios and Eighteenth Century Thought* (Cambridge University Press, 1995)

38. William Carey—*An Enquiry into the Obligations of Christians to Use Means for the Conversion of the Heathen* 1792

William Carey was born August 17, 1761, at Paulerspury near Northampton. His father was a weaver (a descendant of James Carey, curate of that parish from 1624 to 1630), also parish clerk and village school-master, so that William had a fair common-school education. At fourteen he was bound and apprenticed to a shoemaker, but his thirst for knowledge was so quenchless that he habitually worked with a book before him. Finding many Greek words which he could not understand in a commentary, he sought help from Tom Jones, a weaver, who had earlier received something of a classical education but had turned away from it. Carey became familiar with the works of Jeremy Taylor and such other authors as he could gain access to; and Thomas Scott, the Bible commentator, predicted that this *plodder* would prove no ordinary man. He was converted through the testimony of William Manning, his shop mate who was a Dissenter, led him to Christ; and at twenty-two he was baptised in the river New, near Dr Doddridge's chapel, Northampton, by John Ryland, junior. The baptism of a poor journeyman shoe-maker excited little interest, but John Ryland was moved to speak on a prophetic text that day: "The last

shall be First." Carey's chief desire, after his conversion was to qualify himself for usefulness, and his remarkable gift for acquiring languages soon made him master of Latin, Greek, Hebrew, German and French. He set up a small school, but he could not control the children, and this venture was not a success. Soon he moved to Moulton, Northamptonshire, where under the advice of Mr Sutcliffe, he applied to the Church at Olney for admission into the ministry. The body of believers he met there condescended to take him into its membership, and, on hearing him preach, "resolved" that he be "allowed" to preach elsewhere in small places, and that he should meet them again at some future occasion to assess his progress in preaching.

While all this was going on he had developed an interest in geography, and had obtained a copy of Captain Cook's *Voyages Around the World*. He had made a globe of leather, and considering the nations of the world he calculated that 400 millions of people had never heard of Christ.

He moved from his small church in Moulton, where some of its members had given him a great deal of trouble and heartache, to a church in Leicester, Harvey Lane, where he again served as pastor and was predecessor to the famous Robert Hall. It was in Leicester that out of his growing concern for the heathen he wrote his famous book, *Enquiry into the Obligations of Christians to use Means for the Conversion of the Heathen,* first published in 1792. (This was an eighty-seven-page manuscript, popularly known as his *Enquiry.*)

In its introduction, Carey poses the question of whether our Lord's teaching recorded in Matthew 28:18–20 remains an obligation on Christians through all time.

Section 1, includes Carey's treatment of Matthew 28:18–20 in relation to Christians of the late Eighteenth-century.

Section 2, reviews former attempts to convert various peoples of the world to Christianity; in this chapter is Carey's account of Christian missionary history, including exposition of Paul's four missionary journeys as recorded in the Acts of the Apostles.

Section 3 contains a survey of the world's countries, their land size, populations, and religious affiliations. Carey presents twenty-three tables of detailed statistical information, followed by a discussion of the information in the tables.

In section 4, Carey offers a defence in support of sending Christian missionaries to the peoples of the world who had not yet heard the message of the Gospel.

Finally, in the last section, Section 5, he presents an argument in support of the church's duty to promote missionary endeavours to people who had not so far heard the message of salvation.

In Leicester Carey continued to preach in Harvey Lane, also to teach the school, and work at the cobbler's bench, whilst also pursuing his work on languages and his ever-growing interest in the work of overseas mission.

He brought his concern to a meeting of ministers, where he was famously told by Ryland: "When God pleases to convert the heathen, he will do it without your aid or mine."

Though daunted, he was later to find out that Fuller, Sutcliffe, Pearce and the young Ryland shared his views on foreign mission, although Stennett and Booth stood aloof. In the October meeting of ministers, 1791, Sutcliffe preached on being "Very jealous for the Lord of Hosts," and Fuller on the "Pernicious Influences of Delay," when the meeting resolved that "something should be done."

The Association met at Nottingham, May 31, 1792, when Carey preached his famous sermon from Isaiah 54:2–3:

> "Enlarge the place of thy tent, and let them stretch forth the curtains of thine habitations: lengthen thy chords, and strengthen thy stakes;
>
> For thou shalt break forth on the right hand and on the left; and thy seed shall inherit the Gentiles, and make the desolate cities to be inhabited."

In this sermon. Carey represented the church as a poor widow living in a cottage by herself. The voice, "Thy Maker is thy Husband," told her to look for an increase of family; therefore, she must enlarge her tent, and "expect great things from God, and attempt great things for God."

The churches were seized with a sense of criminal neglect; but even then they were about to adjourn without doing anything but weep, when Carey, seizing Fuller's hand, demanded that the first step be taken on the spot. His heart was breaking, and his sobs compelled the assembly to stop. It was resolved, "That a plan be prepared against the next ministers meeting at Kettering, for the establishment of a society for propagating the Gospel among the heathen." Such a meeting was held October 2nd, 1792, and at its closed twelve men met in the parlour of Mrs Wallis, a widow, and formed the first Baptist Missionary Society, originally called, *Particular Baptist Society for the Propagation of the Gospel amongst the Heathen.* Andrew Fuller was made Secretary, Reynold Hogg, Treasurer; with Ryland, Sutcliffe, Carey, and afterwards Pearce, as the Committee of management. They made a subscription out of their penury realising £132s 6d. Pearce preached on the subject in his own church, and soon sent "the surprising sum of £70 to the Society."

In April, 1793, Carey and Thomas set off for India, despite the opposition of the *East India Company*, the indifference of their own brethren, and the disdain of the public; and did such missionary work there as has not been known since the Apostolic Age.

(Based on Thomas Armitage, *History of the Baptists*, pp. 579–581)

William Carey went to India as the first modern missionary to the subcontinent with a burning desire to bring the Gospel of redeeming grace to that benighted people ... He has justly been called by some as *The Maker of Modern India*. The impact of Carey's book, the *Enquiry* and his untiring multiplicity of endeavours to bring the Gospel to the people of India, had far-reaching and enormous beneficial consequences stretching down to the present day. Right from the start he and other pioneer missionaries served that country by turning the various dialects and languages of India into literary languages, which hence became the foundation of Indian modern education. These missionary figures and later Christian civil servants, such as Charles Grant, Charles Trevelyan and the MP for Leeds, Lord Macaulay, were motivated by the idea and vision of giving India the tools for progress, unity and eventual self-government.

William Carey established India's first vernacular college for the purpose of providing higher education, as well as a network of free schools to provide elementary education for the poor. He also regularly lectured on science, astronomy and zoology. India's scientific interest began with his arrival. He excelled in botany, gardening, forestry and agriculture and was the founder of the Royal Horticultural Society of India. He worked hard to challenge the caste system. He translated the Bible into six Asian languages. He challenged the misrule of the East India Company; fought for women's rights, and succeeded in abolishing the practice of Sati (widow burning), researching Hindu law to prove it was in no way commanded by it. He also translated various Indian classics into English. The aim of William Carey and his successors was to liberate India from the misrule of the moguls and to make it a self-governing, democratic country.

Charles Trevelyan, a fellow evangelical Christian and a civil servant employed by the East India Company produced a book in 1838 entitled, *On the Education of the People of India*. He said:

> "The existing connection between two such distant countries as England and India, cannot, in the nature of things be permanent. No effort of policy can prevent the natives from untimely regaining their independence, but there are two ways of arriving at this point.

> One of these is through the medium of revolution; the other through that of reform... Revolution must end in the complete alienation of mind and separation of interests between ourselves and the Indian people, the other, reform, in a permanent alliance, founded on mutual benefit and goodwill. The only means at our disposal for preventing revolution and securing... the result of reform is, to set the natives on the process of European improvement. The natives will have independence after first learning how to make use of it, and we shall exchange profitable subjects for still more profitable allies... trained by us to happiness and independence, and endowed with our learning and political institutions, India will remain the proudest monument of British benevolence."

Charles Grant, a member of the Clapham Sect also mentioned above, authored a book in the 1790s entitled *A Manifesto for Indian Freedom.*

Lord Macauley, a member of the same group and a parliamentarian gave a speech before the House of Commons in 1833, the main points of that speech being:

> A call for greater investment in the development of that country (India).
>
> Avoidance of the rise of racism.
>
> The need to establish a fair and sound legal code.
>
> Reform of the present legal code,
>
> Establishment of moral policies of no discrimination on account of colour, descent, or religion.
>
> Policy of educating Indians for future self-government.
>
> The abolishment of tyrannical oppression.
>
> Building of a sense of duty that flows from God's sovereignty.

This same group supported the establishment of newspapers and a free press in India. They campaigned for the emancipation of women, and sought to abolish waste of money, waste of time, and waste of human lives.

Vishal Mangalwadi, a contemporary Indian historian comments:

> A survey of India's history shows that such commitment on the

> part of 19th-century evangelical Christians was the womb of India's freedom.

The influence of Carey's book continued well into the 19th century. Philip Mason, the author of *The Men Who Ruled India* identifies Sir Richard Temple 1800–1874, who from the 1850s to the 1870s held some of the most important posts in the Government of India, as a man of tremendous vision and ceaseless action, who "went everywhere and saw everything." Municipalities, dispensaries, primary schools, district boards; he surveyed, he created, built, endowed, set up and sometimes severely criticised the way that some organisations were run. He played an important part in the preparation of Indians for democracy. Lord Rippon continued Temples work and issued the famous Local Self-Government Resolution on May 18, 1882. Within a few years, 200 district boards, 500 sub-district boards, and over 700 municipal boards were established. Until then all districts were administered entirely by the British officers of the Indian Civil Service, without local guidance or accountability.

Vishal Mangalwadi, from whose work the above paragraph is derived, comments:

> The Democratisation of local government in India was not a job, assigned by the British Government, to men such as Richard Temple. The inspiration for this effort came directly from William Carey's missionary manifesto and Charles Grant's Evangelical Manifesto for India's freedom.

Temple acknowledged his debt to Carey in London in 1883, during his lecture to the *Baptist Missionary Society* that Carey had founded. Some of the arguments he used in this lecture, came directly from Grant.

> I have felt it my peculiar duty to be present on this occasion because, as Lieutenant-Governor of Bengal, I have been specially acquainted with the Baptist missions in the province. The names of Carey, and Ward, and Marshman, which you read about, are to me, living memories … These are memories of men who were pioneers of civilisation and of humane refinement … India presents the greatest of all fields for missionary exertion … In respect to our moral responsibilities before God and man, India is a country which, of all others, we are bound to enlighten with eternal truth …

> If you believe the Bible, if you are resolved to obey its ennobling dictates, then I ask you whether you are not bound, collectively and individually, to do your utmost to spread over the world, into its very utmost regions and among its most degraded tribes and classes, that light which emanated from Palestine? ... Do you believe that the Providence which permits us to rule over so much of the globe, allows it merely for our national, our temporal, our secular aggrandisement? Remember that every island, every valley, every continent which we occupy politically we are bound (by our Lord) to enlighten morally and spiritually. It should be a matter of thankfulness to us that ... The results of our domination and material progress and civilisation were followed by moral and spiritual enlightenment. Therefore, it is a matter of thankfulness to us to find that the British qualities, the valour and genius, the statecraft and policy, are, under Providence, over-ruled for the good of the human race. And of that good, I venture to think, as a man of the world, as a politician, that one of the most potent instruments consist in those missionary exertions which we are here assembled to advocate and to encourage.
>
> p. 228 V. Mangalwadi quoting Arun Shourie, *Missionaries in India*, op. cit. pp.93–105 from Richard Temple, *Oriental Experience, Essays and Addresses delivered on various occasions* (London: John Murray, 1883).

Finally, we must note that the influence of William Carey's *Enquiry* went far beyond that of India and the mighty work it set in motion. It also was an awakening call to mission amongst the main denominations here in Britain. Carey's *Enquiry* helped to stimulate in 1796 the Congregational churches to commence missionary work. Also, it had an impact on the Scottish Presbyterians who, in 1796 formed the *Glasgow and Edinburgh Missionary Society*. Further, it gave impetus to the founding of the *Church Missionary Society*, in 1799. And later, the various Methodist missionary societies. Soon missionaries were at work in India, Ceylon (now Sri Lanka), China and the islands of the Pacific, Tahiti and Tonga were amongst the first—and later in Australia, New Zealand, the great continent of Africa, South America and the Middle East.

Bibliography

Thomas Armitage, *History of the Baptists* (New York: Bryan, Taylor and Co, 1887)

Vishal Mangalwadi, *The Book that Made Your World* (Nashville: Thomas Nelson, 2011)

Vishal Mangalwadi, *India: The Grand Experiment* (Pippa Rann Books, 1997, Internet)

S. Pearce Carey, *William Carey*, ed. Peter Masters (London: Wakeman Trust, 1993)

39. Hannah More—
Poetess, Writer and Philanthropist
1745–1833

Hannah More was born in the village of Fishponds near Bristol, and spent the early part of her life in the city, where she and her sisters ran a successful school that had been established by her schoolmaster father. At twenty-two she was engaged to a local landowner, William Turner of Belmont. (It appears that the hymn tune *Belmont* was named after his estate). William Turner was twenty years older than Hannah More. Though deeply smitten Edward Turner appears to have been frightened of commitment, and the wedding was postponed three times. When the fourth occasion was proposed Hannah refused any further postponement and her intended settled the matter with a compensation of the sum of £200 per year. This considerable amount in those days enabled her to give up her work in the school and concentrate on writing.

It was after the trauma of this event that she met John Langhorne, at that time vicar of Blagdon. Langhorne is reported to have written with a stick in the sand:

Upon the shore,
Walked Hannah More.
Waves let this record last!
Sooner shall ye,
Proud earth and sea,
Than what she writes, be past.

Langhorne who was much older than Hannah, also proposed marriage, which she refused. However, they maintained their friendship, a literary friendship, which must have helped her overcome her disappointment and further encouraged her to develop and use her literary gifts.

Her first literary works were chiefly in the form of stage plays. One of these entitled *The Inflexible Captive*, was performed at the theatre in Royal Bath. Langhorne wrote the prologue and the renowned David Garrick, the epilogue. It was this contact with David Garrick that first took to her London in 1773.

In 1775, her introduction to London society was at a dinner held by Sir Joshua Reynolds, during which she is reputed to have described herself as "a worm, but a happy worm." This led her to further contacts with such figures as Dr Samuel Johnson, a formidable critic, who, however, encouraged her in her work. Two incidents were to take place which caused her to turn away from stage productions. One was the sudden death of David Garrick, the other was an incident at the end of the performances of her play, *The Fatal Falsehood*, when a rival lady writer fainted in her box, but only after shouting out for all the audience to hear "that's mine!" effectively accusing Hannah More, of stealing her work. The claim was undoubtedly false, but these two incidents were plainly used of God to steer Hannah away from this use of her talents.

This was the age of the London Coffee Houses, where men of influence and ideas met to discuss and debate. Amongst the ladies of good social position and intelligence there were groups forming which became known as *The Bas Blue.* or *The Blue Stockings*, to discuss literature, the arts and current affairs. Through these groups, she came into contact with powerful public figures such as Edmund Burke, Lord North, and John Wilkes. Also in 1780, she came into contact with Horace Walpole and formed a lasting friendship until his death in 1797.

It was during this period, in 1787, that she met John Newton who, despite not approving of drama, (even in Hannah's innocuous form), became one of Hannah's greatest friends, and spiritual mentors.

She initiated the printing and sale of a portrait of a "negro boy"; and urged her friends not to use West Indian sugar. At the same time, she distributed a plan of a typical slave ship, illustrating the terrible overcrowding and denigration of the Middle Passage of the infamous Triangular Run.

The slavers had two policies—to pack the slaves in tightly and run the risk of losing many to disease or pack them less tightly and therefore, although starting with less having more in proportion surviving!

Echo Irving, *A Brief Life of Hannah More* (All Saints Church, Wrington, North Somerset, 2007)

Hannah More met William Wilberforce in Bath in 1787, when she was 42 and he was 28. Wilberforce, together with Henry Thornton went on to finance much of Hannah More's literary and philanthropic work. He also introduced her to the Clapham Sect, the well-known gathering and association of evangelical churchmen. The aims and objectives of this group of Anglican churchmen very much coincided with the vision of Hannah More and each supported the other.

The Clapham Sect had established a colony in Sierra Leone for ex-slaves after the abolition of the slave trade. Slavery ended in Britain in 1807 and in the British colonies in 1833. These notable achievements, owed much to the skilful ability of the group to mobilise public opinion and thus to bring pressure to bear on Parliament. They also were responsible for significant attempts to advance universal education through carefully timed and presented works for the upper classes, such as in Wilberforce's *Practical View*, and for the lower classes Hannah More's, *Cheap Repository Tracts.*

In 1788, she wrote a poem entitled *Slavery* to coincide with Wilberforce's Parliamentary campaign for abolition. The poem dramatically described a mistreated, and enslaved female separated from her children and questioned Britain's role in the slave trade.

I see, by more than Fancy's mirror shown,
The burning village, and the blazing town:
See the dire victim torn from social life,
The shrieking babe, the agonising wife!
She, wrenched forlorn! Is dragg'd by hostile hands,
To distant tyrants sold, in distant lands!
Transmitted miseries, and successive chains,
The sole sad heritage her child obtains!
Ev'n this last wretched boon their foes deny,
To weep together, or together die.
By felon hands, by one relentless stroke,
See the fond links of feeling nature broke!
The fibres twisting round a parent's heart,
Torn from their grasp, and bleeding as they part.

Hold, murderers, hold! not aggravate distress;
Respect the passions, you yourselves possess.

In 1789 she spent the summer with Wilberforce in the Peak District planning the abolition campaign.

In these discussions, however, it was not just the slave trade that was upon their minds, they also wanted to establish a Sunday School Society for "The bettering of the condition and improving the comforts of the poor."

In her endeavours in this direction, she came up against a great deal of opposition from local landowners. In a letter written from the George Hotel, in Bath, she described the chief landowners as "very rich and very brutal." One such landowner warned her that educating the rural poor would be, "the ruin of agriculture and a very dangerous thing."

The wife of another landowner wrote: "the poor were intended to be servants and slaves. It is preordained that they should be ignorant. We cannot alter what is decreed. If a school were to be set up, it would be all over with property and if property is not to rule what will become of us?"

Hannah More established many schools in Somerset, at Nailsea, Shipham, Sandford, Banwell, Congresbury, Yatton, Wedmore and Axbridge. Although some of these schools failed, others continued and by 1840, had become the first *National Schools* which would form the basis for today's village and urban primary schools.

Hannah More also encouraged and indeed established several Friendly Societies. Friendly Societies for men were already established, particularly for farm labourers. These had been set up because of the hardship caused by the *Enclosure Acts*, and the decline of the woollen industry in the area. They had a unique welfare function not matched by any other organisation in those times; however, there was still nothing for women. She wanted these to be run on the same lines as those for men. The first to be established were at Shipham and Roeberrow. By means of a small quarterly payment, medical and pecuniary assistance to married or single females could be given in the event of illness, and a pension for old age could be provided. In addition to this each woman received 10s. 6d. when she gave birth to a child. When a member died, each living member gave sixpence and the Fund contributed £1. 1s. 0d. The idea, which Hannah and her sisters had was that these clubs would form a social centre for the villages.

During all these years Hannah kept on writing, each piece of literature having a spiritual or moral aim. These included *Thoughts on the Importance of the Manners of the Great to General Society; Estimate of the Religion of the Fashionable World; The Churchgoer; Village Politics by Will Chip, a Country Carpenter; The Shepherd of Salisbury Plain;* and *The Story of Sinful Sally.*

Hannah More died at the age of 88, on 7th of September 1833.

> Her mind wandered in the weeks before her death, yet she continued to profess her absolute trust in Christ, the Redeemer; she spoke for the last time, calling out "joy!", on the day before she died. On 13 September she was buried next to her sisters in the graveyard of all Saints at Wrington. She left about £30,000, most of which she bequeathed to charities and religious societies. In his funeral sermon her curate and subsequent biographer Henry Thompson quoted from her book *Coelebs* to describe her guiding principle in life: "If it be absurd to expect perfection, it is not unreasonable to expect consistency."
>
> *Oxford Dictionary of National Biography*

It has been said of Hannah More, "What William Wilberforce was among men Hannah More was amongst women."

Another has commented, "Her efforts formed one of the earliest propaganda campaigns for social reform in England."

Another has called her "A pioneer social novelist."

She has also been called, "The high priestess of 18th and 19th century evangelicalism."

Her writings still challenge corruption and injustice in society today as they did in the 18th and early 19th centuries.

Hannah More's writings have been collected into two volumes, volume 1 containing 807 pages, volume 2 containing 814 pages.

Her life is a demonstration of the power of Christianity to undermine and abolish corrupt institutions and bring about valuable reform. Her work stands as a challenge to engage in holy activism, and also is an example of what can be achieved through faith, prayer and hard work.

She has been criticised for defending the social hierarchical system of the 18th-century, encouraging the poor to accept their station in life, and not to repine against it. At the same time, it must be observed that her efforts in so many ways benefited and empowered the poor to rise above their circumstances and escape their poverty.

It must also be borne in mind that the 1790s coincided with the bloody Revolution in France. These were dangerous times. Her friend and associate Edmund Burke, had written extensively on the dangers of the French Revolution, and Hannah Moore composed a series of tracts that were intended to repress revolutionary tendencies which were circulated at government expense. One of her tracts at this time was entitled *Village Politics* (1792), the first in a series, presenting the homely council of Jack Anvil, the village blacksmith, to live contentedly in a well–ordered England under the wise dispensations of Providence.

David Bebbington continues:

> But if Hannah More insisted on the duties of the poor, she had already written on the obligations of their superiors. In *Thoughts on the Importance of the Manners of the Great* (1788) she castigated the gentry for neglect of their paternalistic role. Like many others in the 18th-century, Evangelicals put their emphasis in social teaching on reciprocal duties, not exclusively on passive acceptance of their lot by the worse off.
>
> Traditionalists they were, by and large, but Evangelicals believed in the conscientious performance of traditional responsibilities. With the growth of their influence in the following century, a much higher proportion of the gentry resided on their estates in order to take a personal interest in their tenants. It has been suggested that evangelicalism was the cause and greater residency the effect. Likewise, ministers of religion were roused to greater zeal in the performance of their duties. Although in Scotland the custom of visiting the flock had been generally maintained, in England, as the clergy rose in income and social status during the 18th century, mixing with their inferiors became less expected of them. The hunting, shooting and fishing parson was a common type. It was the Evangelical movement that prompted the clergy to greater diligence, especially in cottage visiting. Stirring the elite in church and state to care for the poor may have had the effect of reinforcing the social order, but its primary purpose was to ensure that the privileged took a humane interest in the welfare, secular and spiritual, of those committed to their charge."
>
> D. W. Bebbington, *Evangelicalism in Modern Britain, 1730–1980*, pp, 69–70

In Hannah More's works there is a strong emphasis on the spiritual and moral responsibilities of those in positions of leadership and influence. In her paper entitled, *Hints towards Forming the Character of a Young Princess* (Princess Charlotte was in mind) a work running to forty chapters covering two-hundred and one pages, the emphasis throughout is the gaining of wisdom, the development of spiritual and moral character, the reading of books, the knowledge of and the following of great examples, the importance of the Reformation, observance of the Providence of God, the development of a tolerant disposition, an exhortation to read the Scriptures, and the final chapter, emphasising the fact that Christianity is the principle of all noble work and action.

In chapter XV, she writes on *The Distinguishing Characters of Christianity:*

> The great leading truths of Scripture are few in number, though the spirit of them is diffused through every page. The being and attributes of the Almighty; the spiritual worship which He requires; the introduction of natural and moral evil into the world; the restoration of man; the life, death, character, and offices of the Redeemer; the holy example He has given us; the divine system of ethics which He has bequeathed us; the awful sanctions with which they are enforced; the spiritual nature of the eternal world; the necessity of repentance; the pardon of sin through faith in the Redeemer; the offer of divine assistance; and the promise of eternal life. The Scriptures describe a multitude of persons who exemplify its truths; whose lives bear testimony to the perfection of the divine law; and these characters, however clouded with infirmity and subject to temptation, yet, acting under its authority and influence, evince, by the general tenor of their conduct, that they really embraced the religion as a governing principle of the heart, and as the motive to all virtue in the life."

The opening words of this chapter are an exhortation to all of us, to read the Scriptures, and to seek to live our lives in accordance with their precepts whatever our station in life. At the same time to pray that those who have the rule over us, govern their own lives and the decisions they make on behalf of the nation in the light of the same Scriptures of truth.

Bibliography

The Works of Hannah More in two volumes (London: Thomas Tegg, 1840)

Echo Irving, *A Brief Life of Hannah More* (All Saints Church Wrinton, North Somerset, 2007)

Hannah More: The Poet and Writer, The Abolition of Slavery Project, Internet, 2009

The New International Dictionary of the Christian Church, Ed, J.D. Douglas (The Paternoster Press, 1974)

Oxford Dictionary of National Biography (Oxford University Press, 2021)

D.W. Bebbington, *Evangelicalism in Modern Britain* (London and New York: Routledge, 2000)

40. William Booth—
In Darkest England and the Way Out

WILLIAM BOOTII WAS BORN IN SHEINTON, NOW PART OF THE CITY OF Nottingham on 10th of April 1829. The family were nominally connected with the Church of England, but rare attenders at public worship: however, they did send their children to Sunday School.

William once described his father as honest, of considerable force of character, of high spirits and a strong desire to get on in the world. Though his father's business enterprises often failed the family had enough resources to send William to school. This was Biddulph's School, set up by Samuel Biddulph, a Wesleyan Methodist local preacher and a trustee of the prestigious Broad Street Chapel, in Nottingham. This chapel, which boasted a congregation of over a thousand was to play an important role in Booth's early life and conversion. William Booth never completed his education at Biddulph's School, as a period of financial difficulty overtook the family and forced them to withdraw him. They bound him apprentice to Francis Eames, a pawnbroker. Eames was a Unitarian, who William Booth later commented, never spoke about his beliefs, but at the same time, only employed apprentices that showed evidence of good character and moral principle. An amalgamation of the business eventually led to a certain John Knight becoming its head. John Knight was also connected to Broad Street Wesleyan Chapel, and encouraged William to attend there regularly. It is also clear that John Knight was associated with William Booth in his early missionary activities and became a lifelong influence and friend.

The Minister of Broad Street Chapel at that time was Isaac Marsden, who had a formative influence on Booth at that time. He was later to write of Samuel Marsden:

> I shall never forget the words I first heard from Mr Isaac Marsden. I was walking out one evening with two friends at Nottingham, when I was fourteen years of age. Mr Marsden was conducting special services at a Wesleyan chapel, and at that time no one could hear him who had any belief in the great truths of the Bible without being deeply impressed and stimulated.

> We entered the chapel late—in the dusk. I could hardly see the speaker; but just at that moment he was saying, "a soul dies every minute." … I have little doubt that, but for my two friends, I should have stayed that very night and given my heart to God.

Marsden's character is described in Harold Bebbie's book, *William Booth Founder of the Salvation Army*:

> "He would speak to men in his walks, or in houses or shops where he called, in such a fashion that they would fain go and hear him preach. One day, as he went along the street, he saw a woman hanging out clothes. His eyes glanced along the line of garments, and he said, "I say missus, if your heart is not washed cleaner than those clothes, you will never get to Heaven."
>
> *William Booth, Founder of The Salvation Army*, p.23

It seems that it was later under Marsden's ministry that William Booth was converted. He described being seated in a corner of the meeting room where he was strongly convicted of a recent sin. He had received a silver pencil case from a friend in return for a favour, but William felt that he had been guilty of deception. This greatly played upon his mind and he returned the case with a confession, cried out for the Lord's forgiveness, and later, walking back along the pavement, was given a great sense of forgiveness and peace. His conversion experience has been described in the words of the Salvation Army hymn:

> I know my sins are all forgiven,
> Glory to the Bleeding Lamb!
> And I am on my way to Heaven,
> Glory to the Bleeding Lamb!

At this time, 1846, Nottingham was being visited by the controversial evangelist, James Caughey. William Booth seems to have been greatly impressed by Caughey's style of preaching, though many in the Wesleyan body were offended by it. These revival meetings first aroused in William Booth the desire to engage in evangelistic work, but he was too shy to make this known.

Providence then brought him in contact with William Sansom, the son of a well-to-do lacemaker whose father, like Sampson Biddulph, was a trustee of the Broad Street Chapel. He invited William Booth to join him and a group of other young people from the Chapel, who had begun to preach in the poorer parts of Nottingham.

It was at this time he famously led a regiment in the region of 40 ragged boys, into the service at Broad Street Chapel. The Trustees refused to allow them in at the front door. They were however admitted through the back door, and seated discreetly to the right of the high mahogany pulpit. His endeavours at bringing in the urchins off the streets, however, did not meet with any kind of encouragement from the members of the chapel, who frequently complained of arriving to find representatives of the great unwashed sitting in their expensively upholstered seats which they had paid pew rent to occupy.

In spite of these setbacks, however, William Booth eventually became a Wesleyan Methodist local preacher, though at first only being able to minister in outlying country chapels.

By now he was 19 years old and it came to him that there would be better opportunities for employment in London, his father having now died and he was required to support his mother and sisters.

In London, he eventually left the Wesleyans and began to worship at the chapel newly opened by the *Wesleyan Reformers* in Clapham. These were times of great dissension in Methodism, it was believed that Jabez Bunting, the President of the *Methodist Conference* was exerting too much power over the churches. What came to be known as *Fly Leafs*, expressing grievances and the need for reform, were widely circulated amongst the churches. Into this explosive mixture came the famous Leeds, Brunswick Organ Controversy. This arose out of a proposal to install a pipe organ, in this newly built chapel. The decision of the majority was not to install the organ, but the Conference overruled the local democratic decision. All these things led to a division and the formation of the *Wesleyan Reform Church*. This body gave William Booth much greater opportunities to exercise his preaching gifts and the Rev Samuel Dunn gave him great encouragement, as did Edward Rabbits, who encouraged Booth to take up the position of full-time minister/evangelist with this church body, covering all the expense of his appointment himself. Moreover, it was Edward Rabbits who introduced William Booth to Catherine Mumford, who was to become William's wife and help-meet in the great work he was destined to complete. It has been said that the Salvation Army resulted from the last major schism within the Methodist body. (Hattersley p. 31)

Again, in time William Booth grew weary of the contentions amongst these warring factions, and joined what was the longer established group of Methodists, *The Methodist New Connection* in 1854.

His first appointment amongst this body was as assistant pastor in the London Circuit. Rabbits, who had followed him into the *New Connection*, offered to pay the salary of a second minister for the circuit, on condition that William Booth should be appointed to the post. He was appointed to a chapel at Watling Street. Wapping was a poor area where again he came face-to-face with wretchedness and poverty.

The next year, at the New Connection Conference in Sheffield it was resolved that "the Rev William Booth, whose labours have been so abundantly blessed in the conversion of sinners, be appointed to the work of an evangelist."

This however never seems to have transpired, and year after year Booth was appointed to various circuits as a minister. He was very successful in this role, but did not feel this was his calling and eventually, in 1862, he resigned his position in the *Methodist New Connection.*

His son Bramwell Booth later wrote of his situation after he had resigned from the *Methodist New Connexion*:

> For two years after the Churches were closed against him, he wandered about the country without religious domicile… Those two years were probably the darkest in his whole life, at least from the time of his ordination onwards. Small buildings only were available for his services—he who had been accustomed to great congregations … Yet this period, dark and perplexing as it was, was a period in which, I consider, he was being most marvellously fitted the work which, unknown to him, was awaiting his hand in the East End of London.
>
> Robert Sandall, *The History of The Salvation Army*, p. 11

William Booth's own verdict was given when he spoke at the celebration of his sixtieth birthday at the Congress Hall, Clapton;

> I see in all the unpleasant experiences of my early days the hand of God himself, leading me by a way that I knew not—that I could scarcely believe at the time to be His way.
>
> Ibid. p.12

These events took place at the time of the great 1859 Revival. It is sometimes forgotten that there were hostile and certainly unsympathetic attitudes from some of the churches to some aspects of the Revival. Some Church of England clergyman objected to services being held in such places as Sadler's Wells and other theatres in London and other parts of the country. These objections were even carried up so far as the House of Lords, where in February 1860 a resolution was moved condemnatory of the performance of divine worship in theatres and playhouses. The Archbishop of Canterbury at that time, John Bird Sumner said that while he would not have sanctioned the services he could not or would not intervene to put them down. He would not take responsibility for discouraging those who are providing the outcasts and the poor with means of hearing the Word of God. Archibald Campbell Tait the Bishop of London, while not gladly approving of the services would not support the motion for prohibiting them. As a result of these and others withholding their support the resolution was abandoned.

In 1862 the Booths, William and Catherine, were in Cornwall conducting evangelistic meetings in Hayle, St Ives, Redruth and Camborne; it is said that during these meetings, 7000 souls were recorded as being saved.

Eventually, however, because of the disturbances caused by some of these meetings, the local churches withdrew their support and the Booths had to leave.

Local fishermen gave great support to the Booths and later directed them to Cardiff, where they came into contact with the Cory brothers, who were colliery and ship owners, and also with Jonathan E. Billups, a railway builder who provided them with a great deal of financial help. In Cardiff William Booth held meetings in a circus tent, and it is said as a result of his mission the moral tone of Cardiff was so raised that the magistrates had little to do.

From Cardiff he moved to Walsall in the West Midlands, where he adopted the practice of marching through the streets in slum areas, and directing the curious to wagons where the Gospel was preached.

From here they moved on to Leeds; so short were they of funds that Catherine was reduced to pawning her jewellery and lecturing on temperance to gain support. From here they travelled to Nottingham and on to Sheffield and eventually back to London. It was in London's East End that William Booth was to do his greatest work, the work which was to be the foundation and origin of the Salvation Army.

Here, he formed what was originally called *The East London Christian Revival Society*, and as the works spread beyond the East End and further afield still, it was simply renamed *The Christian Mission*. Meanwhile, in the hall in Whitechapel Booth was ministering to gatherings in the region of 1200 people. The hall also boasted of a soup kitchen serving up to 1000 people per day at twopence per bowl. When the annual report of the *Mission* was drawn up it was described as a *Volunteer Army*. Bramwell Booth, William's son, objected that he was no volunteer: and that he had been called of God. William Booth leaned over to the document and crossed out, "*Volunteer*" and substituted "*Salvation*". Thus, in 1878 the *Christian Mission* became known as the *Salvation Army* and the body as we know it today had begun. From this point onwards, Booth began to use military terms to describe the work, prayer became *knee drill*, and putting money in the offering became known as *firing a cartridge*. Uniforms were introduced for the first time, the flag with its motto, *Blood and Fire* came into use and brass bands were formed to attract people to join them as they marched to the *citadels* and to calm those who were intent on disrupting the meetings.

It is well-known that in later years a band passing the entrance to a London theatre as Dr Martyn Lloyd Jones was coming out, convinced him that he should be with the Lord's people rather than the fashionable theatre-goers of the West End.

The blessing of God was on the Salvation Army though many still decried it and mocked it. Even C.H. Spurgeon at the beginning did not approve of it. Darwin's friend Thomas Huxley wrote against it in *The Times* newspaper, describing it as religious fanaticism and prostitution of the mind. The work, however, went from strength to strength. By the end of 1890, the army had to 874 corps, 896 citadels, 9416 officers. The weekly paper, *The War Cry*, was begun in 1879, and by 1890 had a weekly circulation of 300,000 with a worldwide total of 37,400,000 publications in fifteen languages.

It was in the same year, 1890, that William Booth first published his book, *In Darkest England and the Way Out.*

> In 1890, William Booth published, *In Darkest England and the Way Out*. He identified "the submerged tenth of the population" who had little hope of escaping poverty or vice. They included the starving, drunkards, paupers, unemployed, homeless, criminals, prostitutes, sick, lost, and suicidal.

> Booth proposed many avenues of social assistance, saying people have to be "rescued from hell here and hell hereafter". He set up 954 institutions, including city industrial workshops for carpentry, match-making, shoe-repairing, etc. He was careful not to run sweatshops for match-making. He paid more than the going rate and sold at current prices, so as not to undercut other traders. He used red phosphorus to prevent his workers from getting "phossy jaw" through using white phosphorus. Those lacking craft skills lived on self-sufficient agricultural cooperatives. One such establishment survives at Hadleigh, Essex, to this day.
>
> Teams would collect unwanted food and household items from wealthier districts and recycle them for the benefit of the poor. Booth helped released prisoners and established a poor man's bank and rescue homes for women enslaved in the sex trade. By 1890 3000 women in Britain had been helped in 13 homes, and 17 such homes had been established abroad. In all these social ministries, he remained convinced of the need for spiritual rebirth. He said: "spiritual life is divine in its origin; it is a creation of the Holy Spirit. Jesus Christ was at great trouble to teach it. 'Marvel not', he said, 'Ye must be born again.' You must insist on it in your people. The only way to secure conduct of a lasting nature is by affecting the change in nature. Make them new creatures in Christ Jesus, and you will have a Christ-like life".
>
> Nigel Faithful, *Evangelical Times*, November 2012.

It is useful to compare Charles Booth's (no relation to the Salvation Army Booths, a Liverpool ship owner and social researcher) remedy for poverty and the depravation with that of William Booth's remedy. Charles Booth's remedy to the social problem was to recognise the unproductive presence of those he characterised as a class B—whom he described as very poor … of a wretched and casual character… and at all times, more or less in want. These people he recommended should be removed from the society of the deserving poor, to prevent them from infecting industrious workers with their feckless ways. These people were to be placed in state-created communes where they and their children (temporarily separated from their parents) should be educated to become useful members of society. Charles Booth's analysis revealed a callous contempt for those he deemed to be in this class of individuals. This Booth is relying on the power of

SOCIAL TROPHIES 195

'Now what has come out of this beginning?

'1. Here is a list of the various Social enterprises we have in hand. I do not vouch for its completeness; but, anyway, we have here a goodly number of schemes for the benefit of the poor and friendless already in active and useful operation:—

(*a*) For the Starving, we have—
i. Children's Free and Farthing Breakfasts.
ii. Midnight Soup and Bread Brigades for the Homeless.
iii. Cheap Food Dépôts.
iv. Special Relief Funds for cases of Special Destitution.
v. Old Clothes' Dépôts for Slum Families.
vi. Poor Men's Hotels.
vii. Cheap Grain Stores.
viii. Famine Loan Fund for Destitute Indians.

(*b*) For the Drunkards, we have—
i. Drunkards' Brigades.
ii. Midnight Drunkards' Brigades (of use also in any sudden emergency—Fire, Flood, etc.).
iii. Drunkards' Advice Bureaux.
iv. Homes for Inebriates—Men and Women.

(*c*) For the Paupers, we have—
i. Workhouse Brigades.
ii. Salvation Guardians of the Poor.
iii. Pauper Colonies.
iv. Pauper Transportation.
v. Labour Bureaux.
vi. Homes for the Aged.

(*d*) For the Unemployed, we have—
i. Labour Bureaux—Men and Women.
ii. Industrial Homes.
iii. Labour Wood Yards.
iv. City Salvage Brigades.
v. Workshops.

(*e*) For the Homeless, we have—
i. Midnight Scouts.
ii. Shelters for Men and Women.
iii. Metropoles.

196 GENERAL BOOTH

(*f*) For the Criminals, we have—
i. Prison Visitation.
ii. Police-court Work.
iii. Prison-Gate Work.
iv. Probationary Police.
v. Correspondence Bureaux.
vi. Ex-Criminals' Homes.
vii. Criminal Settlements.

(*g*) For the Daughters of Shame, we have—
i. Visitation of Streets, Brothels, Yoshiwaras, Clubs, etc.
ii. Midnight Meetings.
iii. Receiving Homes.
iv. Rescue Homes.
v. Factories, Laundries, etc.
vi. 'Out of Love' Funds.
vii. Service Girls' Brigades.
viii. Shepherding Brigades.
ix. Maternity Homes.
x. Investigation and Detective Department.

(*h*) Slum Work. We have—
i. Visitation.
ii. First-Aid Brigades.
iii. District Nursing.
iv. 'Poorest of the Poor' Aid.

(*i*) For the Sick, we have—
i. Visitation.
ii. Hospitals.
iii. Dispensaries.
iv. Village Dispensing.
v. Leper Hospitals.
vi. Maternity Nursing.

(*j*) For the Lost, we have—
i. Inquiry and Correspondence Bureaux.
ii. Legal Assistance.

(*k*) Prevention and Protective Work for Young Girls. We have—
i. Servants' Homes.
ii. City Institutes.

SOCIAL TROPHIES 197

iii. Theatrical Girls' Home.
iv. Registries.
v. Students' Homes.

(*l*) Anti-Suicide Bureaux. We have—
i. Advice Department.
ii. Loan Department.

(*m*) The Home League.

(*n*) Land Schemes. We have—
i. Emigration.
ii. Home Colonization.
iii. Colonization over the Sea.
iv. Lands and Farm Colonies.
v. Small Holdings.

(*o*) Deep Sea Brigades. We have—
i. Mission Boats.
ii. Life-boat.

(*p*) Training Colleges.

(*q*) Students' Homes.

(*r*) Working-Men's Association.

(*s*) Village Banks.

'The total number of our Social Institutions is now 954.

'The value of properties, etc., held for the use of our Social operations is:—

		£
At Home (U.K.)	... ...	228,000
In other Countries	... ...	747,000
	Total,	£975,000

'2. In the history of the Social Work, nevertheless, there have been, as you will know, any number of shortcomings. We have not realized all our expectations, nor fulfilled all our dreams. It was not to be expected that we should. This is an imperfect world, the Movement has been imperfect, and the people who have carried it on have been imperfect also. Consequently, it is only natural that we have had imperfect results.

the state to remedy the situation, whereas, in stark contrast, William Booth passionately believed the real way out of such darkness, must be through faith in Christ, the light of the world. William Booth said. "Every possible force for good, both spiritual and material, was originated in God … The appearance of progress, which is not dependent on the hope of salvation is a chimera."

Although William Booth in this book was calling for "adequate provision" for the downtrodden, he continually insisted that it was not, in itself, a certain remedy. Constantly he goes out of his way to demonstrate and affirm that society's mistakes can only be rectified by God, through the Gospel of redeeming grace. The Salvation Army could create the conditions in which men and women were offered the chance to lead decent lives, only if those individuals had first experienced the power of the Holy Spirit at work within them, giving them the ability to live good and upright lives. Booth was not advocating a social Gospel in this work.

His analysis of the social crisis which corrupted England at that time, could only be remedied by a stupendous undertaking, and that by men and women who believed in the reformation of human nature in every form.

The book *In Darkest England and the Way Out*, sold a quarter of a million copies in its first publication. It created a tremendous response. Booth appealed for £100,000 to be donated to set the scheme in motion; in fact, he received £104,000 in subscriptions. At the same time, there was much criticism of the book from individuals such as Thomas Huxley and Charles Bradlaugh. These individuals with others demanded a committee of enquiry to be set up to investigate whether all the funds gathered had truly been devoted and used for the purposes donated. Such a committee was set up under the chairmanship of Sir Henry James, whose thorough investigation of the finances confirmed Booth's integrity and demonstrated that no misapplication of monies had taken place whatsoever. *The Times* newspaper also played its part in criticising the scheme. However, in spite of the opposition, the scheme went forward. Booth later summarised and itemised the schemes that had or were being set in motion.

The publication of *In Darkest England and the Way Out*, in spite of its vociferous critics certainly gained the Salvation Army social respect. Bramwell Booth, William's son represented the Army at the Coronation of Edward VII in 1902.

William Booth himself was received at the Palace in 1904. At that same time, before his death he also received the freedom of several cities and a multiplication of honorary degrees.

Mrs Florence Booth (wife of Bramwell Booth) was made the first lady magistrate in 1919, thus paving the way for other women magistrates. Salvation Army officers were invited onto various prison committees, boards of guardians, hospital councils etc. Many of Booth's ideas have now been incorporated into the everyday social welfare provisions we now take for granted.

Though William Booth was never a Calvinist in the accepted sense of the word, he nevertheless fulfilled the Calvinistic vision that the Christian should be involved in all the various realms of public life to the glory of God. As Christians we are supposed to have answers to the various ethical issues that confront us in society and daily life. William Booth's great book certainly sought to fulfil such responsibilities. When Christians only seek the quiet assurance of their own salvation and let the rest of the world go by, mankind becomes dehumanised. We are called to be salt and light in the world, remembering that this world is not all that there is, but whilst we are pilgrims and strangers, we yet have both spiritual and material responsibilities for the well-being of those around us. William Booth's primary priority was for the spiritual, for the saving of souls, and this must be our first priority, but as far as in us lies, we like him, ought to seek to do practical good to all men.

Bibliography

General Booth, *In Darkest England and The Way Out* (International Headquarters of the Salvation Army, 1890)
Robert Sandall, *The History of the Salvation Army*, Vols 1 and 2 (Thomas Nelson and Sons Limited, 1947)
George S. Railton, *General Booth* (Hodder and Stoughton, 1912)
T.F.G. Coates, *The Life Story of General Booth* (Hodder and Stoughton, 1905)
Harold Begbie, *William Booth*, vol. 1 and 2 (Macmillan and Co., Limited, 1926)
Roy Hattersley, *Blood and Fire* (Little, Brown and Company, 1999)
Nigel Faithful, *Evangelical Times*, November 2012

41. C.H. Spurgeon and his Writings

Charles Haddon Spurgeon was born in Kelvedon in Essex on June 19, 1834. His father and grandfather were both Independent/ Congregationalist ministers. He was converted at Artillery Street Primitive Methodist Chapel, Colchester, Essex, turning into this chapel on a snowy morning when he could not get to his own regular church. Later he was baptised and became pastor of Waterbeach Baptist Chapel in Cambridgeshire in 1851. In 1854 he was called to New Park Street Baptist Chapel, Southwark, London, which was soon filled to capacity, necessitating the building of the Metropolitan Tabernacle in 1859.

His ministry was mightily used in the conversion of souls and extended to the founding of the Pastor's College for the training of ministers and the establishing of an orphanage in Stockwell, together with the setting up of many charitable and religious organisations, including Temperance and Clothing Societies, a Pioneer Mission, and a Colportage Association.

Later in his ministry, 1887–89, he became heavily involved in the *Downgrade Controversy* arising out of his deep concern that the growth of liberal teaching among Baptists and other denominations was destroying the churches. He fought long and hard against this trend, seeing clearly the devastating effect it would have on the churches of that time and in subsequent generations. He made his protest but was disregarded, and in 1887 withdrew with others from the *Baptist Union.* His resignation was accepted, but at the same time a motion of censure, (which has never been rescinded) was passed. Spurgeon was a man valiant for the truth, paying the price in a breakdown

of health, which many believe shortened his life. Time however has clearly shown that he was right.

C.H. Spurgeon was an evangelical Calvinist, widely read with a special love for the 17th-century Puritans.

Wilber M. Smith comments on the preaching ministry of C.H. Spurgeon:

> While it may be true that D.L. Moody preached to more people in his lifetime than did Mr Spurgeon, I think it can be safely said that no man in modern times, who remained pastor of one church has preached to as many people face-to-face, as did Charles H. Spurgeon. His own Metropolitan Tabernacle seated about 5,500, and was always full. He often spoke in The Surrey Garden's Music Hall, with a seating capacity of 10,000, occasionally in the Agricultural Hall, seating 20,000, and in the Crystal Palace, London, where 23,000 people gathered. Dr Arthur T. Pearson once estimated that Mr Spurgeon preached to, not less than 10 million people in his 34 years of ministry.
>
> Wilber M. Smith, *The Treasury of Charles H. Spurgeon* (Fleming H. Revell Company, 1955)

Much can be said of this most choice servant of the Lord, but here our focus is upon his writings. Of the writing preachers of the 19th century, few if any, came near to the output or quality of the writings of C.H. Spurgeon. Spurgeon believed very strongly that writing was an essential part of the Gospel ministers work.

> How many souls may be converted by what some men are privileged to write and print! There is, for instance, Dr Doddridge's *Rise and Progress of Religion in the Soul.* Though I decidedly object to some things in it, I could wish that everybody had read that book, so many have been the conversions it has produced. I think it more honour to have composed Watt's *Psalms and Hymns* than Milton's *Paradise Lost*; and more glory to have written Thomas Wilcox book, *A Choice Drop of Honey from the Rock Christ*, or the book that God has used so much, *The Sinner's Friend*, than all the works of Homer.
>
> I value books for the good that they may do to men's souls. Much as I respect the genius of Pope, or Dryden, or Burns, give me the simple lines of Cowper, that God has owned in bringing souls to Him.

> Oh, to think that I may write and print books, which shall reach to sinners hearts!
>
> From a sermon preached at New Park Street Chapel, October 7th, 1855.

The circulation of Spurgeon's sermons has been deemed one of the "miracles" of the 19th century. These were printed every Thursday from 11th January, 1855 and throughout his ministry, such was the volume of sermons preached, the series continued for 25 years after his death, i.e. from 1892 to 1917.

Even by 1905, it was estimated that all the pages of his sermons placed end to end would reach nearly from the Earth to the moon.

The whole of his printed sermons in this series ran ultimately to 62 annual volumes.

The following quotation from Dr Robertson Nicholl, writing in 1898 can be read on the fly sheet of the Banner of Truth editions of the sermons, it reads:

> Our firm belief is that these sermons will continue to be studied with growing interest and wonder; that they will ultimately be accepted as incompatibly the greatest contribution to the literature of experimental Christianity that has been made in this century, and that their message will go on transforming and quickening lives after all other sermons of the period are forgotten.

Spurgeon himself gives in his autobiography, *The Early Years* the following account of the beginning of his printed sermon series:

> The first product of my pen, which found its way into print was Number 1 of a short series of *Waterbeach Tracts*, which bore upon its front page the announcement, "Published by Request of Numerous Friends". This was issued in 1853, and in the same year I sent to *The Baptist Reporter* an account of the conversation I had with a clergyman at Maidstone, which was the means of leading me to search the Scriptures, and to find out the teaching of the New Testament concerning believers' baptism. My letter was printed, although I only gave, for publication, initials for my name, and sphere of labour. Soon after I was settled in London, the Editor of *The Baptist Messenger* then recently started, asked me to write some articles for his Magazine, so I wrote a brief Exposition of Psalm lxxxiv, 6, which was published in September, 1854, under the title,

"The Valley of Weeping". The following month, the next verses furnished me with a sequel, which appeared in the October number under the heading, "Onward and Heavenward". Month by month, I continued to contribute short meditations to the pages of the *Messenger* until my other work absorbed all my time and strength, and from then up to the present, one of my sermons has regularly occupied the first page of each issue of the little Magazine.

On August 20th, 1854, I preached at New Park Street Chapel from the words in 1 Samuel xii, 17: "Is it not wheat harvest today?" The sermon was published by James Paul as No. 2,234 in his *Penny Pulpit*, under the title, "Harvest Time," and was, I believe, the first of my discourses to appear in print. Before I ever entered into the pulpit, the thought occurred to me that I should one day preach sermons which would be printed. While reading the penny sermons of Joseph Irons, which were a great favourite with me, I conceived in my heart the idea that, sometime or other, I should have a "Penny Pulpit" of my own. In due course, the dream became an accomplished fact. There was so good a demand for the discourses as they appeared in the *Penny Pulpit* and *Baptist Messenger*; that the notion of occasional publication was indulged, but with no idea of continuance week by week for a lengthened period; *that* came to pass as a development and a growth.

Spurgeon adds, in relation to his printed sermons, that one brother whom he does not name, purchased and gave away no less than 250,000 copies of them. He had volumes bound in the best style, and presented to every crowned head in Europe. He gave also copies, each containing twelve or more sermons, to all the students of the Universities, and to all members of the two Houses of Parliament, and later began the work of distributing volumes to the principal householders in the towns of Ireland.

Before however, the first volume of my sermons was completed, W. H. Collingridge had published for me, under the title of "Smooth Stones taken from Ancient Brooks", a small volume containing "a collection of sentences, illustrations, and quaint sayings, from the works of that renowned Puritan, Thomas Brooks.

The Early Years, p. 396

In 1855 Spurgeon had printed with Scripture proofs, *The Baptist Confession of Faith 1689*, published, in this case, by Messrs, Passmore and Alabaster, who were to become the chief publishers of Spurgeon's printed works.

In January, 1865 he began what he described as "a new departure." This was the publication of the monthly magazine, *The Sword and the Trowel*; its title was derived from the book of Nehemiah. The motto text which appeared on all the volumes was: "They which builded on the wall, and they that bare burdens, with those that laded, everyone with one of his hands wrought in the work, and with the other hand, held a weapon. For the builders, everyone had his sword girded by his side, and so builded. And he that sounded the trumpet was by me." (Nehemiah 4:17–18)

Although Spurgeon was such a lover of peace, it is significant that he put the battling before the building, not only in the type, but also in the subtitle of the magazine—*A Record of the Combat with Sin and Labour for the Lord*. His purpose in issuing it was clearly to set forth in his opening article, which was headed, "Our Aims and Intentions.":

> Our magazine is intended to report the efforts of those churches and Associations which are more or less intimately connected with The Lord's work at the Metropolitan Tabernacle, and to advocate those views of doctrine and church-order which are most certainly received among us. It will address itself to those faithful friends, scattered everywhere, who are our well-wishers and supporters in our work of faith and labour of love. We feel the want of some organ of communication, in which our many plans for God's glory may be brought before believers, and commended to their aid. Our friends are so numerous as to be able to maintain a magazine, and so earnest as to require one. Our monthly message will be a supplement to our weekly sermon, and will enable us to say many things which would be out of place in a discourse. It will inform the general Christian public of our movements, and show our sympathy with all that is good throughout the entire Church of God. It will give us an opportunity of urging the claims of Christ's cause, of advocating the revival of godliness, of denouncing error, of bearing witness for truth, and of encouraging the labours in the Lord's vineyard.
>
> *The Full Harvest*, p.145

Tom Nettles, in his excellent life of C.H. Spurgeon takes up the subject of his writings and makes the following comment:

> Spurgeon frequently reminded readers of his books and "The Sword

> and the Trowel", that by a little effort on their part to expand the subscription base, or recommend and give his books, they could greatly expand his usefulness, and share in it themselves, without increasing his labour. Even so, he told these young ministers that "it is a surprising thought that what is written today in our study may in a few weeks be read beyond the Alleghanies, and before long may lift up its voice at the Antipodes." So marvellous was the enduring nature of the press that a well-crafted sentence might still be forming a mind 500 years hence." The possibility of doing good to the souls of men is a grand incentive which needs no other to supplement it, and such a possibility beyond all question exists when warm-hearted thought is expressed in telling language, and scattered broadcast in type among the masses.
>
> They should look to their goose quills, "your Gillets, or your Waverleys, and see if you cannot write for Jesus." Spurgeon had seen his share of poor, aggravating literature, and would not mind if a great fire were loosed in London that consumed ninety-nine of a hundred of such books books—a fine purification. As well, he would on bended knee beg most preachers to avoid the temptation to put their thoughts in print. But for the man who begins to burn with something to say, let him practice composition until he can express himself plainly and interestingly and write for readers. Take advantage of periodicals, let them serve the cause of true religion, and dare to be a moulder of the public mind. Though young men should be determined to write, they also should be content to write through serious labour on style and interesting content. Do not print that which costs the writer nothing. "Read good authors, that you may know what English is," Spurgeon advised; "you will find it to be a language very rarely written nowadays, and yet the grandest of all human tongues."
>
> Tom Nettles, *Living by Revealed Truth* (Mentor 2013), p. 395

The above article was written by Spurgeon in 1871 under the title, *Use the pen*. As we can see, Spurgeon was urging the importance of literature in the spread of the Gospel.

He reminded young pastors, (and he himself was only thirty-seven years old at the time) that two fields of usefulness were open to them. They should regard utterance of truth with the living voices their main work, calling for their chief attention, but "the publishing of the same truth by means of the press is barely second in importance, and should be used to the full measure of each man's ability."

C.H. Spurgeon is clearly a perfect example of one who completely paid heed to the warning of John Wesley, "that one could never be a deep preacher without extensive reading, any more than a thorough Christian."

The *Encyclopaedia Britannica* says of Wesley that, "no man in the 18th-century did so much to create a taste for good reading and to supply with books, at the lowest prices."

What Wesley did for the 18th-century C.H. Spurgeon did for the 19th-century and beyond.

To read Spurgeon's comments on books recently published at that time is ample evidence of the depth and breadth of his reading. To read these comments is a theological education in itself as it is a guide to good books on a whole range of topics and subjects.

His famous work, *Commenting and Commentaries* is another extraordinary example of the time he must have taken in reading, and together with prayer and meditation the source of the depth of his preaching and teaching.

The versatility of his style and imagination can be seen in his *John Plowman's Talk*, and his *John Plowman's Pictures*. His devotional writing is perhaps best exhibited in his much used, *Morning and Evening*.

A list of Spurgeon's complete works is a breath–taking insight into his phenomenal output. The following is not a fully comprehensive list, but it does give a good indication of the measure of his output.

The Treasury of David
According to Promise
All of Grace
Smooth Stones Taken from Ancient Brooks
Faith's Check-book
Morning and Evening
Till He come, Communion, Meditations and Addresses
Salt Cellars, A Collection of Proverbs and Quaint Sayings
A Collection of the Letters of C.H. Spurgeon
Lectures to my Students
C.H. Spurgeon's Prayers
Able to the Uttermost
An All Round Ministry, Addresses to Ministers and Students
The Golden Alphabet, Psalm 119

The Beatitudes
God Always Cares
Words of Cheer for Daily Life
The Clue of the Maze
Come Ye Children
Words of Council for Christian Workers
The Words of Jesus Christ
The Down Grade Controversy
Another Word Concerning the Down-Grade
Eccentric Preachers
Farm Sermons I
Farm Sermons II
Faith—What it Is and What it Leads To
Gleanings Among the Sheaves
The Greatest Fight in the World
Christ's Incarnation—The Foundation of Christianity
Christ's Two Appearings
Infant Salvation
The Complete History of a Sermon
Memorable Incidents and Letters
Some Notable Sermons
Pictures from Pilgrims Progress
The Pastor in Prayer
Subjects of Sermons
The Saint and His Saviour
Soul Winning
Sermons on Sovereignty
Speeches at Home and Abroad
Memories of Stambourne
What the Stones Say or Sermons in Stones
Words of Warning for Daily Life
We Endeavour
David and the Temple
Around the Wicket Gate
Words of Wisdom for Daily Life

We may certainly say of the writings of C.H. Spurgeon; "He being dead, yet Speaketh."

Bibliography

Ernest W. Bacon, *Spurgeon: Heir of the Puritans* (London: George Allen and Unwin Ltd., 1967)

Tom Nettles, *Living by Revealed Truth* (Fearn, Tain: Mentor, 2013)

C.H. Spurgeon, *Autobiography, Volume 1: The Early Years* (London: Banner of Truth Trust, 1962)

C.H. Spurgeon, *Autobiography, Volume 2: The Full Harvest* (Edinburgh: The Banner of Truth Trust, 1976)

Wilber M. Smith, *The Treasury of Charles H. Spurgeon* (Fleming H. Revel Company, 1955)

C.H. Spurgeon, *Metropolitan Tabernacle Pulpit*, volume 27, 1881 (London: The Banner of Truth Trust, 1971)

42. Abraham Kuyper—Lectures on Calvinism (1837–1920)

Abraham Kuyper delivered these lectures on Calvinism as the *Stone Lectures* for 1898 at Princeton University. Kuyper was a remarkable individual: one-time journalist and founder of a newspaper, a theologian, a pastor, a Prime Minister and he started a Calvinistic University, the Free University of Amsterdam. Kuyper's Lectures are a battle cry against the so-called liberal and anti-Christian philosophers that he saw gaining ground as the 19th century gave way to the 20th century. Kuyper takes the life-system and worldview of Calvinism, and applies its principles to religion, politics, science, and the arts. He saw Calvinism as furnishing Protestants with a world- and life-view because its principles provide unique answers to the questions concerning man's relation to God, to his fellow men, and to the world. Moreover, Calvinism provides the basis for political justice, and ensures the independence of the Church, the family, and other segments of life, from the encroachments of the state.

He believed that each aspect of human society derives its authority from the sovereignty of God, rather than from the will of the people, or from the state; under God's grace, science, art, commerce, and politics will benefit from the exercise of the principles of Calvinism.

The following summary of these lectures is taken from *Masterpieces of Christian Literature*, edited by Frank N. Magill.

Calvinism is not here equated with the dogmatic beliefs of any church or with any specific doctrine. It refers, first, to the historical course taken by the Reformation, so far as it was neither Lutheran, nor Anabaptist nor Socinian; second, to the system of conceptions that arose under the influence of Calvin in various social spheres; and third, to the political movement which brought political liberty in constitutional statesmanship in Holland, England, and the United States.

Calvinism, an all-embracing system of principles, is able to do more than create a different Church-form. Calvinism can provide human society with a different form of life, with a unified life system, for it offers a peculiar insight derived from a special principle, into three fundamental relations: our relation to God, to man, and to the world. Kuyper's lectures proceed to an analysis of these relations.

First, how does Calvinism interpret our relation to God? Calvinism does not seek God in the creature, nor does it isolate the creature from God, nor does it impose an ecclesiastical middle link between God and man; it proclaims rather that God, the Holy Spirit enters into immediate fellowship with man. There is no divine grace other than that which comes immediately from God to man. The Church is not an office or an independent institute; it is identical with the believers that constitute its membership. Every single believer can have the assurance of eternal salvation and live his life in the immediate fellowship with God, fully persuaded that his entire life is to be lived in the divine presence. (Through faith in our Lord and Saviour Jesus Christ.)

Calvinism's unique view of man's relation to God and God's relation to man is augmented by its own interpretation of the relation of man to man by regarding human life as the immediate concern of God. It views all men, regardless of social or economic status, as lost sinners, who, as equal in the sight of God, are in consequence equal among themselves. No distinctions among men are to be recognised except such as are imposed by God Himself, in that to some He gives authority and greater talents that they might serve those with lesser talents, and thereby also serve God. Calvinism could result only in a democratic view of life in which nations are free, and every man, because he is a man created in the image and likeness of God, ought to be treated fairly, both politically and socially. Man is here placed on a footing of equality with man, not against God, but on his knees before God.

The third basic relation which determines the Calvinistic life-system is man's relation to the world. Calvinism rejects any dualism between a sanctified Church and a demonic world that must be taken into the protective custody of the Church. Calvinism honours man because of his likeness to the divine image; it honours the world as a divine creation. Particular grace works salvation; common grace arrests the corruption of the world and allows our life to develop outside the institutional Church to the glory and honour of God the Creator.

Under the influence of Calvinism, the institutionalised Church is nothing more than the assembly of believers; every sphere of life is emancipated from the dominion of the Church, but not from the sovereignty of God. Family life, trade, commerce, politics, science, and art are restored to their positions of independence. Man is not to retire from the world in a monastery; his duty is to flee from sin alone. His task is to serve God in the world, in every phase of worldly life. Man is duty-bound to discover and to develop potencies hidden by God in nature and in human life. To do so is to keep the divine command given in Paradise: "Subdue and replenish the earth."

Calvinism is a life-system and as such it is offered by Kuyper as the complete evolution of Protestantism, as providing principles which, when embodied in a form suitable to the requirements of our own century, can restore unity to Protestant thought and action. The benefits of Calvinism are to be found in every sphere. Its influence on religion, as such, stresses the fact that religion exists not for man, but for God; it operates directly from the heart, without human interposition; it is not partial in its operations, but affects the whole of our existence, and its character is soteriological, springing from the new man in Christ Jesus.

Calvinism regards the Church as a spiritual organism, with the starting point and centre of its action in Heaven, and not on earth. The Church on earth manifests itself in the form of local congregations of believers, living together in obedience to the ordinances of Christ; it is not an institution for the dispensation of grace. Its purpose is not human or egoistic; it exists merely for the sake of God, for the glory and honour of his name to which end its members are called to conversion, worship, and moral purity.

Calvinism places the believer before the face of God, not only in the Church, but also in his political life, in the domain of the state. The influence of Calvinism on political conceptions springs from its dominating basic principle: the sovereignty of the Triune God over the whole cosmos, including the state. For the magistrates derive their power by the institution of God, by reason of sin. Because of sin, they are indispensable, on the one hand, and because of sin, the people must ever guard against any assumption of power by the magistrates, which would deprive the people of their personal liberty.

Sin alone has made the institutions of governments necessary, but the right to rule over men is a right possessed by God and by him alone. Such authority does not belong to any man or to the people, nor does it originate in the social contract. The authority of earthly governments originates solely in the sovereignty of God, so that every magistrate rules solely by God's grace; the final duty of obedience to civil powers, no matter what form they take, is imposed by God himself.

The sovereignty of God in the political sphere, recognised in the American Revolution, is equally opposed to popular sovereignty, manifested in the French Revolution, and to the state sovereignty, propagated in Germany as a result of philosophical pantheism. To the Calvinist, there is a Court of Appeal beyond that of the whims and desires of men, and whenever men have usurped the power that rightfully belongs to God alone, the Calvinist has not hesitated to appeal directly to the King of kings, and to overthrow the pretender to earthly power, by force, if necessary.

The sovereignty of God is in no way limited to its manifestation in the state. It is equally present in society as a whole, in the family, in business, science and art, and in all other social spheres.

These social structures do not derive their existence from the state, Kuyper claims, but are endowed with their own form of authority; an authority which rules by the grace of God, and not by the grace of the state. The individual, social spheres possess their own individual sovereignty; they have nothing above themselves, but God. The state cannot properly intrude; each social sphere is sovereign in its own domain.

The state bears the power of the sword of justice, to mete out punishment to the criminal; the sword of war, to defend its rights and interests against its enemies; the sword of order, to thwart rebellion at home. But state authority cannot properly be extended into any other social sphere. The life of science, of the family, or of commerce may never properly be enclosed by the stultifying tentacles of the state. This does not mean that the state can never interfere in these autonomous spheres of life. When the different social spheres clash, the state must compel mutual regard for the boundary lines; when power is abused, the state must defend the weak; and it must use coercion to see that each sphere bears its proper personal and financial burden for the preservation of the state. The state, however, must never forget that the source of authority for the social spheres of society is the same as that from which the state derives its own authority; namely, the absolute sovereignty of God.

The Calvinist, in fact, has not always been clear in his conception of the relationship between the sovereignty of the Church and the sovereignty of the state and has invoked the power of the state to defend the truth of his confessions. In principle, however, Calvinism recognises that the magistrate has a spiritual duty towards God, in that he must recognise that it is from God that he derives his power, and that it is, according to God's ordinances that he must rule the people. It is, however, the duty of the government to suspend its judgement concerning which temporal manifestations of the body of Christ is to be found most perfect in the eyes of God. The government must honour the complex of Christian churches as the multiform manifestation of the Church of Christ on earth. The sovereignty of the Church and the sovereignty of the state must both be recognised. The government is to see that the individual liberty and conscience of its citizens is respected, so that every man may serve God, according to his own convictions. For the sovereignty of the Church is limited by the sovereignty of the free personality.

The benefits of Calvinism are not limited to the political sphere, Kuyper contends. With respect to science and learning, Calvinism has fostered, and could not but foster, a love of investigation. For its doctrine of the divine decree of God means that the entire cosmos, instead of being the plaything of chance, obeys law, a fact which permits science to ascend from the empirical investigation of phenomena to the laws and principles which ruled them. Calvinism placed science in its proper domain by acknowledging that nature is God's handiwork; it delivered it from its unnatural bondage to the state and to the Church. Calvinism also provides an answer to the alleged conflict between faith and science by showing that such a conflict is not possible. The real point of dispute is between the assertion that the cosmos as it now exists is normal, that it moves by means of an eternal evolution from its potencies to its ideal, and the assertion that it is abnormal, that a past disturbance has taken place, and that regenerating power alone can bring it to its final goal.

Kuyper contends that in the sphere of art Calvinism did not produce a general art style because Calvinism reached such a high stage of religious development that it's very principles prevented it from expressing religion in visible and sensible forms. In principle, however, Calvinism offers an interpretation of art, which frees it from any slavish interpretation of nature. Art is a gift of the Holy Spirit, and has as its vocation the task of disclosing to man a higher reality then he can find in his sinful and corrupted world. By releasing art from the trusteeship of the Church, Calvinism encouraged and advanced the development of the arts, especially in the fields of music and painting.

The significance of Kuyper's call to a return to Calvinism is not to be minimised. It has been many years now since he delivered his lectures but its message and teaching is still highly relevant. Kuyper's Christian life was given to the struggle to bring the world to a recognition that God is sovereign in every sphere of life, a truth that needs to be recognised again in the fast disintegrating and liberty denying failed secularism of today."

Adapted from, *Masterpieces of Christian Literature*, ed. F.N. Magill

Bibliography

Frank N. Magill, *Masterpieces of Christian Literature*, two volume edition (New York: Salem Press, 1963).

43. John Gresham Machen—*Christianity and Liberalism* 1881–1937

Christianity and Liberalism is an examination of the teaching of liberalism in comparison with the teaching of orthodox Biblical Christianity, and shows that at every point, the two movements are in direct opposition.

So-called liberal Christianity differs from Christianity proper in its view of God, of man, of the seat of authority, and the way of salvation.

So-called liberalism is no mere divergence at isolated points from Christian teaching; it proceeds from a totally different root, and it constitutes, in essentials, a unitary system of its own.

J. Gresham Machen was a member of the faculty of Princeton Theological Seminary from 1906 until 1929. From 1929 until his death in 1937, he was Professor of New Testament in Westminster Theological Seminary, an institution that he helped to establish.

Machen devoted his life to the scholarly defence and exposition of Orthodox Protestantism as contained in the *Westminster Confession of Faith*. His book *Christianity and Liberalism* is said to be the clearest and most-able statement of the conflict between historic, redemptive Protestantism and the modern non-redemptive "liberal" religion.

Machen compares the liberal and the orthodox views of the doctrines of God and man, the Bible, Christ, salvation and the Church, to show that modern liberalism has in fact relinquished everything distinctive of Christianity.

Liberalism frequently regards differences in doctrine as unimportant; it argues that creeds are simply the changing expression of a single Christian experience. From the liberal point of view, creeds are all equally true, if they express Christian experience. Christianity is not a doctrine but a way of life. The liberal puts his trust in the person of Jesus, rather than in what Jesus did; in Jesus' character rather than in the message of his death and resurrection.

Orthodoxy, in contrast to liberalism, contends that Christianity has a doctrinal basis. What Christianity is can be determined by looking at its beginnings. At its inception, the Christian movement was not just a way of life, but a way of life based upon a message, upon an account of facts; that is, upon doctrine. The apostle Paul, for example, certainly did not advocate an undogmatic religion. To remove Paulinism from Christianity is not a solution, the orthodox believer argues, because Paul was not an innovator, as is clear from his relationship to the church at Jerusalem, and to the original companions of Jesus Christ. The primitive Church was concerned with what Jesus Christ had done. It was the proclamation of an event that was to redeem the world. Two elements are contained within the Christian message: the narration of the facts, that is, history, and the narration of the facts together with the meaning of the facts, that is doctrine.

Our Lord's disciples did not distort Christianity by basing it upon an event, for Christ Himself did the same thing. The message our Lord proclaimed in Galilee was the coming of the Kingdom—an event, or a series of events. Christ not only announced an event, but He announced the meaning of the event. Christ's teaching was rooted in doctrine, because it depended upon the presentation of His own person in His Messianic consciousness.

To maintain the doctrinal basis of Christianity does not mean that Christianity is irrelevant to life, nor does it mean that all points of doctrine are equally important; nor does it mean that conservatives and liberals must live in personal animosity, although specifically Christian fellowship between them is impossible, Machen insists.

The distinction between Christianity and liberalism is further evidenced in the contrasting views of God and man. Modern liberalism frequently is indifferent to any conception of God; it would merely feel His presence. Some liberals would become acquainted with God only through Jesus Christ. Some liberals, though perhaps a decreasing number, think of God as a personal God, as a Father. Liberalism as a whole, however, has broken down the sharp distinction between God and the world, and when it is not consistently pantheistic, it tends towards pantheism.

The liberal view of man follows quite naturally from its doctrine of God. Liberalism has lost the awareness of sin and has supreme confidence in human goodness. Liberalism is rooted in the predominant pagan spirit of present-day Western civilisation, a spirit which finds the highest goal of human existence in the harmonious development of existing human faculties.

Orthodox Christianity, in contrast to liberalism, holds that the knowledge of God is the very basis of religion. Theism, the knowledge of one Supreme Person, Maker, and active Ruler of the world is at the very root of the religion of Jesus Christ. Christ believed in the real existence of a personal God. Neither He nor the New Testament supports the modern view of the Fatherhood of God, and its corollary, the brotherhood of man. What is distinctive in the New Testament teaching about the Fatherhood of God concerns only those who have become followers of Christ. Liberalism is lost sight of the very centre and core of Christianity by eradicating the distinction between the creature and the Creator. Liberalism denies the transcendence of God, but orthodox Christianity holds that God is imminent in the world, not because He is identical with the world, but because He has created it, and continues to uphold it.

According to the views of Machen Christianity regards man as a sinner; unlike liberalism. It begins with a consciousness that man is under the just condemnation of God, and that his condition can be changed solely by the grace of God, through faith in Jesus Christ and his atonement, after which change the Christian can proceed to develop every faculty in a higher Christian humanism founded not upon human pride, but upon divine grace.

The two great presuppositions of the Christian message, the fact of sin and the presence of the living God, are disregarded by modern liberalism. The divergence between Christianity and liberalism is, however, not limited to presuppositions, but it affects the message itself. This is not surprising when it is remembered that the Bible is the Book through which the Christian message is delivered, and that the modern liberal rejects the notion that the Bible is a true revelation from God free from error, and that it is an infallible rule of faith and practice. The liberal does not regard the Bible as trustworthy. He may at times give the false impression that Jesus Christ is his authority in religious matters, but the words of Christ which are regarded as authoritative are only such words as the liberal is willing to select. Jesus Christ is not the real authority, then; the real authority is the liberal principle by which the selection within Christ's recorded teaching is made. The real authority for liberals, Machen contends, is "Christian experience," and since individual experience is diverse, such authority is no authority at all.

The foundation of liberalism is the shifting emotions of sinful men. Christianity, on the other hand, is founded upon the Bible. Some Christians accept the central message of the Bible although they believe that the message itself rests upon the authority of reliable witnesses without the supernatural guidance of the Spirit of God.

The view which our Lord Himself seems to have had of the Bible, not only holds that the contents of the Bible are unique, but that the writers have been preserved from error. The Spirit of God did not dictate the Bible in a mechanical fashion. The doctrine of plenary inspiration, espoused by Machen, does not deny the individuality of the Biblical writers; nor does it ignore the use of ordinary means of acquiring information; nor does it involve a lack of interest in the historical situation which gave rise to the books of the Bible. It simply holds that the Bible is free from error; the account that the Bible gives is true, Machen argues, because the Spirit of God kept the writers from falling into error.

Christianity and liberalism are also sharply opposed in their attitudes toward Jesus Christ, Machen points out. Christians stand in the religious relation to Jesus Christ; liberals do not. To the liberal, Christ is an example for faith; to the Christian, Christ is the object of faith. Liberalism regards Jesus Christ as an example and guide; Christianity, as a Saviour. Liberalism regards Jesus Christ as the fairest flower of humanity; Christianity regards Jesus Christ as a supernatural Person, indeed, as a person who was both God and man. Liberalism rejects the Jesus Christ of the New Testament; it rejects His miracles, and finds in Jesus Christ the highest type of humanity, a man who made such an impression upon His followers that even after His death, they could not believe He had perished but experienced hallucinations in which they thought they saw Him risen from the dead. The Jesus of the New Testament, in which Christians believe, performed miracles; He is the Saviour who voluntarily entered into this world for our salvation, suffered for our sins on the Cross, rose again from the dead, and continues to make intercession for us. The imitation of Jesus Christ has a basic place in the Christian life, the orthodox Christian agrees; but the Christ who can serve as an example is the Jesus Christ of the New Testament, not the Jesus of modern liberal reconstruction. The New Testament Christ, the Christ accepted by Christians, primarily offered man not guidance, but salvation.

To the extent that liberalism is willing to speak of salvation at all, it finds salvation in man; Christianity finds it in an act of God. The message of the Christian Gospel is that God has saved man. The cardinal doctrine of modern liberalism is that the world is evil but may be overcome by the world's good.

Christianity teaches that Jesus Christ is the Saviour, not because of what He said, not even because of what He was, but because of what He did, because He took upon Himself the guilt of man's sins, and bore it, on the Cross, in his stead. The atonement taught in the New Testament is a vicarious atonement.

The liberal view of the death of Christ is that it had an effect upon men, not upon God. The Liberal view is correct in holding that the death of Christ is an example of self-sacrifice, which may inspire self-sacrifice in others; it is also true that it shows how much God hates sin and how much He loves men, but these truths are swallowed up in a greater truth, a truth which liberalism denies; namely, that Christ died for man in order to present him faultless before the throne of God.

Christianity is dependent upon history, Machen insists; it is based upon something that happened; it offers tidings of something new; it is exclusive in its claim that Christ is the only means by which man can be saved, so that the Church has the responsibility of proclaiming the Gospel to everyone. Liberalism denies that a person can suffer the guilt of another, but in so doing, it forgets that Jesus Christ was no ordinary person, no mere man, but the eternal Son of God.

Liberals persist in speaking of the sacrifice of Christ, as though it were made by someone other than God, thereby forgetting that according to the Christian doctrine of the Cross, it is God Himself, and not another, that makes the sacrifice for sin. The atoning death of Christ, and it alone, makes sinners righteous in God's sight. On the basis of Christ's redeeming work, the Christian dies unto sin, and lives unto God. The work of Christ is applied to the individual Christian by the Holy Spirit. The believer is thus regenerated, and stands in a new relation to God by an act of justification.

The Christian is saved by the object of his faith, by Christ, so that an act of God becomes the beginning of his new life. The regeneration and justification of the sinner is followed by sanctification. In principle, the Christian is free from the present evil world, but in practice, the battle has just begun.

According to Machen, the liberal regards religion as a means to a higher end; his program has little place for Heaven, and this world is really all in all. The liberal believes that applied Christianity is all there is to Christianity; the Christian believes that applied Christianity is the result of an initial act of God, that man exists for the sake of God, and not conversely.

True Christians are united in the brotherhood of the Christian Church; the true brotherhood of man is the brotherhood of the redeemed, the Church, invisible, which finds expression in the Church visible.

The greatest menace to the visible Church, Machen concludes, comes not from its external enemies but from the presence within its membership of a type of faith and practice, which is anti-Christian to the core. It is highly undesirable that liberalism and Christianity should be propagated within the same organisation.

Adapted from John Gresham Machen, *Christianity and Liberalism*, in Frank N. Magill, *Masterpieces of Christian Literature* (New York: Salem Press, 1963)

Bibliography

Frank N. Magill, *Masterpieces of Christian Literature* (New York: Salem Press, 1963).

John Gresham Machen, *Christianity and Liberalism* (Wm. B. Eardmans)

44. Dr Martyn Lloyd-Jones—His Life and Writings

Dr Martyn Lloyd-Jones was born 20th December 1899, in Donald Street, Cardiff, South Wales. He was the second of three sons born to Henry and Magdalene Lloyd-Jones. His father was a Calvinistic Methodist and a Liberal by political persuasion. His mother however was a Tory and attached to the Church of England.

In 1906 the family left Cardiff and moved to the predominantly Welsh speaking small town of Llangeitho, a rural, old-fashioned and chapel-going town. Large congregations gathered each Lord's Day in the many chapels, but the old revival fire had departed from them.

Lloyd-Jones' father was a shopkeeper cum general dealer, selling a wide range of goods from salted butter to farm machinery. At the beginning of 1914 it was clear that the business was not paying and with great reluctance, and no doubt much apprehension the family realised that they would have to relocate. Lloyd-Jones father intended to immigrate to Canada, and in fact went on ahead of the family, whilst Mrs Lloyd-Jones, and the boys were to remain until they had sat the Welsh School Board exams in June and July of that year. He soon however returned from Canada, seeing that there were few prospects for them there and the family eventually moved to London, 7 Regency Terrace, Westminster.

Two years later Martyn Lloyd-Jones enrolled as a medical student at St Bartholomew's Hospital. He excelled in his field, eventually becoming Junior House Physician to Sir Thomas Horder, one of the most distinguished and brilliant medical men of his age.

Throughout his time in London and up to this point Martyn Lloyd-Jones and his family continued to attend the *Calvinistic Methodist Church* in Charing Cross Road. He had become the superintendent of the Sunday School at the age of eighteen, and considered himself a true Christian.

He himself was later to write:

> "For many years, I thought I was a Christian when in fact I was not. It was only later that I came to see that I had never been a Christian and became one. But I was a member of the church and attended my church and its services regularly. So anybody assuming, as most

> preachers did, that I was a Christian, was making a false assumption. It was not a true assessment of my condition. What I needed was preaching that would convict me of sin and make me see my need, and bring me to true repentance and tell me something about regeneration. But I never heard that. The preaching we had was always based on the assumption that we were all Christians, that we would not have been there in the congregation unless we were Christians. This I think, has been one of the cardinal errors of the Church, especially in this present century."
>
> *Preaching and Preachers*, p. 146

Also in his early twenties he began to understand something about society at the top. Horder had taken him along to various society dinners where he had seen and heard the conversation and behaviour of many of the most prominent and influential figures of that time. His reaction to this was that he was turned away in his mind from ever wanting to become one of them. In the Providence of God, he then began to attend Westminster Chapel on a regular basis, where for the first time he began to hear preaching that made him doubt that he ever was a true Christian.

In other words, Dr Lloyd-Jones came to see that his outward life had been little more than play–acting: the real truth was that he had been seeking to escape from God.

This knowledge did not come to him in days, or even weeks. He put no date to his conversion, it was progressive, like the experience described by Francis Thomson in his poem *The Hound of Heaven*.

To the words of that poem, Martyn Lloyd-Jones could now readily respond:

> I fled him down the nights and down the days:
> I fled him down the arches of the years;
> I fled him down the labyrinthine ways
> Of my own mind; and in the midst of tears
> I hid from him.

After the conflict of his conversion experience, came another wrestling within his mind and spirit. This was the question of whether he should pursue what had all the prospects of a brilliant career in medicine, or respond to what he felt in his heart to be a call to the Christian ministry.

These things came to a head after a friend and his wife invited him to attend a play in one of the theatres of Leicester Square. He didn't really want to go, and gave little attention to the play, all the time he was wrestling in his mind with this sense of call. Coming out of the theatre and into the busy worldly throng of Leicester Square at night, suddenly a Salvation Army band came along, playing familiar hymns. Lloyd-Jones was later to comment, when I heard this band and the hymns I said, "These are my people, these are the people I belong to, and I am going to belong to them."

His first ministry was at the Bethlehem Forward Movement Church, Sandfields, Aberavon, South Wales in 1927. These were days of falling church numbers, times when many in South Wales believed the answer to church decline was a Christianised version of socialism. The Church leaders in Aberavon waited to hear what their new minister's program for reversing decline was to be. They heard with some surprise that his program would consist of regular Sunday Services, Bible exposition, a prayer meeting on Mondays, a midweek meeting on Wednesday, and regular Sunday School work. Moreover, the wooden stage, which occupied part of the church hall on which the church's dramatic society had staged their productions, was to be dismantled.

Dr Martyn Lloyd-Jones served this church faithfully and became its beloved minister until 1939. At this point, just before the outbreak of the Second World War, he was called to serve as assistant to Dr Campbell Morgan at Westminster Chapel, London. The Second World War began the day before Dr Martyn Lloyd-Jones was to be formally inducted as co-pastor of that church. In August 1943, on the retirement of Dr Campbell Morgan, Dr Martyn Lloyd-Jones was called to be his successor. It is on record that a liberal element within the church at that time tried, though unsuccessfully, to prevent his appointment.

It is impossible to sum up in a few lines the extent of influence for good that came from Dr Martyn Lloyd-Jones ministry.

In relation to this present study, mention must be made of his utter commitment to biblical exposition; the Bible and its exposition was central to his ministry.

In regard to the dissemination of good Christian literature he was responsible for bringing the work and vision of Geoffrey Williams, who had begun to make a small library of books available in his local area of Beddington, now known to the wider Christian public, and eventually bringing it to London. The formal opening of The Evangelical Library, took place at 3 p.m. on Monday, January 15, 1945, in which Dr Lloyd-Jones gave its opening address.

In regard to Dr Lloyd-Jones own publications, his *Exposition of the Sermon on the Mount*, his series on Paul's Epistle to the Romans, and Paul's Epistle to the Ephesians requires special mention.

Other publications include:

Exposition of Psalm 51
Faith on Trial, Exposition of Psalm 73
From Fear to Faith: Exposition of Habakkuk
Sermons on Gospel of John
Saved in Eternity
Sanctified through the Truth
Growing up in the Spirit
The Life of Joy, Sermons on Philippians
Sermons on 2nd Peter

Other sermon series, including:

Assurance
Baptism with the Spirit
Revival
War
The Miracle of Grace and other Messages

Evangelistic Sermons:

Evangelistic Sermons at Aberavon
Out of the Depths, four sermons on Psalm 51
The Cross: God's Way of Salvation
I Am Not Ashamed: Advice to Timothy

General Addresses:

The Plight of Man and the Power of God
Creryfydd Heddiw ac Yfory published in English as *Knowing the Times*
Truth Unchanged, Unchanging
The Puritans: Their Origins and Successors

General Addresses and Individual Published Items

Proclaiming Eternal Verities
There Is But One
Christ our Sanctification
Tribute to Dr G. Campbell Morgan

The Wider Evangelism: The Uniqueness of the Gospel
The Position of Evangelicals in their Churches
Address for the Evangelical Alliance, 1948
The Place of Law in the Divine Economy
The Annual Meeting of the Evangelical Library, 1955
Beware that Thou Forget Not, address for the Dedication Service of the IVF New Office Building, 1961
From Puritanism to Nonconformity
Luther and his Message for Today
What is the Church?
The State of the Nation
Funeral sermon for the life of David George Aufrere Legget, Wimborne Minster 1979

Addresses on Christianity, Science and Medicine
An Experimental Study of Malignant Endocarditis
The Christian View of the Universe
Christ and the Unconscious Mind
Healing: Miraculous and Psychotherapeutic
The Approach to Truth: Scientific and Religious
The Doctor Himself, and the Human Condition
Healing and Medicine

In addition, Dr Lloyd-Jones published a number of reviews of various important publications between 1929 and 1964. He also provided in the region of 30 reviews of significant Evangelical publications during his lifetime, and articles and comments by him were published across a range of both English and Welsh magazines and periodicals during his lifetime.

It is said of Dr Martyn Lloyd-Jones, "He came to a city and to a country in which the Reformed Faith of Calvin and the Puritans, of Whitefield and Spurgeon, was almost extinct."

This was the case, and yet even in these dark days of the second decade of the 21st century, we can observe that in many quarters this is not the situation today. James Packer wrote of Dr Martyn Lloyd-Jones in 1968, "It is not given to many of us to change the course of things in the Christian world to the extent that you have been used to change it".

Iain Murray wrote of him:

> Should Martyn Lloyd-Jones' lasting place in Christian history becomes mainly associated with his books, we hope it will be

> remembered that books were always secondary to him, and that he never set out to write them. He was a preacher. He believed in preaching, which was unadorned, and studied (in so far as mere sentences were concerned) but alive, the union of truth and fire, and both humbling and uplifting to the sublime in its effects.
>
> Iain Murray, *D. Martyn Lloyd-Jones, The Fight of Faith*, p.777

Bibliography

The Banner of Truth, Issue 212, May 1981

The Banner of Truth, Issue 231, December 1982

Iain Murray, *D. Martyn Lloyd-Jones, The First Forty Years* (Edinburgh: The Banner of Truth Trust, 1983).

Iain Murray, *D. Martyn Lloyd-Jones, The Fight of Faith* (Edinburgh: The Banner of Truth Trust, 1990).

John Peters, *Martyn Lloyd-Jones, Preacher* (Paternoster Press, 1986)

45. Dr Peter Masters and The 20th Century Revival of the Literature Ministry of the Metropolitan Tabernacle

The history of the Metropolitan Tabernacle is a long and stirring one. It is the story of God's faithfulness, stretching back to 1650 and continuing until the present day. It began at the time of the persecution of Baptist congregations, with a small group of faithful souls meeting in a house.

Over the years it has boasted many godly and excellent pastors each exercising a wide and extensive ministry, most of which have exercised a book ministry. Among them are Benjamin Keach (1640–1704) (author of *Tropologia: a Key to Open Scripture Metaphors, Arguments to prove The Divine Authority of the Holy Bible*, also it is said that he produced in the region of forty-two published works in addition to prefaces and introductions to the books of others. He was the writer of several hymns, and indeed was responsible for introducing hymn singing into Baptist congregations.

His successor, Dr John Gill (1697–1771), one of the most able Hebraists of his day, produced the massive six-volume commentary on the whole Bible. It is said that beside this, Dr Gill produced 10,000 folio pages of theological writings. Dr Gill was succeeded by John Rippon (1751–1836). John Rippon was the author of a short biography of his predecessor, Dr John Gill, and was also the editor of *The Baptist Annual Register*, which included many valuable sketches of the state of religion among the different denominations both at home and abroad. In 1803, he published *A Discourse on the Origin and Progress of the Society for Promoting Christian Knowledge among the Poor*. From 1800 onwards, he began collecting materials relating to Bunhill Fields. The bulk of his manuscript collections occupy eleven volumes, which were purchased

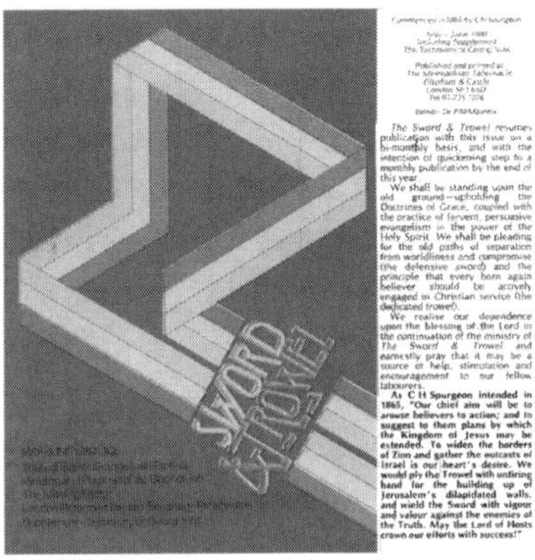

The Sword & Trowel resumes publication with this issue on a bi-monthly basis, and with the intention of quickening step to a monthly publication by the end of this year.

We shall be standing upon the old ground—upholding the Doctrines of Grace, coupled with the practice of fervent, persuasive evangelism in the power of the Holy Spirit. We shall be pleading for the old paths of separation from worldliness and compromise (the defensive sword) and the principle that every born again believer should be actively engaged in Christian service (the dedicated trowel).

We realise our dependence upon the blessing of the Lord in the continuation of the ministry of *The Sword & Trowel* and earnestly pray that it may be a source of help, stimulation and encouragement to our fellow labourers.

As C H Spurgeon intended in 1865, "Our chief aim will be to arouse believers to action; and to suggest to them plans by which the Kingdom of Jesus may be extended. To widen the borders of Zion and gather the outcasts of Israel is our heart's desire. We would ply the Trowel with unfiring hand for the building up of Jerusalem's dilapidated walls, and wield the Sword with vigour and valour against the enemies of the Truth. May the Lord of Hosts crown our efforts with success!"

by the British Museum in 1870. John Rippon is also well-known as the compiler of a *Selection of Hymns from the Best Authors*, which was intended to be an appendix to Isaac Watt's *Psalms and Hymns*. Later *The Comprehensive Rippon* was produced containing 1170 hymns in 100 metres. He also produced an index to Dr Watts *Psalms and Hymns*, a Baptist catechism, and several separate sermons. (*Dictionary of National Biography*, 1885–1900)

The book ministry of C.H. Spurgeon as we have seen was prodigious. From January 1855, one of his weekly sermons was published, and such was the volume of his sermon writing that these continued to be published up to 1917, 25 years after his death in 1892. This collection comprised of 62 annual volumes, and it is said that by 1905 all the pages of his sermons placed end to end would reach nearly from the earth to the moon. It is also recorded that in the region of a hundred million separate sermons were sent out to the four corners of the earth by the end of the 19th century. This of course is over and above, and not including, his numerous other publications.

The Metropolitan Tabernacle was twice destroyed by fire after the end of Mr Spurgeon's ministry. Once in 1898, and again in 1941 by enemy action during the Second World War. The bombing suffered at the time of the Second World War devastated a great deal of the housing in the area of the Metropolitan Tabernacle. This effectively scattered the congregation. After the war few were able to return, and by 1970 the future of the work was in the balance.

However, the great faith of the remaining congregation in the providence of God, called Dr Peter Masters to be their pastor. Thus began one of the most remarkable ministries of the 20th century here in England. Dr Masters' ministry cut across the prevailing trends and fashions of the day. His faithful biblical expository ministry began to attract numbers away from the threadbare liberalism of the mid-20th century churches, and also from the frothy charismaticism that was then on the rise. Faithful evangelism of the local area, (now rebuilt), the creation of a massive Sunday School, the opening of The London Reformed Baptist Seminary in 1976, at the same time the establishing of The Annual School of Theology, the re-commencement of the publication of *The Sword and Trowel Magazine* in 1980. Resulting from these highly significant ministries there has been, under God an ever widening influence of the Metropolitan Tabernacle both in Britain and overseas. Dr Masters has produced, and continues to produce, weekly audio sermons together with in the region of thirty published books.

It is impossible to calculate the extent and benefit that this ministry has brought to our own country and much further afield. Likewise, it would require many pages to sum up the many important emphases and aspects of this ministry, both in regard to the lives of individual Christians and the life of the churches. It has certainly encouraged the churches to have confidence in and hold fast to the teachings of the Bible, to preach the Gospel without recourse to gimmicks or compromise to modern tastes. It has stirred the churches to action, to rebuild the walls of Zion, to go forward with wisdom, much prayer, courage and hard work, in the power of the Holy Spirit to "storm the forts of darkness and bring them down."

A valuable insight into one aspect of this influential ministry is the following summary of the first article in the recommenced *Sword and Trowel Magazine*, May–June 1980.

The Missing Factor

> "Why is there so little power and blessing among British evangelicals? Even where sincere believers stand aside from ecumenical error and worldliness; even where preachers hold to Reformed doctrine, there is little evidence of the life and power, which characterises persecuted unregistered congregations in the Soviet Union.
>
> Why are these friends so different—so zealous and courageous, whether in youth or middle-age.
>
> There is a fatal flaw in British evangelicalism. Sacrificial, committed Christian living has almost disappeared.
>
> The fact is that there are very few sacrificial and committed Christian lives in this land at the present time. There are many born-again believers, and there are quite a number who hold Reformed doctrine, but there are very few sacrificial and committed believers.
>
> And there are very few for this reason—that preachers and churches today seldom require individual Christians to be truly sacrificial and committed. The general standard demanded from evangelical pulpits is amazingly low, it has nothing in common with the New Testament.
>
> As long as there is a certain loyalty in attending the house of God, a

whole hearted intellectual adherence to reformed doctrine and moral fidelity, no other demands will be made. Church members can have beautiful homes, which cost thousands of pounds to furnish and maintain, and no one will worry or trouble them. They can have no avenue of service whatsoever and still be held in high esteem.

So in these days one of the most vital objectives is to try to put back into the thinking of the people of God what we mean by sacrificial committed Christian living.

Paul looked with dismay at one region of believers saying "All seek their own, not the things of Jesus Christ."

How much more would he be dismayed to see British evangelicals today! We even find an evangelical enterprise offering luxury overseas holidays—the ultimate in combining imagined piety with blatant self-interest. Carnally minded, lazy Christians indulge themselves in luxury while touring the sights of Paul's sacrifice and sufferings.

In the seventeenth and eighteenth centuries Christian people had to be far more sacrificial, erect places of worship and support outreach work. People were comparatively poor, yet in those times of austerity the people of God accomplished far, far more than we do today.

The greatest thing that could happen in this land over the next few years would be for the idea to spread among evangelicals that there are two standards of Christian—a born again believer who has received everything from God to become a faithless, shoddy, selfish, mean and lazy believer, and someone who is sacrificial and committed. If we could only get these distinctions proclaimed, an amazing amount could be achieved.

So here is our first objective, and may the Lord help us to achieve it. It is to republish the standards of sacrificial, committed Christian living. May the 1980s be days when many precious servants of God turn away from lovely homes, sitting at ease in Zion, easy timetables, and worldly honours and begin, at last, to really serve the Lord.

The point must be made, and very emphatically, that committed Christian living means a return to holy activism and zealous labour for the Lord.

Revival involves us. When men like Whitefield and Wesley were preaching and working years ago, they were doing so amidst the wholehearted, prayerful labours of all the people of God. The churches of God represented a great hive of activity, and we will never see Whitefield's or Wesley's, unless the people of God are prepared to be fellow labourers. So we must believe in sacrificial, committed Christian living, and we want somehow to get people to see that is not what we have at the moment.

As soon as we talk about holy activism, we discover this point of view, which says that it is our responsibility to be faithful not fruitful, implying that it is possible to be faithful without being fruitful.

The pioneer workers and inspired penmen of the Bible all assert the very opposite, "For as much as you know that your labour is not in vain in the Lord." It is right to be labouring for the Lord, with earnest restlessness and great zeal.

O Christian friends—let us have a return to the old doctrine. But let us also have a whole-hearted return to the old ideology of total, sacrificial commitment to the Lord. Let us learn once again to walk the old paths of burning Calvinistic, evangelistic activism.

Bibliography

Dr Peter Masters, *About the Tabernacle* (London: Metropolitan Tabernacle, Elephant and Castle, 1998)

John Julian, *A Dictionary of Hymnology* (London: John Murray, 1892)

Sword and Trowel Magazine, ed. Dr Peter Masters (London, 1980)

Dictionary of National Biography (London: Leslie Stephens and Sidney Lee, Smith, Elder and Co., 1885), Internet

Conclusion

Other worthy Christian writers of the 20th and 21st centuries could have been mentioned alongside the few referred to in these pages; these centuries are not lacking in their modern major and minor "prophets".

Throughout, this work has only highlighted a small number of the many noble writers of the centuries. What I have included is only a limited sample of the innumerable company of books and writers that we could have described. Some may not have been the most obvious choices or the most spiritually minded of their age, but by including them I have tried to illustrate something of the wide ranging and varied nature of profitable Christian writing produced down through the centuries.

I hope to have given a small insight into this vast storehouse, ever trying to illustrate the treasure trove of Christian volumes available to stir our souls to seek and find; and to make us more able to serve Him who is indeed the Living Word, the only begotten Son of God our Lord and Saviour Jesus Christ.